Clements R. Markham (ed.)

A memoir on the Indian surveys

Clements R. Markham (ed.)

A memoir on the Indian surveys

ISBN/EAN: 9783742874863

Manufactured in Europe, USA, Canada, Australia, Japa

Cover: Foto ©Thomas Meinert / pixelio.de

Manufactured and distributed by brebook publishing software (www.brebook.com)

Clements R. Markham (ed.)

A memoir on the Indian surveys

CONTENTS.

		Page
PREFACE		v
ANALYTICAL TABLE OF CONTENTS		xi
Sections.		
I.	Indian Marine Surveys	1
II.	Major Rennell and the Route Surveys	39
III.	First Period of the Trigonometrical Surveys	44
IV.	First Period of the Topographical Surveys	58
V.	Second Period of the Trigonometrical Surveys	68
VI.	Second Period of the Topographical Surveys	81
VII.	Third Period of the Trigonometrical Surveys	87
VIII.	Third Period of the Topographical Surveys	102
IX.	Fourth Period of the Trigonometrical Surveys	109
X.	Fourth Period of the Topographical Surveys	126
XI.	Supply of Instruments for the Indian Surveys	138
XII.	The Geological Survey of India	145
XIII.	The Archæological Survey of India	170
XIV.	Meteorological and Tidal Observations in India	204
XV.	Astronomical Observations in India	232
XVI.	Physical Geography of India	246
XVII.	The Geographical Department of the India Office	274
	List of the Members of the Great Trigonometrical, Topographical, and Revenue Surveys of India	290
	Members of the Geographical Department of the India Office	301
	Members of the Geological Survey of India	302

MAPS.

I.	Index Chart to the Great Trigonometrical Survey of India	To face page 109
II.	Map of India, showing the extent of the Topographical and Revenue Surveys, on a scale of one inch to mile	„ 136
III.	Index Map to the Geological Survey of India	„ 145
IV.	Index to the Indian Atlas	„ 281

PREFACE.

The object of the present Memoir is to furnish a general view of all the surveying and other geographical operations in India from their first commencement; in order that, in reading reports of current work, ready means of reference to the previous history of each branch of the subject may be at hand. In case it should be desired to follow up an enquiry into the details of any particular operation or series of operations, the references in the foot notes have been made as copious as possible.

It has been difficult to bring together a complete record of the marine surveys, in consequence of the destruction of documents, and it would have been impossible without the aid of several surveying officers of the Indian Navy, who kindly furnished me with the necessary information.* Nothing has been done for many years to continue and complete the admirable work of the surveyors of the Indian Navy, but this state of things cannot last, and it is hoped that, before very long, the section on Marine Surveys will be useful as a means of reference.

The history of the labours of Major Rennell and his fellow route-surveyors is particularly interesting, as the commencement of the vast operations of which they were the precursors. But their work is still extremely valuable in itself. For the decision of important points in physical geography, and of some engineering questions, it is necessary to compare surveys of the same place made at long

* Namely, Captains Jenkins, Lynch, Felix Jones, Selby, Constable, Taylor, Ward, Heathcote, Sweny, and Cruttenden, and Lieutenants Collingwood and Barker, Mr. Marshall, and Dr. Carter.

intervals. The work done by Major Rennell in 1780 enabled Mr. Fergusson in 1863 to argue from data, the absence of which would have left the question he was discussing in doubt; while the want of early observations on the Kattywar coast deprives the present tidal measurements of their comparative interest.

The narrative of the operations connected with the Trigonometrical and Topographical Surveys is an attempt to describe work, the immense value and interest of which admits of no dispute. The main objects of these sections of the Memoir are to enable an enquirer to gain a clear and comprehensive idea of the scope and nature of the surveying operations, to furnish him with the means of prosecuting his researches further, and to enable him to refer at once to the previous history of any particular survey. The account of the surveys is followed by a Section on the arrangements for the supply of instruments, which have been made by Colonel Strange. It contains a brief description of his observatory in Belvidere Road, and some information respecting his plan of examining and testing instruments, and his system of obtaining them.

I have endeavoured, in the section on the Geological Survey, to enumerate the writings of those earlier labourers in this field who did such excellent service before the commencement of the Government Survey; and to describe very briefly the operations of Dr. Oldham and his accomplished colleagues since that period. Besides supplying references to the volumes of the memoirs and records in which the accounts of the surveys are given, a perusal of the Section itself will give a general notion of the nature and extent of the Geological Survey, which has now been so ably and energetically directed by Dr. Oldham for upwards of twenty years; and it ought also to convey some idea of the arduous and perilous character of the service, and of the high qualities necessary for its due performance.

The researches of archæologists are closely connected with the science of physical geography, and therefore naturally find a place in this Memoir. A perusal of General Cunningham's recently published work on the ancient geography of India will show how close is the connection. Moreover, the labours of the archæologist involve very arduous field work, and he therefore belongs to the brotherhood of surveyors and geographical explorers. In the section on the Archæological Survey of India I have enumerated the descriptions of ruins and the interpretations of inscriptions by Sir William Jones and his disciples, and have given a sketch of the interesting labours of James Prinsep and his enthusiastic companions in research. These earlier investigators prepared the way for our living antiquaries and students of Indian monuments, among whom General Cunningham, Mr. Fergusson, Sir Walter Elliot, Dr. Wilson, Colonel Meadows Taylor, and Mr. Thomas take the lead. I have ranged their work under eight heads; and have also given a brief sketch of the recent investigations of General Cunningham, Lieut. Cole, and Mr. Boswell. The Government of India are now fully alive to the value of archæological research; further surveys will no doubt be actively prosecuted; and the foot notes containing references to the various operations mentioned in the text of this section may, I hope, prove useful.

There is a strong disposition in India to establish a system of meteorological observing and reporting on a really satisfactory basis; and a review of previous efforts of the kind, and of the labours of former observers, may be of some service in the consideration of future arrangements. The meteorological section is merely intended to furnish a history of previous operations, and to be useful for purposes of reference. It will serve to show how much conscientious labour is often wasted and lost from want of systematic organization; but it also records much invaluable work, such as that of General Boileau at Simla, and of Mr. Broun in Travancore, as well as the earlier most admirable observations and deductions of Colonel Sykes in the Deccan. Tidal observations have been much neglected in India. The efforts of Dr. Whewell bore scarcely any fruit, and there is little that is satisfactory to record, except the useful computations of Mr. Parkes for the tides at Kurrachee and Bombay. A series of careful observations at other selected points round the coast is urgently needed.

Indian astronomy dates back for more than a thousand years; and old Aryabhata was nobly represented in later times by the learned and energetic Rajah Jey Sing, with his five observatories and colossal instruments. Worthy successors to the famous Rajpoot astronomer have been found in the Directors of the Madras and Trivandrum observatories, and a Memoir on scientific operations in India would be very incomplete without a notice of the labours of the astronomers.

The section on the physical geography of India is intended to give a comprehensive view of the attempts to deduce generalizations from the numerous classes of observations that have been collected by the surveyors, whether geodesists, geologists, antiquaries, or meteorologists; and it also contains some additional references to original sources of information, including a sketch of the labours of botanists and forest conservators. The subject is one which could not be done justice to within the limits of even a large volume, and a mere sketch, such as is contained in this section, can only be of use in supplying references, and possibly in furnishing a few suggestions and incentives to further inquiry; for physical geography is the comprehensive science which utilizes and makes fruitful the observations accumulated by many classes of inquirers. If the triangulations of the geodesists are the skeletons which the topographical surveyor supplies with flesh and blood, it is the physical geographer who clothes these naked bodies with every description of graceful adornment, and gives them beauty and completeness.

The Memoir concludes with some account of the system by which these difficult and expensive operations in India have been reduced to shape, and made serviceable, both to science and to the general public. The work of compilers and map makers forms a necessary supplement to the more arduous labours in the field. The Spanish Council of the Indies established an efficient Department for the utilization of the work of explorers, of which I have given some account; but Hakluyt was the ancestor of our Geographical Department at the India Office, which also inherits the traditions of Rennell, of Dalrymple, and of Horsburgh. These are great names, and conscientious efforts to emulate their services cannot fail to ensure satisfactory results.

In the wild confusion that still prevails respecting Indian orthography, it was considered that the official spelling in Thornton's Gazetteer must be continued, until the authorities have come to a final decision. Meanwhile most of us look forward with some dread to an adoption of the so-called "scientific" system, or to the prosodial marks of Dr. Hunter; and pray for the success of the common sense views of Colonel Meadows Taylor and the Revd. J. Barton.

CLEMENTS R. MARKHAM,
Geographical Department of the India Office.

January 1871.

ANALYTICAL TABLE OF CONTENTS.

Sections.

I.—Indian Marine Surveys.

	Page
1. *Early Voyages and the Bombay Marine, A.D.* 1601–1830	1
First voyages of the East India Company	1
Works of Hakluyt and Purchase	2
Logs and Journals preserved at the India Office	3
Services of the Bombay Marine	4
Ritchie's Survey of the Bay of Bengal, 1770–1785	4
Huddart's observations on the Malabar Coast, 1780–90	5
McCluer and Wedgbrough on the West Coast, 1790–93	5
Blair's Survey of the Andamans	5
Michael Topping's Surveys	5
The Red Sea. Operations of Lord Valentia and Captain Court	6–7
Captain Court as Marine Surveyor General	8
Surveys of the China seas by Daniel Ross	7
Maxfield and Knox's Surveys in the Bay of Bengal	8
Blackwood's harbour	8
Captain Horsburgh	8
Daniel Ross as Marine Surveyor General. His surveys	9
The Old Persian Gulf Survey, by Guy and Brucks	10
Cogan and Peters, Survey of Bombay	12
2. *The Indian Navy, A.D.* 1832–1862	13
Sir Charles Malcolm as Commander-in-Chief	13
Moresby's Survey of the Red Sea	14
Moresby's Survey of the Maldives and Chagos Archipelago	15
Survey of the Gulf of Manaar and Palk Strait, by Powell	16
Arabian Coast Survey by Haines	17
Journey to Sana by Hulton and Cruttenden	18
Whitelock's Survey of the Coast of Kattywar	18
Ethersey's Survey of the Gulf of Cambay	18
Operations of Lieutenant Wood, on the Indus	19
Wood's discovery of the source of the Oxus	19
Survey of the mouths of the Indus by Carless	20
Indus Flotilla under Captain Powell	20
Christopher's experimental voyage up the Indus and Sutlej	20
Sir Robert Oliver as Commander-in-Chief	21
Office of the Draughtsmen of the Indian Navy. Colaba Observatory	21

	Page
Arabian Coast Survey by Captain Sanders	22
Surveys of Grieve and Ward on the Arabian coast	22
Dr. Carter's scientific labours	22
Montriou's operations on the west coast of India	23
Survey of the N. Concan coast by Rennie and Constable	23
Taylor's Survey of the Gulf of Cutch	23
Selby's Survey of the coast from Cape Comorin to Beypore	23
Selby's Survey of the Bombay bank of soundings	23
Operations on the Somali coast Surveys of Carless, Christopher, and Grieve	24
Captain Lloyd as Marine Surveyor General	25
Lloyd's Survey of the sea face of the Sunderbunds	25
Fell's Surveys on the Coromandel and Martaban coasts	26
Ward's Surveys of the Matlah river, &c.	26
Heathcote's Survey of the western entrance of the Hooghly	26
Heathcote's chart of the Bay of Bengal	27
Sweny's Survey of the Coromandel Coast	27
Mesopotamian Survey under Captain Lynch	27
Operations of Captain Felix Jones in Mesopotamia	28
Captain Selby's Surveys in Mesopotamia	30
Bewsher's Survey in Mesopotamia	31
Survey of the Malabar coast by Taylor	31
Survey of Bombay harbour by Whish	32
Marshall's Survey of Port Blair	32
Survey of the Persian Gulf by Constable and Stiffe	33
Current charts by Taylor, Heathcote, and Fergusson	34
Cyclones and hurricanes. Piddington's Memoirs	34
Memoirs on Cyclones by Carless, Buist, and Thom	35
Colonel Fraser's wreck charts	36
Services of the Indian Navy	36
List of Surveys which remain to be executed	37
Arrangement for Marine Surveys made in 1861	37

II. Major Rennell and the Route Surveys, 1763–1800.

Birth and early career of Major Rennell	39
Rennell's Survey of Bengal and Behar	39
Colonel Call as Surveyor General, 1782	40
Route Survey of Colonel Pearse from Calcutta to Madras, 1784	40
Route Surveys of Kelly and Pringle in the Carnatic	41
Colonel Call's map of India	41
Astronomical observations by Reuben Burrow	41
Colonel Wood as Surveyor General, 1788	42
Route Surveys of Emmitt, Colebrooke, Kyd, Hunter, &c.	42
Route Surveys and Map by Colonel Reynolds	43
Liberal encouragement of Surveyors by Government	43

III.—First Period of the Trigonometrical Surveys, 1800–23.

	Page
a. Introductory	44
Measurements of Arcs of the Meridian	44
Birth and early career of Lambton	45
Major Lambton's project for a Trigonometrical Survey	46
The measurement of an Arc of the Meridian in India	46
Trigonometrical Surveying	46
b. Colonel Lambton and the Measurement of an Arc of the Meridian	48
Lambton appointed to conduct the Trigonometrical Survey	48
Instruments supplied to Lambton	48
The longitude of Madras	49
The use of astronomical observations in the Survey	50
Importance of the Madras longitude	50
Commencement of the Great Trigonometrical Survey	51
Measurement of the first base line	51
Measurement of the first Arc of the Meridian	51
Bangalore base line of 1804	51
Measurement of the width of the Indian Peninsula	52
The Tanjore base line	52
Accident to the Cary theodolite	52
Tinnevelly base line. Triangles extended to Cape Comorin	53
Gooty base line. Triangulation to Kistna river	53
Bedar base line, 1815	53
Colonel Lambton's devotion to his work	54
Lambton's difficulties	54
The Survey to be called "The Great Trigonometrical Survey of India, 1815"	54
Appointment of George Everest as Lambton's Assistant	54
Everest's account of Colonel Lambton	55
Everest's operations in Central India	55
Takalkhera base line. Lambton's failing powers	55
Everest's commencement of the Bombay Series	55
Death of Colonel Lambton	55
List of Lambton's works, and of notices of his services	56

IV.—First Period of the Topographical Surveys, 1800–23.

Notice of Colin Mackenzie's services	58
Mackenzie in charge of the Mysore Survey	58
Mackenzie's Survey of the Ceded Districts, and other services	58
Survey of Goa, Sounda, and Coorg, by Garling and Conner	60
Survey of Travancore by Ward and Conner, 1816–21	61
Survey of Malabar by Ward and Conner	61
Survey of Tinnevelly by Turnbull	61
Surveys of Dindigul and Madura by Keyes and Ward	61
Survey of Coimbatore and the Neilgherries	61
Lambton's Peak Range	62
Survey of Trichinopoly and the Carnatic	62

	Page
Mountford and Snell in the Circars	62
Memoirs of the Madras Surveys	62
Colonel Colebrooke as Surveyor General	63
The position of the source of the Ganges	63
Chinese map of the Himalayas of 1717	63
Views of D'Anville, Rennell, and Anquetil	63
Tieffenthaler's Survey	64
Wood's Survey of the Ganges	64
Webb's Survey and exploration of the Ganges	64
Crawford's measurement of Himalayan peaks	64
Colonel Garstin as Surveyor General	65
Colonel Crawford as Surveyor General	65
Survey of Bengal by Dr. Buchanan Hamilton	65
Colonel Colin Mackenzie as Surveyor General	65
Survey of the mountainous region between the Ganges and Sutlej by Hodgson and Herbert	65
Survey of Kumaon by Webb	66
Survey of Gurhwal by Hodgson and Herbert	66
Franklin's Survey of Bundelcund	66
Johnson's Survey of Bhopal and Bairseah	66
Survey of the Sunderbunds by the Morriesons	66
Buxton's Survey of Cuttack	66
Surveys by Monier Williams in Guzerat	67
Dangerfield's Surveys in Malwa	67
Plan of Bombay by Dickenson and Tate	67

V.—Second Period of the Trigonometrical Surveys, 1823–43.

	Page
Sir George Everest, and the completion of the measurement of an Arc of the Meridian	68
Birth and early career of George Everest	68
Difficulties of Everest on taking charge of the Survey	68
Everest takes the triangulation across the Satpoora hills	69
Measurement of the Sironj base	69
Everest goes to England on sick leave	69
The Calcutta Longitudinal Series under Olliver	69
Return of Everest with new instruments	69
Description of Colby's compensation bars	70
Measurement of the Barrackpore base	71
Extension of the Arc Series across the Ganges plain	71
Waugh and Renny join the Survey	72
Approximate Series by Olliver and Rossenrode	72
Erection of masts for selection of stations	72
Ray tracing	72
Day and night signals	73
Description of the permanent towers	73
Measurement of the Dehra Doon base	73
Horizontal angles observed in the plain	74

	Page
Kaliana Observatory - - - - - - - -	74
Astronomical circles adjusted by Everest and Syud Mohsin - -	74
Kalianpoor Observatory - - - - - -	75
Re-measurement of the Seronj base - - - - - -	75
Waugh's revision of the Deccan angles - - - -	75
Observations of stars for difference of latitude - - -	75
Re-measurement of the Bedar base - - - - -	75
Completion of the Great Arc Series of India. - -	75
Colonel Everest, Major Jervis, and the Royal Society - - -	76
Completion of the Bombay Longitudinal Series - - - -	77
The Gridiron Series. The ten Meridional Series across Bengal, Behar, and the N.W. Provinces - - - - - -	78
Retirement of Sir George Everest. His services, and death - -	79
List of works by Sir George Everest - - - -	80

VI.—Second Period of the Topographical Surveys, 1823–43.

The Revenue and Topographical Surveys - - - - - -	81
Colonel Blacker as Surveyor General - - - -	81
Commencement of Revenue Surveys - - - -	81
Colonel Hodgson as Surveyor General - - - -	81
Colonel Everest as Surveyor General - - - -	81
May's Survey of the Nuddea rivers and Hooghly - - - -	82
Revenue Surveys in the N.W. Provinces - - - -	82
Districts surveyed between 1822 and 1842 - - - -	82
New Survey of Bundelcund by Abbot and Stephen - - -	82
Survey of districts round Benares - - - -	82
Wroughton's Survey of the Saugor and Nerbudda territory - -	82
Survey of Orissa by Smyth and Thuillier - - - -	82
Survey of Berar and Nagpore by Norris and Weston - - -	83
Conference of Surveyors of Allahabad - - - -	83
Survey by Waugh and Renny of the sources of the Sone and Nerbudda -	83
The Brahmapootra Surveys by Wilcox and Bedford - - -	83
Pemberton's Survey of Muneepoor - - - - -	84
Richardson and McLeod in Burmah - - - -	84
Fergusson's Sketch Survey of the Lower Ganges - - -	85
Survey of the Nizam's territory - - - - -	85
Revisions of Surveys in the Madras Presidency - - -	85
Surveys in the Deccan by Grafton and Boyd - - - -	85
Survey of the South Concan by Jervis - - - -	85
Map of Sind, from the Route Survey of Burnes - - -	86
Review of Topographical Surveys under Everest - - -	86

VII.—Third Period of the Trigonometrical Surveys, 1843–61.

Sir Andrew Waugh as Superintendent of the Great Trigonometrical Survey -	87
Colonel Waugh succeeds Sir George Everest - - - -	87
The Gridiron system - - - - - - -	87

	Page
Completion of the Meridional Series	87
The Calcutta Meridional Series	89
The N.E. Himalayan Series. Difficulties, and severity of the service	89
Ravages of fever among the Surveyors	90
Measurement of the Himalayan peaks	90
Measurement of the Sonakhoda base	91
South Concan and Khanpisura Series	91
Commencement of the Coast Series	92
Gridiron of triangulation westward of the Great Arc Series	92
North-west Himalayan Series	93
Western section of the Great Longitudinal Series	93
Operations of Captain Strange in the Desert	93
Captain Strange's work in Sind. Difficulties overcome	94
Measurement of the Chach base	95
Measurement of the Kurrachee base	96
Colonel Waugh's volume on the Measurement of Bases	96
The Great Indus Series. Major J. T. Walker	97
Levelling operations	97
The Cashmere Survey under Captain Montgomerie	98
The Jogi Tila Series	99
The Coast Series, under Captain Strange	99
Retirement and services of Sir Andrew Waugh	100
List of documents illustrating Waugh's operations	100

VIII.—THIRD PERIOD OF THE TOPOGRAPHICAL SERIES, 1843–61.

The Revenue and Topographical Surveys	102
Sir Andrew Waugh's administration. Major Thuillier as his Deputy	102
Thuillier's Official Manual of Surveying in India	102
Boileau's Traverse Tables	102
Method of conducting the Revenue Surveys	102
Sir Andrew Waugh's instructions for Topographical Surveying	103
Progress of the Revenue Surveys	103
Failure of the first Punjab Surveys	103
The Hyderabad Survey	104
Operations of Colonel Meadows Taylor in Berar	104
Robinson's Survey of the Sinde Sagur Doab	104
Montgomerie's Cashmere Survey	105
Madras Revenue Survey	106
Ouchterlony's Survey of the Neilgherries	108

IX.—FOURTH PERIOD OF THE TRIGONOMETRICAL SURVEYS, 1862–70.

Colonel Walker and the Great Trigonometrical Survey	109
Colonel Walker succeeds Sir Andrew Waugh. His services	109
The Rahoon Meridional Series	109
The Gurhagarh Meridional Series	109
Sutlej Series	110

Page

Measurement of the Vizagapatam base - - - - - 110
Captain Basevi at work on the Coast Series - - - 111
Survey of Jeypoor by Basevi - - - - - - 111
Completion of the Coast Series by Captain Branfill - - - 111
Re-measurement of the Bangalore base - - - - - 111
Report on Lambton's work, by Professors Airy and Stokes - - 112
Measurement of the Cape Comorin base - - - - - 112
East Calcutta Longitudinal series under Lieut. Thuillier - - 113
Brahmapootra Series - - - - - - - 114
Eastern Frontier Series under Mr. Lane - - - - 114
Captain Haig on the Mangalore Series. Accident to the theodolite - 114
Continuation of the Mangalore Series - - - - 115
Sumbulpore and Jubbulpore Series - - - - - 115
Revision of the old Calcutta Longitudinal Series - - - 115
Beder Longitudinal Series - - - - - - 115
Cashmere Survey completed - - - - - 115
Kumaon and Gurhwal Surveys - - - - - - 116
Exploring expeditions of the Pundits - - - - 117
Kattywar and Guzerat Surveys - - - - - - 118
Levelling operations - - - - - - 119
Astronomical observations - - - - - - 119
Major Tennant's observations of the eclipse of the Sun, 1868 - - 120
Pendulum observations by Captain Basevi - - - - 120
Reduction of observations in the computing office - - - 122
Introduction of photo-zincography by Mr. Hennessey - - - 123
Publication of maps at Dehra - - - - - 123
Verification of the standards of length - - - - 123
Concluding remarks on the Great Trigonometrical Survey. - - 124
Publication of Colonel Walker's History of the Survey. Vol I. - 125
Colonel Walker's Reports - - - - - - 125

X.—Fourth Period of the Topographical Surveys.

Colonel Thuillier and the Revenue and Topographical Surveys - - 126
Colonel Thuillier's services - - - - - 126
Revival of the Revenue and Topographical Surveys - - - 126
Method of operations - - - - - - 127
Captain Melville in Central India - - - - - 128
Mr. Mulheran in the Upper Godavery district - - - 128
Colonel Saxton in Ganjam and Orissa - - - - - 128
Captain Depree in Chota Nagpore - - - - 128
Captain Murray in Rewah and Bundelcund - - - - 128
Captain Godwin Austin in the Garrows and N. Cachar - - 128
The Pegu Survey - - - - - - - 128
Topographical Survey Parties - - - - - 128
Extent of the Revenue Survey operations - - - - 129
Colonel Johnstone and the Punjab Frontier Survey - - - 129
The Sinde Revenue Survey - - - - - - 129

	Page
Revenue Survey Parties in the Lower Provinces - - -	130
Extent and cost of Surveys from 1836 to 1869 - - - -	130
Office of the Surveyor General - - - -	130
Publishing, lithographic, and photographic branches - - -	130
Introduction of photo-zincography - - - -	131
Maps published - - - - - - - -	131
Re-survey of the N.W. Provinces - - - -	133
The Madras Revenue Survey - - - - - -	133
Maps published at Madras - - - - -	134
The Bombay Revenue Survey - - - - - -	134
Survey of Bombay Island by Colonel Laughton - - -	136
Future operations - - - - - - -	136
List of Colonel Thuillier's Reports - - - -	136

XI.—Supply of Instruments for the Indian Survey.

Ancient Hindoo instruments - - - - - -	138
Instruments supplied to Reuben Burrow - - - -	138
Colonel Lambton's difficulties about instruments - - - -	138
Colonel Hodgson's remarks upon the supply of instruments - -	139
Colonel Everest personally superintended the construction of his instruments in England - - - - - - - -	139
Mathematical Instrument Factory at Calcutta, under Mr. Barrow -	139
Mr. Barrow succeeded by Syud Mohsin - - - - - . -	139
Colonel Strange appointed to design and superintend the construction of a new set of instruments for the survey - - -	140
Description of Colonel Strange's Observatory in Belvidere Road -	141
Examination of graduated circles - - - -	141
Examination and testing of meteorological instruments - - -	142
System adopted by Colonel Strange - - - -	143
The new instruments for the G. T. Survey - - - -	143
Lieut. Herschel's Report on the Zenith Sector - - -	144

XII.—The Geological Survey of India.

Mr. Voysey, the first geologist. His labours - - - -	145
Captain Dangerfield on the geology of Malwa - - -	146
Captain Franklin on the geology of Bundelcund - - -	146
Sleeman, Spilsbury, Waugh, Adam, and Finnis - - - -	146
Mr. Hislop on the Nagpore country - - - -	146
Rev. R. Everest - - - - - - - -	146
Nicolls and Keatinge on Nerbudda fossils - - - -	146
M. Jacquemont on the Rewah rocks - - - - -	146
Early examinations of coal fields - - - -	147
Mr. Calder's geological papers - - - - - -	147
Discovery of the Sewalik fossils, by Captains Cautley, Baker, and Durand	147
Dr. Falconer on the Sewalik fossils - - - - - -	147
Reports on Spiti fossils by Strachey, Gerard, and Hutton - -	149

	Page
Sykes and Malcolmson on Deccan geology	150
Captain Newbold's geological labours	150
Cretaceous fossils discovered by Messrs. Kaye and Cunliffe	151
Grant on the Cutch plant bearing formation	151
Christie and Aytoun on S. Mahratta geology	152
Meadows Taylor on the geology of Shorapore	152
Fleming on the nummulitic limestones of the Salinan range	152
Sir Bartle Frere on the Runn of Cutch	152
Geology of Bombay Island by Thompson, Buist, and Carter	152
Nummulitic limestones. Malcolmson, Fulljames, and Rogers	152
Dr. Carter's geological labours	153
Greenough's geological map of India	153
McClelland's geological Report	154
The Geological Survey, 1851–71	154
Arrival of Dr. Oldham. His first operations	154
Organization of the Survey by Lord Canning	155
Dr. Oldham's plan of operations	155
The Blanfords in Cuttack	156
Examinations of coal fields	156
General conclusions respecting the coal fields	156
Mr. Blanford's investigation of Raneegunge fields	157
Returns of the quantity of coal raised	158
The Vindhyan formation	159
Surveys of Medlicott, Oldham, Mallet, and Hackett	159
Mr. Medlicott's Survey of the Sewaliks and Outer Himalayas	160
Messrs. Theobald and Mallet in the Spiti Valley	161
Mr. Mallet and Dr. Stoliczka in the Himalayas	161
The Geological Survey extended to the Madras Presidency	161
Examination of cretaceous rocks by Messrs. King and Foote	161
Cuddapah and Kurnool hills surveyed by C. Oldham, King, and Foote	162
Survey of British Burmah. Blanford, Theobald, Fedden	163
Survey of the Bombay Presidency by Messrs. Blanford, Wilkinson, and Wynne	163
Mr. Blanford in the Central Provinces	164
Mr. Wynne's Survey of Cutch	165
Mr. Wynne on the geology of Mount Tilla	165
Discovery of stone implements in various parts of India	165
Dr. Oldham's superintendence. His numerous journeys	165
The Chanda coal fields	166
Museum of geology. Collection of meteoric stones	167
Publications of the Geological Survey	168
Arduous nature of the service	

XIII.—The Archæological Survey of India.

Importance of an Archæological Survey	170
Descriptions of early travellers	170
Sir William Jones and the foundation of the Asiatic Society	171

	Page
Formation of Societies at Bombay and Madras	171
Early labours in the field of Indian Archæology	171
Deciphering of inscriptions, in the Asiatic Researches	172
Discovery of Sir William Jones, that Chandragupta was the Sandracottus of the Greeks	174
Descriptions of ruins, in the Asiatic Researches	174
Mr. Erskine's account of Elephanta	175
Mr. Salt's account of the caves of Salsette	175
Colonel Sykes on Beejapore and the Ellora caves	175
Great value of the Mackenzie MSS.	175
Daniell's drawings of Indian monuments	176
Notice of James Prinsep	176
Prinsep's labours in deciphering Bhuddist inscriptions	177
Captain Kittoe's discoveries in Cuttack, and excavations at Sarnath	178
The Girnar inscription	178
The Manikyala tope. Researches of Ventura and Court	179
Death of James Prinsep	179
Prinsep's discovery of dates in Indian history	180
Later Indian archæologists	180
Notice of Mr. James Fergusson	180
Fergusson's classification of Indian architecture	182
Prehistoric remains in India	182
Buddhist remains	184
Dravidian architecture	188
Bengalee architecture	190
Chalukya architecture	190
Jaina architecture	191
Saracenic architecture	192
Coins and inscriptions	193
Ruins of Brahminabad	195
General Cunningham appointed Archæological Surveyor	196
Cunningham's operations in 1861–62	196
Cunningham's operations in 1862–63	197
Cunningham's operations in the Punjab in 1863–64	198
Cunningham's operations in 1864–65	198
Examination of temples in Kashmere by Lieut. Cole	199
Casting of the Sanchi gateway, by Lieut. Cole	199
Dr. Forbes Watson's report on the means of illustrating the archaic architecture of India	200
Steps taken by Government to conserve ancient structures	200
Re-appointment of General Cunningham in December 1870	201
Work remaining to be done	202
Report of Mr. Boswell	202

XIV.—Meteorological and Tidal Observations in India.

Importance of Meteorological Observations	204
Series taken at Calcutta by Colonel Pearse, 1785–88	204

Page

Series by Mr. Traill, 1784–85 - 205
General Hardwicke's observations at Dum Dum, 1816–23 - 205
James Prinsep's Benares Series, 1823 - 205
Sir J. Herschel's circular recommending horary observations - 205
Horary observations by Mr. Barrow, Colonel Colvin, and Lieuts. Durand and Baker - 205
Numerous observations by travellers - 206
Registers of Medical Officers. List - 206
Dr. Royle's Series. Series by Cunningham, Strachey, Hooker, &c. - 206
Dr. Lamb's abstract of registers at 126 - 207
Messrs. Schlagintweit's abstracts - 207
The Series taken at the Surveyor General's Office - 207
Dr. McClelland's abstracts for 1843–44 - 208
General Boileau's observations at Simla - 208
The Series taken at the Madras Observatory - 209
The Dodabetta Observatory - 210
The Trivanderum Observatory - 211
The Aghastya Mulla Peak Observatory - 212
Meteorological labours of Mr. Broun in Travancore - 212
Horary observations in the Madras Presidency - 213
Observations in Wynaad and Coorg - 213
Diagram by Dr. Arnold Smith, to illustrate the meteorological condition of Secunderabad - 213
Observations of Colonel Sykes in the Deccan - 214
Discussion of the results of observations by Colonel Sykes - 214
The Colaba Observatory at Bombay - 215
Observations by Mr. Orlebar - 215
Observations by Dr. Buist - 215
General Sabine on Dr. Buist's observations - 216
Dr. Murray's Series at Sattara and Mahabaleshwar - 216
Observations by Mr. Orlebar, Captain Montriou, and Lieut. Fergusson, at the Colaba Observatory - 217
Colonel Sykes on the further progress of Meteorology in India up to 1850 217
Registers of rainfall and temperature by Medical Officers - 219
Mr. Glaisher's Report on the Meteorology of India - 219
Meteorological Committee at Calcutta to establish warnings and forecasts - 220
Appointment of Meteorological Reporters 220
Dr. A. Neil's Reports on Punjab Meteorology - 220
Dr. Murray Thompson on the Meteorology of the North West Provinces - 221
Mr. Blanford on the Meteorology of Bengal - 222
Analysis of Mr. Blanford's Reports - 222
Progress of Meteorology in Madras - 224
Meteorological registers at the Bombay Observatory 224
Concluding remarks by Mr. Blanford - 225

Tidal Observations - 225
Captain Kyd's tidal observations in the Hooghly, 1806–27 - 225
Paper on co-tidal lines by Dr. Whewell - 226
Dr. Whewell's suggestions for tidal observations in India - 226

Page

Mr. Sinclair's table of times of high water at places between Calcutta and Point Palmyras - 227
Madras tides - 227
Chittagong tides by Lieut. Siddons - 227
Tides at Singapore and in the Indian Archipelago - 227
Prediction of tide tables for the Hooghly - 227
Self-registering tide gauge put up at Bombay by Dr. Buist - 228
Captain Montriou's Series - 228
Captain Ross's Bombay Tide Tables, 1835–40 - 228
Tide Tables by Surveyors of the Indian Navy - 228
Tides on the West Coast of India - 229
Captain Taylor's views on the causes of tidal irregularities - 229
Mr. Parkes's computation of Tide Tables for Kurrachee - 230
Mr. Parkes's investigation of diurnal inequality - 230
Mr. Parkes's Bombay Tide Tables - 231

XV.—Astronomical Observations in India.

Antiquity of the study of Astronomy in India - 232
Aryabhata's knowledge of Astronomy - 232
Mr. Spottiswoode on Aryabhata's system - 233
Vahara-mihira, Brahmegupta, and Bhascara - 233
The Arab Astronomers - 233
Ulugh Beg's Catalogue of Stars - 234
The Rajahs of Dhoondar - 235
Rajah Jey Sing appointed to construct tables - 236
Descriptions of the observatories of Jey Sing - 236
Tables and computations of Jey Sing - 237
Colonel Hodgson's observations - 238
The Lucknow Observatory - 238
The Madras Observatory - 238
Mr. Goldingham's labours - 239
Notice of Mr. Taylor. His Catalogue of Stars - 239
Notice of Captain Jacob. His revision of Taylor's Catalogue - 240
Major Worster's Catalogue of Stars - 241
Death of Captain Jacob - 241
Major Tennant in charge of the Madras Observatory - 241
Appointment of Mr. Pogson to the charge of the Madras Observatory - 241
Observations for the determination of the sun's parallax - 241
Catalogue of new small southern stars - 242
Observations of right ascension and polar distance - 242
Discovery of the planets "Sylvia" and "Camilla" at Madras - 242
Share of the Madras Observatory in the Survey of the Southern Heavens - 242
Trivandrum Observatory, Mr. Caldecott - 243
Trivandrum Observatory, Mr. John A. Broun - 243
Bombay Observatory - 245
The Madras Observatory now the sole point for astronomical work in India - 245

XVI.—Physical Geography of India.

	Page
Objects of operations described in previous sections	246
Objects of the present section	246
Enumeration of subjects	246
Structure of the Himalayan mass	247
Early travellers in the Himalayas	247
Captain Herbert's general view of the Himalaya	248
Travellers subsequent to Herbert's time (1818)	249
Cunningham, on the Physical Features of the W. Himalayas	250
Henry and Richard Strachey on the W. Himalayas	251
Dr. Thomson on the W. Himalayas	251
Mr. Hodgson on the Nepaul division of the Himalayas	252
Dr. Hooker's view of the structure of the Himalayas	252
Humboldt on the mountains of Central Asia	253
Recent examinations of the West Himalayas	254
Mr. T. Saunders on the structure of the Himalayas	254
Extent of the area still unexplored in the Himalayas	255
River systems of the Indus and Ganges	255
Cataclysms of the Indus and Sutlej	256
Changes in the Punjab rivers	256
Changes in the course of the Indus	257
Physical features of the Desert and Runn of Cutch	258
Region between the Sutlej and Jumna	258
Mr. Fergusson on changes in the Delta of the Ganges	259
Plateaux of Bundelcund and Malwa	261
Valley of the Nerbudda	262
Satpoora hills and valley of the Taptee	262
The Deccan and Mysore	262
Valley of the Mahanuddy	263
Basins of the Godavery, Kistna, and Cauvery	263
The Western Ghauts	263
Accounts of various sections of the Ghauts	264
Botanical Geography. Early botanists	264
The "Hortus Malabaricus"	264
Notice of Dr. Roxburgh. His works	265
Labours of Dr. Wallich	265
Dr. Griffith	266
Works of Dr. Forbes Royle	266
Works of Dr. Wight	268
"Flora Indica" of Drs. Hooker and Thomson	268
Collections of plants made in various districts	268
Preliminary essay in the "Flora Indica"	269
Effects of human action on the physical condition of the earth's surface	270
Use of forests	270
Forest conservancy	270
Services of Dr. Cleghorn	270
Value of Chinchona plantations	271
Modifications of climate caused by different soils	271

	Page
Changes taking place on the sea coast	271
Concluding remarks	272
Maps to illustrate the physical geography and statistics	273
Mr. Prinsep's maps of the Sealkote district	273
Maps in the Central Provinces. Administration Reports	273
Want of maps illustrating physical features	273

XVII.—The Geographical Department of the India Office.

Importance of a Geographical Department	274
Cosmographers' Department in the Council of the Indies	274
Course of lectures by the Spanish cosmographer	274
Richard Hakluyt, the founder of the Geographical Department	275
Edward Wright, the first compiler of charts	276
Major Rennell's works and labours	276
Rennell's declining years and death	277
A. Dalrymple appointed Hydrographer to the Company	278
Dalrymple's works	278
Notice of Captain Horsburgh	279
Arrowsmith's maps of India	280
Question of the publication of the Atlas of India	280
Notice of Mr. John Walker	281
Mr. Walker appointed to compile and engrave the Atlas	281
Death of Sir Charles Wilkins and Captain Horsburgh	281
Mr. Walker appointed Geographer	281
Mr. Walker's publications	282
Arrangements for engraving the sheets of the Atlas in India	283
Colonel Thuillier returns to India with a staff of engravers	284
Opinion of the Surveyor General on the importance of a responsible Geographical Department at the India Office	285
Mr. Trelawney Saunders appointed Assistant Geographer	285
Value of the collection of maps and records	285
Arrangement of the collection	285
Publication of a catalogue	286
Set of copies of ancient Portuguese plans	286
Copies of Dutch maps and charts at the Hague	287
Arrangements for exchange of maps with the Russian and Netherlands Governments	287
Recovery of lost sheets of the Mesopotamian Survey	287
Repair and cleaning of manuscript maps	288
Memoir on the mountains and river basins of India by Mr. Saunders	288
Map of the central part of British Burmah by Mr. Saunders	288
Completion of the sheets of the Hyderabad Survey	288
Work of the Geographical Department	289

LIST OF THE MEMBERS OF THE GREAT TRIGONOMETRICAL, TOPOGRAPHICAL, REVENUE, AND GEOLOGICAL SURVEYS OF INDIA; AND OF THE GEOGRAPHICAL DEPARTMENT OF THE INDIA OFFICE.

	Page
Survey Department	290
Great Trigonometrical Survey	290
Topographical Survey of India	293
Revenue Surveys under the Government of India	294
Surveyor General's Office	297
Office of the Superintendent of Revenue Surveys	298
Madras Revenue Survey	298
Bombay Revenue Survey	299
Inspection of Instruments for the Indian Surveys	301
Mathematical Instrument Department	301
Geographical Department of the India Office	301
Members of the Geological Survey of India	302

I.—INDIAN MARINE SURVEYS.

1.—EARLY VOYAGES AND THE BOMBAY MARINE. A.D. 1601—1830.

The Surveys of India began along the coasts, and the sailors preceded the shore-going surveyors by nearly 200 years. A sketch of the great services of the Indian Navy, therefore, will fitly precede an account of the operations of the surveyors on land. Before India could be measured, it was necessary to get there: and the history of Indian surveying takes us back to the day when James Lancaster's fleet of four ships and a victualler, got under weigh from Torbay on the 2d of May 1601. The East India Company set forth a voyage every year during the next twenty years; and the Company's sea captains observed for latitude and variation with the greatest diligence, keeping careful journals which must have been full of valuable information for the construction of charts.

Lancaster and Middleton, the commanders of the two first East India fleets, only visited the Eastern Islands, and came home with ladings of pepper and cheerful hearts. It was Captain Keeling, the leader of the third voyage in 1607, who first went to Surat, landed Mr. Finch to form a factory, and sent Captain Hawkins, his second in command, to persuade the great Mogul, at Agra, to order his officers to deal justly and favourably with the English. Then followed Sharpey's unlucky voyage and shipwreck on the shoals of Cambay, the remarkable voyage of Saris to Japan, and the establishment of factories on the Malabar coast by other captains, down to 1621.

The observations of these bold and talented seamen bore good fruit in the shape of "plotts" (charts) and sailing directions, which were condensed into "Rules for our East India Navigations," by the famous Mr. John Davis, of Limehouse, who made five voyages himself.*

* Harris's Voyages, I., ch. xliii, p. 224.

Richard Hakluyt, Archdeacon of Westminster, was the historiographer of the East Indies, receiving the appointment from Sir Thomas Smith, the first Chairman of East India Directors, in 1601. Hakluyt had the custody of all the journals of East India voyages, and made excellent use both of them and of the information he gleaned from "noted seamen of Wapping,"* with whom he constantly conversed. For he freely communicated his knowledge by giving lectures to the students at Oxford, and "was the first that "produced and showed both the olde and imperfectly composed "and the new lately reformed mappes, globes, spheres, and other "instruments of his arte, for demonstration in the common "schooles, to the singular pleasure and great contentment of his "auditory."

While Hakluyt thus made the maps and journals from the Indies useful to the public, Edward Wright, the excellent mathematician and engineer who accompanied the Earl of Cumberland on his voyage to the Azores, was compiling and systematizing the logs and charts. He was the first person appointed by the Company to perfect their charts, in 1616, on a salary of 50*l.* a year,† and was thus the John Walker of the seventeenth century.

Hakluyt died in 1616, and the journals of the East Indian voyages, no doubt with the consent of the Directors, were handed over to the Rev. Samuel Purchas, the quaintest and most entertaining of old writers, but one who was much too fond of taking liberties with his materials. "Purchas his Pilgrimes" was published in 1625, and included the journals of the first twenty voyages set forth by the East India Company, but in a sadly abridged and mutilated form. Several of the originals have disappeared, and only two were ever published separately.‡ Sir Thomas Smith, the Chairman, who was the first to allow the journals to be lent, died on the 4th of September 1625, the year the "Pilgrimes" were published, and Purchas himself died in 1626. The deaths of lender and

* Fuller's Worthies, p. 39.

† Calendar of State Papers, East Indies, p. 284.

‡ I. "A briefe discourse of the voyage of Sir James Lancaster in 1601." This, the first voyage set forth by the Company, has never been printed since, and awaits an editor.

II. "The voyage of Sir Henry Middleton to Bantam and the Maluco Islands, printed for Walter Burre, 1606." A new edition of this voyage was edited and annotated by Bolton Corney, Esq., and printed for the Hakluyt Society in 1855.

borrower, occurring nearly at the same time, possibly account for the loss of some of the earliest journals of the Company's voyages.

The rest are still preserved at the India Office, and are numbered in two series; the first, consisting of 68 volumes, extending from 1606 to 1708; and the second, containing the logs of the East India Company's ships, from 1708 to 1832. The journals of Lancaster, Middleton, and Saris are missing. A copy of the latter (being the eighth voyage of the East India Company) was purchased some years ago, from Mr. Kerslake, a bookseller at Bristol, and is now in the Topographical Depôt of the War Office. The oldest logs, at the India Office, are those of Captain Keelinge in 1606, and Captain Sharpey in 1607. Among the other journals, of the first series, there is a curious treatise on map making in Thomas Love's log kept on board the "Peppercorn" in 1610; Downton's memorial of his second voyage in 1613; the journal of the junk "Sea Adventure," on her voyage from Firando to Siam, kept by Captain Adams; Sayer's journal kept from Firando to Cochin China; the journal kept in 1621 during a cruize off Manilla on board a ship in the combined English and Dutch fleets which sailed from Firando; and journals of other voyages to Aden, Surat, the Persian Gulf, and the Malabar and Coromandel coasts. One only of the Arctic voyages set forth by the East India Company has been preserved, and is about to be printed and edited by Sir Leopold McClintock. It is that of Captain Knight who sailed in 1606, and, landing on some frozen shore, was never heard of again. The discovery of the manuscript of Captain Knight's journal goes some way to exonerate old Purchas, and to show that he did return the journals he borrowed, for Knight is one of his "Pilgrimes." But though many of the logs have fortunately escaped destruction,* a thick darkness closes over the subject of marine surveying, and continues far into the eighteenth century. For in 1860 tons of precious records in the India Office shared the fate of the Alexandrian Library. Among them, the Minutes and Reports of the Committee of Shipping, containing a rich mine of information relating to all that concerned the marine branch of the Company's affairs, as well as the Indian Navy logs that had been sent home,

* The destruction of a log book is little short of sacrilege; and thanks are due, from all literary men, and especially from all who take an interest in the history of our Indian Empire, to Mr. Charles Mason of the India Office, to whose remonstrances the preservation of the old log books is owing.

were consigned to a fate worse than that of warming a true believer's bath.

Thus there is little light to be thrown upon marine affairs in the East Indies, and on the observations and surveys of the gallant seamen belonging to the Company's service for many years; but during those years the Bombay marine was being developed into a service which was destined to produce a noble succession of surveyors. From very early times armed vessels were employed at Bombay to protect the Company's ships from the pirates that swarmed along the coast. In 1742, on a reduced establishment, we find a commodore of the Bombay marine with three 20-gun ships, and several armed gallivats and grabs under his command.* In 1755 Commodore James, with a small force of the Bombay Marine, took the castle of Severndroog, and in the same year Admiral Watson, in taking Gheriah, the stronghold of Angria, with five ships of the British navy and 2,000 soldiers under Clive, had besides nearly a dozen armed vessels of the Bombay marine.

Here then was the material for training surveyors; but it was not until the days of Rennell and Dalrymple that real encouragement began to be bestowed upon marine surveying, and that its great importance was at last appreciated.

Captain John Ritchie was Hydrographical Surveyor to the East India Company from about 1770 to 1785, and surveyed the coasts of the Bay of Bengal and the outlets of the Ganges. His work formed part of the material for Rennell's map of Hindostan. Many of his charts were engraved by Dalrymple, the Company's hydrographer, and a manuscript volume of his remarks is preserved in the Geographical Department of the India Office.† But his lati-

---

* "Anderson's Western India." "Rise of the army and navy at Bombay." "Bombay Quarterly Review, V., p. 265."

† "Remarks upon the coast and bay of Bengal, the outlets of the Ganges and interjacent rivers, according to the surveys of John Ritchie, hydrographer to the United India Company."

Contents.

1. Entrance to the Hooghly, and remarks on its pilotage.
2. Rivers eastward to the Megna, Coast Islands.
3. Chittagong and Islands.
4. Tempests to which the head of the bay is subject.
5. Coast of Arracan.
6. Coast of Ava to C. Negrais.
7. Andaman Islands.
8. Nicobar Islands.

Dalrymple engraved Ritchie's chart of the Coromandel and Orissa coasts (1771), and others.

tudes and longitudes were taken afloat, and his soundings were barely more than sufficient to show the track of his vessel. A Captain Lacam also surveyed the coast at the mouth of the Hooghly in 1770.

Captain Huddart is mentioned by Major Rennell in his Memoir on the map of Hindostan, as having taken a series of observations for latitude and longitude along the Malabar coast between 1780 and 1790. Captain John McCluer, with Lieut. Wedgbrough, in the ships "Endeavour" and "Panther," was employed in surveying the west coast of India from September 1790 to July 1793. Captain McCluer's work was reported to be very incomplete and unintelligible, and there were no astronomical observations in his journal. The resulting chart was drawn by Lieut. Wedgbrough, and many of McCluer's smaller plans were engraved by Dalrymple. McCluer also made one of the earliest plans of Bombay harbour, assisted by Lieutenant Court, which was afterwards corrected by Dominicetti, and Wedgborough made a chart of the Laccadive islands.

Betwen 1777 and 1795 Lieutenant Archibald Blair was very actively engaged in making surveys of parts of the Andaman Islands, the Kattywar coast, Salsette, and other patches here and there.*

In 1788 Captain Michael Topping submitted a journal kept on board the E. I. C. ship "Walpole," in a voyage to Madras, with a chart of the Bay of Bengal. In 1790 he was sent to make a survey of Coringa and the mouth of the Godavery river, a service which he performed most creditably, submitting a chart and a valuable memoir as its results. He was then employed during 1792 in taking observations for determining the course of the currents in the bay of Bengal; and he afterwards took a series of levels of the river Kistnah from the sea to Bezwarra, with a view to the construction of irrigation works. These services led to his appointment as chief surveyor at Madras in 1794, when he drew up a general plan for the improvement of the geography and navigation of India. The bay of Coringa was surveyed again in 1805–6 by Lieutenant Warren, who also made a plan of the roadstead of Vizagapatam.†

* For an account of Blair's Survey of the Andamans, see "Selections from the Records of the Government of India (Home. No. 24)."

† A manuscript memoir of Lieut. Warren's Survey is preserved in the Geographical Department of the India Office. Captain Topping's Memoir on Coringa, with notes by Lieut. Warren and Captain Biden, was published by the Madras Government in 1855.—*Selections, No. xix.*

The expedition to the coast of Egypt led to an examination of the Red Sea in 1799–1800, and Sir Home Popham, who commanded the fleet, drew up some sailing directions for its navigation. But even then it was not entirely unknown. On Lord Valentia's chart the tracks are given of the cruizer "Swallow" in 1776, "Venus" in 1787, and in 1795 Lieutenant Court had taken the "Panther" up as far as Suez. A chart of the Red Sea was drawn by Lieut. Robert White in 1796, for which he received much praise and his promotion. In 1803 Lord Valentia was travelling in India, and while at Calcutta he declared to Lord Wellesley, the Governor General, that he felt it to be a national disgrace that the western coast of the Red Sea should be a perfect blank on our charts; and his lordship volunteered to embark on board one of the cruizers of the Bombay marine and investigate that shore, with a view to prosecuting further inquiries into the state of Abyssinia. The great Viceroy concurred, and Captain Keys of the cruizer "Antelope" was ordered to take Lord Valentia on board at Mangalore, and place himself under his lordship's orders. The "Antelope" sailed for Aden on March 13th, 1804, with Captain Keys as Commander, Lieutenants Hall and Maxfield, Midshipman Hurst, Lord Valentia in the anomalous position of commanding the commander, and Mr. Salt as private secretary. The arrangement did not answer. At Mocha Captain Keys began to show a disinclination for the work, at Dhalac he accused Lord Valentia of wanting to get the credit of discoveries made by his officers, and at Massowa they came to an open quarrel, and only communicated with each other in writing. They returned to Bombay in September, and Captain Keys was put under arrest.

Yet neither Lord Wellesley nor Lord Valentia were disheartened. Two other vessels were ordered to be fitted out for a second expedition under the same arrangement, which this time answered admirably. Captain Court, who had a high character both as a seaman and a man of science, took command of the "Panther," with Lord Valentia and Mr. Salt on board, and two midshipmen named Hurst and Crawford, while Lieutenant Maxfield had the tender "Assaye," a small schooner. They sailed from Bombay on December 4th, 1804, surveyed part of the Dhalac Islands, the great bay to which Captain Court gave the name of Annesley, the island which he called Valentia, and the coast for some distance to the north of Massowah. In July 1805 Lord Valentia landed his secretary, Mr. Salt, at Arkeeko, accompanied by Captain Rudland of the Bombay army, a Mr. Carter, and an adventurous blue-jacket named Pearce, to go on a mission to the ruler of Tigré at Antâlo; his lordship visiting Mocha and other places in the meanwhile. The embassy was a success; but as for geography, Mr. Carter observed for latitude several times at Antâlo, and his result was nearly 40 miles out. In November 1805 the whole party sailed from Massowa, and reached Suez in the end of January 1806. Lord Valentia had agreed perfectly with Court and Maxfield, and had got some useful work done. They parted with regret, and the crew of the "Panther" gave his lordship three cheers when he went over the side. The results of the surveys of Captain Court and his officers are given in a chart of the Red Sea in two sheets, in Lord Valentia's travels.* Lieutenant Maxfield also made a chart of Massowa, and part of the Abyssinian coast, assisted by young Crawford and Hurst; for which he received Rs. 600 from the Government as a recognition of his zeal, and his youngsters were granted Rs. 200 each.

The hydrography of the Indian seas at the opening of the present century was deemed of sufficient importance to warrant the appointment of a Marine Surveyor General at Calcutta, and Captain Court was selected for the post, which he held until 1823. During this period, from 1806 to 1820, Captain Daniel Ross was engaged, with the assistance of Lieutenant Maughan† and others, in surveying the coast of China.‡ Ross made surveys of a portion of the Gulf of Pechili and of the Canton province, as well as of some of the eastern islands. His charts were published as they were completed, and the whole were incorporated into a general chart by Captain Horsburgh. Admiral Collinson, when surveying in China, had opportunities of testing several of the charts drawn from surveys by officers of the Bombay Marine, and he bears testimony to the accuracy of their work. It surprised him to find how much further advanced the Bombay officers were than the marine surveyors of that period in England.

* "Voyages and travels to India, Ceylon, the Red Sea, Abyssinia, and Egypt, in 1802–6, by George Viscount Valentia," 3 vols. (London, 1809).

† In 1804 Lieutenant Maughan had made a survey of the Gulf of Cutch, for which he received Rs. 1,000 from the Government, "as an encouragement to others to emulate his praiseworthy conduct."

‡ "Directions intended to accompany the chart of the South Coast of China, by Daniel Ross and Philip Maughan, Lieuts. of the Bombay Marine. Printed by order of the Directors of the East India Company." (London, 1808.)

The surveys of the Canton river, and of the coast 100 miles on each side, by Daniel Ross, were found by Admiral Collinson to be remarkably correct. Captain Court also had two vessels surveying the Bay of Bengal under Lieutenant Maxfield, and caused searches to be made for various shoals. Captain Knox surveyed a portion of the sea-face of the Sunderbunds in 1803–4; and Captain Maxfield's chart of the coast from Saugor point to Lighthouse point at the mouth of the Hooghly, from a survey executed in 1816, was in use until it was superseded by Captain Lloyd's work in 1841. Admiral Sir Henry Blackwood having reported that H. M. S. "Leander" had been safely at anchor inside the Armagon shoal, north of Madras, for four days during the monsoon, Captain Maxfield was sent to investigate the capabilities of the place, which has since been called Blackwood's Harbour. He went there in 1822 on board the "Henry Meriton," accompanied by Captain De Haviland, but the conclusion come to at the time was that its distance from Madras was an inconvenience which outweighed any advantages it might have as an anchorage.* In 1823, however, the Madras Government hired a schooner called the "Mary Anne" to ride out the monsoon in Blackwood's Harbour, as an experiment.

While Captain Court was Marine Surveyor General at Calcutta, the name of James Horsburgh became indissolubly connected with the Marine Surveys of India. Beginning life as a cabin boy, this bold and diligent Scotch sailor soon rose to the command of a vessel in the Eastern seas, and his innate love of surveying had excellent opportunities for development. After many years he returned to England, and the publication of a set of his charts, engraved by Walker, at once placed him in the first rank of hydrographers. Mr. Dalrymple, who was hydrographer to the East India Company, died in 1807, and the post remained vacant for three years. During that interval Captain Horsburgh published the first edition of his East Indian Directory,† for which the Court of Directors granted him a hundred guineas, and on November 10th, 1810, he was appointed to examine the journals of the Company's ships, and became hydrographer. From that time all charts passed under his

* Chart of Pulicat and Armagon shoals, by Captain Maxfield.

† The second edition appeared in 1817; the first in 1808. A sixth edition is in preparation.

scrutiny, and were published with the benefit of his superintendence until the time of his death in 1836.*

On the death of Captain Court in 1823, he was succeeded at Calcutta by Daniel Ross, "The Father of the Indian Surveys" as he was called. He was indeed the first who introduced a really scientific method. During the Burmese War from 1823 to 1826 the useful operations under his superintendence were interrupted, but he had the "Research" (300 tons) and "Investigator" (450 tons) at work in the Mergui Archipelago; and in 1827, Captain Crawford, the midshipman whose zeal, when with Lord Valentia, had been rewarded by a grant of Rs. 200, surveyed part of the coast of Arracan in a hired brig. John Crawfurd, in his embassy to Ava, speaks in the highest terms of Captain Crawford's surveying work. The "Research" was given up to Captain Dillon to go in search of La Perouse, but the little "Freak" was substituted, and surveys were made along the Martaban coast.

In 1828 there was a fit of ruinous economy. The "Freak" was sold, the "Investigator" was declared to be unseaworthy on account of the ravages of white ants, and Lord William Bentinck ordered the surveying establishment to be broken up.

But stout old Daniel Ross was urgent and importunate in advocating a resumption of the good work: and in 1830 he again had two brigs, the "Flora" and "Sophia," in the Mergui Archipelago, under his assistant, Lieutenant Lloyd, while he himself examined the coast of Arracan.† Captain Ross did his work with great care and regard for scientific accuracy, and it was all on a trigonometrical

---

* Captain Horsburgh's copy of the "Minutes of the Committee of Shipping" is preserved in the Geographical Department of the India Office. The first entry is that recording his appointment on Nov. 10th, 1810, the last is on June 20th, 1837, the year after his death.

Fourteen charts, actually compiled by Horsburgh himself, were published by the East India Company, viz.:—

1. North Atlantic Ocean.
2. South Atlantic Ocean.
3. Part of the Indian Ocean.
4. East Peninsula of India.
5. West coast of Sumatra.
6. Straits of Rhio and Durian.
7. Straits of Banca and Gaspar.
8. Carimata Passage.
9. Strait of Sunda.
10. China Sea (2 sheets).
11. Canton River.
12. East coast of China.
13. Eastern passages to China (3 sheets).
14. Tracks through Pitt Passage and Dampier Strait (1793).

† Captain D. Ross's M.S. sailing directions for the Mergui Archipelago are preserved in the Geographical Department of the India Office.

basis. He measured bases on shore by running a ten-foot rod along a cord stretched tight between the extreme points, and kept in position by stakes, the direction being verified by a telescope. When work on shore was impracticable, recourse was had to measurement by sound. The vessels were anchored when the weather was calm, and the time was taken between the flash and report of a gun, on the assumption that sound travels 1,140 feet per second. All angles were taken with a sextant, and the triangulation was verified by frequent astronomical observations. In Ross's time the Government of India used to strike off a few copies of his charts at Calcutta by lithography, and send the originals to the India House for engraving and publication.*

Captain Daniel Ross resigned his appointment in November 1833, and was succeeded by his able assistant Lloyd. He retired to Bombay, where he was Master Attendant, and President of the Geographical Society from 1839 until just before his death.†

In 1820 the survey of the Persian Gulf was commenced‡ under Captain Guy of the "Discovery" (268 tons), with Captain Brucks as his assistant, in the brig "Psyche." Guy retired, after having examined the Arabian side up to the head of the Gulf.§ His successor, Captain Brucks, was a good sailor, though unfortunately not a scientific surveyor; but he had under him Lieutenants Haines, Kempthorne, Cogan, Pinching, Ethersey, Whitelock, and Lynch, all men of scientific and literary attainments, while the charts were constructed with great taste and ability by Lieutenant Houghton, a most accomplished draughtsman.

It must not be forgotten that surveying was but a small part of the work of the Indian Navy. The influence of England in the Persian

* "Progress of Maritime Surveys." "Journal of the Asiatic Society of Bengal," I, p. 327.

† The following is a return of the cost of the Bengal Surveys from 1821 to 1824 :—

1821-22. Annual expense of survey vessels "Nearchus," "Minto," "Sophia," and "Henry Meriton," Rs. 1,19,055.

1823-24. Annual expense of survey vessels "Research" and "Investigator," Rs. 59,379.

1833-34. Annual expense of survey vessels "Flora" and "Sophia," Rs. 25,055.

‡ The Persian Gulf Survey was commenced by Captain Maughan at Cape Mussendom, but he had done very little when Guy succeeded him

§ The memoir of Captain Guy's portion of this survey, drawn up at his request by Lieutenant Houghton, is preserved in the Geographical Department of the India Office in MS.

Gulf was exercised to suppress piracy and extend commerce, to maintain the *status quo* of the chiefs, to exclude foreign influence, and to root out the slave trade. The English may look upon their connexion with the Persian Gulf with almost unmixed satisfaction. They have hunted down the atrocious hordes of pirates, and have enabled unarmed merchantmen to pass up and down in safety. The successful invasion of Persia in 1856 is amongst the more recent operations of the Indian Navy. The naval head-quarters were at Bassadore, in the Island of Kishm, where there was a guard ship and hospital, and on shore a bázár, five or six private houses, a billiard room, a fives court, and livery stables for the sailors when on liberty.*

The survey occupied ten years, from 1820 to 1830, and Lieutenant Haines also examined the Mekrán coast. The results are given in 14 charts. We also have, as results of the old Persian Gulf Survey, a "Memoir descriptive of the Navigation of the Persian Gulf," being sailing directions by Captain Brucks himself;† notes made by Lieutenant Kempthorne on the identification of places touched at by Nearchus, which would have gladdened old Dr. Vincent's heart; on the ancient commerce of the gulf, and on a visit to the ruins of Tahric;‡ and three papers by Lieutenant Whitelock, one being a description of the islands at the entrance of the gulf, another an account of the Arabs on the pirate coast, and the third a narrative of a journey in Oman.§

Captain Brucks was an old sailor who had been at sea ever since he was 11 years of age, and he had completed 16 years' service in the Bombay Marine. He endeavoured to give his work a trigonometrical basis, and always observed for latitude and longitude on shore, with an artificial horizon, because the refraction was so great as to make it useless to observe with the natural horizon. But in fact only a portion of the survey was trigonometrical, and the bases were measured from ship to ship by sound. The other portion was merely a running survey, verified to some extent by astronomical observations. There was also some confusion in the longitudes. One half of the survey is referred to the meridian of Bassadore, which was fixed by

---

* "Report on Bassadore, with a plan of the roads, by Midshipman Hewett." "Bombay Selections," No. 24, p. 47.

† "Bombay Selections," No. 24, pp. 527–634.

‡ "R. G. S. Journal," v. p. 263. "Bombay G. S. Journal," i. p. 294, and xiii. p. 125.

§ "R. G. S. Journal," viii. p. 170. "Bombay G. S. Journal," i. p. 294.

chronometric measurement from Bombay; but, in those days, Bombay was 7 miles too far to the east. The other half of the survey was calculated from Bushire, the longitude of which had been correctly fixed by Mr. Rich, a former Political Resident, of high scientific attainments. Thus the work does not come up to the standard of excellence subsequently reached by the officers of the Indian Navy, and most of it has since required revision.

At the same time this old survey of the Persian Gulf reflects credit on those who executed it, when the imperfection of their instruments and the difficulties they had to overcome are taken into consideration. Captain Brucks returned to England in 1842, and resided at Exeter, of which city he was mayor. He died in 1850. He was for years employed in preparing a history of the Indian Navy, but the papers collected by him on this subject have never been published.*

After returning from the Persian Gulf, Lieutenants Cogan and Peters made a survey of Bombay harbour and of the coast as far as Bankote in 1832, which was published on a chart of two sheets;† and in the same year Captain Moresby was engaged in a partial examination of the Laccadive Islands.

In 1832 the Bombay Marine was converted into the Indian Navy, by the wish and command of King William IV., and an admirable system of surveying was inaugurated under the auspices of its first Commander-in-Chief, Sir Charles Malcolm.

---

* See "Bombay Times," March 16, 1850.

† The oldest English plan of the harbour of Bombay is in Fryer's work, published in 1698. Next there is one by Mr. Nichelson, master of H.M.S. "Elizabeth," published in 1787; it is stated to be an index to a large one in eight sheets. Then followed that by McClure and Court, corrected by Dominicetti; and then the survey by Cogan and Peters. (See page 32.)

Dalrymple published a plan of Mahim and the north end of Bombay Island by Lieut. Edward Harvey, from a survey in 1777.

2.—THE INDIAN NAVY.

A.D. 1832—1862.

When Sir John Malcolm came out as Governor of Bombay in 1827, his brother Sir Charles was appointed Commander-in-Chief of the Bombay Marine, which was henceforth to be called the Indian Navy.* The change dated from 1832. Sir Charles Malcolm instituted several extensive and important surveys: and the Indian Navy, which came into existence under his auspices, saw its most palmy days during his administration. He was the first Commander-in-Chief of that distinguished service. He was also the founder of the Bombay Geographical Society, an enlightened patron of science and literature, and a warm friend to the officers who served under him.† The first important act of his administration was the formation of the Red Sea Survey.

In 1829 the Indian Government resolved to prepare to open the route by Egypt for steam vessels, and coal was sent from Bombay to Suez in a collier, escorted by the ten-gun brig "Thetis," as a protection from pirates that then swarmed in the Red Sea. The old tub was lost on the reefs north of the Jaffatine Islands, and on the return of the "Thetis" to Bombay a regular survey was resolved upon.

At that time all knowledge of the Red Sea was derived from the chart of 1796 by Lieutenant White, from some sailing directions drawn up by Sir Home Popham during the expedition of 1800, and from Captain Court's charts of part of the western coast, when with Lord Valentia.

Captain Moresby, an excellent seaman and surveyor, was appointed to the "Palinurus" to survey the northern half from Suez to Jiddah, while Captain Elwon, in the "Benares," took up the southern half from Jiddah to Bab-el-Mandeb. The officers were picked men; there

* Sir Charles Malcolm, one of three distinguished brothers, was born in September 1782, and entering the navy served in his brother Pulteney's ship at the cutting out of vessels at Manilla, in 1798. His promotion was rapid, and he saw much service throughout the war. He was knighted by Lord Wellesley at Dublin in 1826, and became a Rear-Admiral in 1837.

† The Bombay Geographical Society was instituted on April 9th, 1831, and Sir Charles Malcolm was its first President, from its foundation until he left India in 1838, when he was succeeded by Captain D. Ross.

were Carless, the future surveyor of the mouths of the Indus; James Young; Pinching; Powell; Barker, the Abyssinian traveller; Christopher, the pioneer of the Indus, who fell gloriously at Mooltan; Wellsted, the accomplished author; and Felix Jones, then a very young officer, but whose skill as a draughtsman was already appreciated. No expense was spared in fitting out the expedition, and all the surveying appliances of the day were provided, besides ample supplies of well-found boats and tenders. The latter were native craft with Arab crews. The sea was then practically unknown, and great dangers and privations were inseparable from such a service.

The first base was measured by a chain at Suez by Captain Moresby in 1830, and the survey was steadily continued, without other interruptions than were necessary to refit the ships and crews, to its completion in 1834, by a system of triangulation down either shore. The work was verified by frequent bases, by almost daily azimuths, by latitudes by the sun and stars observed on shore with artificial horizons, and by chronometric differences.*

The original charts were drawn on a scale of an inch to a mile, but in places where the complicated nature of the channels required greater nicety, scales as high as ten inches were employed.

The original drawings were mostly by Felix Jones.

The noble resolution of all the officers was that the Red Sea Survey should be as perfect as labour and skill could make it; and it has served well to guide thousands of steamers up and down one of the most important and, at the same time, one of the most intricate routes in the world.

The charts were compiled at Bombay from the original drawings by Lieut. Carless, and sent home to be engraved. The northern part of the Red Sea, by Captain Moresby, was published in two sheets in 1833, and the southern, by Captain Elwon, also in two sheets, in 1834. Two sheets of harbours in the Red Sea, and the sailing directions by Captains Moresby and Elwon, were published in 1841. In 1848 Captain Barker, I.N., made a re-survey of the anchorage at Suez;† and Suez Bay, as well as the straits of Jubal, have recently been again examined by Captain Mansell, R.N. In the contemplated partial revision of the survey, called for by the opening of

* "Letter from Captain Felix Jones to the Hydrographer of the Admiralty, July 13th, 1870."

† Captain Barker's chart of Suez Bay was accompanied by a memoir.

the Suez Canal and the great increase of traffic, the original drawings on larger scales would have been of the greatest possible value, but it is feared that they have been carelessly thrown aside and lost.

The literature of the Red Sea Survey is chiefly from the pens of Lieuts. Carless and Wellsted. In the second volume of his "Travels in Arabia,"* Wellsted gives a most interesting account of the proceedings of the survey in the gulfs of Suez and Akaba, and along the coast of Arabia; and he also wrote several detached papers bearing on the work on which he was engaged in the Red Sea, while Carless furnished a valuable memoir on the gulf of Akaba.†

A survey of the coral islands which cross the track of Indian trade had long been considered of the greatest importance to navigation, and Captain Horsburgh strongly urged its necessity.‡ As soon, therefore, as Captain Moresby had completed his work in the Red Sea, he was ordered to proceed in the surveying ship "Benares," with the "Royal Tiger," commanded by his assistant surveyor, Lieut. Powell, and a large decked boat called the "Maldiva," to survey the Maldive Islands. The surveying staff was composed of Lieuts. Robinson, James Young, Barker, Macdonald, Riddle,§ Christopher, Michael Lynch, and Felix Jones. The latter officer drew the original charts, and their execution was so beautiful that they were brought home for the Queen's inspection. The Maldive Islands were almost unknown, and in order to acquire a knowledge of the language, customs, and resources of the inhabitants, Lieuts. Young ‖ and Christopher were landed in June 1834,

---

* "Travels in Arabia, by Lieut. J. R. Wellsted" (2 vols.), 1838.

† "Notes on Bruce's charts of the coast of the Red Sea, compared with the positions of the recent survey, by Lieut. Wellsted."—*R. G. S. Journal*, v. p. 286.

"Observations on the coast of Arabia between Ras Mohammed and Jiddah, by Lieut. Wellsted."—*R. G. S. Journal*, vi. p. 51.

"Memoir on the Gulf of Akabah, from notes during the survey by Moresby in 1833, by Lieut. Carless, I.N."—*Bombay G. S. Journal*, vol. i.

Lieut. Wellsted died in 1843. He also published a work entitled "The City of the Caliphs," 2 vols., and wrote an elaborate memoir on the Island of Socotra, which he visited and explored in 1834, in the *R. G. S. Journal*, v. pp. 129-229, with a map. See also *Journal of the Asiatic Society of Bengal*, iv. p. 139.

‡ Captain Horsburgh had written a paper in 1832 on the "Navigable Channels separating the atolls of the Maldive Islands."—*R. G. S. Journal*, ii. p. 72.

§ Mr. Riddle died from the effects of the climate of the Maldives.

‖ This distinguished officer was lost in a hurricane on the Malabar coast in April 1847, when in command of the "Cleopatra." See a paper on the subject of this hurricane by Captain Carless in the "Bombay G. S. Journal," viii. p. 93.

James Young was engaged at the time of his death in diligently collecting materials for wind and current charts.

and resided for some time at Malé, the principal island. The results of their observations are recorded in a very interesting memoir.* It was found that the Maldivans were a civilized, commercial, and seafaring people, who constructed their own quadrants, and translated our nautical tables into their language.† Having completed the Maldive Survey, Captain Moresby proceeded to the Chagos Archipelago in February 1837, and afterwards surveyed part of the Saya de Malha bank, about five degrees S.E. of the Seychelles. He completed this important work, and returned to Bombay in September 1838.‡

The Gulf of Manaar and Palk Strait, with the Paumben Channel and Ceylon coast, were then taken up by Lieuts. Powell and Ethersey, assisted by Lieuts. Grieve and Christopher, with Felix Jones again as draughtsman. They surveyed the Paumben Pass, the west side of Palk Strait, Adam's Bridge, the west coast of Ceylon from Galle to Colombo, and a small portion of the Tinnevelly coast. After their recall in April 1838, the work was continued by Captain Franklin, R.N., the Madras Master Attendant.§ This officer exe-

* "Memoir on the inhabitants of the Maldive Islands, by Lieut. James Young and Lieut. Christopher."—*Bombay G. S. Journal*, i. p. 54. Vocabulary of the Maldivan language, compiled by Lieutenant Christopher, I. N.—*Journal of the Royal Asiatic Society*, vi. p. 42.

† See a very interesting account of the nautical instruments used by the Maldive navigators, by James Prinsep, in the "Journal of the Asiatic Society of Bengal," v. p. 784.

‡ The charts resulting from these surveys are—

1. Maldive Islands, by Captain Moresby and Lieut. Powell. 3 sheets. 1835.
2. Maldive Islands (reduced).
3. Chagos Archipelago, by Moresby and Powell. 1836.
4. Principal groups in the Chagos Archipelago, by Moresby and Powell. 1837.

Captain Moresby drew up sailing directions for the Maldive Islands and Chagos Archipelago: "Nautical directions for the Maldive Islands and the Chagos Archi- "pelago, by Commander Robert Moresby, I.N., 1839. Printed by order of the "Court of Directors." (London, 1840.) See a Summary of "Moresby's Report on the Maldives" in the "Bombay G. S. Journal," i. p. 102.

§ The resulting charts are—

1. Coast of Madura, by Powell, Ethersey, and Franklin (1838).
2. Western side of Palk Strait, by Powell and Ethersey (1838).
3. Paumben Pass, by Powell and Ethersey (1837).
4. Islands of Rameswaram and Manaar, by Powell and Ethersey.
5. W. coast of Ceylon. Franklin, Powell, and Ethersey. 4 sheets.
6. Palk Strait and Gulf of Manaar. Powell, Ethersey, and Franklin. 2 sheets. (1838 and 1845.)
7. Harbour of Tuticorin. Franklin (1842).
8. Coast of Tinnevelly. Franklin (1842).

Lieut. Christopher wrote an account of Adam's Bridge and Rameswaram, with a plan of the temple.—*Bombay G. S. Journal*, vol. vii.

cuted his survey in a small country craft of 60 tons, between 1840 and 1845. He completed the coast from Cape Comorin to Point Calimere on the Indian side, and made a plan of Tuticorin harbour, and of the pearl banks.* Dalrymple had published a plan of Tuticorin by Van Keulen, in 1782.

While Moresby went to the Maldives on board the "Benares" the old "Palinurus" was fitted out for the survey of the south coast of Arabia, which was commenced in October 1833. Captain Haines received the command, and his officers were Lieutenants Sanders, Cruttenden, Grieve, Rennie, and Dr. Hulton. The survey was intended to cover 500 miles of coast, but it was discontinued in May 1837, and Captain Haines was employed on political work connected with the occupation of Aden, of which acquisition he was the first Political Resident.† He, however, effected the survey of a large portion of the south coast of Arabia, and in October 1837 Lieut. Carless was despatched to survey the coast of Africa about Cape Guardafui, work which was satisfactorily accomplished.

These surveys are utilized by the publication of ten charts,‡ and are also described in several very interesting memoirs. Captain Haines himself has given a graphic account of the Hadramaut and Yemen coasts in two elaborate papers;§ and his assistant, Captain Sanders, has supplemented them by a further paper;‖

---

* Captain Franklin's sailing directions were published by the Madras Government. "Instructions for navigating the Gulf of Manaar and Palk's Bay." (1851).

† Correspondence relating to Aden, Parliamentary Paper, 1839.

‡ 1. Entrance to the Red Sea, by Haines. (1835.)
2. S.E. coast of Arabia. Haines. 3 sheets. (1836.)
3. Several bays near Cape Aden. Haines. (1836.)
4. N.E. coast of Arabia. Sanders and Grieve. (1849.)
5. Gulf of Aden. Haines, Barker, and Grieve. (1847.)
6. Kooria Mooria Islands. Haines. (1837.)
7. Island of Socotra. Haines. (1834.)
8. Islands west of Socotra. Grieve. (1848.)
9. N.E. coast of Africa. Carless. 2 sheets. (1838.)
10. Gulf of Maseera. Grieve. 2 sheets. (1847.)

§ "Memoirs to accompany the chart of the south coast of Arabia, by Captain Haines," Parts I. and II.—*R. G. S. Journal*, ix. p. 125, and xv. p. 104.

Two copies of the original manuscript of the first part of Captain Haines's Memoir, with pen and ink sketches and copies of Himaritic inscriptions at Saná, by Lieut. Cruttenden, are preserved in the Geographical Department of the India Office.

‖ "Short memoir of the proceedings of East India Company's brig 'Palinurus' during the examination of the Arabian coast."—*R. G. S. Journal*, xvi. p. 169.

while Lieut. Cruttenden has given us a journal of his excursion into Dafar.* Dr. Hulton, the surgeon of the "Palinurus," furnished a very interesting history of the Kooria Mooria Islands,† and Lieut. Cruttenden has published a still more valuable account of his visit to Sana, the capital of Yemen, while the "Palinurus" was surveying Mocha roads in 1836.‡ Sana had not been seen by any European since the time of Niebuhr in 1762,§ which gives additional importance to Lieut. Cruttenden's account of the town, and of the coffee-yielding highlands which he traversed to reach it. Dr. Hulton, who was Cruttenden's fellow traveller, was taken ill on the road, and died soon after returning to Mocha.

In 1833, while Moresby went to the Maldives and Haines to Arabia, Lieut. Whitelock, a veteran of the Persian Gulf, commenced a rough survey of the west coast of Kattywar, and had completed it as far as Diu, including the island of Beyt, at the time of his death in 1836. In the following year Lieut. Ethersey zealously took up the work where Whitelock left off, and surveyed the coast round the head of the Gulf of Cambay, and down the east side to Surat, as well as the N. Concan coast from St. John's to Bassein. He performed this work in a miserable native *pattamar* called the "Bhowany," with the water washing up to his ankles under the cabin table.‖ During this service Ethersey laid down the dangerous shoals off Surat called the Malacca banks, on which Captain Sharpey was wrecked in 1607, attentively observed the bore or rushing tide at the head of the Gulf of Cambay for two successive seasons, and explored the fossiliferous tertiary formations on the

---

* "Journal of an excursion into Dafar, by Midshipman Cruttenden."—*Bombay G. S. Journal*, vol. i.

The MS. of Cruttenden's Journal, dated "Palinurus, March 16th, 1836," is preserved in the Geographical Department of the India Office.

† "Account of the Curia Muria Isles, by the late Dr. Hulton."—*R. G. S. Journal*, xi. p. 156; *Bombay G. S. Journal*, vol. iii.

‡ "Excursion to Sána, the capital of Yemen, by Lieut. Cruttenden."—*Bombay G. S. Journal*, vol. ii. and *R. G. S. Journal*, viii. p. 267.

§ The Rev. Mr. Stern, who afterwards suffered a long captivity in Abyssinia, was at Sána in 1855.

‖ The charts representing this work of Whitelock and Ethersey are—

1. Coast of Kuttiawar from Diu to Dwarka. Whitelock. 1833.
2. Kuttiawar from Diu to Perim Isle. 2 sheets. Ethersey. 1836.
3. Diu Harbour. Whitelock. 1833.
4. Gulf of Cambay. Ethersey. 1845.

island of Perim. Besides his charts, the results of his survey are recorded in two valuable memoirs.*

We now come to the important work of the officers of the Indian Navy in the River Indus. When Colonel Pottinger went to Sinde in 1833, he was accompanied by Lieut. Del Hoste, who prepared a topographical memoir with sketch maps, and Alexander Burnes was also exploring the Indus in those days.† The work of Lieut. John Wood in the Indus commenced in about the year 1835, in command of the first steam vessel that floated on the river, when he examined its course from the sea to Hyderabad, and remained in the country to observe its periodical rise and fall. In 1836 Lieut. Wood accompanied Alexander Burnes in his mission to Kabool, and afterwards performed one of the most remarkable journeys that has ever been undertaken in Central Asia. Wood made a survey of the Indus from its mouth to Attock. At Kalabagh, the point where the mighty stream escapes from the Salt Range, he found it impossible to stem the current. Undaunted by the difficulty, Wood landed and went by forced marches to Attock, thence descending the river and completing his survey amidst the falls and rapids. After reaching Kabool he crossed the mountains to Koondooz, and was eventually the first and only European, except Marco Polo, who has ever reached the "Bam-i-Doonya" or roof of the world. Thus in 1838 Wood discovered the source of the Oxus, and for this splendid achievement he received the gold medal of the Royal Geographical Society.‡

---

* "On the bore or rushing tide in the Gulf of Cambay."—*R. G. S. Journal*, viii. p. 196.

"Notes on Perim Island, in the Gulf of Cambay."—*Bombay G. S. Journal*, ii.

"The Bore in the Gulf of Cambay."—*Bombay Selections*, No. 25.

† In the Geographical Department of the India Office there is a MS. "Route book of the mission to Sind in 1833, with sketch maps," by Lieuts. Patterson and Del Hoste. (There is a memoir by Lieut. Del Hoste on Sind in the "Bombay G. S. Journal," i. p. 22.)

Also MS. map of the Indus and Punjâb rivers from the sea to Lahore, by A. Burnes, with a paper regarding the construction of the map.

‡ "Memoranda on the River Indus, by Lieut. John Wood."—*Bombay G. S. Journal*, vol. i.

"Report on the source of the Oxus, by Wood."—*R. G. S. Journal*, x. p. 520.

"Personal narrative of a journey to the source of the River Oxus, by the route of the Indus, Kabool, and Badakshan, by Lieut. John Wood. (1845.)"

Selections from the Records of the Bombay Government, No. 17.

There are several manuscript maps by Lieut. Wood in the Geographical Department of the India Office. A series of sheets of the Indus and a chart of the Indus

At about the same time Lieut. Wyburd of the Indian Navy penetrated into Central Asia, and his fate still remains a mystery.

Meanwhile Lieut. Carless, in the "Palinurus," had carefully surveyed Kurrachee, and the whole coast from the eastern mouth of the Indus to Sonmeanee, in 1837 and 1838.* The Indus mouths were again surveyed, in 1846, by Captain Selby, assisted by Midshipmen Taylor and Stroyan, in the Taptee brig. He drew maps shewing the great swatch-way in which, in a regular line of 9 to 10 fathoms, there is a sudden dip of 40 to 68 fathoms, and so to 120. He concluded this to be the vast bed of the Indus before it had brought down the mountains of soil which now divide its stream into so many channels. These maps have never seen the light. Subsequently the operations of the Punjab campaigns led to the formation of an Indus Flotilla, under the command of Captain Powell, to ascertain the capabilities for navigation both of the Indus and of its Punjab tributaries. In 1847 Lieut. Christopher, with this view, went up the Sutlej and the Chenab in the steam tender "Meanee," with an iron flat laden with merchandise in tow, and made full reports of his observations.† Lieut. Christopher joined the force before Mooltan under Herbert Edwardes in 1848, and was killed during the siege. An elaborate survey of Kurrachee Harbour was

---

from Mittun to Attock in 1838; four sheets, on a scale of two inches to the mile, not coloured.

The original MS. maps, showing the routes of Lieut. Wood in Central Asia, are also preserved in the Geographical Department of the India Office. They consist of a map of the upper valley of the Oxus from Koondooz to its source, showing the new ground explored by Lieut. Wood, 1837-38; a survey of routes from Peshawur to Bamian, with sketches and sections of the Khyber and Hindoo Koosh passes; the route of Burnes's mission to Kabool, in three sheets; and the whole of Burnes's route from Kabool to Bokhara, and thence through Persia to Bushire, in nine sheets, drawn by Lieut. Wood. There are also a set of route surveys in Turkistan (seven sheets), and a reconnoitring survey of the Khawk pass, the most easterly from Kabool to Balkh in Turkistan.

* "Memoir to accompany the survey of the Delta of the Indus, in 1837, by Lieut. Carless."—*R. G. S. Journal*, viii. p. 328. Bombay Selections, No. 17. In the Geographical Department of the India Office there are three copies of a MS. map of the Indus, from Hyderabad to the sea, by Lieut. Carless.

† "Report of an experimental voyage up the Indus and Sutlej, by Lieut. Christopher."—*Bombay G. S. Journal*, viii. p. 144.

"Journal of an ascent of the River Chenab, by Lieut. Christopher."—*Bombay G. S. Journal*, viii. p. 236.

made by Captain Grieve in 1853–54,* assisted by Lieuts. Constable, W. H. Barker, and Stiffe.

Sir Charles Malcolm presided over the Indian Navy from 1827 to 1838. In the latter year Sir Charles was succeeded by Captain Robert Oliver, R.N., who had to recall all the surveys in consequence of the breaking out of war, and from 1839 to 1844 surveying operations were almost entirely suspended. Even when, after the latter date, a few surveys were sanctioned, they were confined to the narrowest limits, the officers were miserably found both as regards vessels and instruments, their allowances were cut down, and the acquisition of all knowledge beyond bearings and soundings was coldly discountenanced.

But officers who had been trained by Moresby and Haines, and whose zeal had been encouraged by Sir Charles Malcolm during so many years of progress, could not so easily be turned from their useful careers. They worked on, in spite of official discouragement. In 1823 an observatory had been formed at Colaba, the sea-girt spit of land south of Bombay, and Mr. Curnin received the appointment of Company's Astronomer, but the instruments supplied to him were so bad that he refused to make use of them. Other instruments were sent out in 1835, and remained unpacked for five years. The transit instrument was put up at last, in 1840; and since September 1841 a regular register of magnetic and meteorological observations, commenced by Mr. Orlebar, has been kept. Time is observed for rating ships' chronometers; but the longitude of Bombay still depends upon that fixed by the Madras observatory. In Sir Robert Oliver's time, the chart office of the Indian Navy was one little corner of the sail loft in the dockyard at Bombay, where numbers of valuable documents were eaten by white ants and cockroaches. The office of the draughtsman of the Indian Navy was afterwards removed to the observatory at Colaba, by Sir Robert Oliver, and here the charts were compiled, drawn, and occasionally lithographed. Captain Montriou held this office from 1847 to 1852, and drew up the information called for in the Parliamentary Paper printed in 1852. He was succeeded by Lieut. Fergusson, who held

* In two sheets on a scale of eight inches to the mile. When Mr. Walker drew up his report on Kurrachee Harbour he acknowledged his indebtedness to the excellent chart by Captain Grieve. This meritorious officer co-operated with Mr. Parkes in his examination of the harbour until his sudden death on Jan. 17th, 1858. Mr. Parkes took Grieve's chart as the general basis of his survey of Kurrachee Harbour.

the appointment until the end came in 1862. The establishment consisted of the draughtsman, and two natives for copying, and its whole cost was under 500*l*. a year.

In 1844 a few surveys were again permitted, but in such a niggard spirit that an officer making geological or other scientific investigations apart from sounding with the lead was obliged to pay his own boat hire! Captain Sanders* was sent in the "Palinurus" to complete the portions of the Arabian coast left unfinished by Captain Haines, assisted by Lieutenants Fell, Constable, Ward, and Whish, and accompanied also by that accomplished naturalist and geologist Dr. H. J. Carter. The work was completed by Lieutenant Grieve in 1848, who also, assisted by Lieutenant Ward, carefully surveyed the islands lying to the west of Socotra.† The second survey of the Arabian coast enabled Dr. Carter to make and record those valuable geographical and geological observations, which have since, from time to time, been published.‡

Sir Robert Oliver, the second Commander-in-Chief of the Indian Navy, died at Bombay, and, after a short interval, was succeeded in 1849 by Captain Lushington, who set several useful surveys on foot, and did his best to restore the service to the state of efficiency it had attained in the days of Sir Charles Malcolm.

* Captain Sanders died at sea, near Malta, on his way home, in 1848.

† The sailing directions for the Arabian coast and Socotra have been drawn up by Commr. Ward: "The Gulf of Aden Pilot, compiled by Comm. C. Y. Ward, H.M.I.N." (Published by the Admiralty in 1863.)

‡ In 1846 Dr. Carter published an account of the ruins of "El Bellad," formerly a town on the shore, in the province of Dafar, on the south-east coast of Arabia, in the *R. G. S. Journal*, xvi. p. 187, and with additions in the *Bombay G. S. Journal*, vii. p. 225, with a plate. In 1847 his notes on the Gurrah Tribe of the south-east coast of Arabia appeared in the *Journal of the Bombay branch of the Asiatic Society*, ii. p. 195, with a plate. Also notes on the Mahrah Tribe of the south-east coast of Arabia, with a vocabulary of their language, and further notes on the Gurrah, iii. p. 339, and a description of the frankincense tree of Arabia (*Boswellia papyrifera*), ii. p. 380. His memoir on the geology of the south-east coast of Arabia is in the same journal for 1852, iv. p. 21, and the second edition, which is the best, will be found in the "Geological Papers on Western India" (1858), p. 551.

Dr. Carter's admirable geographical description of the south-east coast of Arabia, together with an essay on the comparative geography of that coast, was published in the number of the Journal of the Bombay branch of the Asiatic Society for January 1851. It has since been reprinted separately.

He also wrote a paper on the igneous rocks of Muscat and its neighbourhood, and on the limestone formation at their circumference, in the Journal of the Bombay branch, No. XIII. (1850).

From 1844 to 1847 Captain Montriou, assisted by Midshipmen Taylor, Whish, Nixon, Lamb, and Dickson, surveyed the anchorages of Viziadroog, Rutnagherry, and others south of Bombay in the "Taptee" brig, but was frequently called away to assist in quelling the Sawunt-Warree insurrection. Captain Selby, in the "Palinurus," with Lieuts. Stroyan, Sweny, and May, having the "Nerbudda" cutter, commanded by Midshipman Charles Foster, as a tender, trigonometrically surveyed the coast of India from Cape Comorin to Beypoor and the Laccadive Islands, including the Sesostris bank. He constructed a map of a constant circular current prevailing between the Malabar coast and the Laccadives, which was not published, and the want of it caused the loss of one of the P. and O. steamers.* In the memoir which accompanied his drawings, Captain Selby described the remarkable mud bank at Aleppi, and entered at some length on the effects of the fearful cyclone of 1848 in the Laccadive group.

Captain Lushington seems to have systematized and put fresh vigour into this somewhat desultory work. During 1850–52 Lieutenants Rennie and Constable, on board the "Euphrates" brig, filled in the gaps left by Ethersey on the North Concan coast, while Lieutenant Taylor, assisted by Lieutenant Whish, with Barker, Stiffe, and Macaulay, surveyed the Gulf of Cutch and coast of Kattywar on board one little *pattimar* and the "Maldiva" cutter. Lieutenant Taylor's Survey was plotted on four sheets, on the scale of one inch to a mile, then reduced to one sheet by Whish and Stiffe. Their admirable chart is densely covered with soundings, and Taylor pointed out in his memoir the merits of the anchorages to the eastward of Beyt Harbour. Indeed one important result of his labours was to establish the existence of good harbours suitable for the export of Guzerat cotton, which are two days to windward of Bombay.†

Captain Selby was engaged from 1848 to 1850 in making a very important chronometric survey of the Bombay bank of soundings, on board the "Taptee" brig, assisted by Whish, Sweny, Macaulay, and Foster. At a distance of 100 to 150 miles from the shore there is a vast step or precipice some 2,000 feet deep, and the lead is all at once brought from 50 to 300 fathoms and no bottom.

* MS. letter from Captain Selby to Sir Henry Leeke, dated October 13th, 1855.

† "General description and sailing directions for the coast of Kattiwar." (Bombay, 1855.) See also the important paper by Captain Taylor on the harbours of India, read at the meeting of the British Association at Liverpool, 1870.

But within this ridge, the bank, from Diu on the north to Rutnagherry on the south, has a gradual and well-defined slope, so that by the unaided lead, and without seeing a heavenly body for days, the navigator may track his way safely and surely to his port.* Captain Selby also surveyed the entire approach to Bombay harbour from about 17°. 30 N. to 19°. 30 N.; and connected the North Canara with the Guzerat coast, including the tail of the Malacca banks.

The labours of officers of the Indian Navy have been the chief means of bringing the Somali coast of Africa to our knowledge.

In 1838 Captain Carless had made a beautiful survey of the African coast from Ras Hafun to Ras Gulwainee, assisted by Lieutenants Grieve and Selby. The results of Captain Carless's labours would probably have been lost had not the steam frigate "Memnon," under the command of Captain Powell, been wrecked on that coast in December 1843. She was supplied with a little outline chart, the result of Captain Owen's running survey of 1823-26. The question was asked whether Owen's was the best chart in existence, and it then came out that Carless had made an elaborate survey and drawn charts of the coast some years before the wreck of the "Memnon." His chart was *then*, when the mischief had been done, ordered to be engraved. Lieutenant Christopher was at work in 1841 on the African coast, near the mouth of the Juba, and he discovered the Haines river, which flows for many miles parallel to the coast, and terminates in a deep lake about 50 miles N.E. of the mouth of the Juba. Lieutenant Barker examined the coast S.W. of the straits of Bab-el-Mandeb and the Gulf of Tajura in 1840, and two years afterwards he accompanied the embassy of Major Sir W. C. Harris to the Abyssinian King of Shoa, as astronomer. Lieut. Grieve, in 1848, surveyed the Somali coast between Berbera and Ras Gulwainee. The Somali coast was also visited and reported upon by Lieutenant Cruttenden in 1848, who was then Assistant Political Agent at Aden; and Lieut. Stroyan was killed when serving on this coast, with the expedition of Burton and Speke. These officers have recorded the results of their observations in several papers. Lieutenant Christopher kept a journal, and noted down his inquiries into the resources of N.E. Africa;† Lieutenant Barker wrote on the same

* "Bombay G. S. Journal," xii. p. xx.

† "Bombay G. S. Journal," vol. vi. "R. G. S. Journal," xiv. p. 76. There is a MS. extract from the Journal of Lieut. Christopher (H.C. Brig Tigris) on the N.E. coast of Africa, May 8th, 1843, kept in the Geographical Department of the India Office.

subject,* and Lieutenant Cruttenden published two memoirs on Eastern Africa and on the tribes of the Somali coast.†

On the Bengal side, when Daniel Ross retired, his second in command, Captain Lloyd, succeeded as Marine Surveyor General, with J. Young, Fell, Rennie, and Montriou as his assistants. Lloyd had been in the survey department under Daniel Ross since 1823. In 1833 he had one brig, with which he conducted a survey of the inland navigation of Arracan, but, after the first season, his operations were put a stop to by severe illness, contracted by much exposure in that unhealthy climate. On his restoration to health, he, in 1835, surveyed the river Hooghly from Saugor Island to Calcutta, carefully connecting his work with the base line measured by Colonel Everest on the Barrackpoor road. In 1840 he completed the survey of the sea face of the Sunderbunds from Chittagong to Hidgellee, the results of which he submitted to Government in the form of carefully drawn charts and a most valuable and interesting memoir. He compares the state of the coast at the dates of different surveys, and his remarks, in showing the changes that are taking place, prove the urgent necessity for periodical revisions of the surveys. He also describes the remarkable phenomenon at the head of the Bay of Bengal, similar to that reported by Captain Selby off the mouths of the Indus, called the "swatch of no ground." It is a deep chasm, open to seaward and very steep on the north-west face, with no soundings at 250 fathoms.‡ Captain Lloyd also surveyed the Chittagong river, and made additions to Ross's survey of the Mergui Archipelago, a short account of which he published at the time. Ross had laid down the outer islands between 1827 and 1830, and Captain Lloyd filled up the inner portions, and delineated the coast line.§ The coast of the island of Cheduba was surveyed for the Indian Government by Captain Halstead, R.N., in 1840.‖

* "R. G. S. Journal," xviii. p. 130.

† "Bombay G. S. Journal," viii. p. 177, and "R. G. S. Journal," xviii. p. 136. See also a paper by Lieut. Fraser, I.N., relative to the River Juba.—*Bombay G. S. Journal*, xvi. p. 78.

‡ "The nautical remarks to accompany a survey of the sea face of the Sunderbunds, by Captain Lloyd," dated February 1841, are preserved in the Geographical Department of the India Office, in manuscript.

§ Journal of the Asiatic Society of Bengal, vii., pt. ii., p. 1027.

‖ In M. H. B. Childers. See Admiral Halstead's interesting Report on the Island of Cheduba.—*J. A. S. B.*, vol. x., pt. i., p. 349.

On the retirement of Captain Lloyd in 1840 the Marine Surveyor Generalship at Calcutta was abolished; but Captain Fell was employed from 1841 to 1848 on board the brig "Krishna" in finishing detached surveys on the Coromandel coast, along the Pegu and Martaban shores, and on the north coast of Sumatra.* In 1851 he was engaged in compiling a chart, in three sheets, of the whole survey of the Coromandel coast from Pulicat to Bimlipatam.

Captain Ward succeeded Fell in the command of the "Krishna." Between 1851 and 1859 he laid down the Mutlah river, the Preparis north channel, the Bassein and Rangoon rivers, the Malacca strait,† and Penang. Captain Ward also made surveys of the Sittang river and of the main branch of the Irrawaddy, but nothing has been heard of them since he sent in the drawings to the government. Finally Lieutenant Heathcote was engaged upon the surveys of the Bay of Bengal from 1856 to 1862. In the former year he made a survey of the western entrance of the Hooghly, from Kaokali to the Pilot Station at the Sand Heads. It was undertaken because the Gaspar channel, that commonly used, was becoming dangerous owing to accumulations of sand, and threatening to obstruct the traffic to Calcutta. This survey, which required very great exactness, was performed in the surveying vessels "Krishna" and "Spy," and the chart was drawn on a large scale, showing the depth of water to feet. It was accompanied by a report upon all the channels of the Hooghly, comparing their present form with that which they showed upon the last surveys, and showing the amount of accumulation that had taken place in the intervals. The work was connected with the stations of the Great Trigonometrical Survey.

In 1855, Captains Rennie and Heathcote were appointed to accompany Sir Arthur Phayre's Mission to the Coast of Ava, with instructions to make such a survey of the Irrawaddy above the British possessions as the opportunity afforded. The circumstances were favourable for astronomical observations of all kinds. The geographical positions of places and points were fixed, and a sketch

* There are printed sailing directions by Captain Fell for the coast of Pegu and Gulf of Martaban, dated March 4th, 1852, and MS. sailing directions for the north coast of Sumatra, from Achen Head to Diamond Point, in the Geographical Department of the India Office.

† Sailing directions for the Malacca Strait, by Captain Ward, are published in the last edition of Horsburgh's Directory.

survey of the rivers was forwarded to Calcutta, and afterwards lithographed for use in navigation. A section of the Irrawaddy at a point a little above Ava was obtained, and the volume of its discharge at that point calculated.* In 1861, Captain Heathcote was employed by the Admiralty to compile a chart of the bay of Bengal; and in 1857 he had made some additions and corrections on the Arracan coast. He also made a chart of the currents of the S. W. Monsoon in the bay of Bengal, intended as an accompaniment to Taylor's chart of the Arabian sea for the same season. The currents were worked out from a great number of the logs of the old Indiamen.†

Lieutenant Sweny completed the Coromandel coast from point Calimere to Pulicat in 1860.

The survey of the rivers Euphrates and Tigris, and of that region of Mesopotamia, which, for its historical associations, its capabilities, and the importance of its geographical position, surpasses almost any other country in the world, is mainly the work of the Indian Navy.‡ During upwards of 26 years the accomplished and persevering officers who executed the Mesopotamian Survey continued to work in the face of great difficulties and dangers; and for this alone the Indian Navy takes rank among the foremost contributors to geographical knowledge.

After the time of Colonel Chesney, his second in command, who was nearly lost in the ill-fated "Tigris," had charge of the survey in Mesopotamia. This was Henry Blosse Lynch, an excellent scientific observer and daring explorer, who had commenced his career in the Persian Gulf Survey. In 1837 Captain Lynch, C.B., traversed the whole course of the Tigris from its source in Armenia to Bagdad, fixing the chief positions by astronomical observations, and others by cross bearings. He then connected Nineveh, Bagdad, Babylon, and Ctesiphon by triangulation;

* For an account of the manner in which this running survey of the Irrawaddy was performed, see the *Journal of the Royal United Service Institution*, appended to a paper by Admiral Collinson on the Survey of Rivers.

† The chart was sent to the India Office, and is printed, together with the Memoir which accompanied it, in the *R. G. S. Journal for* 1862.

‡ In 1826-30 Lieutenant Ormsby, leaving the Indian Navy, had devoted three years to exploring Mesopotamia. His adventures are described by Wellsted in his "Travels to the City of the Caliphs." (2 vols., London, 1840.)

and, when he completed the Tigris map in 1839,* his mind was full of interest in his work, and he exclaimed that the field of operations, instead of diminishing, appeared to extend.

In October 1841 Lynch commenced the survey of the Euphrates by measuring a base on the level plain between Balis and Giaber. He had the steamers "Nitocris" "Nimrod," and "Assyria," and was assisted by Lieuts. Felix Jones, Campbell, Selby, and Grounds. After ascending the river, it was connected with the Mediterranean by chronometric measurements.† Captain Lynch retired from the survey in 1843, and his assistant, Felix Jones, succeeded him.

Felix Jones had already seen service in the Red Sea Survey, in the Maldives, in Ceylon,‡ and in the Manaar Gulf, and he had reported upon the harbour of Grane or Kowait in 1839, since which time he had been serving under Captain Lynch in the Euphrates. He was stationed at Bagdad, in command of the "Nitocris" steamer, and had other duties besides surveying; but every year he succeeded in completing some interesting and valuable surveys, although for a great part of the time he was almost single handed. In such a region it was impossible to go in any direction without meeting with work well worth the doing, and Felix Jones made the best use of his opportunities. The country, infested by wild tribes of Arabs, was frequently dangerous, and it was necessary to seize upon any chance that offered for exploring and surveying.

In 1844 Captain F. Jones accompanied Sir Henry Rawlinson on a journey to collect information respecting the boundary between Persia and Turkey. The results were a memoir and map of a

* The map is on a scale of 12 inches to a degree.

See "Note on a part of the River Tigris between Bághdád and Samawah."—*R. G. S. Journal*, ix. p. 471.

"Note accompanying a survey of the Tigris from Ctesiphon to Mosul."—*R. G. S. Journal*, ix. p. 441. Captain Lynch was ably assisted in this survey by his brother Michael Lynch, whose constitution did not equal his zeal, as he died from the effects of hard work and exhaustion at Diarbeker. This officer had suffered before from the climate of the Maldives.

† "Memoir of the River Euphrates, in three parts, to accompany the map."—*Bombay G. S. Journal*, vi. p. 169.

"Memoir of the country between Bághdád and the Humreed hills, by Lieut. Grounds."—*Bombay G. S. Journal*, vol. vi.

‡ While employed here he visited and fixed Adam's Peak and the Horton Plains, descending by the Caltura River, of which he made a survey, in company with Major General Adams, who fell at Inkermann. They pushed their way over the higher ranges by the Elephant paths, there being then no constructed roads.

country but little known. In 1846 he made an ascent of the Tigris, from Bagdad to Samarrah, on board the "Nitocris."* In 1848 he undertook a journey to determine the course of the ancient Néhrwán Canal, and to survey the once fertile region which it irrigated,—now a desolate and almost impassable waste. His interesting memoir on the Néhrwán Canal, accompanied by a map, gives the history of the work from the days of its construction in the time of the Sassanian dynasty, and minutely describes its vast brickwork dams and sluices. In April and September 1850 Captain Jones surveyed the old bed of the Tigris, discovered the site of the ancient Opis, and made researches in the vicinity of the Median wall and Physcus of Xenophon. In 1852 he made a trigonometrical survey of the country between the Tigris and the Upper Zab, including the ruins of Nineveh, fixing positions by meridian altitudes of the sun and stars, with chronometric differences for longitude. The results of this work are recorded in the beautiful maps of "Assyrian Vestiges," in four sheets, and in a valuable memoir. During 1853 Captain Felix Jones, assisted by young Collingwood, then a midshipman, completed a map of Bagdad on a large scale, with a memoir on the province full of statistical information;† and in 1854 he sent home his maps of Babylonia. They consisted of three sheets with a detailed memoir, and included the country from Museyb, north of Hillah, down to the N.W. end of the sea of Nejf. Unfortunately these maps were lost in the India House.‡

In 1846 Captain Felix Jones compiled a general map of Mesopotamia, from Scanderoon on the Mediterranean to Bussorah, which was based on the surveys by Chesney, Lynch, and himself. Captain Jones retired from the Mesopotamian Survey, to take up the post of Political Resident at Bushire in the Persian Gulf, in 1855. He possessed all the knowledge and tact which were necessary for an officer in his position. For the work of the Mesopotamian Survey several acquirements were essential in addi-

* "R. G. S. Journal," xviii. p. 1.

† The memoirs and maps by Captain Felix Jones will be found in the "Bombay Selections," No. xliii. (New Series). Most of the memoirs were reprinted in the Transactions of the Bombay Geographical Society.

‡ On the Survey of Nineveh and Babylon he was much indebted to Dr. J. M. Hyslop of the Bombay Army, for valuable aid in the field operations, and to Mr. T. K. Lynch, now Consul General for Persia in London, who entered "con amore" into the work from a love of research alone.

tion to those of a surveyor; such as an acquaintance with the language and ancient history of the country, tact and judgment in dealing with wild Arab tribes, and capacity for enduring fatigue and privations. All these were possessed by Felix Jones in an eminent degree. In 1857, while he was Political Resident at Bushire, the Persian war broke out. This he had foreseen and provided for by furnishing to the government of India an elaborate plan for invasion, containing itineraries through Persia, and guides for the Commissariat Departments of the Army and Navy. This paper obtained for him great commendation under Earl Canning's own hand.* Assisted by Captain Malcolm Green, he made a survey of the Shat-el-Arab, including the Karoon, which enabled Sir James Outram to attack Mohammerah.

Captain Selby took charge of the Survey of Mesopotamia in 1855. He had previously done very important service in the spring of 1842, by ascending the Persian rivers Karoon and Dizful in the E.I.C. steamer "Assyria," thus demonstrating their navigability.† He had with him in the Mesopotamian Survey Lieuts. Collingwood and Bewsher as assistants. These officers made a trigonometrical survey of the region west of the Euphrates, including the sea of Nejf, which is fed by that river, and embracing the classic sites of Meshed Aly, Birs Nimrood, Kerbela, Kufa, and Babylon, and the portion of Mesopotamia from Samarrah on the Euphrates to a point about 10 miles above Bagdad on the Tigris. The former portion was completed and sent home in 1861, with an elaborate memoir by Captain Selby. But both maps and memoir were lost, through some unaccountable carelessness. The original maps and field books have, however, been procured from Bagdad, and the maps have been redrawn by Lieutenant Collingwood, and are to be engraved. Lieutenant Collingwood also surveyed and drew maps of the Shat-el-Arab from Bussorah to Makil, and of the course of the old Hindiyeh Canal, near Meshed Hoossein. It is feared that this valuable work is also irretrievably lost. Captain Selby and Lieutenant Collingwood, while tracing the old bed of the Euphrates with great care, and surveying the Bahr el Nejf, were exposed to much harrassing work among the marshes. They also sent in accurate plans of the irruptions from the Tigris, and showed

* Indian Records, Political and Secret.

† "R. G. S. Journal," vol. xiv. p. 219.

that, before long, if no efficient steps were taken to check the evil, that river would be as unnavigable as the Euphrates now is.

The latter portion of the survey from above Bagdad to Tel Ibrahim, and from Tel Ibrahim to Samarrah on the Euphrates, was commenced in October 1862. In the end of that year Captain Selby retired, and Lieutenant Bewsher, who then took charge of the work that had thus been begun, completed it in 1865. The maps (seven in number) have been engraved in two sheets, and Bewsher's memoir * contains an interesting account of the ancient canals which can still be traced, and some details respecting the humbler modern system of irrigation. The ability and learning shown in this memoir are proofs that Lieutenant Bewsher would have been a worthy successor of the earlier surveyors; but he died of diseases contracted during the service, and the Government abruptly put a stop to the survey, leaving it incomplete, and with much work still to be done.

The survey of the west coast of India, south of Bombay, with the exception of some roadsteads and detached bits of coast laid down by Montriou, and the portion from Beypoor to Cape Comorin by Selby, had not been revised since the old charts were drawn by McCluer in the last century. This most important work was entrusted to Lieutenant A. Dundas Taylor, who received the command of an old *pattimar*, the "Pownah," afterwards exchanged for the "Bheema." He was assisted by Lieutenant Sweny, and mates May, Bewsher, Williams, and Lewis, and commenced work in 1853. The whole of Taylor's work is admirably executed on a trigonometrical basis, with bases measured on shore, and is included in six sheets of the coasts of the South Concan, Canara, and Malabar.† It occupied six years, from 1853 to 1859. He also surveyed the harbour at Carwar, the anchorages at Beypoor and Cochin, and the Bay of Coringa ‡ on the east coast in 1857. There is no man living who

* "On the part of Mesopotamia contained between Sheriat el Beytha, on the Tigris, and Tel Ibrahim." By Lieut. Bewsher, I.N.—*R. G. S. Journal*, xxxvii. p. 160.

† John Edye, Esq., who was master shipwright at Trincomalee in 1832–38, wrote a valuable paper on the sea ports of the Malabar coast, with remarks on the poon spars, coir fibre, and a list of timber in the forests; and another describing the native craft in use on that coast. *See* "Journal of the Royal Asiatic Society, I., p. 1, and II., p. 324.

‡ Coringa Bay, it will be remembered, was surveyed by Michael Topping in 1790, and Lieut. Warren in 1805. *See* p. 5. There is also a chart by Lieut. Fell, 1846; and Dalrymple engraved a plan of Coringa roads by Wm. Stevens, dated 1773.

is so intimately acquainted with the anchorages on the Indian coast from the mouths of the Indus to those of the Godavery, or who so completely understands their capabilities for improvement. Since his return to England he has drawn up a volume of sailing directions for the west coast of India.* Lieutenant Williams afterwards completed the coast from Boria to Bombay. These coast surveys were ably supplemented with deep sea soundings by Lieutenant Foster in the cutter "Nerbudda."

In 1859 Lieutenant Whish examined and reported upon the harbour in Bahrein Island and on a channel called the Khaur-el-Bab,† and in the following year he made a complete survey of Bombay harbour on several sheets on a large scale, which has since been reduced and published by the Admiralty.

In 1860-61, under instructions from the Government of India, Mr. William Marshall, senior midshipman of H.M. gunboat "Clyde" of the Indian Navy, then stationed at the Andaman Islands, made a trigonometrical survey of Port Blair, which has since been published by the Admiralty. ‡He also made rough surveys of Port Meadow, Middle Straits, and part of Great Coco Island, all of which were lithographed in India. The natives of these islands being very savage, the surveys were executed in boats fully manned and armed, and before taking observations on shore it was generally necessary to station outposts in the jungle to prevent surprises. Mr. Marshall also discovered, by several chronometric measurements taken between Bombay, Madras, and Calcutta, that the Andaman Islands were placed eleven miles too far to the westward on the charts, and that the Great Coco Island was placed six miles too far to the westward of Port Blair.

The last and not the least important work of the officers of the Indian Navy has been a careful revision of the old survey of the Persian Gulf in 1857-60, by Captain Constable, assisted by Lieutenant Stiffe.

Captain Constable had for many years taken a deep interest in the maritime geography of the Persian Gulf, and had gradually collected a large mass of material with a view to preparing a sailing directory,

* "West Coast of Hindostan Pilot, including the Gulf of Manar, the Maldivh and the Lakadivh Islands, compiled by Com. A. D. Taylor, H.M.I.N." (Published by the Admiralty in 1866.)

† "Memoir on Bahrein, by Lieut. Whish, I.N."—*Bombay G. S. Journal.* xvi. p. 40.

‡ See pages 119-120.

with a description of the shores and islands. A vast number of omissions and inaccuracies had been discovered in the old survey from time to time, and there was a weight of evidence to show that the knowledge of the gulf was very imperfect. One remarkable instance of the unreliable character of the old charts was furnished by Commodore Carless in 1848, when entering the gulf on board the "Elphinstone." He found that a shoal marked on the chart as three miles from the Persian coast, really extended seven or eight miles to seaward. Numerous other discoveries of the same character had been reported. There is no published chart of the Shát-el-Arab from Bussorah to the sea,* and no marine survey of the Island of Karrak.† In 1846 Captain Carless‡ went to the gulf with eight chronometers and proved that the longitude of Bassadore was nearly correct with reference to Bombay: but that Bushire was eight miles too far west.§

It was abundantly clear that there existed a pressing necessity for a revision of the Persian Gulf Survey, and Lieutenants Constable and Stiffe were commissioned to execute it in 1857. They had the brig "Euphrates" from 1857 to 1858, and the schooner "Marie" from 1858 to 1860. Their revision of the old survey consisted in carefully determining certain positions round the gulf by observed latitudes (the altitudes all being taken with artificial horizons) and longitudes by chronometer, with as much triangulation in the vicinity of the fixed positions as time would admit of. They compiled a general chart of the Persian Gulf in two sheets in 1860, which is thus a correct skeleton of the islands and principal points round the gulf, with some detail of the coast line round the fixed positions triangulated, and the remainder adopted from the old charts.‖

---

* Lieut. Collingwood made one, and so, I believe, did Capt. Felix Jones, but both have been lost.

† Dalrymple published a plan of this island from a French MS. in 1787; and Ensign Anderson (afterwards murdered at Mooltán) made a trigonometrical survey on a scale of 6¾ inches to a mile in 1839, on which every ravine and fissure is accurately laid down; but there is no marine survey of its shores.

‡ This officer died in 1848.

§ "Memoir relative to the hydrography of the Persian Gulf, by Lieut. Constable, I.N."—*Bombay G. S. Journal*, xii. p. 98.

‖ "Persian Gulf Pilot, including the Gulf of Oman, compiled by Capt. C. G. Constable and Lieut. A. W. Stiffe, I.N. Published by the Admiralty." (London, 1864.) Captain Constable's chart of the Persian Gulf was published by the Admiralty

Lieutenant Stiffe now holds the post of Director of the Persian Gulf Cable. He is one of the most able, scientific, and accomplished of those surveyors who made the Indian Navy famous, and though his immediate duties are now unconnected with surveying, he has never missed an opportunity of improving, correcting, or adding to the charts. Mr. Girdlestone, formerly a midshipman in the Indian Navy, and now in the Topographical Survey Department, is about to be sent to the Persian Gulf to complete the survey of the reefs and channels between Bahrein Island and El Katiff.

The subject of winds and currents in the Indian seas, to which Major Rennell devoted so much attention, has been carefully studied since his time. Lieutenant A. D. Taylor compiled a chart of the Arabian Sea with great care, showing the winds and currents during the S.W. monsoon, by a comparison of upwards of a hundred logs of vessels of the Indian Navy* and Lieutenant Heathcote made a similar wind and current chart of the Bay of Bengal. Lieutenant Fergusson, the draughtsman of the Indian Navy, also prepared three sets of charts, each set containing a chart for every month in the year, showing the winds and currents of the Red Sea, Persian Gulf, and Indian and China seas.†

Henry Piddington, of Calcutta,‡ was, however, the great contributor to the study of the law of storms. His attention was first turned to the subject by the reviews of Colonel Reid's work; and he tells us that it was, to him, a subject connected with many associations of his early life, and more especially with one instance in which to the veering of a hurricane alone he owed his safety from shipwreck, after cutting away the mainmast of the vessel he then commanded. His first memoirs on cyclones or circular storms were published in 1839. In the following year he received extracts from numerous

---

and the hydrographer, the late Admiral Washington, sent it to the Great International Exhibition of 1862 as a good specimen of English chart drawing.

Dr. Carter reported on the geological specimens brought from the Persian Gulf by Constable and Stiffe, in the "Journal of the Asiatic Society of Bengal," No. 97, N. S., p. 41.

* Sent home with a letter dated January 16, 1852, in which Captain Lushington called attention to Lieut. Taylor's zeal, assiduity, and ability. The chart was published in 1853, with a memoir.

† Published in 1856.

‡ Captain Piddington was Foreign Secretary to the Agricultural Society of India, Sub-Secretary to the Asiatic Society of Bengal, Curator of the Museum of Economic Geology and President of the Marine Court of Enquiry at Calcutta.

logs preserved at the India House, furnishing records of hurricanes from 1780 to 1841;* and he thus accumulated proofs that these great storms are circular, that they turn from right to left, north of the equator, and that they are progressive. He also made out the tracks on which they move, and their rates. Mr. Piddington continued to publish accounts of all important cyclones that occurred in the Eastern seas from 1839 to 1851. This involved immense labour and research, the untiring and persevering collection of materials, and no small ability and judgment in their arrangement. Each memoir was accompanied by a chart showing the course of the storm. Mr. Piddington was zealously assisted in his labours by Captain Christopher Biden, the Master Attendant at Madras.†

The impetus thus given by the zeal of Captain Piddington to the study of the law of storms was communicated to the western side of India. The great hurricane of April 1847, in which the "Cleopatra" was lost, was carefully observed, and remarks upon it were published by Captain Carless, of the Indian Navy,‡ and by Dr. Thom, of the 83rd foot.§ Dr. Buist afterwards collected accounts of hurricanes on the west coast from 1647 to 1847, and wrote a careful memoir on the subject of cyclones,‖ to which he added another reviewing the course of storms from 1854 to 1859,¶ and Lieut. Fergusson published an account of the cyclone of November 1862.**

At Madras, Mr. Franklin, the master attendant, published an account of the storms of October 20th and November 25th, 1846, with diagrams,†† and Lieutenants Mullins and Hemery of the Engineers described the cyclone at Nellore and Cuddapah on November 2nd, 1857.‡‡ The full report on the Calcutta cyclone of October 5th, 1864, was drawn up by Colonel Gastrell and Mr. H. F. Blanford, with maps and diagrams. At the end there is a list

* Journal of the Asiatic Society of Bengal, vol. xi., pt. ii., p. 605.

† Mr. Piddington published 23 memoirs on cyclones, in volumes 8, 9, 10, 11, 12, 13, 14, 15, 16, 17, 18, 19, 20, 21, and 23 of the Journal of the Asiatic Society of Bengal. He also published "A Horn Books of Storms." Calcutta. (Second edition.) 1845.

‡ "Journal of the Bombay Geographical Society," viii. p. 1.

§ "Journal of the Bombay Geographical Society," viii. p. 93.

‖ "Journal of the Bombay G. S.," vol. xii. p. xxv.

¶ "Journal of the Bombay G. S.," vol. xv. p. 19.

** "Journal of the Bombay G. S.," vol. xvi. p. 127.

†† "Madras Journal of Literature and Science," xii. p. 146.

‡‡ Ibid, iii, N. S., pp. 65 and 70.

of recorded storms in the Bay of Bengal from 1737 to 1865, chiefly from Piddington's Memoirs.

In 1864 Colonel Fraser, who erected the lighthouses on the coast of British Burmah, made a proposition that monthly returns of wrecks should be furnished, with a view, first, to show the positions of wrecks on a chart; second, to show the general causes of losses at sea; and, third, to give a table of loss of life, cargo, and ships, with the value. In accordance with this idea, the first wreck chart of India for 1864-65 was produced in 1865. Another was published at the Surveyor General's office for 1866, and a wreck chart of the approaches to Bombay harbour has been prepared with reference to the urgency of its being adequately lighted. It shows the wrecks from 1826 to 1866, and was compiled by the Master Attendant. Nor must the chart by Colonel Fraser, showing the lighthouses on the Burmese coast, with printed directions, be omitted in an enumeration of valuable publications for the use and guidance of navigators.

In 1862 the Indian Navy ceased to exist, and all the surveys were abruptly stopped and left incomplete. In his anniversary address to the Geographical Society for that year, Sir Roderick Murchison said,* "The war services of the Indian Navy, as well as the beneficial and "enduring results of its repression of piracy and the slave trade, "are well known. These services have been varied, honourable, "and useful; but in the eyes of geographers the wide-spread "and lasting utility of the excellent surveys made by officers of the "Indian Navy hold an equally prominent place."

Before the Indian Navy had become a thing of the past, there was a destruction of the materials for its history. Previous to 1860 there were many and most valuable records of that service in the India Office; but in that year nearly all were reduced to pulp. The charts, with the copper plates, original drawings, and sailing directions, were transferred to the Admiralty in 1861.

In 1862 four of the leading surveying officers of the Indian Navy submitted a memorandum to the late hydrographer of the Admiralty,† showing the surveys which remain to be executed. They are as follows:

1. Bank of soundings on the S.W. side of Socótra.

* "R. G. S. Journal," vol. xxxiii. p. cliii.

† Memorandum on the present state of the coast surveys of India, signed by Capt. C. G. Constable, H.M.I.N. (March 3rd, 1862).

2. The coast of Africa between Ras Bir and the entrance of the Red Sea, lying at the junction of two surveys, which has never been examined at all.
3. Anchorage of Soor, near Muscat, on the Arabian coast.
4. Revision, from Muscat to the entrance of the Persian Gulf.
5. Shat-el-Arab from Bussorah to the sea. The charts of Captain Felix Jones and Lieut. Collingwood appear to have been lost.
6. Outer soundings on the Mekran coast, with a search for some reported shoals.
7. More soundings at the entrance of the Gulf of Cutch.
8. The reef off Danu.
9. The Gulf of Cambay and Malacca banks require revision, as they have altered much since Lieut. Ethersey's survey in 1835–37.
10. Deep-sea soundings in the Gulf of Manaar, between Cape Comorin and Colombo; and soundings in Palk Strait, between Point Pedro and the coast of India.
11. The east coast from the Santapilly rocks to point Palmyras.
12. The coast from Chittagong to Akyab is very inaccurate, and requires to be re-surveyed.
13. A re-survey of the coast from Cheduba Island to Cape Negrais.
14. Outer soundings in the Gulf of Martaban.
15. The coast from Amherst to Tavoy, with the islands off it.
16. Outer soundings from Tavoy to Pakchan river.
17. A survey of the Andaman Islands.
18. A survey of the Nicobar Islands.
19. Outer soundings on the east side of the Bay of Bengal.
20. A revision of the meridian distances in the Bay of Bengal.
21. The survey of the Saya de Malha banks requires completion.
23. Several doubtful dangers on charts of the Indian Ocean should be investigated.

In August 1861 it was arranged that the portions of the survey of the coasts and harbours of India that were incomplete or required verification should be completed by vessels and officers of the Indian Navy, and that all further surveys that might be required should be conducted by the Royal Navy, and at the expense of the Imperial Government as in other parts of the world. In April 1862 Admiral Washington, who was then hydrographer to the Admiralty, submitted a list of the surveys that should be done by the Indian Government, under this arrangement.

The surveys enumerated in the memorandum of 1862 remain untouched in 1870. But some marine survey operations have recently been carried on by the Bengal Government on the Chittagong and Orissa coasts, to provide for local exigencies.

The whole subject of Marine Surveys is about to receive the serious consideration of the Government.

The official records of the Bombay Marine and Indian Navy have been almost entirely destroyed. Its history can now only be traced in the fragmentary memoirs, papers, and reports which have already been quoted and indicated by references. Some statistical details will be found in a Parliamentary Paper called for by Mr. Joseph Hume, and printed in August 1851.* It is much to be desired that, before the generation of Indian marine surveyors passes away, one of their number would gather together the recollections of his colleagues, and with the aid of such fragments as have survived the general destruction, give to the world a history of the work done by the Indian Navy in war and during peace. The history of its war services, containing such episodes as the gallant capture of the "Media" by Henry Meriton, and many deeds of daring in Persia, Burmah, and China, combined with the splendid services of its surveyors, would form a very noble record.†

* "Statement of the nature and locality of the maritime surveys undertaken by the East India Company since 1820, and other papers connected with the subject."

† A work entitled "The Land of the Sun" (1870) has been published by Lieut. C. R. Low, late of the Indian Navy, giving an account of his services in the Red Sea and Persian Gulf, with notices of Aden, Perim, the Somali coast, the Andamans, and the ports in the Persian Gulf, &c.

Note.—The following are some of the surveys made by officers of the Indian Navy, but never published :—

1. Large-scale plan of Masireh Island and Straits, by Sanders and Grieve. 1846.
2. Plan of Makullah, by Haines. 1835.
3. Large-scale plans of Khor Jerámah, Bundar Kheiran, and Bundar Jezzar, by Lieut. Grieve. 1848–49.
4. Plan of the Deïmaniyeh group, by Com. Constable and Lieut. Stiffe. 1858.
5. Chart of Soonminny and Kuráchee Bays, by Captain Carless. 1838.
6. Plans of Porbunder and Veráwul Roads, by Lieuts. Constable and Stiffe. 1853.
7. Beyt Harbour : corrections to 1859, by Lieut. Taylor.
8. Capt. Selby's chronometric measurements between Minicoy and the Malabar coast, and chart of the currents in that part of the sea.
9. Chart of Hooringottah River, by Lieut. Sweny.
10. Mouths of the Indus from Hajamri to Waree, by Captain Selby and Lieuts Taylor and Streyan.
11. Charts of Sittang and Irrawaddy rivers by Captain Ward.

II.—MAJOR RENNELL AND THE ROUTE SURVEYS, 1763-1800.

The land survey and mapping of British India have advanced with the acquisitions of territory; they were commenced when the first battles were fought, and the first provinces gained. Rennell, the father of Indian geography, served under Clive, the conqueror of Plassy.

At that time all existing knowledge of India, derived from routes of solitary travellers and rough charts of the coasts, had just been collected and utilized by the great French geographer D'Anville.* His map of India appeared five years before the date of the battle of Plassy; and eight years afterwards Rennell was at work in the newly acquired territory of Bengal and Bahar, laying the foundations for the construction of a map which was destined to succeed the admirable work of D'Anville.

James Rennell, the son of a captain in the artillery, was born at Chudleigh in Devonshire in 1742. He entered the navy, and distinguished himself as a midshipman at the siege of Pondicherry; but soon afterwards took service in the army under Clive, rose to the rank of major, and was eventually, but when still quite a young man, appointed Surveyor-General of Bengal.

Major Rennell's labours in the field extended over a period from about 1763 to 1782, when he finally left India. In Section II. of his memoir he describes this survey as covering an area about 900 miles long by 300 to 240 wide, from the eastern confines of Bengal to Agra, and from the feet of the Himalayas to Calpee. The distances appear to have been chained, and observations were taken for latitude and longitude at certain stations. The measured distances are said to have accorded minutely with observations for latitude, and closely with those for longitude.

Rennell's maps of the rivers Ganges and Brahmapootra, reduced from the original surveys by himself, are preserved in the Geographical Department of the India Office. They are on a scale of two miles to an inch. A portion of the original surveys in

* The English edition of his map by Herbert, with a memoir, appeared in 1754.

15 sheets, on a scale of 500 yards to the inch, is also preserved. These are not only interesting memorials of the great geographer who executed them; but, looking to the changes which have since taken place in the rivers, are still useful in the study of the causes which operate to effect these changes. For instance, Rennell's Surveys were turned to good account by Mr. Fergusson, in his thoughtful and well-considered paper on the recent changes in the delta of the Ganges.* The maps of the districts of Bengal and Bahar are of course entirely superseded by those of the Revenue Survey, and now have only an historical interest. They are on a scale of five miles to an inch (that of Chittagong being rather larger), and were compiled, by Major Rennell, from 500 original surveys made by himself and nine assistants. These maps were published in 1781 as the "Bengal Atlas."†

Major Rennell returned to England in 1782, the very year of D'Anville's death; and thus as it were received his mantle, and commenced that useful career of nearly 50 years' duration, which has won him a place in the first rank of geographers. The story of his labours in England belongs to another section of this memoir.

Colonel John Call, who had made some route surveys of the southern part of the peninsula,‡ succeeded Major Rennell as Surveyor General of India in 1782; and the following years saw much good and zealous geographical work done by the disciples of Rennell. Colonel Pearse was engaged in making astronomical observations at Calcutta from about 1774 to 1782, and in the latter year he undertook a journey to Madras, for the purpose of fixing positions, and laying down the intermediate coast line, for a distance of 700 miles. He observed for latitude by stars' meridian altitudes, for longitude by immersion of Jupiter's satellites, and measured the distances with a perambulator. This work occupied two years, from 1782 to 1784; and

---

* "On recent changes in the delta of the Ganges," by James Fergusson, F.R.S.—*Quarterly Geological Journal*, xix. p. 321. (1863.)

† The originals are now in the Geographical Department of the India Office. They were taken home by some official, and treated by him as private property, till they were accidentally discovered in the collection of a lady of rank, and purchased for 100*l*. by their lawful owners, the Court of Directors.—*Bombay Quarterly Review*, iii. p. 140.

‡ In the "Philosophical Transactions" for 1772, vol. 62. p. 353, there is a letter from John Call to the Astronomer Royal, Nevil Maskelyne; on the signs of the Zodiac he had observed on the ceiling of a choultry near Cape Comorin.

Colonel Pearse was ably assisted by young Colebrooke, the future Surveyor General, who latterly took all the observations. During this period intelligent surveyors accompanied every army in the field, and good route maps were thus obtained. In 1783, Colonel Kelly is reported to have made a most valuable collection of routes and maps of the Carnatic during a long course of service, some of which had proved valuable guides to General Sir Eyre Coote. Captain Pringle also made maps, and measured 2,000 miles of road, in the Carnatic, during the war with Hyder Ali.

Thus materials were rapidly accumulating, and Colonel Call, the Surveyor General, undertook the compilation of an Atlas of India in 20 sheets, to be collected afterwards into one general map on a smaller scale. In 1787 it was nearly completed, and the Bengal Government ordered that a fair copy of it, on a scale of four inches to a degree, should be made, and hung up in the Council Room at Calcutta for constant reference. Colonel Call went home in 1788, but died soon after he landed in England; and his map, which must have entailed an enormous amount of labour and expense, appears to have been lost.

In 1787, when Colonel Call was compiling his map of India, he found so many contradictions and absurdities in the various surveys, that he requested Mr. Reuben Burrow, an experienced marine surveyor and an accomplished mathematician,* to consider the subject, and draw up a plan for determining astronomically the positions of the principal places in Bengal. Eventually Burrow received orders from Major Wood, Colonel Call's successor, to determine the latitude and longitude of Moorshedabad, Rajmahal, Monghyr, Patna, Dacca, Goalpara, and Chittagong. But there was great difficulty in procuring the necessary instruments. It sounds strange in these days, that the equipment of this Government

---

* Reuben Burrow contributed several mathematical papers to the "Asiatic Researches":—

1. "Hints relative to friction in Mechanics," i. p. 171.
2. "Method of calculating Moon's parallax," i. p. 3.
3. "Remarks on the Artificial Horizon," i. p. 327.
4. "Demonstration of a Theorem concerning the Intersection of Curves," i. p. 330.
5. "Corrections of the Lunar Method of finding the Longitude," i. p. 433.
6. "A Proof that the Hindoos had the Binomial Theorem," ii.
7. "Method of Reducing Practical Tables," iii.

expedition could only be secured by borrowing a sextant here, a watch there, and a quadrant in another quarter, from different officers at Calcutta who happened to possess them.

In addition to the work sketched out for him, Reuben Burrow went up the Ganges as far as Hurdwar, taking observations, and making careful notes of everything he saw.* It is remarkable that Rennell should not allude to the survey by Reuben Burrow in his second edition of the memoir, published in 1792.

Colonel Call was succeeded in the office of Surveyor General of India by Colonel Wood, who was strongly impressed with the importance of making the marches of troops subservient to the promotion of geographical knowledge. He actively collected information and materials for correct maps wherever it was to be obtained. In 1792 he received the surveys by Lieut. Emmitt, of portions of the Deccan, made during the previous war, which are said to have been both reliable and elegant. In 1793, Colonel Wood's assistant, Lieut. Colebrooke, submitted a map of the part of Mysore traversed by the army under Lord Cornwallis, with a memoir, and received Rs. 6,000 for his trouble. In the same year Major Kyd surveyed the route from Seringapatam, through Coorg, to the west coast, and Dr. Hunter, the surgeon to the Residency at Scindia's Court, sent in route surveys made on marches from Delhi and Agra to Gwalior and Oojein.† A map of Calcutta and its environs was made by a Mr. Upjohn in 1794, who secured liberal patronage from the Government; and in 1795 Lieut. Hoare received instructions to make a survey of the River Jumna. When Captain Symes went on a mission to the Court of Ava in 1795, he was accompanied by Dr. Buchanan and Lieut. Wood. The latter officer surveyed the route, and afterwards submitted a map of the Irrawaddy from Rangoon to Amarapoora, with a paper of astronomical observations. Mr. John Crawfurd, when he went over the same ground in 1826, bore witness that Wood's survey was still the best extant.‡

---

* "Remarks made in the Ganges and Burrampooter Rivers in 1787, by Reuben Burrows," MS. volume preserved in the Geographical Department of the India Office. See also his tables of latitudes and longitudes determined from astronomical observations, in the "Asiatic Researches," iv. p. 325.

† See also Dr. Hunter's Astronomical Observations, taken during a journey from Upper Hindoostan to Oujein, in the Asiatic Researches, iv. p. 41.

‡ Syme's Embassy is in Pinkerton's Voyages, ix. p. 216; and was also published separately in 1800.

On the Bombay side Captain Moncrieff surveyed the district of Canara in 1799, while Colonel Charles Reynolds made a careful route survey of Malwa and part of Bednore. Colonel Reynolds was for years engaged in collecting materials for a great map of India, which was at last completed and sent home in 1798, but it was never published.* Reynolds measured one long line of route with great care, checking it at each end by observations for latitude, and established it as a base to which all other diverging routes were referred, the intervals being filled in from native information. But such work was of course very inaccurate; and the maps of that period were only of service while India was an unknown region, to be traversed by armies, and ceased to be tolerable when that vast country became a British imperial possession, requiring to be administered.

At the commencement of the present century the great triangulation was begun, which was to furnish a permanent geodetical basis of the highest order of accuracy, for all future surveying operations in India. The process of constructing maps from route surveys and astronomical observations has since been gradually discontinued in the provinces which are under the immediate control of the British Government, though it is still necessarily practised in geographical explorations beyond the frontier, and more particularly in the Trans-Himalayan regions.

Yet the labours of Rennell and his school were not only useful at the time, but also served as incitements to encourage their successors; and the names of those first pioneers of the Indian Surveys will ever be held in reverence by geographers. It is particularly pleasant to note the liberal and hearty encouragement which was given to young surveyors by the Government in those days, by granting them a good round sum of money for their services whenever they submitted creditable results of their labours in the field. This was done to show them that their hard and meritorious work was appreciated, and to excite a feeling of emulation and zeal.

---

* Some rough sheets for this map are still preserved, but the great map of India by Reynolds itself, a work of considerable value and interest, appears to have been lost in the destruction of precious records which took place at the time of the abolition of the East India Company.

III.—FIRST PERIOD OF THE TRIGONOMETRICAL SURVEYS. 1800–23.

(*a.*) Introductory.

It was not until the end of the last century that a trigonometrical survey was generally allowed to be the only accurate basis for the mapping of a country. The observations for ascertaining the shape of the earth by measuring an arc of the meridian were commenced a few years after the death of Sir Isaac Newton, but not by his countrymen; and these observations were the forerunners of the great trigonometrical surveys. The famous French expedition of Condamine and Bouguer went to South America in 1735, and the admirable work of these savans, aided by the Spanish brothers Ulloa, consisted in the measurement of two bases connected by a series of triangles, one north and the other south of the equator on the meridian of Quito, the arc being 180 miles long. It is to be regretted that while France and Spain were thus combining in the interests of science, England was less nobly engaged in burning churches and cutting off supplies from the Peruvian coast.

The labours of Condamine were followed by the measurement of an arc in Lapland, of another in France, and finally the countrymen of Newton took up the work at which they should have been foremost.* The idea of a Trigonometrical Survey of Great Britain was first conceived by General Watson, after the Scottish rising of 1745. It was intended to extend over the disaffected parts of the High-

* The particulars of the measurements of various arcs are as follows:—

Date.	Observers.	Country.	Latitude of Middle of Arc.	Arc measured.	Length of Degree in feet.	Length of Degree in Ordnance Tables.*
			° ′ ″	° ′ ″		
1739	Maupertuis re-examined by Svanberg	Lapland	66. 20. 10 N.	1. 37. 19	365,782	365,878
	Struve	Russia	58. 17. 37 ,,	3. 35. 5	365,368	365,144
1802	Roy and Kater	England	52. 35. 45 ,,	3. 57. 13	364,971	365,097
	Lacaille	France	46. 52. 2 ,,	8. 20. 0	364,872	364,730
1790	Delambre and Mechain	France	44. 51. 2 ,,	12. 22. 13	364,535	364,590
1755	Boscovich	Rome	42. 59. 0 ,,	2. 9. 47	364,262	364,479
	Mason and Dixon	United States	39. 12. 0 ,,	1. 28. 45	363,786	364,335
1750	Abbé Lacaille	Cape of Good Hope	33. 18. 30 S.	1. 13. 17½	364,713	363,871
1835	Everest	India	16. 8. 22 N.	15. 57. 40	363,044	363,044
1808	Lambton	India	12. 32. 21 ,,	1. 34. 56	363,013	362,959
1735	Condamine and Bouguer	Peru	1. 31. 0 S.	3. 7. 3	362,808	362,758

* Geodetical Tables based on the elements of the figure of the earth given in the Account of the Principal Triangulation (of the Ordnance Survey). London, 1858. Quarto, 13 pages.

lands, and the design was subsequently extended so as to include all Great Britain and Ireland. The work was committed to General Roy in about 1784, when he measured his famous base on Hounslow Heath. He died in 1790, and Colonel Mudge was engaged in the measurement of his arc from Dunnose to Clifton in Yorkshire, in 1802.* Thanks to the genius and resolution of one man, to whom the early commencement of similar work in the east is due, British India was only a few years behind France and England in beginning a great trigonometrical survey; a stupendous work, which has occupied the lifetime of several noble and devoted surveyors, and which, when completed, will be among the most glorious monuments of British rule in the east.

The man who originated the great Indian Survey was an infantry officer serving in the army of General Harris, in the war with Tippoo. William Lambton was born in 1753. He was very reserved in all particulars respecting his origin or family, and it is not known where he was born or who were his parents. But his name points to the county of Durham, and he certainly passed his boyhood at Darlington. For many years he devoted a large portion of his pay to the support of one of his parents. He obtained a commission in the 33rd Regiment, and his proficiency in surveying obtained for him the work of measuring land granted to settlers in America. He was appointed barrack master in Nova Scotia, and applied himself for several years to the study of mathematics. Lambton was entirely self-educated. In 1795 the Duke of York issued an order that all officers in civil employment were to be struck off the strength of their regiments. Lambton, therefore, gave up his barrack-mastership, and joined the 33rd at Calcutta, after an absence of 13 years from regimental duties. He was well acquainted with the methods of observing and computing which were in use among the learned men who had recently been engaged in the measurement of arcs in Europe. He rejoined the 33rd Regiment, then commanded by Sir Arthur Wellesley, at Calcutta in 1797,† was brigade major during the Mysore campaign, and distinguished himself by leading the left column, after all his superior officers had been disabled, in the storming of Seringapatam.

After the fall of Tippoo, Lord Wellesley took measures for explor-

* "Philosophical Transactions," 1803.

† While at Calcutta, Lambton contributed two mathematical papers to the Asiatic Researches :—1. "Observations on the Theory of Walls," vi. p. 93.

2. "On the Effects of Machines when in Motion," vi. p. 309.

ing and collecting accurate information respecting the vast territory which had thus been thrown open to the English. Dr. Buchanan was employed to report upon the agriculture and products of Mysore and Malabar. Colin Mackenzie proceeded with his admirable topographical surveys and memoirs: and it was then also that Major Lambton submitted his project for the measurement of an arc of the meridian, and for a trigonometrical survey across the peninsula.

The measurement of an arc in the peninsula of India was, in a purely scientific point of view, of the highest importance. By it the exact figure of the earth was to be ascertained; and it should be remembered that this was not, as has been asserted, an object of mere curiosity. It affects some of the tables used in navigation, especially all those of which the moon's parallax is an element, and is therefore an investigation of the greatest practical consequence to the whole civilized world. Moreover, the measured base line, the series of accurately measured triangles, and points fixed by numerous astronomical observations, all which are necessary for ascertaining the shape of the earth, were the basis from which, as a back bone, the triangulation was eventually to be extended over the whole of India. The primary triangles formed guides by which the topographical and revenue surveyors were enabled to fill in the details, and delineate all the main features of the country within fixed limits of error.

Trigonometrical surveying is divided into three distinct branches. First, the selection of sites for base lines to form the ends of certain ranges of triangles; their setting out; and their measurement with the utmost attainable accuracy. The base line becomes the side of a triangle, the length of which is thus known, and by trigonometry the distance of other points, visible from its extremities, can be ascertained through angular observations with suitable instruments. Second, the construction of the range of triangles. This is done by ascertaining the position of selected points on the earth's surface by angles taken at first from the ends of a measured base, and then carried on from point to point in succession so as to form a network of positions fixed by this triangulation along a belt of country. The accuracy of the work is checked by the base line which terminates it. The primary triangulation is completed by a sufficient number of such belts across the area of the survey, both in the direction of latitude and longitude. Third, as a further check to the triangulation, astronomical observations for latitude and longitude are made at selected points.

The positions of a sufficient number of places spread over the area of survey are in this way fixed with the greatest accuracy; and they become the starting points from which the topographical surveyors proceed to fill in the detail, as well as checks upon their accuracy.

But from the first, the staff of the great trigonometrical survey was distinct from that of the topographical and revenue surveys. The nature of the work, the training, and the objects, were distinct; and even the time required for each, and the calls of the public service rendered it impracticable that they should be carried on together. The trigonometrical surveyor was obliged to secure extreme accuracy, both in his terrestrial measurements and in his celestial observations. The same stars had to be taken over and over again, and it was often necessary to wait for days until they were in the desired positions. His mathematical attainments must be of the highest order, and he would have neither the time nor, as a rule, a special aptitude for the collection of topographical details for filling up the exact skeleton furnished by his scientific labours. The two kinds of work are distinct, and require a different training in many respects, and a different turn of mind. On the other hand, the topographical and revenue surveyors found the main landmarks on which their maps were to be based, already fixed and established to their hands. Their work consisted of secondary triangulation, and filling in the details with the plane table. It was their duty to examine and delineate all the natural features of the country, to mark boundaries, and collect information of all kinds. While they would never be detained so long at one spot, as would often be the case with the trigonometrical surveyor, they would be longer in one district, filling in and completing the maps. Thus, though their work was in some respects similar, and even may be said to dove-tail at certain points, it was on the whole so distinct that it has generally been found most convenient to carry on the two surveys apart from each other.

By the trigonometrical survey a network of primary triangles was formed with numerous fixed positions. By the topographical and revenue surveys the details were filled in, and the data for the maps collected. These points will be brought out more clearly as the narrative of the surveys proceeds. The labours of each system will be recorded separately, in the successive periods. The first period covers the work of Major Lambton, and will be divided into two sections; first that treating of the trigonometrical surveys of Lambton himself from 1800 to 1823; and secondly that under which the topographical surveys of Colin Mackenzie and his followers in the peninsula, and of other workers in the Bengal Presidency, must be recorded, covering the same period of time.

III.—FIRST PERIOD OF THE TRIGONOMETRICAL SURVEYS.

1800–23.

b.—COLONEL LAMBTON AND THE MEASUREMENT OF AN ARC OF THE MERIDIAN.

Major Lambton's proposal for a mathematical and geographical survey of the peninsula and the measurement of an arc of the meridian in connection therewith was supported by Sir Arthur Wellesley and approved by the Madras Government. It is a curious coincidence that two of the most energetic and influential Supporters of Lambton's proposal, Mr. Petrie and Mr. Andrew Scott, should have been first cousins of the father of the future superintendent of the surveys, Sir Andrew Waugh. Lambton was himself appointed to conduct the measurement, but it was not until 1802 that he was furnished with the necessary instruments. Meanwhile he organized an efficient staff, and obtained the able assistance of Lieut. Warren of the 33rd,* and Lieut. Kater.†

Lambton's instruments were a theodolite, zenith sector, and steel chains. The three-foot theodolite, by Cary, was captured on the passage to India by the French frigate "Piemontaise," and landed at Mauritius; but it was eventually forwarded to its destination by the chivalrous French Governor, De Caen, with a complimentary letter to the Governor of Madras. The zenith sector was one of 5 feet radius by Ramsden. The chain was one that had been sent as a present to the Emperor of China, with Lord Macartney's Embassy, and refused. It was handed over to Mr. Dinwiddie, the astronomer to the mission, apparently as part payment for his services, and he brought it to Madras with the zenith sector.‡ Both

* Author of the Kala Sankalita. This officer was descended from a noble French family, by the mother's side.

† Kater, afterwards so well known for his pendulum and other scientific observations in England, was appointed an Assistant in the Survey in October 1803. He invented a very ingenious method of ascertaining the amount of moisture in the atmosphere, while serving under Lambton. He observed that the bearded seed of a species of grass called in Tamul *yerudooraul pilloo* (*Andropogon contortum*, Lin.), possessed an extreme sensibility of moisture, and he constructed a hygrometer of this material. Asiatic Researches, IX., p. 24 and 375."—Henry Kater was born at Bristol in 1777, and went out to India in 1794, as an Ensign in the 12th Regt. Ill health obliged him to return to England in 1806. He is most generally known in connexion with his labours for the construction of standards of weights and measures. Captain Kater died in 1835.

‡ According to another account, these instruments were bought from Dinwiddie at Calcutta, and sent down to Madras.

were bought by the Government for Major Lambton's survey. The chain was 100 feet long, consisting of 40 steel links of 2½ feet each. In May 1802 another steel chain arrived from England, manufactured by Ramsden, and having been set off from his bar at a temperature of 50°. This was never used in the field, but reserved as a standard with which the old chain was compared both before and after measurement. There was also a standard brass scale by Cary, 3 feet long, for use if the standard chain failed.

The fixed position or point of departure of the Trigonometrical Survey of India is the Madras Observatory; and its longitude was always a matter of some moment. Observations had been taken since 1787; but the building was erected in 1792. It contained a 20-inch transit, and a 12-inch altitude and azimuth instrument by Troughton. From 1796 there is a regular series of meteorological reports, and the astronomical results are recorded in huge folios printed at Madras.* Mr. Goldingham, who seems to have succeeded Michael Topping, was the Madras astronomer contemporary with Colonel Lambton. He made experiments with the pendulum at Madras, and on the equator near Bencoolen in Sumatra; other careful experiments for ascertaining the velocity of sound; and observed regularly for latitude by the transit of heavenly bodies over the meridian, and for longitude from eclipses of Jupiter's satellites and lunars. Since 1787 a regular series of observations of eclipses of Jupiter's satellites had been taken, and about 800 lunar distances. The means of the eclipses gave a longitude of 80° 18′ 30″ E., but the results from the lunars were 2′ 55″ more to the east. In 1815 Lieutenant Warren had charge of the observatory during Mr. Goldingham's absence in England, and reduced the longitude to 18° 17′ 21″ E. These figures were adopted by Colonel Lambton in the survey; but they were destined to further change. Mr. Taylor succeeded Mr. Goldingham as astronomer at Madras in 1831, and was supplied with a new set of instruments consisting of a five-foot

---

* "Astronomical Observations," by J. Goldingham. 4 vols. (folio) *Madras*, 1825–27, "Madras Observatory Papers," by John Goldingham, Astronomer.—(*Madras*, 1827.)

"Results of Astronomical Observations made at the H. E. I. C. Observatory at Madras," by T. G. Taylor. 4 vols. *Madras*, 1831–37.

See also Journal of the Asiatic Society of Bengal. ii. p. 380. The Meteorological Reports of the Madras Observatory will be found in the Madras Journal of Literature and Science.

transit instrument, a mural circle, and a five-foot telescope equatorially mounted. He specially devoted his attention to the positions of 2881 fixed stars, to observations of planets passing the meridian, moon culminating stars, and occultations. He reduced the longitude of Madras to 80° 14′ 19·5″ E., by observations between 1830 and 1847.*

It must be borne in mind that the astronomical observations of the surveyors were not taken only for the purpose of fixing points for geographical purposes. The object of the astronomical observations was also to measure the angular, as distinguished from the linear, length of a degree. Thus, supposing observations for latitude were taken at two points distant from each other exactly one degree or sixty minutes of a celestial arc; then by triangulation the distance of these points in yards, feet, inches, and decimal parts of an inch, might be ascertained by angular observations referred to a measured base line; or the distance itself might possibly be measured by the same method as a base line; or it might be traced or staked on the ground, measured, and corrected for irregularities of the surface by levelling operations. By such means the length of a degree of latitude on the earth's surface would be ascertained if the two points were on the same meridian; or of a degree of longitude if they were on the equator or a parallel. So also the actual form of the earth's circumference, and any departure of it from the regularity of the celestial arc can be obtained.

The longitude of Madras is important, as that of the secondary meridian, or substitute for the prime meridian of Greenwich Observatory, from which observations for longitude in the Indian Survey are reckoned. Every station and place in that Survey will be erroneous if the longitude of Madras is in error. In other words, the accuracy with which the entire map of India, as a whole, will be placed on the globe, will correspond precisely to the accuracy with which the geographical position of the Madras observatory has been

* Mr. Taylor was followed, at the Madras Observatory, by Captain Worster, Major Jacob, Major Tennant, and Mr. Pogson. According to Findlay, in the new edition of his Directory, the last result (80° 14′ 19·5″) was from observations by Major Jacob. The observations of Worster and Jacob were also published, and extend from 1848 to 1852.

Besides the publications of Goldingham, Taylor, and Jacob, see "Philosophical Transactions," vol. 112, p. 408, Memoirs of the Astronomical Society, xxxi. p. 83. (1861–63), and a short account of the observatories in India, in the "Times of India," for June 15th, 1850.

determined. At present three different authorities, commenced at different periods, are based on the three different results, accepted as accurate at the time of adoption. The Indian Atlas adopts 80° 18′ 30″ E. as the longitude of Madras; the Survey Department in India uses 80° 17′ 21″; while the Admiralty, on their charts, have 80° 14′ 19·5″. The point will be again investigated when the longitude is ascertained through the electric telegraph from Greenwich.

The actual work of the Great Trigonometrical Survey of India was commenced on the 10th of April 1802, by the measurement of a base line near Madras. The ground selected by Major Lambton for this operation was a flat plain near eight miles long, with St. Thomas's mount near its northern, and Perumbauk hill near its southern end. The chain was fitted into five coffers of wood, each 20 feet long, which were supported on tripods with elevating screws. The base line was 7½ miles long, and the measurement was completed on the 22d of May, when observations were taken to determine the angle of the base with the meridian.

Major Lambton, by means of triangulations from this base line, then proceeded to measure an arc of the meridian, and the length of a degree at right angles with the meridian, in the neighbourhood of Madras. These operations were conducted with great care; and the Major himself devoted 16 nights to the observation of the star Aldebaran at each of the stations at the extremities of the arc; while Lieutenant Warren filled in the topographical details of this part of the survey, from Cuddalore to Paudree, north of Madras.

But these preliminary labours were only first trials in which the young surveyors were, as it were, trying their wings. Sir George Everest says, in one of his letters to the Duke of Sussex, that they were afterwards rejected by Major Lambton himself, and never adverted to by him in his latter days, but as failures.

From the Madras base line a series of triangles was carried up to the Mysore plateau, and a second base was measured near Bangalore in 1804, by Lieutenant Warren; as a datum for extending the triangles to the Malabar coast; and as a base of verification for the triangles brought from the Madras base.* Lieutenant Warren also made some experiments to estimate the effects of terrestrial refraction.† Lieutenant Kater was next despatched to select stations in the moun-

* A base, which afterwards appears to have been rejected, was measured by Lambton himself at Bangalore between October 14th and December 20th, 1800.

† "Asiatic Researches" ix. p. 1.

tains of Coorg and Bednoor, whence the flag staves on the western sea coast could be intersected. A series of triangles, in two degrees of latitude, was then carried across the peninsula; the flag staves at Tellicherry, Cannanore, and on Mount Delly, being intersected from the summit of Todiandamole, the highest peak in Coorg; but no base line was measured on the Malabar coast.

The distance across the peninsula, at this point, was found to be 360 miles; while the best maps had hitherto given it as 400 miles. Thus 40 miles had to be taken off the width of the peninsula at one swoop, and the absolute necessity for a Trigonometrical Survey, owing to the hopeless inaccuracy of other methods, was thus demonstrated. This work was completed in 1806.

Having connected the two sides of the peninsula, Major Lambton devoted much of his future labors to the measurement of an arc of the meridian, and the series of triangles that was measured for this purpose is known as the "Great Arc Series." He first brought the series down from the Bangalore base line towards Cape Comorin; and a new base line was measured in Coimbatoor in 1806. But this was very far from representing the whole of his work, which included a network of primary and secondary triangles, almost covering the peninsula.

In 1808 a base line was measured at Tanjore, and on this occasion Major Lambton dispensed with the tripods, and made the measurement on the ground, drawing out the chain by means of two small capstans. In this flat country Major Lambton availed himself of the *goperams* or lofty towers of the pagodas, on which scaffoldings were erected, and thus the triangles were formed, connecting Tanjore with Nagore and Negapatam. But, in hoisting the three-foot Cary's theodolite to the summit of the Tanjore pagoda, a most serious accident occurred. One of the guys carried away, and the instrument was dashed with great force against the wall of the pagoda, the blow falling upon the tangent screw and clamp, and quite distorting the limb. Ordinary men would have been disheartened at such a mishap, but Lambton was endowed with indomitable resolution, and was full of resource. He hurried back with the theodolite to Bangalore, where there was an establishment of ordnance artificers, and shut himself up in his tent, refusing admittance to all comers except a few of the workmen who assisted him. He then took the instrument entirely to pieces, cut out a circle of the exact size on a flat plank, and gradually drew the limb out so as to fit into the circumference by using wedges, screws, and pullies. In six weeks he had brought it back nearly to its original form, and the same instrument was used for all the subsequent observations up to 1830.

A base line at Tinnevelly was measured in 1809, and the primary triangles were extended thence to the sea shore at Punnae, eight miles north-east of Cape Comorin. This terminal station is a square building with two doors and two arched windows, and a solid pillar in the centre, on the top of which is a large circular stone with a hole through it. It is a mile south-east of the village of Punnae, and about 700 yards from the beach. Major Lambton devoted 28 days to fixing the latitude of the Punnae Station, during which time he took 236 astronomical observations. In addition to the "Great Arc Series," another series of triangulations was carried across the peninsula from Negapatam to Ponany and Calicut, and another round the coast from Rameswaram, through Travancore and Cochin, to Calicut.

The Arc Series was thus completed from Cape Comorin to Bangalore; and in 1811 Major Lambton and his staff turned their whole attention to its extension northwards, in the direction of the Himalayas. Major Lambton himself, ever hopeful and buoyant, calculated on personally completing it as far as Agra. A base was measured at Gooty, with triangles connecting it with that near Bangalore, and others extending to the river Tumbuddra. The Gooty base is also the foundation of a series of triangles connecting Masulipatam with Goa; and bases of verification were measured near Guntoor, on the beach at Coomta, and at Cape Ramas. Thus an accurate basis of triangulation was formed from Cape Comorin to the Kistnah river, enabling the Topographical Surveyors to proceed with the mapping of the country; and the heights of peaks and table lands were carefully measured.

Major Lambton then crossed the Tumbuddra and entered the territory of the Nizam, continuing the Great Arc Series to the neighbourhood of Beder, where another base line was measured at a station called Dumargidda in 1815. Astronomical observations were taken with the zenith sector to determine the celestial arcs of amplitude, and nothing remained to the completion of near 10 degrees of the meridional arc from Cape Comorin to Beder. In concluding his fifth report, the enthusiastic surveyor thus writes: "In 20 years devoted to this work I have scarcely experienced a "heavy hour. Such is the case when the human mind is absorbed "in pursuits that call its powers into action. A man so engaged, "his time passes on insensibly, and if his efforts are successful his "reward is great, and a retrospect of his labors will afford him an

" endless gratification. If such should be my lot I shall close my " career with heartfelt satisfaction, and look back with unceasing " delight on the years I have passed in India."

Yet the difficulties in the field were not the only obstacles with which Lambton had to contend. He was called upon, from time to time, to demonstrate the utility of his work; even Major Rennell came forward to maintain that route surveys on an astronomical basis were equally accurate and more economical, and Major Lambton's resources were crippled and starved by the Finance Committee at Madras.* Nor did he receive any encouragement from scientific bodies in Europe during the early years of his survey, when such support was most needed, and would have been most welcome. Professor Playfair reviewed his work in the Edinburgh in 1813, and he received one letter from Nevil Maskelyne at a time when he was surrounded by difficulties, and when he was vainly endeavouring to impress the nature and utility of his operations on the local Government. He used to dwell on this letter from the Astronomer Royal as the event which had most cheered him under all his toils. But for many years he never received one word of encouragement, sympathy, or advice, either from the Government or from the Royal Society. Indeed it was a foreign nation that was the first to recognize the importance of his services. In 1817 Major Lambton was made a corresponding member of the French Institute, but it was not until the following year that the Royal Society tardily followed the example, and elected him a Fellow.

The Governor General, "not unaware that with minds of a certain " order he might lay himself open to the idle imputation of vainly " seeking to partake the gale of public favour and applause which " the labours of Lieutenant-Colonel Lambton have recently at- " tracted," at last recognized the great importance of the survey. He transferred it to his immediate control on January 1st, 1818; and ordered it to be denominated for the future, "The Great Trigonometrical Survey of India." Captain Everest was appointed as Colonel Lambton's chief assistant, and Dr. Voysey as medical attendant to the surveying parties, and geologist.†

In the end of 1818 young Everest joined Colonel Lambton at Hyderabad. The assistant describes his chief, at this time, as an old man with a bald head fringed with a few snow white hairs,

* "Calcutta Review," vol. iv., p. 80 (1815.)

† For a notice of Dr. Voysey's work, see the section on the Geological Survey, p. 145.

about six feet high, erect, well formed, and muscular. His complexion was fair and his eyes blue, but dimmed and weakened by time. Yet when he aroused himself to adjust the great theodolite, they shone with the lustre, and his limbs moved with the vigour, of full manhood. "His high and ample forehead gave animation and dignity to a countenance beaming with intellect and manly beauty." But these moments of activity were like the last flickerings of an expiring lamp. The old surveyor was gradually wasting away, and in June 1819 was the last occasion of his ever taking part in the work of triangulation.

Central India was then in a most unsettled state; and instead of attempting to push forward the Great Arc Series, Lambton employed his parties in completing the triangulation between the rivers Kistnah and Godavery. In June 1819 Everest was despatched upon this duty, into a wild country, where each village had its mud fort defended by jinjals, and many districts were in rebellion against the Nizam's government. He overcame the difficulties arising from the disturbed state of the country; but he and his party, working in a region teeming with malaria under a tropical sun, were at length prostrated by jungle fever, and in 1820 Everest himself went to the Cape of Good Hope for the recovery of his health.

Meanwhile the indefatigable but now aged and broken chief of the survey once more began to push forward the Great Arc Series. He measured a base line with the steel chain stretched on the ground by capstans, at Takalkhéra in the valley of Berar, in the winter of 1822; but the standard had got rusty, and was unreliable. Old Colonel Lambton during this time, was constantly at work with the zenith sector, exposed to a tropical sun, and unaided, for his assistants were all sick owing to the reckless exposure to which he had subjected them. He himself took no rest at night, but continued to work at the zenith distances of stars. His constitution received its death blow, while his observations proved wild, and were confusedly registered. "Men cannot last for ever," wrote his assistant, "and the Colonel's infirmities had evidently subdued all but his " spirit, at the time of his last effort."

On Everest's return from the Cape, he was detached, in October 1822, to bring up a series of triangles connecting Bombay with the Great Arc Series. Colonel Lambton set out from Hyderabad to Nagpoor, to make arrangements for continuing the Great Arc operations. But he died on the road at Hingunghat, now one of the great Berar cotton marts, on the 20th of January, 1823, aged 70.* His assistants and servants were affectionately attached to him and looked upon him as a father; and in 1822 he counted three generations of them in his camp. His assistants, De Penning and Rossenrode, attended upon him in his last hours. A tomb was erected over his remains at Hingunghat, by Mr. Jenkins, the then Resident at Nagpoor.

Colonel Lambton, the first Superintendent of the Great Trigonometrical Survey, completed the triangulation of 165,342 square miles in the peninsula of India, at a cost of 83,537*l*. In concluding his last report he says, "I sincerely hope that, after I relinquish "the work, somebody will be found possessing zeal, constitution, "and attainments wherewith to prosecute it; and it would indeed "be gratifying to me if I could but entertain a distant hope, "that a work which I began should at some future day be extended "over British India."

That hope was fulfilled in the appointment of George Everest as his successor.

The labours of Colonel Lambton are recorded in the following manuscript volumes, deposited in the Geographical Department of the India Office.

Vol. I. (Part 1.)—Trigonometrical Operations, 1802—3, with a map.

„ (Part 2.)—Trigonometrical Operations, 1803—6, with a map.

Vol. II.—Operations, 1807—11.

Vol. III.— „ 1811—14. Dated at Hyderabad in 1818.

Vol. IV.—Missing from the Geographical Department of the India Office.

Vol. V.—Operations to Jan. 1823. Signed W. Lambton, and counter-signed in 1832 by Everest.

Vol. VI.—End of Lambton's Reports, with an Appendix by Everest, relating to his own operations under Lambton in 1822—23, and to Capt. Garling's in 1816—17. Signed by Everest in 1832.

Abstracts of these accounts will be found in vols. 7, 8, 10, 12, and 13, of the Asiatic Researches. The first three of these were reviewed in the 21st volume of the Edinburgh Review (1813) by Professor

* The Government Gazette of the time gave his age at 75.

Playfair. Colonel Lambton published an abstract containing the results of all his measurements from Punnae to Dumargidda in the Philosophical Transactions of 1818. See also Everest's "Account of the Measurement of an Arc of the Meridian (1830)," and his series of letters to the Duke of Sussex (London 1839), for some further interesting particulars respecting Colonel Lambton and his services.* The operations of the survey under Colonel Lambton are also described in the "Account of the operations of the Great Trigonometrical Survey of India," vol. i., by Colonel J. T. Walker, R.E., F.R.S. (Dehra Doon, 1870.) There is a "Biographical Sketch of the late Colonel Lambton" in "Gleanings in Science," vol. ii., p. 27, (Calcutta, 1830,) and an article "On the Measurement of the Indian Meridional Arc," in the same work, vol. iii., p. 337. The whole of Colonel Lambton's operations are shown in a chart of eight sheets engraved by Mr. Walker.

---

* Major Jervis published some extracts from Colonel Lambton's Notices of Malabar (Coimbatore ?) in the *Bombay Geographical Society's Journal*, vol. iv., (1840).

IV.—FIRST PERIOD OF THE TOPOGRAPHICAL SURVEYS.

1800–23.

Hitherto, the maps of Indian districts had been based on military route surveys. The initiation of detailed topographical surveys, based on triangulation, is due to Colin Mackenzie, one of the most indefatigable surveyors and persevering collectors of information that ever served this country.

Colonel Mackenzie commenced his exploring labours after the close of the war of 1783. In that and the following years he was at work in Coimbatoor and Dindigul. In 1790–94 he was engaged in surveying Nellore, Guntoor, and the Ceded Districts; and his journal in manuscript is one of the most interesting relics in the Geographical Department of the India Office.* In 1799 he was appointed to conduct the topographical survey of Mysore.

It was Mackenzie who suggested the establishment of the Madras Military Institution, which, under the able superintendence of Captain Troyer, trained most of the surveying officers who, under Mackenzie and others, carefully surveyed the peninsula of India.

Mackenzie was engaged on the Mysore Survey during several years. His system of triangulation was independent of Colonel Lambton's, and the two officers do not appear to have worked harmoniously. Mackenzie measured five bases in the Mysore country, in convenient situations, each from three to five miles long, and connected them by triangles. His results were a topographical

---

* "Remarks on a journey in the countries of Cummum, Purwatbum, and Canoul; being a continuation of the survey of the frontier and passes between the Pennair and the Krishna in 1794, by Captain Colin Mackenzie." This manuscript volume is in the form of a journal, with archæological and other notes, and sketches on the margins.

The following manuscript maps, drawn by Colin Mackenzie at this period, are also preserved in the Geographical Department of the India Office :—

1. Nizam's dominions and Mysore, showing acquisitions of territory, 1799.
2. Military chart of the Carnatic, 1802.
3. Roads from Bangalore to Nellore, &c., 1793.
4. Survey of passes leading from the Carnatic to Kurnool, 1792.
5. Passes between the Pennair and and the Krishna, 1794.

Mackenzie's account of the Perwuttun Pagoda is published in the *Asiatic Researches*, v., *p*. 303.

survey comprising 40,000 square miles, a general and seven provincial maps, and a valuable memoir in seven folio volumes, containing, besides a narrative of the survey, much carefully digested statistical, historical, and antiquarian information. The copies of all these precious records, formerly in the India House, are now missing! !

In 1809 Mackenzie was removed from the Deccan Surveys, and became Surveyor General of Madras. In 1811 he went with the expedition to Java, where he got through much work with his usual zeal and energy, and resumed his post at Madras on his return in 1815. He superintended the continuance of the survey of the Ceded Districts, commenced in 1809, until he was removed to Calcutta, and took up the appointment of Surveyor General of India.

But his surveys were only a part, and, indeed, a small part of the stupendous labours of Colin Mackenzie. He devoted himself to the study of Indian antiquities, and visited every place of any interest, from the Kistnah to Cape Comorin, accompanied by a native staff of assistants, copying and collecting records. He got together 3,000 sassanums or tenures inscribed on stone or copper; and the Mackenzie collection consists of 1,568 manuscripts in different Indian languages, 8,076 inscriptions, 2,630 drawings, 78 plans, 6,218 coins, and 106 images. He sent some beautiful sculptured stone work from the Amravatee tope to the India House before 1820, and published various papers on historical and topographical subjects.* Among the results of his labours were the discovery of the existence of the Jain religion, and of other sects, and the descriptions of tumuli of early tribes.

After Colonel Mackenzie's death, Horace Wilson volunteered to examine and report upon his manuscripts, and the result appeared in 1828.† Our knowledge of the literature and early history of Southern India is almost entirely due to the Mackenzie MSS.

* In Dalrymple's Oriental Repertory are papers by Mackenzie on routes in Nellore, and on the source of the Pennaar. In the Asiatic Annual Register for 1804 are his Life of Hyder Ally, and his Histories of the Bijayanuggur and Anagoondy Rajahs; and in vol. ix. of the Asiatic Researches he first brought to notice the religion and monuments of the Jains.

† "Mackenzie Collection of Oriental Manuscripts, by H. H. Wilson, Secretary to the Asiatic Society." 2 vols. (Calcutta, 1828). A further series of Reports on the Mackenzie MSS. was made to the Madras Government by Revd. W. Taylor. They are printed in vols. vii., viii., ix., of the Madras Journal of Literature and Science. See a notice of Colin Mackenzie in the Journal of the Royal Asiatic Society, i., p. 333, and Madras Journal of Literature and Science, ii., p. 262.

In 1811 Lieutenant Garling, an élève of the Madras Military Institution, commenced the survey of the Portuguese territory of Goa. A base was measured at Cape Ramas, and the survey was completed in 1812. Besides the maps, Lieutenant Garling wrote a memoir in four volumes, containing a general description of the Goa territory, and detailed accounts of the coast, anchorages, rivers, population, and villages, with tables, cultivation, towns, and roads and passes.

As soon as the Goa Survey was completed, Lieutenant Garling, with Lieutenant Conner and three sub-assistants, commenced work in Soanda and Bilgy, in North Canara, in 1813. The topographical survey of Soanda is founded on the base measured near Goa, whence a net of triangles was extended over the new country, and united with the stations of Lambton's Trigonometrical Survey. The detail was taken up by plane tables on a scale of one inch to a mile, and all topographical objects that could be expressed on the scale were embraced in the survey. The field work was completed in March 1815, and the descriptive memoir, in two volumes, contains an account of the general aspect of the region surveyed, with details respecting the cultivation, water supply, inhabitants, tenures, trade, routes, and history.

Lieutenant Conner then proceeded to conduct a survey of the little mountainous principality of Coorg, exactly on the same plan as that of Soanda. Colonel Lambton had carried his primary triangles through Coorg, so that Conner could use them as a basis on which to construct his secondary series. He commenced work in 1815, and completed the survey in October 1817. The memoir, in one volume, intended to illustrate the map, contains details respecting the boundaries and extent of Coorg; a table of areas of the districts; accounts of the principal places; descriptions of the mountains, rivers, forests (with a catalogue of trees), animals, agriculture, implements of husbandry; a register of villages; and tables of triangles, and of bearings and distances.

Travancore and Cochin were surveyed by Lieutenants Ward and Conner between 1816 and 1821. Their memoir, in seven volumes, contains a journal; tables of triangulation; and descriptions of the districts, villages, forests, productions, and passes. Extracts from it, describing the hill tribes of Travancore, were published in the Madras Journal of Literature and Science, vol. i., pp. 1 and 54.

Malabar was surveyed by Lieutenants Ward and Conner between 1825 and 1829. Their memoir, in one volume, furnishes a special description of each talook, including Wynaad, but Ward refers to the great work of Buchanan for fuller details.*

Tinnevelly was surveyed by Assistant Surveyor Thomas Turnbull and others, between 1807 and 1813, and the memoir which accompanied the map is most valuable, but, unfortunately, it was left unfinished, owing to the death of its author. Tinnevelly was a portion of the ancient Pandian kingdom, and the memoir describes inscriptions on granite walls; the temples and other religious monuments; the climate, population, products; and gives details respecting the boundaries, the resources of each talook, and the roads. This was the best account of the people in the extreme south of India that had appeared since the publication of the "Lettres Edifiantes." The Tinnevelly surveyors, however, could not be induced to penetrate into the forest covered mountains towards the Travancore frontier, from a not altogether erroneous idea that they were unhealthy; and there is still a large blank space on the atlas in that direction.

The provinces of Dindigul and Madura were surveyed between 1815 and 1824 by Assistant Surveyors Thomas Turnbull and William Keyes, and afterwards by Lieutenant Ward. Their memoirs are well written and most valuable, containing full details respecting those provinces, and an account of the wild and little known hill region bordering on Travancore. The account of the Pulney hills, from Lieutenant Ward's memoir, is published in the Madras Journal of Literature and Science (vol. vi., p. 280.)

Ward and Keyes also surveyed the Coimbatore district between 1821 and 1824, and a descriptive memoir accompanied their maps. They were the discoverers and explorers of the Neilgherry hills; and Ward completed a map and memoir of that mountain knot in 1821. An isolated range of hills, with a remarkable peak, separated

* The memoir on Malabar, by Captains Ward and Conner, was communicated by Major Jervis to the Bombay Geographical Society, and published in their vol. iv. (May 1840). The map of Malabar was drawn on a scale of one inch to a mile, but there is only one sheet of it in the Geographical Department of the India Office. A beautiful reduction of it was drawn in 1832 at Madras, on a scale of two inches to the mile, by C. Ignatio, (draftsman), a complete copy of which is preserved in the Geographical Department. The portion including Wynaad has been lithographed separately at Madras by Colonel Priestley.

from the Neilgherries by the Bhowany river, was named after the founder of the Great Survey, and is known as Lambton's Peak Range.

The Carnatic was topographically surveyed by the officers of the Military Institute, and Trichinopoly by Lieutenant Ward, whose memoir, in two volumes, contains registers of triangles; tables of bearings and distances; maps of roads on a scale of one mile to an inch; and accounts of the system of irrigation, trade, and agriculture.

The eastern districts of Ellore, Rajahmundry, and Guntoor were surveyed between 1816 and 1823 by Lieutenant Mountford and the officers of the Military Institute. The memoir on the Ellore Survey is in three volumes. That of Rajahmundry, in two volumes, by Captain Snell, contains tabulated routes with coloured maps. For this survey a base was roughly measured on the borders of the Colair Lake in May 1820, and connected by triangulation with two of Lambton's points near the Kistnah. The map was on a scale of one mile to an inch. The survey of the Nizam's territory, commenced in Colonel Lambton's time, occupied upwards of 30 years.

Thus full materials for a map of the whole peninsula of India south of the Kistnah, based on Lambton's Great Trigonometrical Survey, were furnished. The memoirs, with a few exceptions, are preserved in the Geographical Department of the India Office. Those that are wanting are the memoirs of the Mysore Survey in seven volumes,* those of Madura and Dindigul, that of the Neilgherries by Ward, and the two first volumes of the Travancore Memoir, which were lent many years ago to some one who never returned them. These manuscripts appear to have been placed in the hands of Mr. Montgomery Martin, for publication, by the Court of Directors. A small portion of the Coorg Memoir appeared in two parts in the Colonial Magazine during the year 1842, and extracts from the Travancore and Dindigul Memoirs were published in the Madras Journal of Literature and Science; but, with these exceptions, and that of the Malabar Memoir in the Bombay Geographical Society's Journal, the whole of these valuable and interesting memoirs remain in manuscript.

* We have, however, a manuscript volume by Colin Mackenzie, entitled, "Report on the State and Results of the Survey of Mysore, in a geographical, statistical, and historical view, up to July 1st, 1807, with a map explanatory."

While the topographical surveyors of Madras were thus energetically filling in and completing Colonel Lambton's work, their brethren in the north of India were not idle.

That indefatigable geographer, Colonel Colebrooke, was Surveyor General at Calcutta from 1803 until his death in 1810. He had previously made a series of astronomical observations in the Carnatic in 1791, consisting of latitudes by meridian altitudes of stars, and longitudes by eclipses of Jupiter's satellites; and in the previous year he had made similar observations during a voyage to the Andaman and Nicobar Islands.* He also made a survey of the Ganges; but only one of the original sheets has escaped destruction, and is now in the Geographical Department of the India Office.† Colebrooke's attention was early called to what was, at that time, one of the most interesting problems in Indian geography,—the position of the source of the Ganges. The only knowledge then attainable of the Upper Himalayas and Tibet was derived from Chinese sources through the Jesuit missionaries. It appears that a map of Tibet was put into the hands of Father Regis at Pekin, in 1711, and that he reported its defects to the Emperor Kang-hi, who resolved to procure one that was more accurate and reliable. Two lamas, who had been instructed by the Jesuits at Pekin, were sent to prepare a map from Sining to Lassa, and the source of the Ganges. The results of their labours were given to the missionaries in 1717, by whom they were communicated to Du Halde, and published in Paris. Much of this map was from oral information; but all that was derived from personal observation appears to have been well laid down. Our knowledge of Tibet and of the course of the Sanpoo was entirely derived from this source, until the journeys of Captain Montgomerie's pundits corrected the old lamas' work, within the last few years, while confirming its general accuracy. The map published by Du Halde was re-examined by D'Anville, who moved the source of the Ganges further north; and Rennell, in his first map, copied D'Anville almost exactly. Afterwards, Anquetil du Perron obtained the results of some observations along the course of the Ganges from a Jesuit missionary named Tieffenthaler, who did not, however, carry his compass survey beyond

* Asiatic Researches, iv., p. 317, and p. 321.

† No. 3, Mouth of the Cossimbazar to Colgong. It is dated 1796. There are also three sheets of another incomplete set by Colebrooke, dated 1801.

Hurdwar, the rest being laid down from native information.* Rennell, in his second edition, adopted the position of the source of the Ganges from Tieffenthaler, which was based on no better authority than that of the lamas, namely, the reports of natives.

Thus this important geographical question was left in a state of doubt; and Colonel Colebrooke considered that, as Surveyor General, and for the honour of his country, it was his duty to attempt its solution.

In 1800, Lieutenant Wood, the former surveyor of the Irrawaddy in 1795, had, "by order of General Sir James Craig, K.B., commanding the Army in the Field," made an elaborate survey of the Ganges from Hurdwar to Allahabad;† and in 1808, Colonel Colebrooke resolved to complete the examination of the sacred river from Hurdwar to its source. Captain Guthrie and Mr. Daniell the artist in 1789, and Colonel Hardwicke in 1796, had already penetrated as far as Sreenuggur, and the observations of these officers had enabled Rennell to correct the error of Tieffenthaler in placing Sreenuggur N.N.W. instead of E.N.E. of Hurdwar. But the source of the Ganges had not yet been reached.

Such was the state of knowledge when Colonel Colebrooke obtained the sanction of the Government for his expedition. But while he was preparing to set out, the Surveyor General was seized with a fatal illness, and the execution of the project devolved upon Captain Webb, who was accompanied by Lieutenants Raper and Hearsey. They surveyed the course of the Ganges from Hurdwar to near its source at Gangotri, and fixed the position of Sreenuggur, on the Aluknunda, and other points, between April and June 1808.‡

In 1805, Colonel Crawford, while conducting a survey in Nepal, measured some of the peaks of the Himalayas, and was the first to

* There is a copy of this curious map of the Ganges, published by Anquetil, in the Geographical Department of the India Office, entitled, "Carte Général du cours du Gange et du Gogre, dressée sur les cartes du Tieffenthaler, Missionaire. Par M. Anquetil du Perron. Paris, 1794."

† This survey is beautifully drawn and coloured on several sheets. The MS. is preserved in the Geographical Department of the India Office, and there is also a second set of sheets of Wood's Survey on a reduced scale. But both are in a disgraceful state from long neglect.

‡ The Manuscript of Webb's Survey of 1808, in 12 sheets, from Hurdwar to Gangotri, is preserved in the Geographical Department of the India Office. The narrative of his expedition was written by his companion, Lieutenant Raper, and published in the Asiatic Researches, xi., p. 446–63.

announce their immense height, but the journal of his survey is unfortunately lost. Mr. Colebrooke, the Sanscrit scholar, and kinsman of the Surveyor General, took a great interest in the question of the height of the Himalayan peaks, hereafter to be finally settled by Andrew Waugh, and wrote a paper on the subject.*

After the untimely death of Colonel Colebrooke, the office was held by Colonel Garstin from 1810 to 1814, and Colonel Charles Crawford succeeded him. During this period many useful route surveys were made by officers who accompanied the armies in Oude and Rohilcund; and in 1807, Dr. Buchanan, who had so ably reported upon Mysore and Malabar, was nominated by Lord Hastings to make a statistical survey of Bengal, with an account of the condition of the people, their religion, agriculture, productions, &c. He had efficient assistants and draftsmen, and his labours extended over seven years, from 1807 to 1814.†

In 1816, Colonel Colin Mackenzie, who had been working in the Madras Presidency for more than 30 years, became Surveyor General at Calcutta, where he reduced and compiled many useful maps, and set several surveys on foot. He eventually died there of old age in 1821, and was temporarily succeeded by Colonel Hodgson.

After the termination of the Nepaul War, Lord Hastings, in 1815, appointed Captain J. A. Hodgson and Lieutenant Herbert to survey the mountainous regions between the Sutlej and the Ganges, which are bounded on the north by Chinese Tibet. A base was measured by Lieutenant Herbert with staves made of *deodára* wood, latitudes were fixed by stars' zenith distances, and longitudes by observations of Jupiter's satellites;‡ but, although the scientific basis

* In the Asiatic Researches, vol. xii. For interesting particulars respecting early measurements of Himalayan peaks, see also "Murray's Discoveries in Asia," ii., p. 382, "Baillie Fraser's Journal," p. 323, "Buchanan Hamilton's Nepal," and the Quarterly Review, No. 34. The reviewer challenges the accuracy of the observations, and, like a true conservative, declares that the Andes will be found to be higher than the Himalayas.

† Dr. Buchanan's Survey cost 30,000*l*. His MSS. were sent home in 1816, and in 1838 Mr. Montgomery Martin got leave from the Court of Directors to publish extracts, which accordingly appeared in three thick volumes. There are a series of manuscript maps of the Bengal Districts, drawn for Dr. Buchanan, in the Geographical Department of the India Office, but they are merely compilations to illustrate his reports, and were engraved by Mr. Walker in 1838 for Mr. Montgomery Martin's book.

‡ The original manuscript map showing the base measured by Hodgson and Herbert near Saharunpore, and the triangulation founded on it, to ascertain the heights of peaks, is preserved in the Geographical Department of the India Office.

of the survey is highly creditable to the officers employed, the interior filling in was scanty and inaccurate.* Captain Webb was employed to continue the survey over the province of Kumaon, from 1815 to 1820, and in 1818 Hodgson and Herbert were engaged† in Gurhwal.

Between 1815 and 1821, Captain James Franklin, a very accomplished officer, surveyed the whole of Bundelcund, and produced a valuable map of that region, and a memoir on its geology. A survey based on routes and cross routes was also made in 1821 by Captain Johnson, of Bhopal and Bairseah, in Central India.‡

The Sunderbunds were surveyed between 1812 and 1818 by two young brothers, Lieutenants Hugh and W. E. Morrieson. They were much annoyed by tigers and alligators, and they relate how a tiger sprang from a branch just over their theodolite while in the act of observing, and how the shaking of the ground near them made the instrument vibrate, owing to the tread of huge monsters in the jungle. Hugh died of jungle fever at Jessore in 1818, and his brother was killed in an action with the Goorkhas.§

A rough survey of Cuttack was commenced in 1818 by Lieutenant Buxton; a survey of Backergunge was instituted in 1819; and those of the Sylhet frontier, and of Azimghur and Jounpoor were com-

---

* Interesting accounts of these operations will be found in the Asiatic Researches, vol. xiii., p. 297, and vol. xiv., p. 60 and p. 187.

The operations of Hodgson and Herbert were also published in a work entitled "Astronomical Observations in various parts of Hindustan, and a Survey of the sources of the Ganges and Jumna," by Capt. J. A. Hodgson; "with operations for "determining the heights of peaks in the Himalayas, by Captains Hodgson and Her-"bert, 1817." It contains an account of their measurement of a base, with drawings of the apparatus.

There is a copy of this work in the Geographical Department of the India Office, bound in red morocco and gilt, with a manuscript title page.

In 1829, Herbert commenced a periodical at Calcutta, called "Gleanings in Science," to which James Prinsep was a frequent contributor. Herbert became Astronomer at the Lucknow Observatory in 1831, and Prinsep took his place as editor. In 1832 the "Gleanings" were converted into the "Journal of the Asiatic Society of Bengal," and have been published monthly ever since. Herbert died at Lucknow on September 24th, 1833.

† The original "Journal of the Survey of Gurhwal," by Lieutenant J. D. Herbert, 8th Regiment N.I., in 1818; is preserved in the Geographical Department of the India Office.

‡ The field books of Captains Franklin and Johnson are preserved in the Geographical Department of the India Office.

§ Their field books are preserved at Calcutta. *See* "Calcutta Review," vol. 63 (1859).

menced in 1818. A line of country was also surveyed by Lieutenant Jackson, from Midnapore to Nagpore in 1818, with a view to ascertaining the practicability of making a road.*

In the Bombay Presidency, during this period, Colonel Monier Williams made a careful survey by compass and perambulator of Guzerat, Cutch, and Kattywar, between 1813 and 1820; and some maps were compiled from route surveys in the Deccan, but none were based on triangulation. Captain Dangerfield was engaged on geographical work in Malwa, and between 1812 and 1816 Colonel Dickenson and Captain Tate surveyed the town and islands of Bombay and Salsette, and this map was accompanied by a statistical memoir.†

* See a dispatch from Lord Hastings, dated February 15th, 1821.

† The map of Bombay, by Dickenson and Tate, was lithographed for Major Jervis in 1843, on a scale of 1 inch to 1,200 yards; but it is very inaccurate.

V.—SECOND PERIOD OF THE TRIGONOMETRICAL SURVEYS.

1823–43.

Sir George Everest, and the completion of the Measurement of an Arc of the Meridian.

On the death of Colonel Lambton in 1823, his assistant George Everest was appointed to succeed him as Superintendent of the Great Trigonometrical Survey of India; and thus the hope of the veteran surveyor, expressed in his last Report, was fulfilled. "A " man was found, after he relinquished the work, possessing zeal, " constitution, and attainments wherewith to prosecute it."

George Everest, son of Tristram Everest, Esq., of Gwernvale in Brecon, was born on July 4th, 1790. He began his education at Marlow, and completed it at Woolwich, where he passed a brilliant examination. He sailed for Bengal as an Artillery Cadet in 1806, and executed a reconnaissance survey for Sir Stamford Raffles in Java in 1814–16,* when he became the friend of Mr. John Crawfurd. In 1817 he was employed in establishing a telegraph system from Calcutta to Benares, and joined the survey in 1818.

He had been Colonel Lambton's chief assistant for upwards of five years. At the time of his chief's death he was engaged on the Bombay longitudinal series. On taking charge of the survey, he found the most northern work to be a base line measured at Takalkhéra in the valley of Berar, but the triangulation had not been extended so far. Here Everest commenced work in November 1823.

He was surrounded by many difficulties. His colleague, Dr. Voysey, died in December 1823, and Lambton's principal assistant, Mr. De Penning, a half caste from Madras, became weary of the service, and retired in February 1824. The rest of Lambton's staff consisted of Madras men, who were unwilling to go so far from their homes, and there were no trained hands to take their places.

* The MS. volume containing the original route survey of Java in 1814–16 is preserved in the Geographical Department of the India Office.

Everest himself was attacked with a severe fever, and his limbs were paralyzed. Still he resolutely persevered, lest, if he broke down, the establishment should be scattered, and the trained men be lost, whom it would be impossible to replace. He was lowered into and hoisted out of his seat by two men, when he observed with the zenith sector.

He now had to take the meridional arc series across the Satpoora hills,* which bound the valley of Berar to the north, about 15 miles north of the Takalkhéra base. He anticipated that the density and magnitude of these mountains would cause a considerable deflection of the plumb line, and made some careful observations with a view to deciding the point. He then carried the triangulation across the Satpoora hills as far as the plain of Sironj, where a base line was measured with the old chain in November 1824. In January 1825 a series of observations was taken at Kalianpoor near Sironj, and then at last the Superintendent's health completely broke down. He was obliged to go to England on sick leave, but still retaining his appointment, in 1825.

During Colonel Everest's absence, a longitudinal series of triangles was extended from the Sironj base to Calcutta, over nearly 700 miles of difficult and little known country. This important work was entrusted to Mr. Joseph Olliver, who had been Everest's pupil from the time he first joined the survey in 1818, and whom he called his "right arm."

Colonel Everest was in England from 1825 to 1830; and his time was fully employed in studying the newest improvements and superintending the construction of instruments on the most approved principles. When he returned to India in 1830, he was provided with the best instruments that could then be produced. He had a large theodolite with an azimuth circle 36 inches in diameter, by Troughton; and two double vertical circles three feet in diameter, by Troughton and Simms. But the most important improvement introduced into the survey by Everest, at this time, was the measurement of the bases by compensation bars, instead of the old inaccurate method by chains.

One of the objections to the chain method was the impossibility of determining the temperature of its different parts while in actual

* He calls them the Mahadeo hills.

use. Colonel Colby, of the Irish Survey, invented the method of measuring bases by compensation bars,* founded on the principle of eliminating the errors arising from changes of temperature by compensation or self correction. Advantage is taken of the unequal expansion of various metals to eliminate the effects of variations of temperature altogether. Two bars, one of brass and one of iron, each about 10 feet long, are firmly clamped together in the middle so that no motion can take place near the centre; and any expansion from change in temperature must be towards the extremities. At a temperatue of 62° the two bars are precisely the same length. At each end of both bars an aperture is worked out to admit a conical pivot, and the two pivots, one in the brass the other in the iron bar, are adjusted to a flat iron tongue. When the temperature rises, the brass bar will be lengthened more than the iron one, and the tongues will incline inwards, and *vice versâ*. Consequently there is a point on the tongues at which theoretically the expansion of the bars is compensated by the inclination of the tongues. This point is marked with a dot on each tongue, and the distance between these dots is, as nearly as it can be made, ten feet. The bars are supported on brass rollers and enclosed in deal boxes, from which the tongues only project. Before going to India, Colonel Everest tried the compensation bars in Lord's cricket ground. Two iron standard bars were made of 10 feet each, called A. and B., and two brass standard scales of six inches, also A. and B, with which the compensating bars and microscopes were frequently compared. All the measurements were referred to these standards.†

Colonel Everest arrived at Calcutta in the autumn of 1830, with six sets of bars, and well supplied with the most improved instruments. He combined the appointments of Surveyor General and Superintendent of the Great Trigonometrical Survey in his own person. He found that Mr. Olliver had nearly completed the Calcutta longitudinal series, which originates at Kalianpoor, and terminates at

---

* It is said that a base 100 feet long in Ireland was measured six times with Colby's compensation bars, and that the extreme difference between the measurements did not exceed half the breadth of a sharp steel point on a plate of metal, observed with a microscope.

† "Transactions of the Physical Class of the Asiatic Society of Bengal." 1839. This was an interesting lecture by Everest on the compensation bars, the substance of which will be found in the *Asiatic Researches*, xviii. p. 189.

Fort William, Calcutta. On Everest's arrival he resolved to measure a base line of verification for this series, which is interesting as the first base line in India that was measured with the compensation bars. Mr. Taylor, the Astronomer at the Madras Observatory, was deputed to Calcutta to assist Colonel Everest at the measurement of this base. It extends for $6\frac{1}{2}$ miles along the road from Government House at Calcutta to Barrackpore. The extremities are marked by two towers 75 feet high, which overtop the trees and houses.* The measurement was commenced on November 23rd, 1831, finished on January 21st, 1832, and the triangulation of the Calcutta longitudinal series was completed on July 2nd, 1832.†

In 1832 Colonel Everest resumed the work connected with the meridional arc series, and in the commencement he had to encounter difficulties which could only have been surmounted by a combination of qualities which are rarely found united in one man. His staff had to be trained to the work, and, in addition to his incessant labours in the field, he had to transact all the business connected with his office as Surveyor General.

Hitherto the meridional arc series had been conducted over the elevated plateau of the Deccan, where numerous rocky heights offered excellent sites for stations. But in extending the triangulation beyond the Sironj base, the surveyors entered upon a much more difficult country for their work. Here the great plateau of Central India terminates with the high land round Gwalior, and the valley of the Chumbul commences. From this point the east flank of the meridional series is on flat land, while the western side rests on low hills as far as Delhi. But from Delhi a wide plain, overgrown with groves of mango and tamarind, intermingled with lofty peepul and banian trees, and thickly scattered over with villages, extends for 101 miles to the foot of the Sewalik hills, the first outwork of the Himalayas. At a distance of a few miles from the observer on the great Gangetic plain, the trees appear to form a continuous belt of foliage, while clouds of dust often obscure the view.

* The following officers were engaged in measuring this base. Lieutenants Western and Bridgman, Mr. Taylor the Madras Astronomer, Messrs. Logan, Olliver, Peyton, Torrick, Rossenrode, and Lieutenant Wilcox the surveyor of Assam. There is an account of the measurement in the *Journal of the Asiatic Society of Bengal*, i. p. 71. See also James Prinsep's determination of the constant of expansion of the standard, i. p. 130.

† The area surveyed was 33,442 square miles. Total cost 13,074*l.*

In entering upon this difficult country, Colonel Everest was supported by able and zealous young assistants. In 1832, Andrew Waugh*, his future successor, and Renny joined the survey, and Olliver and Rossenrode had already been in training for some years.

It is the practice of the survey, before commencing the main triangulation of a series, to execute an approximate series by which the stations for observing the angles of the main series are selected, and the positions of the triangles sketched out.

Mr. Olliver commenced the new work by exploring the tract north of the Chumbul, while Mr. Rossenrode was deputed to carry on an approximate series along the meridian of the great arc as far as the Chumbul river. It then became necessary to erect permanent towers for stations on the Gangetic plain; and in order to select their positions, Colonel Everest designed a mast 30 feet high, with a circular table, 40 inches in diameter at the top, round which a square scaffolding of large bamboo was built. This was intended to observe from; and 13 other masts, 70 feet high, with cross bamboo staves having an ignited blue light at one end, and a sway rope at the other, were placed on the surrounding stations.

On December 5th, 1833, Colonel Everest arrived at Muttra, the station for collecting bamboos for the masts and scaffolding. The instrument used on the top of the observing mast was a Troughton and Simms 12-inch theodolite, constructed in 1830. The signals at the pinnacles of the other masts were blue lights, burnt by sets of four, at intervals of 10 minutes. But, owing to the distance between the stations, the signals were scarcely ever visible to the naked eye, and it was necessary to lay the telescope in the proper direction, to be calculated beforehand by a series of minor triangles. This system, invented by Colonel Everest, was called "*ray tracing.*" By May 1834 all the 35 stations between the Chumbul and the foot of the Sewalik hills had been selected. Day and night, at all hours, from December to May, Everest was perpetually at work. Colonel Lambton had used masts and flag staves as signals. But, owing to the nature of the atmosphere, objects of this kind cannot be easily bisected in the day time during the healthy season, and are often invisible for days together. So Lambton chose the rainy season, when the atmosphere is very clear, for field observations. The con-

* Nominated July 2nd, 1832.

sequence was a reckless waste of life and health, besides much suffering and discomfort. But luminous objects were found to succeed best in the dry healthy season. Everest therefore substituted the heliotrope* for day observations at short distances, and reverberatory lamps with argand burners,† or blue lights, for the night.

The position of each station having thus been fixed, 17 permanent towers were erected. They are square at the base, about 50 feet high, with walls five feet thick at the bottom and two at the top. The roof or terrace is supported by two large stone beams on which rests a cylindrical well of masonry surmounted by a circular slab of sandstone. At right angles to these stone beams, and 3½ feet above them, are rafters supporting the stage for the observer, round which is a hand rail with rings for the observing tent. Thus the instrument is completely isolated from the stage on which the observer stands. The instrument is hoisted up by a crane at one angle.‡

These important but tedious preliminaries having been completed, the great work of measuring the most northern base for the great arc series was commenced in the end of 1834. The region selected for this measurement was the Dehra Doon, a beautiful valley between the Sewalik hills and the Himalayas, 2,000 feet above the sea. The western end of the base line is 1,886 and the eastern 2,073 feet above the level of the sea. The measurement was commenced on December 1st, 50 comparisons having first been made between each of the six compensation bars and the iron standard, while the standards A and B were compared with each other 101 times. As soon as the base was measured, it was remeasured in reverse order by Waugh and Renny, the error being 2·396 inches. The whole distance was 7·42 miles. On March 28th, 1835, the work of measuring was completed. The uncultivated part of the country, over which the base line passes, was afterwards purchased by Captain Kirke, who called it Arcadia, in compliment to the great arc series. Colonel Everest's head quarters were at Hatipaon, in the Dehra Doon, whence

* The heliotrope is a circular mirror, 10 to 12 inches in diameter, fitted for vertical and horizontal motion.

† The lamps constructed in 1830 consisted of a parabolic reflector 12 inches in diameter, applied to an argand burner, the whole enclosed in a wooden shed with a glass window, which served as a packing case in travelling.

‡ See an article on the detail of the working of the Great Trigonometrical Survey, describing the duties in the field, the rules for selecting stations, the heliotrope and other apparatus, in the "Professional Papers on Indian Engineering," vol. iv. p. 303.

he commanded a view of the lovely valley. The base was transferred, by triangulation, to the peaks of the Sewalik hills, called Amsot and Banog, which are visible both from Dehra and from the Gangetic plain. During this period Colonel Everest's health suffered very severely, and he was ordered home, but this was impossible, as none of his staff could then have taken his place.

Between October 1834 and June 1835, all the horizontal angles across the plain, from the Chumbul to the foot of the Sewalik hills, were taken. The instruments used were two three-foot theodolites, one by Troughton and the other by Mr. Barrow, the instrument maker whom Colonel Everest had brought out from England, and established as head of a factory at Calcutta. Barrow's theodolite was partly composed of portions of the old instrument of Colonel Lambton, and the circle was graduated at Calcutta by Barrow. Members of the surveying staff were now rapidly gaining knowledge and efficiency.

An observatory was formed at Kaliana, near the foot of the Sewalik hills. It consists of a room 20 feet long by 12, terminated at either end by a semicircular bow, and two side rooms. Pillars are passed up through the floor, and free from contact with it, and opposite each there are two meridional apertures 24 inches wide. Here one of the double vertical circles was placed on a column of carved sandstone, surmounted by a capital of brass. The instrument is three feet in diameter, and consists of two circles with a telescope between them. These astronomical circles were found to vibrate so much as to render accuracy impossible. At first this was attributed to the wooden tripods on which they were placed, but the same defect was apparent when they were removed to the stone columns, and it became evident that they were top heavy. Everest set himself resolutely to work to devise a remedy. He was ably assisted by Syud Mohsin, a native of Arcot, who came to Calcutta under the patronage of Colonel Blacker, the Surveyor General, and was engaged by Everest in 1830. The task was one of great delicacy, and requiring an intimate knowledge of the subject, as well as much mechanical skill. Finally, however, the great surveyor and his native colleague achieved a complete success.

On the 1st of October 1836, Colonel Everest took the field with both the large theodolites, and four 18-inch altitude and azimuth instruments. He divided his staff into two distinct parties, under himself and Andrew Waugh, and by February 1837 they had connected the Dehra Doon base with that measured on the Sironj plain near Kalianpoor in 1824. At the latter place another observatory was erected, exactly like that at Kaliana.

It then became necessary to re-measure the Sironj base with the same instruments that had been used in the Dehra Doon. This work was commenced on December 1st, 1837, and completed on January 18th, 1838. The old base proved to be too short by 2·825 feet, and the error was attributed to want of means of knowing the true length of the chain and the true temperature.

In October 1838 Captain Waugh was sent south to revise the angles in the Deccan with Troughton's large theodolite, and he completed a series of triangles over a meridional distance of 260 miles, returning to Dehra in June 1839. To show the wonderful accuracy of these observations, it may be stated that the difference between the length of the Dehra Doon base as measured, and as computed by triangulation from the Sironj base, was only 7·2 inches.

The difference of latitude between the Kaliana and Kalianpoor observatories, which are on the same meridian, was fixed by simultaneous observations of the same stars with the two great astronomical circles.* The stars selected for simultaneous observation were 36 in number. On the 25th of November 1839 Captain Waugh reached the Kalianpoor observatory, with the instrument called "Troughton," while Everest and Renny remained at Kaliana with "Simms." The series of observations was completed on the 23rd of January 1840, and an arc of amplitude was thus determined on this section of the meridian. Waugh then went south to Dumergidda near the old Beder base line, and Everest came down to Kalianpoor. Simultaneous observations of 32 selected stars were then commenced on November 24th, 1840, and completed on January 11th, 1841, and another arc of amplitude was determined. From Kaliana to Kalianpoor the arc is 5° 23′ 37″, and from Kalianpoor to Dumargidda 6° 3′ 55·9″ In 1841 Waugh proceeded to re-measure the old Beder base line, after making 57 comparisons between the compensation bars and the standard. The difference between the length as measured, and as computed from the Sironj base, was 4·296 inches.

Thus were brought to a close the operations of the great arc of India series, which extends from Cape Comorin to Banog in the

* By the simultaneous observation of the same stars, the errors in the catalogued places of stars were eliminated.

Himalayas. The portion from Cape Comorin to Dumargidda and the Beder base is dependent on Lambton's chain measurements. That from Dumargidda to Banog depends on the iron standard bars A and B, and the brass standard scales. B was sent to England in 1843-4, and deposited at Southampton. A was at first deposited in the fort at Agra, and now remains with the rest of the apparatus in charge of the officers of the Survey.

In these observations Everest deemed symmetry essential to accuracy in his triangles ("triangles bien conditionnés), and allowed no angles to be less than 30° or greater than 90°. The total cost of Everest's Great Arc Series was 89,833*l.*, and the area covered 56,997 square miles.*

In 1835 Colonel Everest had had a serious and almost fatal illness, and at one time his recovery was pronounced to be beyond all hope. In September 1837 the Court of Directors appointed Major Jervis, an engineer officer who had been engaged in some of the surveys in the Bombay Presidency, to succeed Colonel Everest as Surveyor General in the event of his death, that the work might not be impeded. Major Jervis had made himself well known in England by reading papers and submitting proposals for improved methods of conducting the surveys;† and eventually the President and several Fellows of the Royal Society addressed a memorial to the Directors of the East India Company, urging them to adopt the views of Major Jervis, without alluding to the great services of Colonel Everest and his admirable staff. This proceeding excited great indignation in those distinguished officers who had borne the heat and burden of the day, and gave rise to a series of letters addressed to the Duke of

---

* There was an interesting discussion on the Great Indian Arc and the figure of the earth, between Archdeacon Pratt and Captain Tennant. See the Philosophical Transactions 1855 (p. 78); papers read before the Astronomical Society in January and June 1857; and the Journal of the Asiatic Society of Bengal, XXVIII. p. 20. Archdeacon Pratt held that it would be necessary to allow for the effect of mountain refraction on the plumb line, in calculating the curvature of the earth. See further on at page 121.

† See his "Address delivered in the Geographical Section of the British Associa- "tion at Newcastle on August 26th, 1838, on the state and prospects of the Surveys "in India, with a prefatory sketch of the principles and requirements of Geography, "by Major Jervis, appointed provisionally Surveyor General of India; with intro- "ductory remarks. By Sir George Back, Vice-President of the Section."

It is published in Vol. IV. of the Bombay Geographical Society's Journal, pp. 157–89. (1840,) and was printed separately at Torquay.

Sussex* as President of the Royal Society, from Colonel Everest, remonstrating against the conduct of that learned body. These letters are written in a vein of humorous sarcasm, and they so completely gained the writer's object that nothing more was ever heard of Major Jervis in connection with the Surveyor Generalship. Useful service was, however, unintentionally done by arousing the great Surveyor's indignation, for his letters contain many interesting details which would otherwise have been lost.

The labours of Colonel Everest, as Superintendent of the Great Trigonometrical Survey of India, are by no means comprised in the Great Arc Series. He also completed the Bombay Longitudinal Series, and designed and partly carried out a scheme for covering Bengal and Behar with a gridiron of triangles.

The Bombay Longitudinal Series had been commenced by Everest himself, as long ago as 1822, and he had reached as far as the meridian of 76°, when he received the news of Lambton's death. This portion was revised by Lieutenant Jacob in 1840-41. During Everest's absence in England, Captain Jopp, the Deputy Surveyor General at Bombay, proposed the continuation of the work in 1827, and Lieutenant Shortrede† was appointed to undertake it. But these officers committed the great mistake of commencing from a base of their own, unconnected with Lambton's triangulation, and this too, in the teeth of remonstrances from Colonel Hodgson, then Surveyor General at Calcutta. They measured an independent base on the Karlee plain, 40 miles east of Bombay, with a steel chain made by Cary. The rest of their work, as regards observations of angles and celestial azimuths, was considered by Colonel Everest to be slovenly and objectionable, and he set it aside. When Lieutenant Shortrede resigned in 1836, Lieutenant Jacob was appointed to succeed him, and took the field in October 1837.‡ His labours were completed with the revision of Everest's old work by himself and Waugh, and thus the Bombay Longitudinal Series was finished in 1841. It is

* Published in a pamphlet by Pickering, in 1839.

† Author of "Logarithmic and new Astronomical and Geodesical Tables, by Robert Shortrede, Captain E. I. C. S." (Edinburgh 1844.) He afterwards had charge of the Punjab Revenue Survey, from 1849 until 1856. General Shortrede died at Blackheath in 1868.

‡ Between 1845 and 1848 Jacob made a catalogue of double stars from observations at Poona, with a five-foot equatorial by Dollond. (*Memoirs of the Astronomical Society*, XVII, p. 79.) He afterwards had charge of the Madras Observatory, from 1848 to 1856. See the section on Astronomical Observations in India.

315 miles in length. The area surveyed is 15,198 square miles. Total cost 13,742*l*.

A complete revision of the famous old survey by Major Rennell was also designed by Everest. He resolved to originate several Meridional Series from the Calcutta Longitudinal Series, to terminate at the foot of the Himalayas, and eventually to be connected by another Longitudinal Series along the base of the mountains. This is the gridiron, in contradistinction to Lambton's network system of triangles. The plan was approved in 1832, and nine stations about 60 miles apart, were selected on the Calcutta Series, as origins of as many Meridional Series; namely,

1. *Budaon*, passing through Gwalior and the western part of the North-West Provinces to Dehra.
2. *Rangheer*, through the western part of the North-West Provinces.
3. *Amua*, going through the central part of the North-West Provinces and Oude.
4. *Karara*, do. do.
5. *Gurwani*, do. do.
6. *Gora*, going by Goruckpore, through the eastern part of the North-West Provinces.
7. *Hurilaong*, through the Lower Provinces.
8. *Chindwar*, do. do.
9. *Parisnath*, which goes both north and south from the Calcutta Series, through the Lower Provinces.
10. *Maluncha*, also going north and south, through the Lower Provinces.

Thus the North-West Provinces, Rohilkhund, Oudh, Bahár, and half Bengal would be crossed by lines of primary triangles, sixty miles apart.

The first series taken in hand was that of Parisnath, under Lieutenant Western. The northern portion was executed between 1832 and 1835, and the southern part, extending to Bálasore, under Colonel Boileau, between 1835 and 1840. The Budaon Series was commenced in 1832 by Lieutenant Roderick Macdonald, who died at his post, and finished by Captain Renny.* The Rangheer Series was begun by Captain Waugh in 1834, and completed in April 1840. The Amua Series was begun in 1834, and finished in June 1839.†

* Vol. ix., pt. i. † Vol. ix., pt. iii.

The northern connecting series was also proceeded with in Colonel Everest's time. Captain Du Vernet connected the Great Arc Series with that of Rangheer between 1841 and 1843, and in November 1842 Captain Waugh continued the work thence to the head of the Amua Series, through the Terai north of Rohilcund, a fever haunted country covered with dense forest and brushwood. Everest designates this piece of work by Andrew Waugh "as complete a specimen of rapidity "combined with accuracy of execution as there is on record in the "volumes."*

The Superintendent of the Great Trigonometrical Survey finally quitted the scenes of his labours and triumphs in 1843, and retired from the service after having been connected with the surveys for twenty-five years. He refused the knighthood which was then offered to him, but accepted it with a C.B. in 1861. He had completed one of the most stupendous works in the whole history of science. No scientific man ever had a grander monument to his memory than the Great Meridional Arc of India. Everest's was a creative genius. The whole conception of the survey, as it now exists, was the creation of his brain. He entirely altered and revolutionized the old system of Lambton by substituting the gridiron for the network method. He introduced the compensation bars which have measured every base in India down to the present day. He invented the plan of observing by heliotrope flashes, and the system of ray tracing, and designed the plan for the towers. There have been modifications and improvements since his time; but nearly everything in the surveys was originated by the great geodesist. Sir George Everest died in 1866. In one of his letters to the Duke of Sussex, he speaks of two of his assistants as having "attained a degree of "accuracy and perfection of skill which it would be impossible to "surpass." One of these, now Sir Andrew Waugh, was his successor.†

Records of the labours of Sir George Everest are to be found in the following published and manuscript books:—

1. "Account of the Measurement of an Arc of the Meridian."—(London, 1830. 4to.)

---

* Budaon Series, cost 17,259*l*. Area 12,468 sq. miles.
Rangheer Series, cost 11,837*l*. Area 16,087 sq. miles.
Amua Series, cost 10,495*l*. Area 5,565 sq. miles.

† The other was Major Renny Tailyour.

2. "Account of the Measurement of two sections of the Meridional Arc of India," by Lieut.-Colonel Everest.—(London, 1847. 4to.)
3. Account of the Compensation Bars, in the *Asiatic Researches*, xviii. p. 189.
4. Edinburgh Review. (1848.) Vol. 87, p. 372.
5. A Series of Letters addressed to H.R.H. the Duke of Sussex, by Lieut.-Colonel Everest. (London, Pickering. 1839.)
6. The operations of the Trigonometrical Survey from January 1823 to 1837. Great Arc Series, Beder to Seronj and Dehra. Vol. 7, parts I. and II., with Maps and Appendix to part II., MS.
7. Calcutta Longitudinal Series, with a map. Vol. 8, part I. MS.
8. Bombay Longitudinal Series, with a map. Vol. 8, part II., MS.
9. Budhon Series. Vol. 9, part I., MS. (Skeleton maps.)
10. Rangheer Series. Vol. 9, part II., MS. (Maps.)
11. Amua Series, &c., with maps. Vol. 9, part III., MS.
12. Himalaya Longitudinal Series. Vol. 9, part IV., MS.
13. Pilibit Series. Vol. 9, part V., MS.
14. "Remarks respecting the errors likely to arise from the false position of the fixed axes of the pendulum," by George Everest. *Memoirs of the Royal Astronomical Society*, iv., p. 29.
15. "On Instruments and Observations for Longitude for travellers on land," by Colonel G. Everest. *Journal of the Royal Geographical Society*, Vol. xxx., p. 315.
16. "Geodesical operations in India," by Sir George Everest. *British Association Reports*, 1844, p. 3, and 1845, p. 25.

The obituary notice of Sir George Everest, by Sir Roderick Murchison, in his anniversary address for 1867, will be found in the *Journal of the Royal Geographical Society*, Vol. xxxvii., p. cxv.

There is another obituary notice in the address of the President of the Astronomical Society, on February 8th, 1867. *Proceedings*, vol. xxvii. p. 105.

VI.—SECOND PERIOD OF THE TOPOGRAPHICAL SURVEYS.

1823—1843.

The Revenue and Topographical Surveys.

During the period from 1823 to 1830 there was a Surveyor General at Calcutta, and Deputy Surveyors General at Madras and Bombay. The post at Calcutta, from 1823 to 1827, was held by Colonel Valentine Blacker, whom Sir Andrew Waugh speaks of as, with the exception of Everest, the ablest and most scientific man that ever presided over the department.* The revenue surveys in the North-West Provinces were commenced under his auspices; and his thorough appreciation of the importance of the surveys on a geodetic basis is shown in his able paper on the subject, which has been reprinted by Sir Andrew Waugh. Colonel Blacker died of fever in 1827, and was succeeded by Colonel Hodgson, who had previously held the office from 1821 to 1823, and who now held the post until 1829, when he returned to England, in the expectation of being employed on the engraving of the Indian Atlas.† Major H. Walpole acted as Surveyor General for a short time in 1829-30. In the same year Colonel Everest assumed the duties both of Superintendent of the Great Trigonometrical Survey and Surveyor General of India; and about 1834 the posts of Deputy Surveyor General at Bombay and Madras‡ were abolished.

There was convenience in placing the whole department under one head; but it must be confessed that, owing no doubt to the absorbing nature of Colonel Everest's duties connected with the great arc, and to the difficulties which surrounded him in the organization of his department, the progress of the geographical delineation of

* Parliamentary Paper, April 1851.

† This is the same officer who surveyed part of the Himalaya with Captain Herbert. (See page 65.) John Anthony Hodgson was born at Bishop Auckland on July 2nd, 1777, and went to India as a cadet in 1799. After his return to England, he lived at Durham. He became a Major-General in 1845, received a command in India, and died at Umballa on March 28th, 1848. Hodgson was also an accomplished astronomer. See the section on Astronomical Observations.

‡ Captain D. Montgomerie had been Deputy Surveyor General at Madras since July 1829. A map of the peninsula of India, to be compiled from the surveys, had been called for so long ago as 1819; and in 1830 Montgomerie submitted a map of most of the Madras Collectorates on a scale of four miles to the inch, with a sketch map of southern India, on a scale of 24 miles to the inch, as a key.

the country had languished in some degree during the period of his incumbency.

In 1828, Mr. J. S. May, the Superintendent of the Nuddea rivers, surveyed and made maps of the Hooghly, Bhagruttee, Jellinghee, and Matabhanga; and J. Prinsep lithographed maps of the Hooghly and Ganges, from old surveys by Colebrooke, corrected up to his own time from May's work.

The revenue surveys in the North-West Provinces were commenced in 1823. They were undertaken mainly with a view to forming a settlement for the land revenue, and the correct delineation of boundaries of estates was considered of more importance than accurate topographical detail; while rapidity of execution, rather than good mapping, was the object of the surveyor. The revenue survey was divided into two parts, scientific and native. The scientific survey laid down, on a scale of four inches to the mile, the village boundaries, and the main geographical features of the country. The native survey consisted of a rough plan of the village and fields, called a *shujreh*, and the list of the fields with their measurement, or *khusrah*.

Between 1822 and 1842, the districts west of the Jumna (Hurreeanah, Paneeput, Bhuttiana, Delhi, Rohtuk, Goorgaon, Muttra, and Agra,) were surveyed in this way by Captains W. Brown, Simmonds, Oliver, Wroughton,* and Fordyce; the districts of the Dooab by Captains Fraser, H. Lawrence, Wroughton, W. Brown, Abbott, and Stephen; and those of Rohilcund by Captains Birnie, Brown, Bedford, Wroughton, Fraser, and Abbott.

Abbott and Stephen, between 1839 and 1842, completed a survey of Bundelcund in three maps, which superseded the old route survey of Franklin, and showed great changes in the country. Several villages marked on Franklin's map are not found in the later survey.

The districts round Benares were surveyed from 1839 to 1841 by Abbott, Wroughton, Maxwell, Fordyce, and H. Lawrence, whose work superseded the old route surveys. A survey of the Saugor and Nerbudda country was completed by Captain Wroughton in 1842, while that of Behar and Bengal was commenced in 1837, and was still progressing at the time of Everest's retirement.

Lieutenant Thuillier, who entered the service in 1832, and is now Surveyor General of India, was engaged on the survey of Ganjam and

* See a statistical return of the Muttra District (Act 1835), by Captain Wroughton. —*Journal of the Asiatic Society of Bengal*, v., p. 216.

Orissa, in conjunction with Lieutenant Smyth,* from 1839 to 1842; and afterwards surveyed the districts of Silhet and Cachar. A rough survey was also made of Chittagong, for a district map, between 1835 to 1841; and in 1831 Lieutenants Norris and Weston surveyed the Berar and Nagpore country, and made a map, which contained much detailed geographical information.

The topographical details of these Revenue Surveys were tolerably well executed until 1834, when a conference of surveyors was held at Allahabad, by order of Lord William Bentinck. The great object was to get the surveys done, in order to commence a new system of revenue settlement. A new plan was therefore adopted, introducing economy and rapidity, and sacrificing quality for quantity. The maps were only required to delineate village boundaries and sites, with rough outlines of roads and the courses of rivers, and were mere skeleton sketches. They preceded the Great Trigonometrical Survey: and thus a proper connexion was not in the first instance established between the two operations. Major Bedford was appointed Superintendent of the Revenue Surveys of Bengal, under Colonel Everest, in the end of 1838.

On the first appointment of Captains Waugh and Renny to the Trigonometrical Survey in 1832, Colonel Everest sent them to explore the wild jungly country between Chunar and the sources of the Sone and Nerbudda, up to Jubbulpoor. They completed this service, and submitted a topographical and geological report in 1834.†

The breaking out of the Burmese War led to the acquisition of much valuable geographical information in the direction of the north-east frontier of Bengal, and of that vast unknown region beyond, which then, as now, was delineated only from the maps of d'Anville. Captain Bedford and Lieutenants Wilcox and Burlton were sent to explore the Brahmapootra towards its source in 1825, under instructions from Colonel Blacker, then Surveyor General. Burlton surveyed the Brahmapootra as far as Sudiya, Bedford went up the

* Their memoir on the Ganjam district is preserved in the Geographical Department of the India Office. It contains an account of the boundaries, area, divisions, soil, productions, population, ports, lakes, &c. Their new map is in 15 sheets, (and an index) on a scale of four miles to the inch.

† A manuscript volume, containing the journal of the route from Shergotty to Chunar, and thence to Jubbulpoor, by Lieutenants Waugh and Renny, is preserved in the Geographical Department of the India Office. At the end there is a "Geological Journal," with coloured sketches of the route.

rivers Dihong (Sanpu ?) and Dibong until he was stopped by wild frontier tribes, and Wilcox made one journey beyond the frontier up the Brahmapootra valley, and in another penetrated to the banks of the Irrawaddy.* Captain Boileau Pemberton surveyed the territory of Muneepoor and surrounding country, and portions of Cachar, between 1825 and 1830; and from 1830 to 1837 Dr. Richardson and Captain McLeod made exploring journeys from Moulmein to Ava and to Kiang Hung near the Chinese frontier. To this day no explorer has succeeded in adding, in any appreciable degree, to the knowledge conveyed by the discoveries of Bedford and Wilcox, as regards the region beyond our north-east frontier, and towards the sources of the head waters of the Brahmapootra and Irrawaddy. Captain Pemberton's exceedingly valuable large map, compiled from the route surveys of all these officers, was lithographed at Calcutta in 1838.†

In 1830 a survey was commenced to connect the map from Goalpara, where it terminated in Captain Wilcox's survey of the Assam valley, with the surveys of the Ganges. In 1834 Lieutenant Ommanney was engaged in tracing the line of the Brahmapootra from Goalpara, round the difficult country at the root of the Cossyah

---

* "The Memoir of the Survey of Assam, 1825–28," with a detailed account of the discoveries, and a map, by Lieutenant Wilcox, will be found in the Asiatic Researches, vol. xviii., p. 314.

† The record of these surveys will be found in the following printed and manuscript books:—

Vols. xvi. and xviii. of the Asiatic Researches.

No. xxiii. of the selections from the records of the Bengal Government. (1855.)

Report on the Eastern Frontier of British India, by Captain Pemberton. (Calcutta, 1835.)

Journal (abstract) of an expedition from Moulmein to the Chinese frontier, in December 1836, by Captain McLeod.—*Journal of the Asiatic Society of Bengal, VI., Pt. II., p.* 989. The manuscript journals of Captain McLeod's and Dr. Richardson's expeditions are preserved in the Political Department of the India Office. They were printed by order of the House of Commons in 1870, with a map compiled by Mr. Saunders. Captain McLeod's original map appears to be lost.

Original Journal of Captain James Bedford on the Brahmapootra and Dihong. 1824–25. MS.

Note book of route from Kusan on the Dihong, towards the source of the Irrawaddy in 1826, by Lieutenant Wilcox. MS.

Field book of the survey of part of the Brahmapootra in 1825. MS.

Survey of the Brahmapootra from Goalpara to Bisheuath in 1828. MS.

These manuscript volumes are preserved in the Geographical Department of the India Office.

hills, to within thirty miles of Dacca, when a sudden order of the Government directed the work to be suspended, thus rendering it comparatively useless for want of the connecting link which it would only have taken three months to complete.*

In 1835 Mr. Fergusson made a sketch survey of the lower Ganges and Brahmapootra, from Jaffiergunge to the sea, which was combined in a small atlas published at Calcutta by Mr. J. B. Tassin; and a topographical survey of the river Hooghly from Bandel to Garden Reach was compiled and published in 1841, by Mr. Charles Joseph.†

The survey of the Nizam's territory was progressing throughout the period of Colonel Everest's incumbency, having been commenced in 1816. The officers engaged upon it were Captains Garling, Young, Macpherson, Du Vernet, Morland, and Crisp. The survey, based on the trigonometrical operations of Colonel Lambton, progressed systematically and steadily. It was conducted on the principles of the Madras Military Institution Survey, and the maps are full of topographical detail. They were accompanied by several volumes of memoirs, which are deposited in the Geographical Department of the India Office.

Several districts were re-surveyed, and the surveys of others were completed in the Madras Presidency, including Nellore, Vizagapatam, Salem, Ganjam, and the Arcots, between 1833 and 1840, by Captains Snell and Macpherson. In the Bombay Office some maps were compiled, from compass and perambulation surveys not based on triangulation, of Cutch, Kattywar, part of Guzerat, Ahmedabad, and Surat. Captain Grafton and Lieutenant Boyd were surveying in the Deccan in 1829, and a survey of the South Concan was executed in detail by Captain Jervis, between 1824 and 1829, but it was grounded on imperfect triangulation, and is now obsolete.‡ This is the officer who was to have succeeded Colonel Everest, and, during the time that he was in England in 1837, he obtained a donation of 1,000*l.* from the Court of Directors, "as a testimony of their high sense of the value of his labours."§ In the same year he wrote a memoir

* "James Prinsep. In the Journal of the Asiatic Society of Bengal," iv. p. 63.

† See the "Calcutta Review," iii. p. 428.

‡ "Bombay Quarterly Review," iii. p. 133.

§ Nov. 10th, 1837. (No. 2,670.)

on the surveys in India, which is published in the Journal of the Royal Geographical Society.*

In 1841 a map of Sind was compiled from the survey of Alexander Burnes and other sources.

The Revenue Surveys were under Major Bedford from 1830 to 1840; and in 1844 Major Wroughton succeeded, and was Superintendent until 1847, when he made over the work to Captain Thuillier, and died in 1849.

On the whole, although much was done both as regards exploration and the filling in of topographical details, the incumbency of Sir George Everest will be more memorable for the great scientific results of his labours as a geodesist than for the quantity of reliable material that was furnished to the map makers. It was said of him that "he would have nothing to do with researches which he " did not think admitted of the accuracy he cultivated, lest his " assistants, whom he had trained with so much care and labour, " might lose their aptitude for his objects."†

---

* Vol. vii., p. 127. (1837.) It is re-published in the *Madras Journal of Literature and Science, vol. VII., p.* 424. Major Jervis retired in 1842. In 1845 he published a translation of Baron Hügel's travels in Cashmere and the Punjab. In 1855 he was appointed the first Director of the Topographical Depôt of the War Department, and died in 1858. See an Obituary Notice of Major Jervis, by Professor Phillips, in the Transactions of the Geological Society.

† "Proceedings of the Astronomical Society," xxvii. p. 105.

VII.—THIRD PERIOD OF THE TRIGONOMETRICAL SURVEYS. 1843-61.

Sir Andrew Waugh as Superintendent of the Great Trigonometrical Survey.

When Sir George Everest retired, he recommended that his able and indefatigable lieutenant, Andrew Waugh, should succeed him. In doing so he thus spoke of his successor: "He is beloved and "respected by all the subordinate members of my department, and "held in honour and esteem by all who know him personally. His "talents, acquirements, and habits as a scholar, a mathematician, "a gentleman, and a soldier, are of a high order." Colonel Waugh took charge in 1843,* and, like his predecessor, received the appointments both of Superintendent of the Great Trigonometrical Survey and Surveyor General of India. His first work was to complete Sir George Everest's project for the triangulation of the important region between the Great Arc Series and Calcutta, including the North-West Provinces and Bengal.

Lambton's system had been to throw a network of triangles over the whole face of the country. But Everest considered this to be unnecessarily laborious, and that nothing more was required than to execute meridional series about a degree apart, tied together at their ends by longitudinal series. This is termed the gridiron system, and is analogous to the French and Russian methods. Sir George Everest had projected a gridiron of which the Great Arc and a Calcutta Meridional Series formed two sides, the Calcutta Longitudinal Series and a Series along the base of the Himalayas being the other two; and ten Meridional Series, 60 miles apart, originating from the Calcutta Longitudinal, and ending in the Himalayan Series, forming the grating. It has been seen that three of these, namely, Budaon, Rangheer, and Amua, had been completed in Everest's time. On assuming the command, Colonel Waugh set himself steadily to work to finish his old chief's project.

The Karara Meridional Series comes next to the Amua, emanating from a hill called Karara on the Calcutta Longitudinal Series, and

* Andrew Scott Waugh, son of General Gilbert Waugh, the Military Auditor General at Madras, was born in 1810. He entered the corps of Bengal Engineers in 1827, became garrison engineer at Allahabad in 1830, and joined the survey in 1832.

passing through Rewah, Allahabad, and Lucknow, to the Terai. The first part passes through a hilly country covered with pestiferous jungle, and the rest is in the Gangetic valley. The work was commenced in February 1838, under Mr. Scully and Lieutenant Jones; but the whole party was prostrated with jungle fever, of which Mr. Scully died. In February 1842, Lieutenant Shortrede took charge of the Karara Series, but he retired in 1845. It was then arranged that Mr. Armstrong should advance from the south, while Lieutenant Du Vernet carried a series of triangles from the Amua Series to the meridian of Karara, and thence turned south until a junction was effected with Armstrong's work. In May 1845 this junction was established. The area surveyed covered 5,819 square miles, at a cost of Rs. 1,34,908.*

Next comes the Gurwani Meridional Series, 235 miles long. It was begun in December 1845 by Lieutenant Du Vernet, and completed on May 24th, 1847, the 18-inch theodolite by Syud Meer Mohsin being used for measuring angles in the first season, and Colonel Waugh's 24-inch in the second. The positions of Jounpoor, Oude, and Fyzabad, were fixed by secondary triangulation. The area of the operations covered 6,298 square miles, and the cost was Rs. 53,019.†

The next is the Gora Series, 208 miles long, which was commenced by Lieutenant Jones in 1844, but he died of jungle fever. Lieutenant Garforth then took charge, and completed the series. Of the stations, six were on hill tops, and 23 were towers in the valley of the Ganges. The area is 4,416 square miles, surveyed at a cost of Rs. 76,948.‡

Then comes the Hurilaong Series, 208 miles long, which was executed by Mr. Armstrong between 1848 and 1852. Of the 32 stations 7 were placed on hills, and rest were marked by towers. The series crosses the rivers Ganges and Gogra near their junction.

Then follows the Chundwar Series, 181 miles long, of which 86 is through hill country, with 11 stations, and the rest in the Gangetic valley, where 19 towers had to be erected. It was commenced by Mr. Logan, in December 1843, and completed in April 1846. The area is 3,565 square miles, surveyed at a cost of Rs. 64,504.§

* Vol. x., pts. 1 and 2.
† Vol. x., pt. 3.
‡ Vol. x., pt. 4.
§ Vol. xi., pt. 2.

The Parisnath North Meridian Series* was completed by Mr. Nicolson between 1850 and 1852; and lastly the Maluncha Meridional Series was commenced by Captain Renny Tailyour in 1844. But he was called away to serve as Brigade Major of Engineers in the Gwalior campaign, and was present at the battle of Máhárájpoor. Lieutenant Reginald Walker then took up the work, and completed it in 1846. The length is 157 miles, a large proportion being over very unhealthy ground. The area was 4,765 square miles, and the cost Rs. 52,878.†

The eastern side of Everest's gridiron is formed by the Calcutta Meridional Series, originating from his base line in the Barrackpoor road, passing north parallel to the Hooghly and Bhagruttee rivers, and ending at a new base line at Sonakhoda, near the foot of the Darjeeling mountains. The preliminary work of selecting stations was begun by Mr. Lane in December 1843, Mr. Peyton took charge in 1844, and the series was completed in 1848. It consists of a simple series of triangles, and all the 56 principal stations necessitated the building of a tower. The area surveyed is 4,136 square miles, at a cost of Rs. 1,10,302.

We now come to the North-Eastern Himalaya Series which connects the northern ends of all these meridional series, and the dangers and difficulties in the execution of which were far greater than have been encountered in the majority of Indian campaigns. Military service, plentifully rewarded by the praise of men and by prizes of all kinds, is neither so perilous nor so honourable as that of the Indian Surveyor, who devotes great talent and ability to scientific work in the midst of as deadly peril as is met with on the field of battle, and with little or no prospect of reaping the reward that he deserves. His labours, unlike those of a mere soldier, are of permanent and lasting value; but few know who obtained the valuable results, except the gallant surveyor's immediate chief and colleagues. The North-Western Himalaya Series was the most desperate of these grand undertakings, and the average slaughter was greater than in many famous battles.

This memorable series was commenced in 1845, and completed in 1850, and was the longest series between measured bases in the

* Vol. xi., pt. 4.

† Vol. xii., pt. 2.

‡ Vol. xii., pt. 4.

world, being 1600 miles long from the Dehra Doon base to that of Sonakhoda, in Purneah. It was originally intended to have been carried along the Himalaya Mountains, but the Nepalese Govern- refused to allow the operations to enter their territory. So, after crossing the hills of Gurwhal and Kumaon, the triangles were brought down into the Terai near Bareilly, whence they continued to pass through the deadly tracts of marsh and jungle which fringe the Himalayas. The first and second parts were, as has already been stated, performed by Du Vernet and Waugh himself; and the next section, as far as the head of the Chundwar Series, was completed, amidst great difficulties, by Mr. Logan, who did the work admirably, observing with Barrow's great theodolite. In one season 40 natives died of jungle fever; Mr. Logan was himself prostrated, and in 1847 the whole surveying party was conveyed in a helpless condition from fever to Goruckpore. In 1847 Lieutenant Reginald Walker took charge; but he also was attacked by the terrible scourge. He hurried towards Darjeeling, and was found dead in his dooly when it arrived, on April 24th, 1847. Mr. Charles Lane completed the eastern end in 1848, when Colonel Waugh himself joined the party, to carry on operations for fixing the heights of Himalayan peaks. The completion of the worst part of this series is due to the ability, courage, and perseverance of Mr. George Logan, who died from the effects of diseases contracted in the Terai, about three years afterwards. Of the five officers who had charge of the series at different times, two retired, and two fell victims to the climate.

The mightiest of the Himalayan peaks are visible from the principal trigonometrical stations of this series, and were fixed by measurements with the great theodolite. The primary difficulty of the computer was the identification of numerous points, the positions of which had been observed by different persons from different points of view. The series was carefully projected on a scale of four miles to an inch, and the rays emanating from the stations of observation exactly drawn. Their intersection defined the points sought for. The area of the largest triangle to a Himalayan peak is about 1,706 square miles, with a side 151 miles long. The heights of 79 peaks were fixed, of which 31 have names, and the rest only numbers. Their positions are correct within a quarter of a second as regards latitude, and half a second as to longitude, and the heights are probably true to within 10 feet, all being too low, if anything, owing to deflection due to mountain refraction. No. 15 peak, the highest of all, 29,002 feet above the sea, was well named by Colonel Waugh, after his old chief, Mount Everest.

The N.E. Himalayan Series* covered an area of 15,826 square miles, exclusive of the operations of the mountain peaks in Sikkim, which included 73,920, or a total area of 89,746 square miles. The cost of the survey was Rs. 2,14,257.

Colonel Waugh then proceeded to measure a base at the junction of the N.W. Himalaya and Calcutta Meridional Series, to verify both triangulations, and with a view to the future extension of operations eastward into Assam. The site selected was an unbroken level plain near Sonakhoda, and the measurement was performed in the season 1847–48. Waugh was assisted by Captain Renny Tailyour, Mr. Logan, and Mr. Lane; but the whole party suffered severely from fever. Colby's compensation apparatus, brought out by Everest in 1830, was used, and the measurement was proved by a system of minor triangulation in four sections. The bars were compared with the standard 53 times before measurement, 60 at the middle, and 80 times afterwards.†

With the Sonakhoda base Colonel Waugh completed the project of Sir George Everest, for placing a gridiron of trigonometrical series over the North-West and Lower Provinces. Accurate data were now supplied for the complete filling in and mapping of this important region.

Operations were progressing to the south at the same time. In 1842 Captain Jacob had commenced the South Concan Series from a side of the Bombay Longitudinal Series, but was obliged to go home owing to ill health. He was succeeded by Lieutenant Harry Rivers of the Bombay Engineers, who worked with an 18-inch theodolite, made by Dollond under instructions from Kater. This series is not, in Colonel Waugh's opinion, in the first rank of geodetical operations, but it is sufficiently accurate for geographical purposes. The series passes through Mahabuleshwur, and goes south as far as Goa.‡ It was completed in 1844, and Rivers then took up the North Concan and Khanpisura Series, which extends north as far as Neemuch.

* Vol. xv., of the Trigonometrical Operations, M.S.
"Calcutta Review," vol. xxxviii. (1863).
"Journal Asiatic Society of Bengal," vol. xxxi. (1862), p. 32.

† Vol. xii., pt. iv.

‡ Vol. xiv., pt. i.

Sir George Everest had also projected the execution of a chain of triangulation along the east coast of India, from the Calcutta base line to the observatory at Madras; and two of the Meridional Series, namely, those of Parisnath and Maluncha, were to be extended south from the Calcutta Longitudinal Series, to join it. The South Parisnath Series was commenced as early as 1832 by Lieutenant Western, assisted by Lieutenant Boileau. The next year Captain Macdonald was sent to take charge, but fell a sacrifice to the arduous nature of the work, and in 1835 Boileau and the whole party were prostrated by sickness. The series was completed in 1839. The work is second rate, but will answer all purposes of geography.*

The Coast Series was commenced by Captain Thorold Hill, who had previously, from 1845 to 1847, been engaged on the South Maluncha. He was supplied with a new 24-inch theodolite in 1847, and began the coast operations from the Calcutta base line, but found extreme difficulty in crossing the flat swampy country, intersected by creeks, between Calcutta and Balasore. His health suffered so much that he was obliged to go to sea for two years, and thus progress was very slow. He was replaced by Mr. J. Peyton.

After the measurement of the Sonakhoda base, Colonel Waugh was free to undertake a work originated by himself, and the acquisition of Sinde and the Punjab offered a vast field for fresh operations. He conceived a project for forming a gridiron of triangulation to the westward of the Great Arc Series, to include all the newly acquired territory, which entailed more labour and was on a grander scale even than Everest's gridiron to the eastward. Colonel Waugh's plan commenced with the Great Arc Series, having the Dehra Doon base at the north, and the Sironj base at the south end. From the Dehra base a N.W. Himalaya Series was to be extended to near Attock, where a new base was to be measured; while from the Sironj base the line of the Calcutta Longitudinal Series was to be extended to Kurrachee, to be called the Great Longitudinal Series (Western Section). At Kurrachee another base was to be measured, and a Great Indus Series was to form the western side of the quadrilateral. Finally, a set of intermediate Meridional Series was to complete the gridiron. This magnificent project was commenced

* Vol. xiii. pt. i.

in 1847–48, with the Longitudinal Series from the two bases at Debra Doon and Sironj.

Lieutenant Du Vernet began the North-West Himalaya Series in 1847 from the Dehra Doon base; but in the following year an insurrection in the Jaswán Doon drove the party from their work. The triangulation was proceeded with by Mr. Logan, who reached Attock in 1853. The series consists of 77 principal triangles, in quadrilaterals and polygons, covering an area of 33,000 square miles. The direct length is 416 miles, and there are no towers, as all the stations are on mounds or hill tops.

The western section of the Great Longitudinal Series was commenced from the Sironj base by Captain Renny, assisted by Captain Strange of the Madras Cavalry, in the end of 1848. After the first season Renny, who had done such excellent service during 16 years, retired from the Survey Department,* and Captain Strange took charge of the series. He was assisted by Lieutenant Tennant, R.E., Mr. C. Lane, Mr. Rossenrode, Mr. Burt, and Mr. McGill. The triangulation had to be taken across the rugged range of Aravulli mountains, then over the great Thurr or desert to the north of the Runn of Cutch, and finally across the Indus valley to Kurrachee, which place was reached in April 1853, after five seasons of very severe work. This series is 668 miles long, consisting of 173 principal triangles, and covering an area of 20,323 square miles. Of the 117 stations only 22 are towers.

A few details respecting the progress of Captain Strange's party will give a general idea of the obstacles to be encountered in work of this kind. The great difficulty, peculiar to this series, was the crossing of the desert. No geodesical operation of the first order had, at that time, ever been conducted in a desert, and experience was therefore totally at fault as to the probable obstacles to be encountered. Stations had to be selected, in the first instance, by an advanced party. At each station a masonry platform had to be erected in a country entirely composed of sand, and destitute of building materials. After this had been accomplished, the main party engaged in taking the final observations, numbering 200 men,

* On the death of his father in 1849, he succeeded to the estate of Borrowfield, in Forfarshire, and retired from the service, taking the name of Tailyour. He is now Major Thomas Renny Tailyour, of Borrowfield. His eldest son is named after his old colleague, Waugh.

had to be maintained in the desert during a whole season. The desert furnished only three things useful to man or beast, namely, grass, immediately after the rainy season; limited supplies of milk; and brackish, or, more correctly, salt water in deep wells, scattered at wide intervals. The approximate series was conducted by Mr. J. Rossenrode, to whose courage, energy, and sagacity as a pioneer Captain Strange attributed, in no small degree, the success of the undertaking. The information gained by Mr. Rossenrode while conducting the approximate series with a small party was invaluable in organizing the arrangements necessary to maintain the main body during the succeeding season. These arrangements involved the supply of provisions of every description for 200 men during several months, and also the distribution of these provisions to the numerous detachments into which the party was necessarily divided. For this purpose, depôts had to be established beforehand, throughout the tract to be crossed. Special arrangements were also necessary for supplying the people with water from distant wells. Being favoured with good weather, and immunity from sickness, the final triangulation of the desert was completed in one season, 1851–52. In November 1852 Captain Strange's party finally marched across the desert from Deesa to the verge of the Indus valley, and commenced work in Sinde. These arrangements, requiring so much calculation and forethought, remind one of the precautions and minute attention to details which alone enabled McClintock to explore the Arctic Regions in search of Franklin. Like McClintock, the leader of the Great Longitudinal Series had to form depôts of food at certain intervals for his people, and to calculate exactly the weight of the food consumed by each man, and the weight his camels (the sleighs of the Thurr) could carry at each trip.

The principal stations in Sinde are from 12 to 20 miles asunder, each defined by masonry pillars four feet in diameter, surrounded by a platform for the observer's tent, according to Sir George Everest's pattern. They vary in height from 8 to 35 feet, according to the nature of the country intervening between two points of observation. When the only practicable view is obstructed by trees or houses, the practice is to remove them, paying the owners fair compensation, in communication with the village authorities. Captain Strange's party reached the borders of Sinde, and commenced operations on the 8th of December 1852. The first station was Chortlee, where it was necessary to observe from a tower 37 feet high, the side being 22 miles long, and crossed by the Indus. The view was obstructed by a dense *babool* jungle, intersected, in many places, by sheets of water. It was a tedious task to clear the line, and then it was long before the signal could be made out at the other station of Helaya, 22 miles away. After a wearisome detention of 25 days, and much painful straining of the eyes, occasional faint glimpses of Helaya were caught, and at length the angle was satisfactorily observed. At the next station of Kanad there were fresh misfortunes. The tower, 39 feet high, began to emit a crackling sound towards evening, and luckily the great theodolite had not been placed, when one of the angles fell in. These Sind towers were built of alternate layers of wetted earth and stout branches, but this one had been carelessly thrown up. In rebuilding it a ramp was raised round the walls for two thirds of their height. At another place the great theodolite narrowly escaped destruction from a hurricane, and was rescued by the desperate efforts of its guardians, amidst the roar of the tempest, in a night of inky darkness. Such are the sort of harassing difficulties and delays which form the daily life of the surveyor, but which are ever cheerfully faced and overcome. Captain Strange and his party had their full share; but at length their work was completed, and the last angle of the series was taken at Muggur Peer Station, on the 22nd of April 1853.

At the western terminations of these two Longitudinal Series it was necessary to measure bases.

Accordingly, Colonel Waugh selected a site for the northern base in 1851-2, in the Chuch Doab, near Attock, and the chief officers of the survey, Walker, Montgomerie, and Strange, were summoned to assist at the measurement. George Logan was also there at the commencement. He adhered to his post, with undaunted resolution, though the hand of death was on him. He had been at the measurement of every base since 1831, but here he was forced to succumb, and this brave and zealous officer died at Mussouree, on the 10th of June 1854, aged 45.

The ground at the Chuch base was more level than at any previous one: and as the plain was studded with ancient mounds, the termini were placed on two of them. The stone piers used by Everest in 1834 for bar comparisons, were brought all the way from Dehra Doon in a platform cart, and set up on Dec. 2nd, 1853. On the 6th there was a violent shock of earthquake. Many comparisons were made with the standard, but the length of the compensation bars was found, as on former occasions, not to be constant during a single hour of the day, owing to the dissimilar radiating power in the brass and iron. The only available remedy was to compare them with the standard, under circumstances exactly identical with those prevailing during the measurement.

The verification triangles of the Chuch base were executed by Lieutenant Montgomerie, with Barrow's great theodolite.

On the completion of this measurement, the apparatus was sent down to Kurrachee, where Mr. Rossenrode had already selected the ground. It is a nearly uniform ascent from the south to the north end, with masonry towers at the termini. The verificatory triangulation was effected by Lieutenant Tennant previous to the measurement, and the apparatus was delivered over to Captain Strange, who had the principal charge of the Kurrachee base operations, under Colonel Waugh. Syud Mohsin, the mathematical instrument maker, came round by sea from Calcutta. The Surveyor General himself had been overworked with his multifarious duties, and had been prostrated by fever; but he joined the party at Kurrachee, on December 6th, 1854. Montgomerie, Tennant, and Nasmyth were also present.

The measurement was commenced on December 6th, 1854, and completed on January 20th, 1855. Lieutenant Tennant also took 810 observations to fix the latitude of Kurrachee.

Colonel Waugh took especial pains in the preparation of the volume recording the measurement of the Chuch and Kurrachee bases; and previously drew up instructions for the selection of sites, and a memorandum to serve as a guide for other base lines that may hereafter be measured. No man living has had so much experience, and he made the volume* as complete as possible, furnishing detailed instructions and suggestions for every conceivable contingency. His final conclusion was that Colby's compensation system was unsatisfactory; and he recommended that the Survey should be equipped with a new apparatus of the most perfect kind, free from all its defects. Careful observation, extending over many years, showed that the relative length of the bars changed according to some law independent of temperature. He would, therefore, discard the compensation principle, and substitute simple iron bars 10 feet

* MS. Vol., not numbered.

long, coupled by a pair of microscopes revolving round an axis regulated by a level.

It remained to complete the quadrilateral by connecting the two bases at Chuch and Kurrachee along the Indus valley. This operation is comprised in the Great Indus Series, which was commenced at both ends, the parties to meet and connect their work half way. The approximate triangulation of the southern half, commencing from Kurrachee, was effected in a remarkably short time by Mr. W. C. Rossenrode.* Major J. T. Walker took charge of the northern section of the Indus Series in October 1856, with Lieutenant Basevi as his assistant. One flank was placed in the Sinde Sagur Dooab, and the other in the Derajat, with the Indus between them, as far as Sukkur; but below, the series is taken along the western bank of the Indus to Kurrachee. At the conclusion of the season of 1857 the mutinies broke out: and Major Walker joined the moveable column under General Chamberlain at the siege of Delhi, where he was wounded. This threw back the work a year; but in 1858 it was resumed. The Indus Series was completed in 1860. It is 706 miles long, and covers an area of 2,925 principal and 8,157 secondary triangles. Of the 148 stations, 122 in the flat valley of the Indus are towers. The heights of numerous peaks in the Suliman mountains were fixed, but political considerations prevented the exploration of that range.†

In 1856 Colonel Waugh determined to institute a series of levelling operations to determine the height of the base lines in the interior. These heights had already been approximately measured by vertical observations between the principal stations. The method of determining heights of stations above the sea by taking reciprocal vertical angles, which was the plan which had hitherto been pursued in the Survey, is susceptible of a high degree of accuracy, provided that the observations are taken during the period of minimum refraction,

* This series formed the basis for the Sinde and Khelat Boundary Survey, for the conduct of which Captain Strange drew up a set of instructions. The line begins at Cape Monze, follows the River Hubb for 80 miles, and then approaches close to the sides of the triangles of the Indus Series. The boundary pillars were all connected with the Indus Series. This boundary survey was entrusted to Mr. J. Rossenrode.

† Blue Book. Report for three years, ending 1858–59.

"Calcutta Review (1863)" vol. 38. Major Walker has contributed an interesting paper on the Suliman Range, to the Geographical Society, entitled "On the Highland region adjacent to the Trans-Indus frontier of India." By Major Walker of the Bombay Engineers.—*Journ. R. G. S.*, xxxii. p. 303.

which occurs between 1 and 3 p.m. But the series of triangles is the longest in the world, and it became necessary to check the results of the observations by vertical angles, by instituting a series of levelling operations.

The series was commenced in the Indus valley in 1858, under the superintendence of Major Walker, and has connected Kurrachee with the Chuch, Dehra, and Sironj bases. The spirit levels used were 21 inches focal length, and had been made for the Punjab Canal Department. The levelling staves were painted, and divided on both faces to feet, tenths, and hundredths, one face being white with black divisions, and the other black with white. The operations were commenced by three observers working over the same ground; and the results, as regards agreement with heights previously determined trigonometrically, were remarkably satisfactory. The distance from the sea to the Chuch base is 706 miles, and the difference between the result by vertical angles and that by spirit levelling was found to be only 3 feet 2 inches. At Dehra the difference was 5 feet 1 inch; and at Sironj, in levelling from Dehra, 1 foot and 8 inches; and from Kurrachee to Sironj 2 feet 1 inch.*

As soon as the measurement of the Kurrachee base was completed, the survey of Cashmere, and the mighty mass of mountains up to the Tibetan frontier, was commenced, under the superintendence of Captain Montgomerie, who began work in the spring of 1855 with the 14-inch theodolite by Troughton and Simms. Great difficulties were encountered from the outset, and manfully overcome. The Cashmere Series originates from that of the North West Himalaya between Sealkote and Goordaspoor, and during the first season it was taken across the Pir Panjal range into Cashmere. Two of the stations were 13,000 and 15,000 feet above the sea. Building materials had to be dug out of the snow for the station pillars, and the observers were detained at one station for 22 days, owing to the storms of snow and the foggy weather. Afterwards, as the party penetrated into the mountains, the height of the stations averaged 17,000 feet, and luminous signals were used from peaks 19,000 and even 20,000 feet above the sea. Between 1855 and 1861 the triangulation was extended over 93,500 square miles. Mr.

* Tables of Heights in Sind, the Punjab, N.W. Provinces, and Central India, for May 1862. (Calcutta 1863.) Major Walker communicated a paper on the methods of fixing the heights of Stations, in use in the Great Trigonometrical Survey of India, to the Astronomical Society.—*Memoirs. Astronomical Society.* xxxiii., p. 103.

Johnson, one of the party, took observations from a station which was 20,600 feet above the sea, and marks were erected on peaks as high as 21,480; while a peak on the Karakorum range temporarily called K. 2. was found to have a height of 28,290 feet, and to be second only to Mount Everest. This most difficult and laborious survey is remarkable for its accuracy: and in a circuit of 890 miles, only a discrepancy of $\frac{3}{10}$ of a second in latitude and of $\frac{1}{10}$ in longitude was found. In the Cashmere Series the topographical filling in by plane table advanced with the triangulation, both being under Captain Montgomerie.

Of the Meridional Series forming the bars of Colonel Waugh's gridiron, the Jogi Tila, executed by Captain Walker and Lieutenants Tennant and Brownlow, passes by Jhelum, and is stopped by the Great Desert. The Gurhagarh Series is on the meridians of Amritsir and Ferozepoor, and extends south, joining the Arumlia Series by Captain Rivers, at Ajmeer. It was commenced by Lieutenant Tennant, but almost entirely executed by Mr. Shelverton. It was designed for the incorporation of the Revenue Survey with the general map of the Punjab. Captain Nasmyth, after triangulating Kattywar and Cutch, connected his work with the Great Longitudinal Series.

In 1855 Captain Strange was appointed to take charge of the Eastern Coast Series, succeeding Mr. Peyton, who was invalided. Captain Strange left head quarters at Mussouree on the 17th of October for Cuttack, and visited the fine observatory at Lucknow on his way.* The early reports of this Coast Series record a yearly succession of disasters, disappointments, and failures; and it takes rank among the most difficult of the whole survey. Captain Strange was ably assisted by Mr. W. C. Rossenrode, who pushed forward the approximate series, and by Mr. Clarkson. The difficulties consisted in an inaccessible country, unhealthy climate, unfavourable state of the atmosphere, and an inefficient native staff. At one station the party was detained for 19 days before they could obtain observations. In 1856–57 Mr. Clarkson completed the Sumbulpore Series, Mr. Shelverton commenced a secondary series from the Chilka lake to Balasore, to fix the coast line, and some progress was made in the main triangulation. But the whole party suffered from a jungle

* This observatory, with its instruments and the whole of its valuable series of observations, was entirely destroyed during the mutiny.

fever, producing the utmost debility and depression both of mental and physical powers, and six men died of cholera. In 1857–58 further progress was made; but in August 1860 Captain Strange, in consequence of his promotion, regimentally, to the rank of major, was obliged to retire from charge of the series, and from the Survey Department, after a service in it of thirteen years. In addition to his ability as a surveyor, his rare knowledge of the mechanism of mathematical and astronomical instruments, his never failing resource in an emergency or when any accident happened, and his inventive faculty, rendered him a pre-eminently valuable member of the Survey. He was succeeded in the charge of the Coast Series by Captain Basevi.

The Superintendent of the Survey designed and saw the commencement of two more important Longitudinal Series, one from Calcutta to the eastward, and the other extending from the Sonakhoda base into Assam.

Sir Andrew Waugh became a Major General, and was knighted, in 1861. He retired in March 1861, after having held the appointment for 17 years. When he returned to England, he took with him the appreciative thanks of his Government, and the attachment of a splendid staff of surveyors who had been trained under his auspices.* He had pushed forward the great work with such ability and energy that his successor could see his way to its completion in a specified number of years.

The results of Sir Andrew Waugh's labours will be found in the following volumes:—

(1.) Vol. 10, parts 1, 2, 3, and 4. Accounts of the Kárara, North Longitudinal connecting Amua and Karara, Gurwani, and Gora Series. MS.

(2.) Vol. 11, parts 2, 3, and 4. Chundwar, Hurilaong, and North Parisnath Series. MS. Part 1 of this volume is wanting.

(3.) Vol. 12, parts 2, 4. Maluncha Series. Calcutta Meridian Series. Measurement of the Sonakhoda base. MS. Parts 1 and 3 are missing.

(4.) Vol. 13. Part 1. Southern Parisnath Series. MS. The remainder is missing.

(5.) Vol. 14. Part 1. South Concan Series in the Bombay Presidency. MS. The remainder is missing.

* The whole staff, 197 in number, presented Sir Andrew Waugh with a service of plate in 1862.

(6.) Vol. 15, and appendix in a separate volume. The North-East Longitudinal Series. MS.

(7.) Volume on the Chuch and Kurrachee base lines; not numbered. MS.

(8.) "Report by Colonel Waugh on the extent and nature of the operations of the Grand Trigonometrical Survey," with Appendices. Called for by Mr. Joseph Hume, and presented to Parliament in April 1851.

(9.) Report on the Surveys of India, by Sir Andrew Waugh, for the three years ending 1858-59.

(10.) Report on the Surveys of India, by Sir Andrew Waugh, dated January 31st, 1861, being his last.

(11.) "Calcutta Review" for 1842, vol. 4, p. 62. On the Great Trigonometrical Survey.

(12.) "Calcutta Review" for 1863, vol. 38. On the Great Trigonometrical Survey. This article is by Colonel Walker.

(13.) "Journal of the Asiatic Society of Bengal" for 1862, vol. 31, p. 22.

The labours of the survey under Sir Andrew Waugh were brought to public notice in several of the annual addresses of the Presidents of the Royal Geographical Society,* and in 1856 he was awarded the gold medal.

A history of the operations of the Great Trigonometrical Survey down to the time of Sir Andrew Waugh's resignation, compiled from the reports, by H. Duhan, personal assistant to the Surveyor-General, will be found in five articles in the "Professional Papers on Indian Engineering," edited by Major J. G. Medley, C.E., (Roorkee), vol. ii., p. 285 and p. 398, and vol. iii., pp. 94, 305, and 402. The articles are illustrated by a map showing the direction of the series and by prints of the astronomical circle by Troughton and Simms, of a sketch representing the measurement of a base line, of an observing tower, and maps of the Tso-Morari lake and of the Baltoro glacier in Tibet, as surveyed by Captain Godwin Austen. The fifth article describes the operations of the Cashmere Survey.

* By Sir R. Murchison in 1844 and 1845, Lord Colchester in 1846, Mr. Hamilton in 1848 and 1849, Admiral Smyth in 1851, Lord Ellesmere in 1855, Admiral Berchey in 1856, and Lord de Grey in 1860.

VIII.—THIRD PERIOD OF THE TOPOGRAPHICAL SURVEYS.

1843—61.

The Revenue and Topographical Surveys.

Great progress was made in the Topographical and Revenue Surveys during the administration of Sir Andrew Waugh, who was admirably supported by Major Thuillier, his Deputy in the Surveyor General's Office, from 1847.

In 1851 the Official Manual of Surveying for India, by Captains Smith and Thuillier, was published;* a thick volume divided into five parts:—

1. Geometry and trigonometry.
2. Surveying instruments.
3. Surveying.
4. On native field measurement (khusrah).
5. Practical astronomy, and its application to surveying.

Captain Boileau prepared a new and complete set of traverse tables, chiefly for the use of officers of the Revenue Survey. It was the first that was calculated to single minutes, or carried out to five places of decimals.†

The Revenue Survey is conducted as follows:—The settlement officers mark the boundaries of the pergunnah, and furnish the surveyor with a rough sketch demarcation map, called *thak-bust*. With this map men go round, fixing the stations and clearing the ground for measurements. The surveyor then runs a line from station to station, as near the boundary as possible, entering every measurement in a field book, and parties of village boundary surveyors do the same with the villages. The *khusrah*, or field measurement by natives, is checked by the general survey; and the physical details are filled in by the plane table. The pergunnah maps are

---

* "Manual of Surveying for India, detailing the mode of operations in the Revenue Survey of Bengal, compiled by Captains R. Smyth and H. L. Thuillier." (Calcutta, 1851.) "Calcutta Review," vol. xvi., p. 321, 1851. A second edition of the Manual, with additions, was published in 1860.

† "A new and complete set of traverse tables, shewing the differences of latitude and the departures to every minute of the quadrant, and to five places of decimals; together with a table of the lengths of each degree of latitude and corresponding degree of longitude from the equator to the poles, with other tables useful to the Surveyor." By Captain J. T. Boileau. (2nd ed. London. 1839.)

drawn on a scale of one mile to an inch, and the zillah or district maps four miles to an inch. The plans of cantonments are drawn on a scale of 12 or 18 inches to a mile.

One important object of the Revenue Survey is to fill up the outlines fixed by the Great Trigonometrical Survey, and, as the Calcutta Review expresses it, "to put sinews and flesh on the colossal skeleton which that survey constructs."

In 1861 Sir Andrew Waugh published his Instructions for Topographical Surveying, in which, adopting the rules laid down in Thuillier's Manual as a basis, he developes the system best suited to surveys purely topographical in character.* The special province of the Revenue Surveys is to define the boundaries of estates; while Topographical Surveys are mainly for the measurement and delineation of natural features in wild districts or native states. The stations of the Great Trigonometrical Survey give the topographical surveyor four initial elements required for commencing a survey, namely, a point of departure with latitude and longitude, a base, an azimuth or true direction of the meridian, and the height above the sea. But the great stations are too far from each other for use in filling up topographical details, and the principal triangles have, therefore, to be broken up into smaller ones by the Ray Trace System, introduced by Sir George Everest.

Rapid progress was made with Revenue Surveys under Sir Andrew Waugh, by Blagrave in the Julinder Dooab, Gastrell in the Sunderbunds, O'Donel in Arracan,† and Van Renen in Nagpore. The Hyderabad Survey, which had been progressing since 1818, was suspended in 1852, owing to the mismanagement of the officer in charge; but in 1855 it was resumed by Mr. Mulheran, an excellent surveyor, who made good progress, and successfully carried a branch series of triangles from the Great Arc to Nagpore, during the rising of Tantia Topee. A survey in Ganjam and the Cuttack Mehals proceeded under Captains Saxton and Depree.‡

The first *khusrah* survey of the Punjab proved a failure. It was made by plane table to which native-made compasses were attached,

---

* "Instructions for Topographical Surveying, by Lieut.-Colonel Sir Andrew Waugh, for the use of the Surveying Department." (Roorkee, 1861.)

† See "Notes on the tribes of the Eastern Frontier, by J. H. O'Donel." Nos. 1, 2, 3, in the *Journal of the Asiatic Society of Bengal*, vol. 32 (1863.)

‡ Registers of computations of triangles, &c., &c., for the Ganjam Survey from, 1845 to 1864, are preserved in the Geographical Department of the India Office.

which were in the last degree uncertain and confounding. A book of instructions was issued for their use, and a great deal of work was done with them at a very considerable expense. The surveyors to be employed were the putwarees of villages. In 1856 it was reported that all the work done in this way was utterly useless, and that the system had broken down. Colonel Meadows Taylor had meanwhile been ordered to introduce it into the Hyderabad Assigned Districts, but had reported that it would be quite impossible to work out the system as proposed. He was, however, ordered to use the plane table, instead of the cross staff and chain used in the Bombay revenue surveys, and he adopted a plan of his own, by working by back and forward sights only, as with a theodolite. The method was readily learned by native assistants, who became wonderfully expert and correct. The work had been cheap and comparatively rapid, and when tested by scientific processes in connexion with the points of the Great Trigonometrical Survey, it had proved very satisfactory. A good deal of work was done in 1856-57 in the Nuldroog district, and Colonel Meadows Taylor was ordered to prepare an establishment for the Revenue Survey of the whole of the Assigned Districts, of which he was to have been the head. But the mutiny broke out in 1857, causing a suspension of work, and when quiet was restored a part of the Bombay Revenue Survey establishment was set to work in Berar.

The most interesting and valuable of the topographical surveys executed in Sir Andrew Waugh's time are undoubtedly those of Cashmere and the Sinde Sagur Doab, under Montgomerie and Robinson.

After the Sutlej campaign, Captain Robinson was employed on a military reconnaissance of the Hazarah hill district, and as soon as the second Punjab war was over he was ordered to survey the Salt Range. Sir Andrew Waugh speaks of the result as an admirable work, to which Captain Robinson's great talent for topographical delineation has imparted the highest character for fidelity and beauty of execution.

Robinson's work comprises a complete survey of the whole highland country of the Sinde Sagur Doab, between the rivers Indus and Jhelum.* From the nature of the country, this was a work of great

* General Report of the Survey of the Kohistan of the Sind Sâgur Dooab, by Captain D. G. Robinson, Bengal Engineers, F.R.G.S.; Seasons 1851–59. M.S. Volume

difficulty. The area amounts to 10,551 square miles, and the cost of the survey was Rs. 1,93,465. The region is the scene of some of the exploits of Alexander the Great, and includes the site of ancient Taxila, the burial place of Bucephalus. Here too is the line on which India has been invaded from the days of Alexander to those of Nadir Shah. The country abounds in strong positions, and an elaborate and accurate map is important in a strategic point of view, and in facilitating public works operations. The map, which is on eight parts published in 28 large sheets on a scale of one inch, comprises the whole of Rawul Pindi and Jhelum, including the Salt Range, and the hilly parts of Shahpoor and Leia. The greater portion consists of elevated plateaux of marl and clay, resting in basins of sandstone and limestone, supported by the Salt Range and several parallel ridges, which run east and west. These ridges, some of them rising like fish fins, others expanding into mountains nearly 10,000 feet high, protect the surface from denudation; but the water, acting on the underlying sandstone, is constantly washing it away, and cutting up the country into a series of deep and intricate ravines, in the bottoms of which the richest cultivation is found. The drainage of the country thus becomes exceedingly complicated; but it was made the fundamental part of the field sketching, and is delineated on the map with admirable exactness.* Captain Robinson trained 17 surveyors. The work was commenced in 1851 and completed in 1859.

The Topographical Survey of Cashmere proceeded *pari passu* with the main triangulation, and both were under the superintendence of Captain Montgomerie. The filling in was executed by the plane table, on a scale of two miles to the inch for the valleys, and of four miles for Ladak and the wilder region. A plan of the city of Cashmere, with the lake and suburbs, was also executed on a

---

in the Geographical Department of the India Office, with an introduction by Sir Andrew Waugh.

* Colonel Robinson speaks of this service as eight years of hard but pleasing labour. He says of the maps, that "they are not likely to be of great interest as mere indi-"cations of the geography of that part of India, but they are valuable as indicating, "with complete fidelity, the extraordinary geographical contortions of that wild district, "and it is much to be regretted that the adjacent countries have not been surveyed "with the same care"—*Letter from Colonel Robinson to C. R. Markham, Oct.* 1866. In 1865 Captain (now Colonel) Robinson quitted the Survey Department, and was appointed Director General of the Telegraph Department.

scale of two inches to the mile. This work was in full swing when Sir Andrew Waugh retired; and several of those who are now leading officers in the survey, such as Montgomerie, Basevi, Godwin Austen, and Melville, were partly trained in the Cashmere mountains. Godwin Austen, especially, sketched some most difficult ground with great taste and skill, including the enormous glaciers of Little Tibet, one of them 36 miles long. One of the most distinguished of the Cashmere surveyors was Elliot Brownlow, who was slain at the siege of Lucknow. "His adventures and achieve-" ments in the snowy mountains, and his hardihood and endurance, " were the theme of much praise amongst his brother surveyors. He " had intended to devote his rare and splendid qualities as a mountain " surveyor to the exploration of Central Asia on rigorous principles."*

Between 1849 and 1853, Lieutenant Walker, the future successor of Sir Andrew Waugh, executed a military reconnaisance of the Trans-Indus region from Peshawur to Dera Ismael Khan, single handed.

The subject of a Revenue Survey of the Madras Presidency, with a new assessment of the land, had engaged the attention of the local Government for upwards of ten years, but it was not until the end of the year 1855 that they submitted the final result of their deliberations to the Court of Directors and the Government of India, for approval. At that time no regular survey had ever been made, and in many districts the land revenue demand was based merely on the unchecked statements of the curnums. The object of the survey was to correct the measurements of superficial areas, and to ensure a fair and just assessment on each description of land, by a classification of the different fields in each village.

But the Board of Revenue at Madras were at first disinclined or at least indifferent to the geographical aspect of the question, and objected to the survey being conducted in connexion with Colonel Lambton's triangulation. They urged that they only required field maps for fiscal purposes; and that geodesical operations would cause extra expense and delay, which they strongly deprecated. Major Thuillier, on the other hand, in a letter dated May 6th, 1857, represented that no general survey of the Madras Presidency ought to be

* Colonel Thuillier, in a paper read before the Asiatic Society at Calcutta, on July 6th, 1859.

commenced without full and ample precautions being taken for making the materials subservient to the general purposes of geography. At the same time he showed that the utmost facilities existed for connecting the Revenue Survey operations with the trigonometrical points of Colonel Lambton.

Fortunately, Colonel Thuillier's opinion prevailed; the Court of Directors approved of the arrangements on December 17th, 1856, and on August 18th, 1857, Captain Priestley, of the 74th Highlanders, was appointed Superintendent of the Madras Revenue Survey. This officer had entered the service in 1838, and became a captain in 1853. He had already acquired considerable experience, and had been conducting an experimental survey in South Arcot since 1854.

The area to be surveyed was assumed at 60,000 square miles, or 38 million acres, and it was originally expected that the survey would cost Rs. 38,40,000, and be completed in 14 years. The survey is conducted on an English and not on an inaccurate native method, such as the *khusrah* of Bengal; and it is designed to show all the principal variations in the surface of the soil, such as hills, jungles, woods, channels, tanks, topes, houses, cultivated and cultivable land, whether *nunjah* (irrigated) or *punjah* (unirrigated), and the area of each field. The village maps are on a scale of 16 inches to the mile, the talook maps one inch to the mile, and it was intended that, from these materials, district maps should have been compiled on a scale of half an inch to the mile. The work is connected with the Great Trigonometrical Survey by the following method. The first operation is the identification of the Great Trigonometrical Survey stations. From one of these the traverse work commences, and runs along a village or talook boundary until it reaches a convenient point to connect it with another trigonometrical station. These traverses embrace circuits of from 50 to 100 square miles. The bearing of station lines is ascertained at intervals by astronomical observations, and the traverses are corrected by comparison with the sides of the Great Trigonometrical Survey triangles, the errors being proportionately distributed. Thus corrected, the work of the Madras Revenue Survey adapts itself exactly to Lambton's triangulation. At every tri-junction point the boundaries of villages are marked by masonry pillars, two feet square and three feet high.

Captain Priestley commenced work with an establishment consisting of 18 surveyors and deputy serveyors, 30 survey ameens,

30 gomastahs, 20 draftsmen and computers, 77 peons and measurers, and 19 station markers, at an annual cost of Rs. 31,338. Mr. Newill was appointed superintendent of the new assessment, and the two officers worked in concert. In 1857 two talooks, one in South Arcot and the other in Trichinopoly, were surveyed. In 1858 the survey was commenced in the Rajahmundry district; in 1859 Masulipatam was taken up; and in 1860 there were parties in Nellore, Trichinopoly, and Salem.

In 1859 a survey was undertaken of the important coffee-growing district of Wynaad, under Lieutenant Hessey, who had been working with Captain Priestley since 1855, and had, by his untiring exertions, contributed much to the success of the experimental survey in South Arcot. The main object of the Wynaad Survey was to define the boundaries of the coffee estates, and Lieutenant Hessey began it in the Nelloornaad Umshum near Manantawaddy, the principal station. The district had been surveyed as a part of Malabar by Captain Ward in 1826,* who fixed 16 stations from those of Lambton's Triangulation; but the sites of villages and pagodas are said to have been very loosely laid down in Ward's survey. Hessey commenced work in 1860, forming a system of secondary triangulation from Ward's points, and filling in the detail by the plane table.

A lithographic press, with a suitable staff, was established at Madras, under Mr. Paczensky, for the publication of the talook and village maps, and during 1859 the number printed was 145, comprising 4,495 copies. The work of the Madras Revenue Survey, which has been conducted under the superintendence of Colonel Priestley from the first, is still progressing.†

In 1851 and 1852 the Neilgherry and Koondah hills were surveyed, under the superintendence of Colonel Ouchterlony. The map is in 16 sheets, on a scale of 1,000 feet to an inch, and is accompanied by a geographical and statistical memoir.‡

* See page 61.

† For an account of the Madras Revenue Survey, see the voluminous correspondence published in the Selections from the Records of the Madras Government, No. LIII. (1858) and No. LXXIV. (1863.)

‡ Published in the "Madras Journal of Literature and Science," XV. p. 1. Also presented to Parliament.

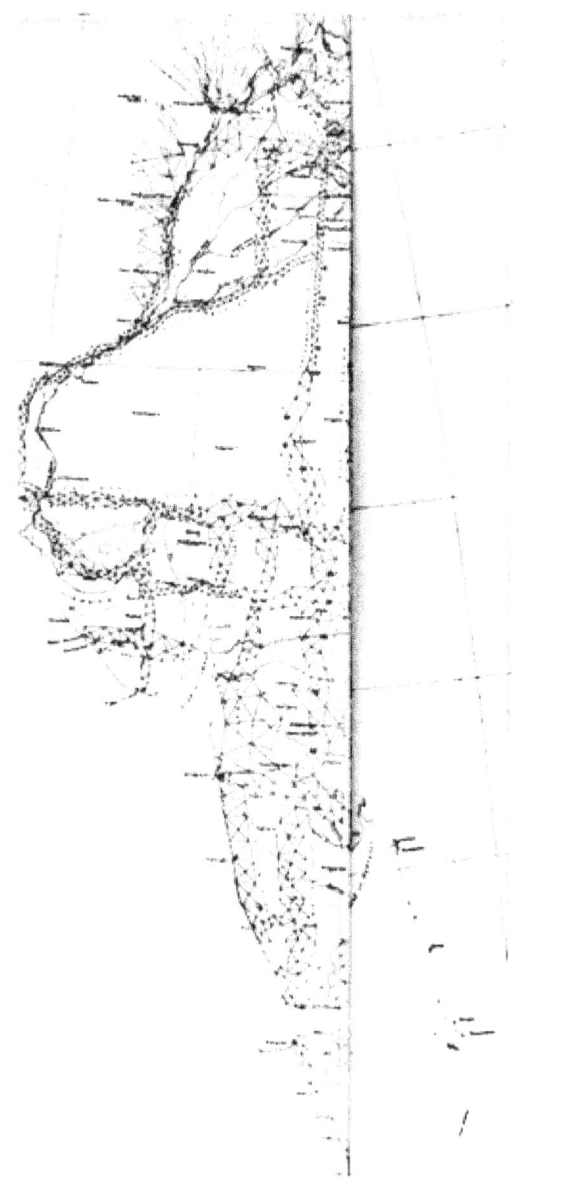

IX.—FOURTH PERIOD OF THE TRIGONOMETRICAL SURVEYS.

1862—70.

Colonel Walker and the Great Trigonometrical Survey.

On the retirement of Sir Andrew Waugh, the two offices of Surveyor General and Superintendent of the Great Trigonometrical Survey were once more separated, after having been united in one person since 1830. Colonel Thuillier became Surveyor General; and Colonel Walker was appointed Superintendent of the Survey, on the 12th March 1861. James Thomas Walker joined the Bombay Engineer Corps on December 9th, 1844, and served in the Punjab campaign at the siege of Mooltan and battle of Gujerat, and in various affairs on the Trans-Indus frontier under Sir Charles Napier, Sir Colin Campbell, and Sir Neville Chamberlain. After the annexation of the Punjab in 1849, he was ordered by Lord Melville, who then commanded at Peshawur, to make a military survey within ten miles radius of that station; which was afterwards extended to embrace the whole of the British territory beyond the Indus, as far south as Dera Ismael Khan. On the completion of this important work, he became a member of the Great Trigonometrical Surveying Department, and had latterly been in charge of the Great Indus Series, and of the spirit levelling operations. In 1857 he was wounded at the siege of Delhi. He assumed charge of the Great Survey, with the invigorating prospect, which had been denied to his predecessors, of completing the grandest series of survey operations ever undertaken in the world, during his own incumbency.

As Sir Andrew's first work was the completion of some of the Meridional Series in Everest's eastern gridiron, so Colonel Walker's opening labour was the completion of the great north-western gridiron, designed by Sir Andrew Waugh. The Rahoon Meridional Series, after six years of work, was finished by Mr. Keelan in 1863, by being connected with the Great Longitudinal Series (western branch). It is 457 miles long; its triangles cover an area of 23,620 square miles, and the total cost was Rs. 2,01,609. The Gurhagarh Series, under Mr. Shelverton, having occupied five years, was completed in 1862, by being joined to the Arumlia and Khanpisura series brought up from the Bombay Longitudinal Series to the Great Western Longitudinal Series and thence from Bombay to Ajmeer by Captain Rivers. Its length is 587 miles, covering an area of 19,096 square miles, and the cost was Rs. 1,08,212. An oblique series was also brought up from Mittunkote near the junction of the Indus and Garra, to a side of the Gurhagurh Series, being 300 miles long, with an area of 8,142 square miles. It was begun by Lieutenant Herschel in 1860, and completed by Mr. Shelverton in 1863, Mr. Ryall working zealously under him, and clearing 300 miles of trace. This is called the Sutlej Series, and cost Rs. 80,743.

But Colonel Walker's first work was the measurement of a base line at Vizagapatam, nearly in the same latitude as Bombay, at which point the Longitudinal Series, from Bombay to the Beder base line, was eventually to touch the east coast. The Coast Series in charge of Captain Basevi, had already been completed from Calcutta to Vizagapatam. Captain Basevi was engaged during the season of 1861 in selecting a site, but he met with much difficulty, owing to the numerous irrigation tanks with which the district is studded. At length he found a suitable site on an undulating plain near the military station of Vizagapatam, and about 15 miles from the port of Bimlipatam. Trenches were dug to carry away the rainfall of the monsoon; but, notwithstanding this precaution, the line was submerged in the following October, and was not drained off without much trouble and exertion.

In the autumn of 1862 Colonel Walker arrived with Colby's compensation bars and microscopes, the same that had been brought out to India by Sir George Everest, and had measured every base line since that time. Colonel Walker was assisted by Captains Basevi and Branfill, and Lieutenant Campbell. The base line measurement occupied two months, and was finished on the 5th of November 1862. The line is 6½ miles long, and was divided into three verificatory sections, checked by a double series of triangles, one on each flank of the base. These tests of accuracy were most satisfactory. The difference between the measured length, and the length as computed from the triangles commencing at the Calcutta base, was ¼ of an inch. When it is considered that the distance from Calcutta is 480 miles, and that the Coast Series passes through a region of dense jungle, such accuracy is perfectly marvellous. Colonel Walker, mindful of the maxim that "the ends of a base line should be guarded with religious veneration," gave much attention to the measures for their preservation at Vizagapatam. In India such marks are viewed with cupidity not unmixed with fear. The natives have an idea that money is buried under these mysterious monuments erected by the western strangers, while they feel a dread that they may cast a spell over the district. Hence they are exposed to a double danger, and those at Sironj were actually destroyed. At Vizagapatam substantial domes of cut stone masonry without openings were built over the marks at each end of the base line, and put in charge of the police.

After the measurement, Captain Basevi was sent to make a reconnaissance in the almost unknown Jeypoor territory, with reference to the extension of the Bombay Longitudinal Series to the East Coast. The whole party was attacked by fever, but the result was a good preliminary map of Jeypoor, and a valuable memoir by Captain Basevi.*

Meanwhile Captain Branfill connected the Vizagapatam base line with the principal triangles of the Coast Series, and in December 1863 he commenced work near Guntoor, with a view to the extension of the Coast Series to Madras. The Madras Observatory is the only one in India at which systematic observations for longitude have been taken, for a number of years; and it was very important to connect the Coast Series with it. It will be remembered that this Madras Observatory was the fixed point from which Colonel Lambton started with his triangulation in 1802. It was the pivot on which the whole fabric rested.† Now, after a lapse of 62 years, Captain Branfill was bringing back the triangulation to the old starting point. Unluckily several trees interrupted the view between the nearest station and the observatory, and extravagant compensation was demanded for permission to remove them. One man wanted Rs. 300 for a single branch of a casuarina tree. Eventually a pillar had to be erected to overlook the intervening obstacles, and a scaffolding was raised at the observatory, so that the theodolite could be fixed at a height of 63 feet from the ground. Thus, in 1864, the Coast Series from Calcutta to Madras was completed.

In 1865–66, Captain Branfill and his party observed a Longitudinal Series over Colonel Lambton's old ground, from the Madras Observatory to the Bangalore base line. It is 118 miles long, and consists of 23 principal triangles, covering 2,641 square miles. Secondary triangulations were also completed from Guntoor to

* "Report by Capt. J. P. Basevi, R.E., on a reconnaissance of part of the Jeypore Territory," forms an Appendix to Colonel Walker's Report for 1862–63.

† See Page 49.

Masulipatam, to fix the positions of the lighthouses on the coast. Most of the party were struck down by fever, and Captain Branfill himself was obliged to go home on sick leave.

In the season of 1866–67, Lieutenant Campbell took charge of the party at Bangalore. He extended the triangulation for some distance to the westward, and south for 60 miles in the direction of Cape Comorin. He also successfully re-measured two of the last years' triangles, which had been rejected owing to the grazing of the rays of light against the slope of an intervening hill, which caused an error of 3"·8. This error was reduced to 0"·7.

Colonel Walker now gave orders for the re-measurement of the Bangalore base line. In 1861 Professors Airy and Stokes, at the request of the Royal Society, had reported upon Colonel Lambton's Surveys. They were of opinion that, owing to his instrumental appliances having been far less complete than at present, his work, though executed with the greatest care and ability, admitted of being improved in every part; and they expressed a hope that the whole of his survey would be repeated with the best modern appliances. The Superintendent, therefore, resolved to re-measure the bases at Bangalore and Cape Comorin, and to revise the intervening triangles.

In 1867 Lieutenant Campbell selected a site for the new base near Bangalore. Colonel Lambton's terminal marks were still in existence, and in good preservation, but the surface of the country was much changed. Irrigation tanks, as well as a lofty railway embankment, now cross Colonel Lambton's base line. Hence the necessity for a new site.

Colonel Walker was prevented by a severe accident from going south to measure the new Bangalore base, and he deputed Mr. Hennessey, one of his most trusted assistants, to take his place. The length of the base line is 6·84 miles, and, like that at Vizagapatam, it was divided into three verificatory sections, with triangulation on both flanks. The difference between the result by measurement and that by calculation from the Vizagapatam base was again only a quarter of an inch. Lieutenant Rogers, a young officer who now commenced his career in the survey, connected the base with the main triangulations, and with Lambton's base and his astronomical station at Dadagoontah.

Captain Branfill then proceeded to Cape Comorin, to select a base line site at the southern extreme of the Great Arc. He found the country studded with rocky precipitous hills, and large groves of palmyra palms, but at last he found a site near Lambton's old station at Punnae, and prepared the ground. The measurement of the base, during the season of 1868–69, was entrusted by Colonel Walker to Captain Basevi, with Branfill, Herschel, and Rogers to assist him. This is the last base necessary for the verification of the triangles within the limits of India proper, and the tenth that was measured with the compensation bars brought out to India by Sir George Everest in 1830. The system adopted was to divide the line into three sections, measure the central one, which is 1·68 miles long, four times over, and determine the length of the other two from the central one by triangulation on both flanks. The latter operation was performed by Lieutenant Rogers, and the result of the measurement was highly satisfactory.

While this important revision of Colonel Lambton's work was proceeding, the Superintendent continued to push forward the other survey operations with vigour and judgment. In September 1862 he formed the party under Lieutenant Thuillier for the East Calcutta Longitudinal Series, to extend from the Calcutta Meridional Series to the eastern frontier, and form a basis for the survey of the districts of Nuddea, Jessore, and Dacca. Operations were commenced at Chinsura in November, but the party encountered great difficulties. In working through jungle it is first necessary to cut a narrow glade in a perfectly straight line in the direction required for a station, for 8 or 10 miles. The ground is then reconnoitred for a suitable site, to which a glade is cut from the trial line. Two sides and the included angle thus give the data to ascertain the direct line between the two stations, which is then cleared to bring them in sight. Immense labour is thus involved, and, in a populous country like Lower Bengal, the difficulty is increased by having to make bends to avoid houses and gardens, and by being exposed to worrying litigation for compensations. The towers of unburnt bricks were found to be unsafe in so moist a climate, and masonry walls round the central pillar will be essential.

The country which was the scene of Lieutenant Thuillier's operations was perfectly level, covered with malarious swamps, and intersected by great rivers, with densely wooded banks. In the season of 1864–65, 174 miles of trial lines and 314 of final lines were cleared through the jungle. Cholera and fever were raging in the country, and twenty men of the party fell victims. Yet Thuillier remained steadily at his post, and made satisfactory progress, completing the series as far as the eastern frontier in 1866–67, on the parallel of 23°. It is 210 miles long, and consists of 41 triangles, every station necessitating the erection of a tower.

Lieutenant Thuillier then commenced a Meridional Series on the meridian of 90°, called the Brahmapootra Series, to complete the basis for the surveys of Nuddea, Jessore, Dacca, and other parts of Eastern Bengal. Again the ground was level and covered with vast swamps. During 1867–68 upwards of 700 miles of glades were cleared through heavy jungle, and ten towers were built, the season being entirely devoted to preliminary operations. But in 1868–69 the measurement of the triangles was commenced with a 24-inch theodolite by Troughton and Simms. At the same time Lieutenant Larminie commenced a chain of secondary triangles to be carried through the valley of Assam, where the Revenue Survey operations are in progress. A series of triangles from Calcutta to Port Canning was commenced by Mr. Ryall, but it was permanently interrupted by litigious fellows through whose gardens the line had to be taken. Half Mr. Ryall's time was passed in the courts of law; and Colonel Walker represented the urgent necessity for extending the provisions of Act VI. of 1857 to the officers of the Survey Department.

The Eastern Frontier Series was commenced by Mr. C. Lane in 1861–62, near the western extreme of the Assam valley. He was ably seconded by Mr. Rossenrode, and in 1862–3 they were in Independent Tipperah, and working down towards Chittagong. The physical difficulties to be overcome were very great.* In 1865–66 Mr. Rossenrode assumed charge, and the series was brought down to the eastern frontier towards Akyáb, and through Arracan. In 1867–68 and the following year the party crossed the difficult range of hills between Arracan and Prome, and pushed their operations into British Burmah.

In the Bombay Presidency a series of triangles was commenced by Captain Haig south of Bombay (on the meridian of Mangalore). He, however, first revised a large portion of the old Bombay Longitudinal Series. In the season of 1862–63 good progress was being made, when a tower, on which the large theodolite had been placed for observing, gave way on one side, and the instrument was so

* See Extracts from a "Report on Independent Tipperah, by C. Lane, Esq." in Colonel Walker's Report for 1862–63. (Appendix.)

severely injured as to be incapable of further use until it had been repaired in England. It was sent out again overland, reached Bombay in November 1864, and work was re-commenced. The design was to take the series south to Mangalore, and thence east to the Bangalore base line. In 1866-67 Lieutenant Trotter took charge, when the work was still 180 miles from Mangalore, and on the verge of the dense and deadly jungles of North Canara. The whole party was struck down with fever, and Lieutenant Trotter himself was obliged to go home. When completed this series will extend from the northern frontier of Cashmere to Mangalore, over 22° of latitude. Lieutenant Heaviside is now taking astronomical observations upon it.

Two additional Meridional Series are designed to pass south from the old Calcutta Longitudinal, called the Sumbulpore and Jubbulpore Series. They were in charge of Mr. Keelan and Mr. Shelverton, who commenced their operations by a revision of a large portion of the Calcutta Longitudinal Series from the Sironj base to the Gora hill station. Mr. Keelan then worked south, through wild tracts covered with almost impenetrable forest, where his party suffered severely from fever, intending to run into the Coast Series near Madras. Mr. Shelverton's operations were on the meridian of Jubbulpoor. From 1864 to 1866 he worked through the Central Provinces, and was prostrated by fever, but satisfactorily completed the series in the latter year. It is intended, hereafter, to extend it down the east coast to the straits of Manaar, and so connect it with the island of Ceylon.

As soon as the Jubbulpoor Series was finished, Mr. Shelverton was employed to continue the Bombay Longitudinal Series from the Beder base line to the Vizagapatam base. In 1868-69 he had completed the portion between the Great Arc and the Jubbulpore Series; receiving much assistance from the Nizam's Government, which was urgently required, as 72 hill tops had to be cleared of forest for observing stations. This series is called the Beder Longitudinal Series.

In the Cashmere Survey Sir Andrew Waugh first combined trigonometrical and topographical work in the duties of one party. Colonel Walker continued this principle in two or three instances, in anticipation of the completion of the trigonometrical survey, foreseeing the importance of having his officers trained to topographical work, that their services might eventually be available in filling in the mighty skeleton, which their accurate observations and high mathematical attainments will have completed.

During 1862-63 great progress was made with the Cashmere Survey east of Leh. Stations were fixed on the Chinese frontier, and peaks were determined at a distance of a hundred miles from it. On the 21st of April 1864 Lieutenant Carter joined the party as second Trigonometrical Assistant, and helped Captain Montgomerie in observing for latitude, while Godwin Austen and Johnson turned out much effective topographical work. At the close of 1864 the Cashmere Series was completed. It consists of a surveyed area of 70,000 square miles, in every variety of climate and scenery. There is not a valley in these wild regions of perpetual snow that was not visited by the surveyors, the triangulation covering Jamoo, Cashmere, Khagan, Ladak, and Little Tibet; and peaks were fixed, some of which (among them that named K 2) being second only to Mount Everest. In 1865 Mr. Johnson crossed the frontier, and visited Ilchy, the capital of Khotan, obtaining two observations for latitude there, and reconnoitring an area of 21,000 square miles.*

After ten years of uninterrupted labor in Cashmere, Montgomerie went home on leave, and Lieutenant Carter received charge of the party, which was sent to commence a topographical survey of Kumaon and Gurhwal, on a scale of one inch to the mile, with a survey of the tea plantations, eight inches to the mile, and of the stations of Mussouree and Landour, 12 inches to the mile. Lieutenant Carter pushed the work forward with much zeal and ability during the time that he was in charge, and on May 1st, 1867, Captain Montgomerie returned, and resumed his labors.

While he has made good progress with the surveys of Kumaon and Gurwhal, Captain Montgomerie has been also busily engaged in superintending the geographical explorations of regions beyond the Himalaya. The Chinese authorities would not allow English officers to penetrate beyond the frontier, and the use of Asiatics for purposes of exploration was first proposed, and approved by Government, in 1861. Colonel Walker engaged two pundits from one of the upper valleys of the Himalaya, who were trained to the use of the sextant, compass, and hypsometer.

* For an account of the Cashmere Survey see the "Journal of the Asiatic Society of Bengal," vol. xxix. p. 20, and vol. xxx. p. 99.

The first expedition was undertaken by one Muhamed i Hamed, who went from Ladak to Yarkand by the Karakoram pass, and fixed the latitude of Yarkand, but died soon after his return. The second was by a pundit who started in January 1865, and went by Khatmandoo and the valley of the Sanpoo, to Lassa, the capital of Tibet. He was obliged to conceal his object, and profess devotion to Buddhism. In his hand he carried a prayer wheel, which consists of a hollow cylindrical copper box revolving round a spindle, one end of which is the handle. But inside, instead of the usual scroll with a prayer on it, the cunning pundit had slips of paper for entering his bearings and distances. He took 31 observations for latitude, 30 for boiling point, and laid down 1,200 miles of route survey. In 1867 a third pundit was sent across the basins of the Sutlej and Indus into Great Tibet as far as the gold field of Thok Jalung; another got as far as Rudok, and a fifth penetrated to the lofty region in the rear of Mount Everest. A Mohammedan named Mirza Sooja, under the same auspices, reached the Pameer Steppe and the distant city of Kashgar.

The stupendous character of the glaciers and mountains, and the geographical interest attaching to the explorations of these pundits, has attracted special attention to Captain Montgomerie's operations in the Himalaya.

So far as the Royal Geographical Society is concerned, this interest had first been excited, long before, by the valuable papers of the two Stracheys on Tibet and Kumaon, in 1851 and 1853, and by Dr. Thomson's in 1849, on the Karakorum Pass; while, in 1851, Mr. Purdon communicated some account of the Cashmere Survey.* H. Strachey and Dr. Thomson received gold medals in 1851 and 1865. Their communications were followed by papers written by the actual surveyors, Godwin Austen and Johnson; and

---

* R. G. S. Journal, 1851, p. 57. On the physical geography of the provinces of Kumaon and Gurhwál, by R. Strachey.
„ „ 1853, p. 1. On the physical geography of Western Tibet, by H. Strachey.
„ „ 1849, p. 25. Successful journey to the Karakórum Pass, by Thomas Thomson, M.D.
„ „ 1861, p. 14. On the trigonometrical survey and physical configuration of the valley of Kashmir, by William H. Purdon (Ex. Eng. Punjáb).

Montgomerie gave a most interesting account of the explorations of the pundits. The Geographical Society awarded a gold medal to Captain Montgomerie in 1864, and in 1867 presented a gold watch to the pundit who reached Lassa.*

Colonel Walker has another topographical survey party at work in the Bombay Presidency. In 1865 it was engaged, in Bombay Island, in forming a basis of triangulation for a detailed cadrastal survey; and in 1866 it was transferred to Kattywar, under Captain Haig, to resume the survey commenced in 1864, but suspended in consequence of a famine in 1865. Topographical operations are also being commenced in Guzerat, where an attempt is being made to utilize the details of the fiscal surveys which have been carried over British Guzerat by the Bombay Revenue Surveyors, and which have been mapped on a scale of from 8 to 12 inches to the mile, by native surveyors, but with no attempt at delineating the configuration of the ground.

The Kattywar survey has progressed satisfactorily. It differs from all other topographical operations in that the plane table or field sections are drawn on an enlarged scale of two instead of, as is usual in India, one inch to the mile. The maps are prepared on three scales of 2, 1, and ½ inches to the mile. Dr. Oldham, of the Geological Survey, has suggested that points should be selected on the south coast of Kattywar during the operations, to determine the existing relative level of land and sea by a series of tidal observations (the stations being connected by a line of levels), with reference to the changes in the relative level of land and sea that are believed to be going on in various parts of the Bombay Presidency.

* R. G. S. Journal, 1861, p. 30. Notes on the valley of Kashmeer, by Captain H. Godwin Austen, Topl. Asst. G. T. S.

" " 1864, p. 19. On the glaciers of the Mustákh Range, by Captain Godwin Austen.

" " 1867. Report on his journey to Ilchi, the capital of Khótán, in Chinese Tartary, by W. H. Johnson, F.R.G.S.

" " 1867, p. 343. Notes on the Pangong Lake District of Ladak, from a journal made during a survey in 1863, by Captain H. Godwin Austen, F.R.G.S.

" " 1868, p. 129. Route survey by the Pundit, from Nepál to Lhasa, and thence through the upper valley of the Brahmaputra to its source, by Captain Montgomerie, F.R.G.S.

See also Notes on the Pangong District of Ladakh, made in 1863, printed in the end of Colonel Walker's Report for 1864–65; and Mr. Johnson's Report on Ilchi in that for 1865–66.

Colonel Walker has not failed to push forward those important spirit levelling operations which he himself commenced in Sir Andrew Waugh's time. In 1862 Mr. Donnelly had completed 242 miles of levelling up the valley of the Ganges, when he was compelled, by severe illness, to close work near Bhagulpoor. In 1863 Captain Trotter took charge of the levelling party, and got as far as Allahabad, though he and his party were prostrated by fever. He found the levels of the railway officials to be very inaccurate. In 1864 Trotter brought the series of levellings up to Agra. Kurrachee is connected with Calcutta by a line of levels 2,200 miles long, being the longest and probably the best ever executed, besides 830 miles of branch lines, the origin or datum being the mean sea level of Kurrachee, and the terminus the sill of Kidderpoor Dock, at Calcutta.

In 1866-67, branches were taken from the main line of levels to connect the levels of canals and railways at Delhi, Lahore, Mooltan, and other places. In 1867-68 a line was brought through Rohilcund, and in 1868-69 a line was taken from Bareilly for 350 miles to Lucknow, Cawnpore, and Fyzabad.

A second volume of levels has been published under Colonel Walker's instructions, recording a portion of these operations;* and two sheets of a series of maps showing the various levels of trigonometrical stations, canals and railroads.†

During the last few years there have been parties engaged on purely astronomical observations. In 1861, Mr. Nicolson was sent to fix the positions of the Andaman and other islands which were erroneously placed on the charts; but after taking a series of observations at Port Blair, and fixing its position, this work was handed over to the marine surveyors.‡ In 1863, however, two astronomical parties were organized to fix the latitudes of trigonometrical stations, at moderate distances, all over India. One was to begin at Calcutta, and observe at each of the stations along the Calcutta Longitudinal Series, whence the Meridional Series of Sir George Everest's grid-

* "Tables of Heights in N.W. Provinces and Bengal, to May 1865 (Roorkee, 1866)," with an introduction by Lieutenant Trotter.

† "Spirit Level and Trigonometrical Heights of the Great Trigonometrical Survey of India, with canal and railway levels, compiled from various sources." Sheets 1 and 3 photo-zincographed at Dehra Doon in 1867. These two maps comprise the districts of Umballa, Suharunpoor, Dehra Doon, and Mozuffurnuggur; and are accompanied by printed sheets describing the bench marks, and giving other information.

‡ See page 32.

iron started; while the other was to work north and south at certain stations, about a degree apart, on the Great Arc Series. The latitudes were to be observed from the zenith distances of pairs of north and south stars. Mr. Taylor, Lieutenants Campbell and Heaviside, and latterly Captain Herschel, have been employed on these operations.*

In 1868 the total eclipse of the sun in India gave some additional work to the scientific surveyors. The observations were entrusted to Major Tennant, whom we last met with at the measurement of the Kurrachee base, and who had since been in charge of the Madras Observatory. He came out from England with instruments supplied by the Royal Astronomical Society, and was joined by Captain Branfill. After much careful inquiry, it was decided that the most favourable positions for observing the eclipse, as regarded the probable absence of clouds and rain, would be Beejapoor, and Guntoor on the east coast. Tennant and Branfill observed at Guntoor, Herschel, Campbell, and Haig, at Beejapoor, and the conclusions arrived at from their investigations were that the *corona*, in an eclipse, was but slightly, if at all, self-luminous, while red flames were.†

There is a method, independent of triangulation, by which the ellipticity of the earth can be determined, and it seemed important that it should be tested over the same ground as was traversed by the Great Arc Series. This method is by observing the pendulum. The force of gravity increases from the equator to the poles: and a pendulum, which makes a certain number of vibrations in a given time at the equator, will make a greater number at all other points, the number increasing, as a rule, with the latitude. The experiment consists in determining the number of vibrations which a given pendulum of invariable length makes in 24 hours, at the position selected for the operations. Previous observations had been taken chiefly on islands and near the coast, notably by the veteran observer, General Sabine. It was a desideratum to obtain experiments in the interior of continents to combine with those taken near the sea. The Russian Government had caused them to be taken at the principal stations of the Great Russian Arc, and General Sabine was anxious that a series should be observed in India.

* At Isanfur, near the northern end of the Punjab plains, the difference between the observed latitude and that computed from triangulation was only 0G".! ! !

† See an article on the eclipse observations for 1868 in the "Professional Papers on Indian Engineering," vol. vi., p. 93. See also "Revista de España" Tom. xvii., No. 67. (Madrid, 1870.) "El eclipse de sol considerado bajo el punta do vista fisica."

The tendency of the plumb line to deviate from its normal direction in consequence of local irregularities of the earth's crust, is a source of error which requires the most careful investigation. The plummet is supposed to be attracted by mountains and repelled by oceans; and even on level plains deflection is said to exist when the rocks below are of unequal densities, on either side of the plummet. Archdeacon Pratt, after close examination of the effects of this attraction on the operations of the Trigonometrical Survey, came to the conclusion that the probable error caused at Kalianpoor, by proximity to the Himalaya, was one fourth of a mile; but this only affects astronomical observations. In the triangulations the correctness of the relative distances is of course unaffected.*

The pendulum observations will give an independent determination of the ellipticity of the earth, and throw light on its physical constitution, by determining the intensity of the force of gravity.

Captain Basevi, while he was on leave in 1864, learnt the use of the apparatus that had been used by General Sabine in the course of his pendulum operations at Kew, and in March 1865 the apparatus was sent out to India. Captain Basevi then received charge of the pendulum experiments, which have been carried over the Great Arc from Dehra Doon to Cape Comorin, in compliance with a suggestion from General Sabine.†

The two pendulums are of Kater's pattern, and slightly longer than a seconds pendulum. (Nos. 4 and 1821.) They are swung in a vacuum, to be free from all disturbing currents, and the vacuum apparatus, with its air-pump, requires incessantly watchful care. The pendulum is set up in front of the pendulum of an astronomical clock, the first being slightly the longest, and vibrating more slowly. The clock pendulum gains on the other, and they diverge more and more up to a certain point, then commence converging, and once more coincide after an interval. It is thus known that the pendulum has

* "A series of papers on mountain and other local attraction in India, and its effect on the calculations of the Great Trigonometrical Survey, by John H. Pratt, M.A." (Calcutta, 1862.) These papers are reprinted from the Transactions of the Royal Society.

† This is not the first series of pendulum observations that has been taken in India. In June 1809, Captain John Warren, Colonel Lambton's able assistant, made experiments for determining the length of the seconds pendulum, and M. le Gentil made similar experiments at Pondicherry and Manilla. Warren's result at the Madras Observatory was 39.026273 ins., which he compared with those of other observers, in a paper in the "Asiatic Researches," vol. ix., p. 293. Subsequently, John Goldingham conducted a series at the Madras Observatory in 1821. The apparatus was sent out to him by Captain Kater, and was similar to the one used by Kater at the

made two vibrations less than the clock in a given interval indicated by the clock. With this datum and the rate of the clock, the number of vibrations in 24 hours is computed.*

Captain Basevi also commenced a series of magnetic observations for variation, dip, and intensity. In 1867 he observed at Mussooree, Dehra, Meerut, Agra, and Kalianpoor. In 1868 he had reached Bangalore; and in 1869 the pendulum observations on the Great Arc were completed to Cape Comorin. He will also observe at certain points on the coast, and on Menikoy Island; while a series of magnetic observations have been taken in Kumaon and Gurwhal by Captain Montgomerie.

One fact of great scientific importance has been ascertained by these experiments, namely, that the density of the strata of the earth's crust under and near the Himalaya is less than that under the plains to the south.† It is also a noticeable feature of Captain Basevi's observations, and one already observed in comparing pendulum observations made in other parts of the world, that at inland stations gravity appears to be in defect of that observed at coast stations in similar latitudes. The cause of this is still uncertain.

The superintendence of work in the field only forms a part of Colonel Walker's anxious and absorbing duties. The labors in the computing and drawing office also require his close attention, and here he has been ably assisted by Lieutenants Herschel and Mr. Hennessey. One matter for careful thought is the dispersion of unavoidable though minute errors in the observation of latitudes, longitudes, and azimuths, in such a manner as to obtain the closest approach to accuracy. This is a consideration of great intricacy and difficulty, and the preliminaries for eventual calculations have been carefully elaborated in the computing office. All the observations are reduced *de novo*, which involves an enormous amount of calculation. In 1865 Mr. Hennessey, who had studied at Cambridge and Southampton while he was in England, resumed charge of the computing

---

stations of the Trigonometrical Survey of England. Goldingham's result was as follows:—

Kater's length of a seconds pendulum in London (temp. 70°), 39.142213 ins.
Goldingham's ,, at Madras ,, 39.026302 ,,

From this he computes the diminution of gravity from the pole to the equator to be 0052894, and ellipticity $\frac{1}{[illegible]}$.—*Philosophical Transactions for* 1822, *vol.* 112, *p.* 27.

* See a paper on the pendulum operations in the "Professional Papers on Indian Engineering," vol. v., p. 305.

† " See note at page 76.

office. He commenced the printing of the observations of all the principal angles, which, except the Great Arc Series, published by Sir George Everest, had hitherto been only in manuscript.* He also introduced photo-zincography, having learnt the process at Southampton, and the sheets of topographical surveys were rapidly re-produced.† Photographic apparatus had been in use in the drawing office some years before, for copying and reducing. Here the Cashmere maps were compiled, and one of Central Asia, by Mr. Scott, in 1866, and many others.

In 1866–67 Colonel Walker was engaged, with Mr. Hennessey, in the verification of the standards of length. At the measurement of each base the relative length of the standard bar A and the six compensation bars was found to be altering; and as all the bars told the same tale, it seemed probable that their lengths had remained constant, and that the standard had changed. While Colonel Walker was in England, in 1864, two new standard bars, one of brass and the other of iron, were constructed for him. They arrived at Dehra Doon, in 1866 and were compared with A, having first been compared with B at Southampton. The comparison showed that the relative length of A and B was nearly the same as in 1834, when they were last compared together. Then B was 1·28 millionths longer than A. Now B is 3·08 millionths longer. Thus the old standards have not altered appreciably, and the changes must be due to the compensation bars.‡

The tables to facilitate the calculations of the Survey Department were also revised and extended, under the direction of Colonel Walker, in 1866, by Mr. Hennessey.§

In 1867 the Cashmere and Ladak maps were completed, together with a series of maps with lines of levels‖; and in 1868 a valuable new map of Central Asia, in four sheets, was compiled and published. Preliminary charts of triangulation for the use of surveyors, and new maps of the Himalaya, are also in course of preparation, and many maps have been photo-zincographed. All this useful work is done under the immediate supervision of the Superintendent at

---

* One copy at the India Office and another at Calcutta.

† See page 131.

‡ See "Professional Papers on Indian Engineering," vol. v., p. 305.

§ "Auxiliary Tables to facilitate the Calculations of the Survey Department" (Dehra Doon, 1868).

‖ See page 119 (*note*).

his head quarters, and is independent of the more voluminous labors of the Surveyor General at Calcutta, whose operations will be the subject of the next section.

The magnificent work, so ably commenced by Colonel Lambton in the first year of the century, is now nearly completed. The topographical surveying of the present day is so much more accurate than it was in Lambton's, or even in Everest's time, that a smaller amount of triangulation suffices as its basis. When the remainder of the Beder Series, that from the west coast to Bangalore, the continuation of the Jubbulpoor Series to the southward, and some revisions of old work, are finished, there will be nothing more left to do in India Proper. In Burmah there will be further triangulation, and probably two bases to measure; and, in some future day, the great arc will doubtless be carried northward over the mountain barriers to the shores of the Arctic ocean. A preliminary approximate series would extend our geographical knowledge of Central Asia, while it would establish the practicability of a final measurement. Sir George Everest looked forward to an arc of the meridian extending from Cape Comorin to the northern shore of Siberia, as the final achievement by which his successors would complete his labours.*

Colonel Walker, the fourth in succession of the great surveyors who have superintended this most difficult and important work, will, in all human probability, have the high honour and satisfaction of being at his post when it is completed. It is, and has been, a very noble band, that body of surveyors who have been trained and have worked under Lambton, Everest, Waugh and Walker. It is no small honour to be at their head. These men must combine the knowledge and habits of thought of a Cambridge wrangler with the energy, resource, and presence of mind of an explorer or a backwoodsman, and they must add to this the gallantry and devotion which inspire the leader of a forlorn hope. The danger of service in the jungles and swamps of India, with the attendant anxiety and incessant work, is greater than that encountered on a battle field; the per-centage of deaths is larger; while the sort of courage that is required is of a far higher order. The story of the Great Trigonometrical Survey, when fitly told, will form one of the proudest pages in the history of English domination in the east.

---

* See the preface to "An account of the measurement of two sections of the meridional arc of India," p. 7.

Since Sir Andrew Waugh's time, the manuscript volumes containing the Superintendent's reports and the triangulations for each series have not been forwarded to the India Office. Preliminary charts containing all requisite data for Topographical Surveyors and Geographers are published by photo-zincography annually, but the reports are kept back until the whole of the results can be printed in a final and complete form. A considerable portion of the original observations is already in the press.

Colonel Walker has completed the first volume of this series, being a history of the Great Trigonometrical Survey of India, which includes an introductory account of the early operations of the Survey during the period 1800–30; and sections on the standards of measure and on the measurement of base lines. The complete work will consist of about twenty volumes.* Accounts of Colonel Walker's work are to be found in his annual printed Reports, and in the abstracts of them which he has from time to time communicated to the Journal of the Asiatic Society (Bengal.)† The progress of the Survey is noticed in the anniversary addresses of the President of the Royal Geographical Society, and there are articles on the Survey in the Calcutta Review for 1863,‡ and in the Quarterly Journal of Science for October 1870, the latter by F.C. Danvers, Esq.

The annual reports by Colonel Walker, in the Geographical Department of the India Office, are as follows:—

1. Report on the operations of the Great Trigonometrical Survey of India, 1862–63. An abstract of this report is also given in vol. i., p. 180, of the "Professional Papers on Indian Engineering" (Roorkee) 1863.

2. Report on the operations of the Great Trigonometrical Survey of India, 1863–64.

3.	"	"	"	1864–65.
4.	"	"	"	1865–66.
5.	"	"	"	1866–67.
6.	"	"	"	1867–68.
7.	"	"	"	1868–69.

* "Account of the operations of the Great Trigonometrical Survey of India," vol. i. By Colonel J. T. Walker, R.E., F.R.S., Superintendent of the Survey. (Dehra Doon, 1870.)

† Vol. xxxii., (1863,) p. 111. Vol. xxxi. (1862,) p. 32.

‡ Vol. xxxviii., No. 75.

X.—FOURTH PERIOD OF THE TOPOGRAPHICAL SURVEYS.

1862–70.

COLONEL THUILLIER AND THE REVENUE AND TOPOGRAPHICAL SURVEYS.

Colonel Thuillier succeeded Sir Andrew Waugh as Surveyor General of India, on the 13th of March 1861. Henry E. Landor Thuillier entered the Bengal Artillery in 1832, and joined the surveying service in 1836. He had been Sir Andrew's Deputy in charge of the office at Calcutta since 1847, and during those fifteen years the general usefulness of the surveying operations had been increased a hundredfold. Thuillier's energy and talent for organization had been devoted alike to improving the system of surveying in the field, and making its results more readily accessible to the public. In all this he was well supported by his chief. In one of his early reports Colonel Thuillier "records his sense of the "valuable and hearty support always rendered by Sir Andrew "Waugh's method of conducting the great triangulation to meet "the necessities and requirements of the Revenue Survey, and of "his forethought and great consideration for the important objects "of the extension of the geographical knowledge of India."

The revival of the Revenue and Topographical Surveys may be dated from the appointment of Colonel Thuillier, at the end of the first Punjáb war in 1847. Since that date they have been conducted with ever increasing efficiency, and with annually improving arrangements for extending the sphere of their usefulness. The previous history of the surveys will have shown that the great triangulation has, as a rule, been prosecuted by a distinct staff, and separate from the operations of filling in details for the maps. Men trained for the strictly scientific work of the great triangulation are not always adapted for the detail surveys, or vice versâ, while the two classes of operations must be conducted on distinct principles.* The revenue and topographical surveys must be undertaken with reference to the public requirements, while the triangulation is regularly proceeded with on a fixed plan. But it has always been Colonel Thuillier's care to follow in the track of the different trigonometrical series, and thus have the advantage of fixed stations on which to base his detail surveys.

---

* See pages 47 and 86.

The Revenue Branch conducts a capital detail survey of all British revenue paying districts on a scale of four inches to the mile, showing the limits of every village community. The operations of this branch are much influenced by local civil requirements, are under local Governments, and subject to local budgets. The Topographical Surveys, on the other hand, usually on the scale of one inch to the mile, are simply intended for Native States or non-regulation British districts of a wild rugged character and small value, as regards revenue, where only a military map on a smaller scale is required. Both are carefully connected with the great triangulation; the revenue by a chain and theodolite system of measurement fixing all boundaries of estates and villages; the topographical by breaking up the large triangles into minor triangulations with sides sufficiently short to give bases for plane table sketching. The chain is not generally used by the Topographical Surveyor because it is politically obnoxious to independent tribes, and is looked upon as the sure harbinger of loss of territory. The number of points used by the surveyor with the plane table in delineating the ground is the criterion of the value of his survey;* and lines are run across the ground, either with chain or perambulator, to test the accuracy of the work, by traverse.

The Revenue Surveyors are at work in several districts of the Bengal Presidency, turning out about 15,000 to 20,000 square miles a year.

The Topographical Surveys, when Colonel Thuillier took charge in 1861, consisted of four parties in Central India, the Nizam's Territory, Ganjam, and Chota Nagpore, comprising a total area of 43,316 square miles. When this was completed, there still remained 319,338 square miles to be done in the Native States, and 21,134 in the wild hills of Eastern Bengal. In 1862 a fifth party was organized to survey Rewah.

In 1864, after 18 years of uninterrupted and arduous service in charge of the Surveyor General's Office at Calcutta, Colonel Thuillier

* The work is divided into sections, 15 minutes in latitude and longitude containing 270 square miles. The surveyor fills in the details round the trigonometrical points already projected on his plane table, and at each trigonometrical station he draws a series of rays to neighbouring objects, the positions of which are determined by intersection. The points of intersection are then visited, and a similar process is gone through. The position of each detail need not be more than $\frac{1}{50}$ of an inch in error on the maps, but there is often great difficulty when the points are concealed from each other by jungle.

went home for 20 months on sick leave, Colonel Walker officiating for him as Surveyor General and Superintendent of the Topographical Surveys, and Colonel Gastrell as Superintendent of the Revenue Survey.

During the two seasons, 1864-66, Captain Melville was at work in Central India. Mr. Mulheran was at work in the upper Godavery district, in the midst of heavy forest and tangled underwood. He fell a victim to his own unceasing exertions in the survey of the Nirmul jungles, a most pestilential tract on the Wurda and Godavery rivers; and added one more to the long list of zealous and devoted surveyors who have laid down their lives in the service of their country.

Colonel Saxton continued his severe work in Ganjam and Orissa, regions of a uniformly deadly and malarious nature, where the majority of the officers who were associated with him had perished. The survey in Chota Nagpore was conducted by Captain Depree, and that in Rewah and Bundelcund was under Captain Murray. Godwin Austen, the topographer of the lofty region of the Pangong lake, had accompanied Mr. Eden's Bhotan mission, and had served with the Dooar field force. He now headed a sixth topographical party, to survey the forest covered and pestilential Garrows, the Cossyah and Jynteah hills, Nowgong, and North Cachar.

The Pegu Survey is distinct from these, and is on a scale of four miles to the inch. The survey was commenced in about 1854; but when Captain Fitzroy took charge, in 1860, he rejected the work executed by his predecessors, and commenced *de novo*, which gave rise to considerable delay. In 1865, Captain Edgcome, the Principal of the Madras College of Civil Engineering, took charge of the Pegu Survey. He completed the field work, constructed *teik* or district maps on a one-inch scale, besides the quarter-inch geographical map, and prepared a memoir containing much valuable statistical information.

Colonel Thuillier returned to India, and resumed charge on the 12th of December 1866; but he was again in England from the 10th of May 1868 to the 7th of January 1869, when his duties were shared by Colonel Walker, Colonel Gastrell, and Captain Montgomerie. On the latter occasion Colonel Thuillier was on duty, maturing arrangements for the transfer of the engraving of the sheets of the Indian Atlas from London to his own office at Calcutta.

During the two last seasons there have been seven parties of topographical surveyors in the field in Rajpootana, the Central

Provinces, and the wild region on the N.E. frontier. The country under survey embraces every variety of ground, from the arid and sandy tracts of Beekaneer to the mountains of Cossyah and Jynteah, which are deluged with a rainfall of 600 inches in the year. The surveyors penetrate into the wildest and most secluded spots. In the Central Provinces they came upon a tract utterly devastated by a tigress which had killed 50 people, and driven the inhabitants from 13 villages. In many parts they traversed regions hitherto not only unmapped but unknown. Their system of work is suited to native states; their operations with the theodolite and plane table, and no chain, excite little jealousy, and they usually succeed in establishing friendly relations with the wildest hill tribes.

The last Revenue Survey Report, that of 1868–69, shows an area of 19,369 square miles surveyed by 17 parties,* at a total cost of Rs. 3,90,314. The revenue surveys are divided into an upper and lower circle; the former comprising the North-West and Central Provinces, Oude, Punjab, and Sinde, under Colonel Gastrell, and the latter including the Lower Provinces and British Burmah, under Van Reuen.

Colonel Johnstone, of the Punjab Frontier Survey, accompanied the Huzara Field Force in October 1868 and following months, with his staff of surveyors, and completed a sketch map of 400 square miles of hitherto unexplored and unknown country during the expedition, resuming his regular duties on its return. The work was amongst glaciers and mountains of perpetual snow. Johnstone fixed stations on peaks that had hitherto been pronounced impracticable, and made an important geographical discovery respecting the true course of the Indus, between Astor and the Black Mountain.

The Sinde Revenue Survey was commenced in 1855–56, and will be completed in 1869–70. During 1868–69 about 6,000 square miles were surveyed in the plain of Omercote, and in Thurr and Parkur. All that remains, to complete this survey, is the Shahbunder district.†

* Four in the Central Provinces, one in Oude, two in N.W. Provinces, one in the Punjab, one in Sinde, six in Lower Provinces, one in Burmah, and one in Punjab cantonments.

† Work completed:

Seonee,	commenced	1865,	finished	1869.
Kheree,	„	1865	„	1869.
Thurr & Parkur	„	1862	„	1869.
Huzara	„	1865	„	1869.
Camroop	„	1865	„	1869.
East Dooars	„	1867	„	1869.
Palamow	„	1863	„	1869.

Six parties have been at work, during 1868-69, in the Lower Provinces, chiefly in Cooch Behar, and in the Camroop and Luckimpoor districts of Assam. In Luckimpoor Lieutenant Barron had most severe work, cutting his way through dense jungles with imported labor, and his health has suffered much by it. His services have been specially recognised in a despatch from the Secretary of State.

Since Colonel Thuillier took charge of the office at Calcutta in 1847, down to 1869, the out-turn of work has been as follows:—

	Square Miles surveyed.	Cost.
(1836-69) Topographical Surveys	97,028	Rs. 35,14,281
(1846-69) Revenue - -	400,162	1,15,14,371
	597,190	Rs. 1,50,28,652

A large office establishment is required for the reduction, compilation, and publication of such a mass of geographical materials; and in its efficient management the great talent for organization which distinguishes Colonel Thuillier has perhaps been most conspicuously displayed. Certainly it is in the system by which he year by year extends and increases the general usefulness of the surveys, by making their results rapidly and easily accessible, that his services have borne most fruit.

In the Surveyor General's office at Calcutta there is a drawing and compiling, a lithographic, and a photographic branch. The publishing branch may be said to have been completely formed by Colonel Thuillier. Originally there was only one small lithographic press, but during the term of Colonel Thuillier's tenure of office, the establishment has been gradually increased, until now the printing branch has 20 presses continually at work, besides three small type presses for departmental forms. In addition to the map printing, all kinds of work are executed, as the different Government Departments indent on the Surveyor General's Office to print any diagrams, sketches, or illustrations that they may require to accompany reports. It is worthy of remark that the first postage stamps ever used in India were lithographed at the Surveyor General's office. Until within the last few years, all the maps of the Indian Survey, (with the exception of the Atlas sheets,) were put on to stone by hand drawing on transfer paper, a very laborious process, and very liable to error, particularly when executed by natives who cannot read English, and who simply copy what they do not understand. The climate of Calcutta also militates very much against the successful transfer from paper to stone. Latterly natives, who have acquired a small knowledge of English, have been easily attainable, and apprentices have been carefully trained to write on stone, and thus better and more certain results are obtained.

The greatest advance of all was the introduction of photo-zincography into the office. The credit of having first introduced the process into India is due to Mr. Hennessey of the Great Trigonometrical Survey,* and the first photo-zincograph was executed by himself in the office of the Superintendent at Dehra Doon. Before Mr. Hennessey's return to India in 1865, maps had been copied by photography both in the office at Calcutta and in that at Dehra Doon. Colonel Thuillier had two serjeants employed in his office, who were sent out, after receiving instruction in photo-zincography at the Ordnance Survey office at Southampton, but their attempts were not very satisfactory. Photo-zincography cannot be said to have been fairly introduced into Calcutta until 1866, when survey officers, who had been trained in the process under Mr. Hennessey, were available to take charge of this branch. Since that year progress has been steadily made, the establishment has been enlarged, and the out-turn of work, already enormous, is yearly increasing. It must be remembered that the great demand in India is not for highly finished, but for rough accurate maps, published as soon after survey as possible. By means of photo-zincography the results of the surveys are immediately made available for general use. Captain Melville and Lieutenant Waterhouse have ably superintended this department,† and during the year 1868-69 as many as 44,092 copies of maps were struck off. In the same year 97,647 were lithographed; so that the total out-turn amounted to 141,739 maps. The demand, both from official‡ and general sources, is in proportion to the supply, and these branches are not only self-paying but remunerative. The value of the work turned out by the

---

* See page 123.

† See "Report on the Cartographic Applications of Photography, and notes on the European and Indian Surveys, by Lieutenant J. Waterhouse, R.A." (Calcutta, 1870.)

‡ 21,848 maps supplied.

litho and photo-zincographic branches very considerably exceeds the cost of the working expenses, and as most of the initial expenditure has been incurred, the returns will probably increase year by year.

Colonel Thuillier has compiled and published many useful general maps; among which may be mentioned his small scale maps of India; his new map of India, on a scale of 32 miles to an inch; his eight sheet map of the Punjab; his Punjab and its dependencies, in four sections, on a scale of 16 miles to an inch; and his maps of Sinde and Oude.

In concluding this very inadequate sketch of the recent operations of the Revenue and Topographical Surveyors, it will be well to glance at what remains to be done in India under this head.

Since the appointment of Colonel Thuillier in 1847 the work has been thoroughly well done, and there are excellent surveys of the Punjab, Oude, Sinde, the Lower Provinces, and of all the districts included in the operations of his parties. But unfortunately the surveys of the North-West Provinces were executed before his time. It will be remembered that, at the conference of surveyors held at Allahabad in 1834, it was resolved to sacrifice everything to cheapness and rapidity of execution.* The consequences of this resolution have been most disastrous. The surveys of the North-West Provinces were made at a galloping rate each season, owing to the pressure of the revenue officers, who wanted to complete the settlement. The result was, that the maps were the merest and most inaccurate skeletons, while topographical details were altogether omitted. The surveys were confined to the actual definition of village boundaries, and the work on opposite sides of a river was never even connected. As geographical material, they are perfectly useless, and there is now no reliable map of the North-West Provinces for engineering or local purposes. These were the materials from which the geographical maps on a scale of four miles to the inch were lithographed at Allahabad, after having been reduced by native draftsmen. They have no trigonometrical points, and no basis of any kind; yet from these maps the sheets of the Indian Atlas have been filled up.

Most of the original village plans, bound up in folio volumes, were destroyed in the mutinies; but those of twelve districts were saved, and deposited in the Surveyor General's office at Calcutta.

---

* See page 83.

The time has now arrived for a second settlement of the North-West Provinces, and the local Government proposed to dispense with a proper survey, because they thought that the *khusrah* or measurement of fields by a native *ameen* was so accurate that nothing more was required; and that, if anything further was wanted for geographical purposes, a bare survey like that made in the native states would suffice. Thus we are threatened with a repetition of the lamentable and short-sighted mistake that was made thirty years ago.*

In reality the *khusrah* measurements, however carefully made, having no basis or fixed points, must necessarily have an ever accumulating error. In the Revenue Survey the maximum error allowed is half an acre per cent., and that is considered bad work; while the *khusrah* error, when unchecked, is from 3 to 7 per cent. The regular surveys check the gross village areas, and furnish reliable village maps on a scale of 4 inches, and district and pergunnah maps of 1 inch to the mile. It is most surprising that such a proposal as to dispense with accurate surveys should have been made in these days, when it is well known that it would be ridiculous to attempt to use the old revenue skeleton maps of the North-West Provinces as a basis on which to work for preparing any engineering project, or indeed for any useful purpose.

A good survey of the North-West Provinces, similar to those of other districts already mapped, will have to be executed; and the *khusrah* or field measurements ought to be taken out of the hands of the native ameens, and handed over to the professional surveyors, so that the whole operation may proceed on one regular and scientific system.

The Madras Revenue Survey has been steadily progressing, under the superintendence of Colonel Priestley, since 1856, and it has the great triangulations as its basis. It consists of an admirable cadastral field survey on a scale of 16 inches to the mile for every village in British revenue paying districts, and many thousands of square miles are completed. The maps are well drawn, and are lithographed very shortly after survey. But all tracts of lands which are held by rent-free tenures were omitted until quite recently. Now, however, these gaps have been ordered to be filled in, by means of a topographical survey on a moderate scale; so that the materials for compiling geographical maps will be complete.

---

* See page 103 for an account of the consequences of adopting a native system of surveying in the Punjab.

The reduction of the results of the Madras Survey to maps of convenient size is making some progress. But the truth is that Colonel Priestley and his staff have as much to do as they can possibly get through, and there is no machinery for utilizing their work for geographical purposes. There can now be no doubt that the abolition of the office of Deputy Surveyor General at Madras, in 1834, was a great mistake. The beautiful old Military Institute Maps of the early part of the century remain in manuscript. They were used for the sheets of the Indian Atlas, but have never been published on their own most useful scale of an inch to a mile. Since those maps were drawn, geographical interests have somewhat languished in the Madras Presidency. Yet a good deal has been done at various times. Colonel Scott, the Quartermaster General of the Madras army, compiled an excellent map of the Presidency on two sheets, on a scale of 24 miles to the inch, in 1863. Large maps of the Presidency on a scale of 8 miles to the inch, showing all the works of irrigation, finished and in progress, have been compiled for the Secretary of State, from information supplied by the superintending engineers, in 1858, 59, 60, 63, 64, and 65. In 1862 a map showing the extent of cotton cultivation, on a scale of 24 miles to the inch, was published to illustrate the official cotton hand-book. Maps of the talooks have also been compiled from the old surveys on a scale of two miles to an inch, and published, but they are meagre, and contain few of the names given on the original maps. A map of the Tanjore irrigation channels, of the Denkanicotta range, showing the Salem forests, some road maps, and a few others, have also been engraved. But much remains to be done. The Revenue Surveys should be reduced, and compiled on a scale of 4 miles to the inch, and results of general utility should thus be secured, from the excellent work of the surveyors.

District maps of Kurnool, S. Arcot, Tinnevelly, and Vizagapatam, 17 talook maps, 8 maps of parts of the town of Madras, 76 plans of Wynaad coffee estates, and 5,650 village maps were on the way to the Geographical Department of the India Office, from the Madras Government, in January 1871.

A minute revenue survey of the Bombay collectorates was commenced in about 1836 by Major Wingate and Mr. Goldsmid, of the Civil Service, the latter aiding in the revenue portion. Major Wingate carefully elaborated the original design of the Survey. It consists of a cadastral measurement of fields, by means of the cross staff and chain;* but this operation has not, and, I believe, cannot be generalized and reduced into a convenient scale, on a proper basis. There is no basis to build upon, and when any attempt is made to join the component parts of this field survey together nothing but failure results.

There is a quartermaster general's map of the Presidency on a scale of 20 miles to the inch, but this is all that exists of nearly half the entire area of the Presidency, for the rough lithographed maps of districts and collectorates are so badly executed, and so meagre as regards details, that they are of little use.

The consequence is, that the Baroda and Ahmedabad Railway, and the Great Indian Peninsula Railway, south of the Taptee, exist on the maps solely by guess work.

The triangulation of the Great Trigonometrical Survey is now well extended over the Bombay Presidency as a basis; and it is, therefore, much to be regretted that, as in Madras, the field surveys were not connected with it, so as merely to require reduction to be made useful for general geographical purposes. As it is, sixteen sheets of the Indian Atlas, belonging to the Bombay Presidency, remain unpublished.

I understand that it would now be impossible to connect the Bombay field surveys with the Great Trigonometrical points. When the lands of a village have been surveyed by cross staff and chain, and mapped, the work is tested by theodolite; but the points of the Great Trigonometrical Survey form no part either of survey or proof. Another defect is the absence of topographical features, such as hills, in the maps, though the rivers and streams are partially entered. The Bombay field survey is available for revenue purposes only.

The state of the case, as regards Bombay, is at present as follows. Sind has been surveyed by Colonel Thuillier's parties, Kattywar and Guzerat have been taken in hand by Colonel Walker, and the North Concan is fairly well surveyed. There remain about 80,000 square miles to be surveyed by future parties, working on the basis of the great triangulation. But the parties do not exist, and the work has not yet been commenced.

---

* See a paper "On the Principles and Practice of the Bombay Revenue Survey," by Lieutenant-Colonel A. Cowper, R.E. (1866), in the "Professional Papers on Indian Engineering," vol. iii., p. 184.

One excellent and most creditable piece of work, connected with the Bombay Presidency, has just been completed. This is the new survey of the island and city of Bombay by Lieut.-Colonel Laughton, for the municipality, some sheets of which have been photozincographed. They are to be engraved on scales of 40 and 100 feet to an inch.*

There may be various desultory Surveys in existence, but there is a pressing necessity for a more systematic organization of the Surveys in the Bombay Presidency, first to utilize all existing materials, and to compile a good map of the Presidency from them, and afterwards to superintend the surveying operations of the future.

Thus there is a vast field for future work in India, in the North-West Provinces, in Madras and in Bombay; besides that of parties still progressing in Central India and Eastern Bengal. Yet year by year a good out-turn of work is produced; the system is admirable, and ere many decades have passed the whole structure of accurate triangulation will be clothed with useful and reliable topographical detail.

The history of Colonel Thuillier's work is to be found in his own annual reports. Those now in the Geographical Department of the India Office are as follows:—

1. Report of the Revenue Surveys (*Lower Provinces*), 1854–55.
2. " " " (" "), 1856–57.
3. " " " (*N. W. P., Punjab, Sind*), 1856–57.
4. " " " (" "), 1857–58.
5. General Report of the Revenue Surveys, 1858–61.
6. Report of the Revenue Surveys (*Lower Provinces*), 1861–62.
7. " " " (*Upper Provinces*), 1864–65.
8. General Report of the Revenue Surveys, 1865–66.
9. Report of the Revenue Surveys (*Upper Circle*), 1866–67.
10. " " " ("), 1868–69.
11. " " " (*Lower Provinces*), 1868–69.
12. General Report on the Topographical Surveys, 1860–62.
13. " " " " 1862–63.
14. " " Topographical and Revenue Surveys, 1863–64.

* See the Annual Reports of the Municipal Commissioner of Bombay, 1867, p. 20; 1868 p. 13; 1869 p. 13.

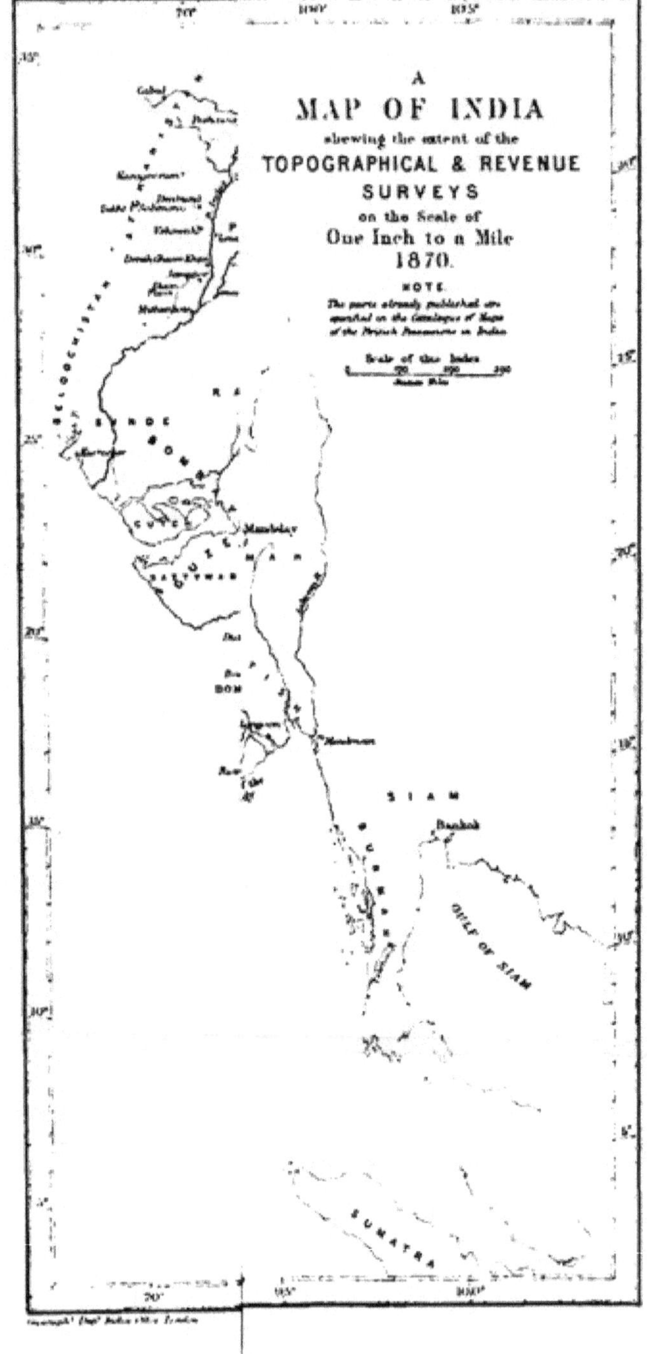

A
MAP OF INDIA
shewing the extent of the
TOPOGRAPHICAL & REVENUE
SURVEYS
on the Scale of
One Inch to a Mile
1870.
NOTE
SYNDE
CUTCH
SIAM
Bankok
GULF OF SIAM
SUMATRA

15. Topographical Surveys (With Colonel Walker's G. T. S. Report), 1864–65.

16. „ „ („ „ „), 1865–66.

17. General Report on the Topographical Surveys, 1866–67.

18. „ „ „ „ , 1867–68.

19. „ „ „ „ , 1868–69.

See also "Selections from the Records of the Government of India (Home Department)," No. LXXIV. (1869).

For details of the mode of working, see "Report on the Cartographic applications of photography, &c.," printed in Calcutta in 1870; and prepared by Lieutenant Waterhouse, under the direction of Colonel Thuillier.

XI.—SUPPLY OF INSTRUMENTS FOR THE INDIAN SURVEYS.

The superiority of modern surveys rests mainly on the perfection to which the manufacture of instruments has attained. Observers in the old days were as careful and thoughtful, but this availed them little without the needful appliances. What could the most learned Hindoo astronomer achieve with such instruments as Sir Robert Barker found on that terrace at Benares in 1777?—Quadrants with a 20-foot radius, and the arc carved on a stone wall, so that to take an angle a Brahman, how high soever his caste, must have been slung in a bowline knot, and hoisted up and down with guys. Rough approximations would be all that an observer with such an instrument could hope for.*

When Englishmen became the rulers in India, the instruments they brought with them were certainly improvements on the wonderful structures in the observatories at Delhi and Benares; but at first the difference was not so very great. Reuben Burrow, in starting upon a Government survey, had to borrow his tools anyhow, and complained that among them he got a wretched quadrant from Captain Ritchie. It was probably such an instrument as Bruce took with him to Abyssinia, which it required four men to carry.

Colonel Lambton was in constant difficulties with his instruments, for, though he was eventually provided with the best that the artists of that period could produce, he had no means of getting repairs done, and no trusty coadjutor in England to refer to, until Captain Kater went home. It will be remembered how, when the guy carried away, and the great theodolite was violently bumped against the tower of the pagoda at Tanjore, Lambton shut himself up in a tent for weeks, and repaired the damage with his own hands. When, in the evening of his days, difficulties arose respecting the measuring chains,† he felt the want of a proper system for the supply and

* "An account of the Bramin's Observatory" at Benares, by Sir Robert Barker (May 1777). Philosophical Transactions, vol. 69, pt. 2. See also "Benares, Ancient and Modern," by FitzEdward Hall.

† The first bases were measured with wooden rods. Colonel Roy, after a careful series of experiments on the dilatation of various bodies, adopted glass tubes 20 feet long. Then the 100-foot steel chains came into use; and finally the compensation bars.

testing of instruments. In those days it was the custom of the service, until the first Burmese war, for officers to supply their own instruments. Colonel Hodgson, when he was surveying, had instruments and books of his own to the value of Rs. 13,000, and nothing belonging to Government. As Surveyor General he considered this to be a better system than the supply by contract, and declared that the instruments sent out for the Revenue Survey of 1821, by contract, were not such as a good observer would consent to use.

Everest saw these evils, and provided a remedy. He personally superintended every detail in the construction of his instruments while he was in England, watching their progress day after day, and examining them at every stage. When he returned to India with them in 1830, he took an accomplished maker, Mr. Barrow, out with him, and established a mathematical instrument manufactory at Calcutta. Yet even these precautions were insufficient, and when Colonel Everest began to observe with the large astronomical circle he found that it was top heavy from faults in the construction, and unreliable. Again the Superintendent of the Survey was thrown upon his own resources, and, with the aid of Syud Mohsin, invented and applied the remedy with his own hands.*

Mr. Barrow was established at the head of a useful factory at Calcutta, where instruments of all kinds could be repaired, and much good work done. Indeed the second great theodolite, known as Barrow's theodolite, which has measured the angles of several of the Trigonometrical Series, was made at the mathematical instrument manufactory, under Colonel Everest's direction. The graduation of the circle was performed by Mr. Barrow, and the instrument was built out of old musket barrels, and parts of Colonel Lambton's trusty old theodolite that was damaged by a blow against the pagoda at Tanjore. Lambton's old zenith sector is laid up in ordinary at Calcutta. When Mr. Barrow retired he was succeeded by Syud Mohsin, a native of Arcot, possessed of great mechanical talent. Colonel Everest, like most men of genius, had a sort of intuitive perception in selecting the right man, and at once singled out Syud Mohsin as an able mechanician. He was right. This native of India, though he could not read English, would have taken a leading place even among European instrument makers. When he died

* See page 74.

his place was taken by a mechanician from Mr. Cooke's establishment at York, and the factory continues to turn out plenty of useful work.

But all important instruments, and all that require nicety and accuracy in their construction, must still be made in Europe; and, moreover, they must have the benefit of scientific supervision of the highest order if they are to prove efficient in such a service as the Indian Survey. It was obvious that the Superintendent of the Survey could only occasionally be in England, at intervals of several years, while the supervision of instruments was a constant requirement.

In 1862 the supply of a complete new set of instruments was sanctioned for the Great Trigonometrical Survey, and in the following year the importance of having all instruments for India subjected to special scientific examination became apparent.

It would be impossible to find half a dozen men in England who combine the experience of India, knowledge of the highest branches of mechanical science, fertility of resource, and inventive genius, which are required in the officer to whom the superintendence of the manufactory of instruments for the Indian Surveys can be properly entrusted. Most fortunately the services of Colonel Strange were secured, an officer who possesses all these qualifications. Colonel Strange was a member of the Great Trigonometrical Survey from 1847 to 1860. It will be remembered that he conducted the Western Longitudinal Series, superintended the measurement of the Kurrachee base, and for a short time was in charge of the Coast Series. He thus had had considerable practical experience in trigonometrical surveying, while his mechanical genius, and knowledge of mathematical, geodetical, and astronomical instruments, is not surpassed by any man in England.

In 1862 the Secretary of State for India entrusted Colonel Strange with the task of designing and superintending the construction of a set of geodetical and astronomical instruments of the first order, for the Great Trigonometrical Survey; and in 1863 he was appointed to examine and test all instruments ordered for India.

A set of instruments was required for the efficient discharge of his duties, and a special observatory for testing was an absolute necessity. The provision of these requisites was sanctioned in 1864 and 1865, and the observatory was erected at the warehouse of the Store Department of the India Office in Belvidere Road (Lambeth), where Colonel Strange's office was established.

The site of the observatory at Lambeth is on the banks of the Thames, close to a railway, and is exposed to much vibratory motion; while it is essential to secure rest and complete isolation for the proper examination of astronomical and geodetical instruments. Colonel Strange found it necessary to pierce right through the London clay, and established a basis on the underlying gravel, in order to ensure stability for his instruments during the process of testing.

For this purpose twelve screw piles were wormed into the gravel, which here lies 24 feet below the surface of the London clay. Broad heads of cast iron were keyed upon the top of the piles; and stone slabs were laid on the pile heads, the space beneath being filled in for a depth of three feet with concrete cement. A circular platform of brick work was built on the flag stones. A solid column of masonry was then erected in the centre, and two semi-circular segments of wall were raised round the circumference. In order to secure complete isolation between the observer and the instruments resting on the piled foundation, the wooden flooring, between the central column and the circular wall, lies upon beams which are supported from beyond the brick work built over the piles. The observer thus walks on the floor, without shaking, or affecting in any way, the instruments on the wall or column. The floor is reached by a flight of stairs.

This arrangement is on the principle designed by Sir George Everest for the towers of observation in India, a central column for the instrument, with complete isolation for the observer.

For the examination of graduated circles for taking horizontal angles, the instrument is placed on the central column. Four collimators are fixed on different parts of the circular wall. These are horizontal telescopes containing marks for observation. In one there are diagonally crossing spider threads, in another horizontally and vertically crossing threads, in a third an artificial star or speck of light. The angular intervals between the collimators are 30°, 60°, 120°, and 150°; an arrangement which admits of twelve different angles being taken, by varying the sets of collimators. The positions of the collimators themselves also admit of alteration. The angles between them must have exactly the same values, whichever part of the circle is employed. This forms a severe and searching test.

There are contrivances in the roof of the observatory for enabling observations of celestial bodies to be taken; and verticle circles are tested, when necessary, by observing stars as they pass the meridian.

There are two clocks, built into the circular wall, one for mean, the other for sidereal time, the mean time clock being connected by electric wires with Greenwich.

The methods for testing spirit levels and telescopes to small surveying instruments are equally complete and searching. These operations are performed in the observatory.

In another room, in the body of the building, are the standard barometer and thermometer. They have been compared at the observatories at Kew and Greenwich, and it is an important fact that the two comparisons do not exactly agree. So that there is no fixed standard in England to which observations can be referred, a deficiency which Colonel Strange has brought to the notice of the Royal Society; but no steps have yet been taken to remedy this defect in physical science. Colonel Strange, therefore, gives the error on both for every instrument that passes, and is sent out to India.

Every kind of meteorological instrument is tested and examined. There is a most ingenious contrivance for comparing the aneroids. They are placed in a reservoir connected with the receiver of an air pump in such a way that the channel of communication is crossed by a diaphragm of porous porcelain. When the receiver of the air-pump is exhausted to a certain degree, the exhaustion of the reservoir containing the aneroids goes on very gradually through the porcelain. Thus the action of the instrument is exactly the same as it would be in the pocket of a man slowly ascending a mountain. At every half inch of change the aneroid is compared with an accurate mercurial barometer.*

As many as 7,000 instruments of more than a hundred different kinds are examined yearly, and the number is largely on the increase.† The system, ably and thoroughly worked out by its talented founder and inventor, is a complete success.

---

* See an article by Dr. Mann, in the "Quarterly Journal of Science," entitled "The Lambeth Observatory," which gives an excellent popular account of Colonel Strange's operations. The article is also printed in "Scientific Opinion," in the numbers for July 21st and 28th, and August 4th, 1869.

† It is curious to compare the return of instruments in store in the office of the Surveyor General and in use in the surveys, which was drawn up by Colonel Hodgson in 1828, with Colonel Strange's Return, showing the number of instruments ordered in 1868 and 1869.

The following system has been adopted by Colonel Strange. All pattern instruments have been abolished, for he considers patterns to be an obstacle to improvement, and no two batches of important instruments have been sent out by him which have been identical in construction. But the abolition of patterns adds enormously to his labour, and keeps the inventive faculty constantly on the stretch. A sufficient amount of competition, both in price and quality, is ensured by employing at least two makers for each separate class of instruments. At the same time competition in price has been abolished. This was formerly the chief, if not the only competition relied on, and the consequence was that the prices became such as no really good conscientious maker could compete with. The supply thus fell into fifth-rate hands. The selection of makers is made chiefly with reference to two points, character and general manufacturing power in the first place, and secondly special knowledge of particular branches of the profession. Thus makers of meteorological instruments are seldom distinguished for the excellence of their surveying instruments. All instruments are subjected to rigorous inspection, Colonel Strange's decision on them being accepted, in every contract, as final.

Colonel Strange's most absorbing work has been the designing and superintendence of the construction of the grand new set of instruments for the Trigonometrical Survey. They consist of a great theodolite with a three-foot horizontal circle, and two zenith sectors, by Troughton and Simms; two five-foot transit instruments, and two smaller ones by Cooke of York; two 12-inch vertical circles by Repsold of Hamburgh; two galvanic chronographs for registering transit observations, by MM. Secretan and Hardy of Paris; and three astronomical clocks by Frodsham.

The five-foot transit instruments have very powerful telescopes of five inches clear aperture, with a hollow axis of aluminium bronze, cast in one piece. They are provided with four levels for rendering the axis horizontal; and there are peculiar methods for adjusting the axis vertically and azimuthally, the object sought being to exclude shake, obviate strain, and cause the expansions to take place from the centre outwards. These adjustments are exceedingly delicate in their action, and very stable.*

* "On a transit instrument and zenith sector, to be used on the Great Trigonometrical Survey of India, for the determination, respectively, of longitude and latitude," by Lieutenant Colonel A. Strange, F.R.S.—*Proceedings of the Royal Society, No. 90.* 1867.

The zenith sectors are designed by Colonel Strange, on a new plan, his endeavour being to combine maximum power with minimum weight. The weight is 595½ lbs. One of them is already in India, and Lieutenant Herschel, whose astronomical talent is inherited, was observing with it at the Coimbatore base in March 1870. His report is most satisfactory. He takes about 50 stars at each station, three times each; and 36 stars observed in six hours will suffice to give a result whose probable error will not be greater than ⅕ of a second. When he wrote, Lieutenant Herschel had taken about 1,200 zenith distances with the instrument. He says, "There can "be no better proof of forethought and efficiency of design and "execution in an instrument than that it allows of rapidity and "certainty and comfort in manipulation, and spares the observer "mental and physical distraction and distress. The graduation "seems to be almost perfect."

Such testimony must be most gratifying to the designer of the instrument, whose time had been so long absorbed by the trials and experiments to which it was necessary he should subject it, before its despatch to India.

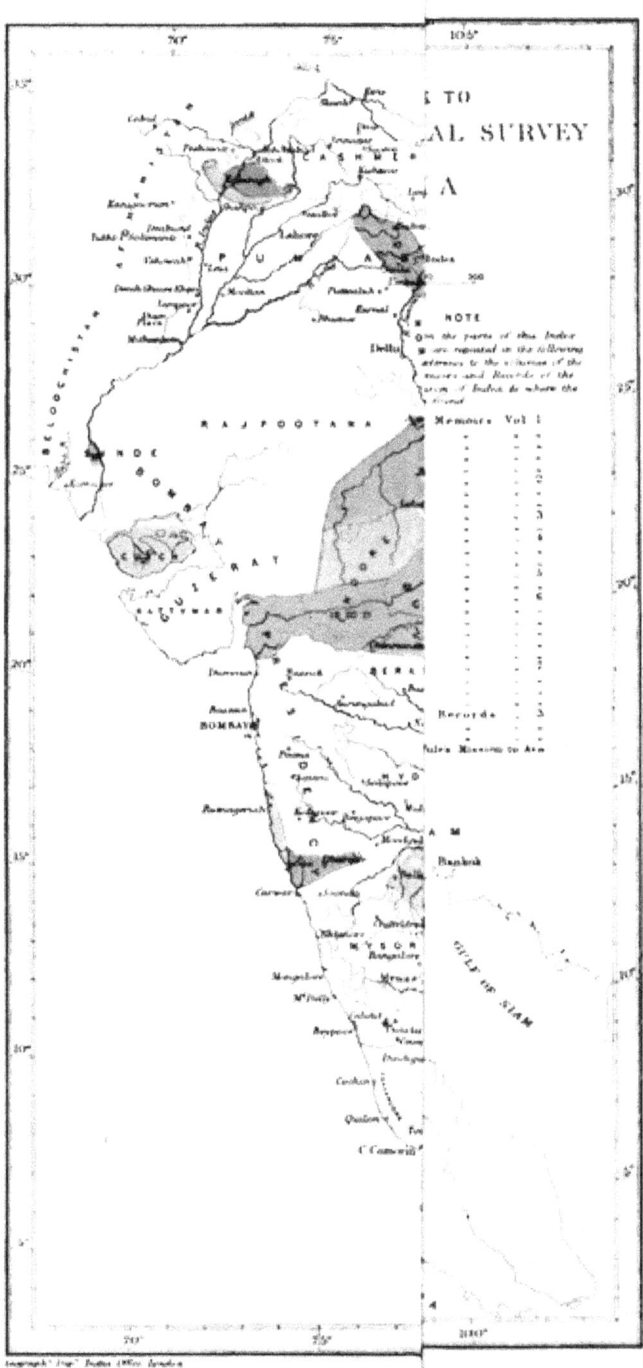
AL SURVEY
A
NOTE
Memoirs Vol 1
Records
RAJPOOTANA
CASHMERE
GUZERAT
BOMBAY
Delhi
GULF OF SIAM
C Comorin

XII.—THE GEOLOGICAL SURVEY OF INDIA.

A Geological Survey of India, regularly organized and working systematically, has not reached the fifteenth year of its existence. But ever since cultivated Englishmen have been at work in India, in the surveying, military, clerical, or medical services, there have been keen observers of everything worth observing; and the Indian rocks and minerals, viewed sometimes from a practical and at others from a purely scientific point of view, have had their due share of attention. Thus there have been many geological reports on various Indian districts in the years preceding the regular establishment of the Survey; but it will only be possible to enumerate those that are best known.

It will be remembered that when Sir George Everest first joined Colonel Lambton in 1818, he had with him, as a colleague, Dr. Voysey, who was surgeon and geologist to the Survey. This was probably the first official appointment of a geologist in India*, when the science was in its infancy, and Dr. Voysey's papers refer to the Wernerian and Huttonian systems. He was sent by Colonel Lambton to reconnoitre the country in advance, as far as Agra. He accompanied Everest in his severe work on the Godavery, and was one of the earliest writers on the rocks of the Deccan. He explored the Nalla-Malla mountains between Cummum in Cuddapah and Amrabad north of the Kistnah, and wrote an interesting account of the diamond mines in southern India. He also wrote papers on the building stones of Agra, and on petrified shells in the Taptee valley.† This able and zealous officer died of fever, on his way to Calcutta, in 1823.

* A Mr. Laidlaw was appointed as mineralogist and geologist to the Survey in Kumaon under Captain Webb (see page 64) in June 1817, but his allowances were stopped in 1819.—*Despatch from Lord Hastings*, Feb. 15th 1821. Laidlaw was a very able man, and is said to have been badly treated.

† See "Asiatic Researches," xviii., p. 187, and xv., p. 429 and p. 120. Dr. Voysey's Private Journal during 1819 was published in the "Journal of the Asiatic Society of Bengal," xix., p. 201. See also "Gleanings in Science," ii. p. 27 (Calcutta 1830). Dr. Voysey's 1st and 2nd Reports, on the geology of Hyderabad, are in the "Journal of the Asiatic Society," vol. ii., pp. 298 and 392. Dr. J. H. Carter speaks of "the sagacity, ability, and truthfulness which characterise Dr. Voysey's observations."

Dr. Voysey was followed by various other observers, who reported upon the rocks and minerals in different parts of India. Captain Dangerfield wrote a notice of the geology of Malwa, the result of careful observation, previous to 1823;* and Captain Franklin, while executing the topographical survey of Bundelcund in 1828, also reported on its geology.† Colonel Sleeman discovered fossils near Jubbulpoor in 1830,‡ Dr. Spilsbury made further collections,§ and the geological investigations of Sir Andrew Waugh and Major Renny Tailyour have already been mentioned. Lieutenant Finnis wrote upon the rocks of the country between Hoshungabad and Nagpore in 1834,‖ and in 1842 Dr. Adam described the rocks of Bundelcund, north of Spilsbury's work.¶ The Rev. S. Hislop also wrote various papers on the geology of the Nagpore country,** and in 1831 the Rev. R. Everest recorded his geological observations between Calcutta and Ghazeepoor. He also criticized Captain Franklin's work in a paper entitled "The Sandstones of India."†† James Prinsep wrote papers, in his journal, on the fossil bones found in the Jumna and Nerbudda valleys.‡‡ In 1854 Captain Nicolls made large and valuable collections of fossils from the inter-trappean lacustrine limestone deposits at Saugor, and from the Nerbudda valley; and Lieutenant Keatinge collected fossil ammonites and bivalves of what was supposed to be the Cretacean age, at Bagh, near the Nerbudda.

There are some geological notices on the rocks of the Rewah table land, and other parts of India, in the valuable work of M. Jacquemont.§§

---

* Published in 1823 in Sir John Malcolm's "Central India," ii. p. 320.

† Papers in the "Journal of the Asiatic Society of Bengal," and in the "Transactions of the Geological Society."

‡ "Journal of the Asiatic Society of Bengal," i. p. 456.

§ Ibid., ii. p. 549, and xiii. pt. ii. p. 765.

‖ Ibid., iii. p. 71, and xi. p. 20.

¶ Ibid., vol. xi., p. 392.

** There is an account of the inter-trappean freshwater and estuarine formations of the peninsula of India, by Mr. Hislop, in the "Quarterly Journal of the Geological Society," xvi. p. 154; and Professor Owen described the fossil cranium of a labyrinthodont reptile, obtained by Mr. Hislop from the sandstone of Mangoli, 60 miles south of Nagpore, in the "Quarterly Journal of the Geological Society," xi. pt. i. p. 37.

†† "Gleanings in Science," iii. p. 129 and 207.

‡‡ "Journal of the Asiatic Society of Bengal," iii. p. 396.

§§ "Voyage dans les Indes Orientales."

Attention was early turned to the coal bearing rocks of Bengal and the Nerbudda valley. Coal was known to exist in the Dammoodah valley so long ago as 1774, and was actually worked in 1777. Mr. Jones described the coal fields and opened mines in 1815,* and in 1830 there were several collieries in the Raneegunge country. Mr. Hislop wrote a paper on the age of the coal strata in Western Bengal, and a description of the coal fields in the Dammoodah valley by Mr. Homfray was published in 1842.† But the Raneegunge coal field was first carefully examined and reported on by Mr. Williams in 1845, who was appointed Geological Surveyor to the East India Company.‡ Mr. Williams died of jungle fever at Hazareebagh in 1849. The earliest explorer of the Nerbudda coal region was Colonel Ouseley, who tried a quantity of the coal in 1838.§

In 1833 Mr. Calder wrote a general review of the geology of India, which forms a sort of introduction to various geological papers in the 18th volume of "Asiatic Researches," by Franklin, Voysey, Hardie, Jones, and Coulthard.

The most interesting geological work in India, before the commencement of the Survey, was undoubtedly the examination of the Sewalik hills by Dr. Falconer and Sir Proby Cautley, and the famous discovery of their wonderful fossil fauna.

Dr. Falconer took charge of the government gardens at Saharunpore in 1832, and at once began to investigate the geology of the Sewalik hills. This is a ridge running parallel to the great chain of the Himalaya, and consisting of rocks of very late formation. In strictness the Sewalik are the range of hills rising from the plains between the Ganges and Jumna, but the term is usually applied to the outermost ridge along the whole length of the Himalaya.‖

Herbert had examined and reported on the Sewalik rocks when engaged on the Survey;¶ but Captain Webb is said to have been the first to prove the existence of fossil bones. Yet they were

* "Description of the N.W. Coal District, stretching along the river Damoodah." —"Asiatic Researches," xviii. p. 163.

† "Journal of the Asiatic Society of Bengal," vol. xi. pt. ii. p. 723.

‡ "A Geological Report on the Damoodah Valley, by D. H. Williams, Esq., late "Geological Surveyor in the Service of the East India Company." (London 1850.) The work was reprinted in Calcutta.

§ "Journal of the Asiatic Society of Bengal," iv. p. 648.

‖ Rennell applied the name to the hills from Hurdwar to the Sutlej.—"Memoirs," p. 233.

¶ "Journal of the Asiatic Society," vol. xi. (App.)

known to Feroze III. as long ago as 1360. Ferishta tells us that this monarch, while cutting through a hill with 50,000 workmen, to lead the waters of the Soorsutty into the Seliona, came upon bones of giants three yards long.

Dr. Falconer was led to expect the discovery from the nature of the rocks, and he had noted the above passage in Ferishta. At that time three officers, who have since linked their names indissolubly with the history of Indian irrigation, Sir Proby Cautley, Sir William Baker, and Sir Henry Durand, were at work on those Jumna canals, the heads of which are close to Dr. Falconer's abode at Suharunpore; and he had them as fellow labourers in the same field of research.

Falconer and Cautley both found fossil bones in 1831, and Cautley energetically followed up the search by blasting operations in the Kalawala pass of the Sewalik. These discoveries were not fortuitous, but were results led up to by previous special study. In 1834 Baker and Durand discovered the great ossiferous deposit near the valley of the Markunda, below Nahun. Two days after they got their first specimens, Falconer was on the spot, and collected 300 specimens of fossil bones within six hours.

Thus was a sub-tropical mammalian fossil fauna brought to light, which was unexampled in richness and extent in any other region then known. The history of the discovery is recorded in various papers published in Scientific Journals, and the whole was to have been embodied by Dr. Falconer in a great work entitled "Fauna Antiqua Sevalensis." It was commenced, and 1123 specimens were figured, but Dr. Falconer was not spared to complete it. He died in 1865, and all his papers bearing on this subject have been ably edited and published by Dr. Murchison.* Dr. Royle, in his great work on the Himalayas, both figures and describes the Sewalik fossils.†

* "Palæontological Memoirs and Notes, by Hugh Falconer," 2 vols. 1868.

His first account of the Sewalik is in the "Journal of the Asiatic Society of Bengal," i. p. 96. (1832). Cautley's first memoir is in the "Asiatic Researches," vol. xvi. In vol. xix. of the "Asiatic Researches" are seven papers by Falconer, Cautley, and Durand. On the fossil camel at p. 115, fossil tiger, p. 135, fossil bear, p. 193. See also Baker's papers in the "Journal of the Asiatic Society," iv. p. 506, 694, 706, v. p. 729. There is also a paper by Cautley in the "Geological Transactions (2nd Series)" v. p. 276 (1836). Cautley's paper on a fossil giraffe in the Sewalik is in the "Journal of the Asiatic Society," vii. pt. ii. p. 658, and Falconer's on the quadrumana of the Sewalik, ibid. vi. pt. i. p. 354.

† "Illustrations of the botany and other branches of the natural history of the Himalaya mountains," by J. Forbes Royle. (London, 1839. 2 vols.)

These important discoveries have thrown light upon the state of India in the most remote ages. On their authority we may conceive an ancient sea to have occupied the valleys of the Indus and Ganges, washing the bases of the Himalaya on one side, and the Vindhya of the Deccan on the other, and receiving all the silt bearing rivers from both. In course of time the sea was filled up, and the alluvial valleys teemed with the animals whose bones are now imbedded in the Sewalik. Similar remains exist in Sinde. They were also found by Mr. Crawfurd on the banks of the Irrawaddy in 1826,* by Dr. Spilsbury in the Nerbudda valley, and by Captain Fulljames on the island of Perim in the gulf of Cambay.† These points indicate the vast area over which the Sewalik animals of that remote tertiary age roamed. There were mastodons, elephants, five species of hippopotami, rhinoceroses, giraffes, horses, pigs, camels, stags, antelopes, hyænas, dogs, and cats, monkeys, ostriches, and huge cranes. There are also the sivatherium, a bull the size of an elephant with four horns and a roman nose; and the colossachelys atlas, a gigantic tortoise 6 feet high and 22 feet long.

The upheaval of a narrow belt of the plains of India, at the foot of the Himalayas, into hills 3,500 feet high, seems to mark the time when the present epoch commenced in India, as these hills form the grave and monument of an earlier and distinct fauna.

The investigation of the Sewaliks was followed by Colonel Richard Strachey's examination of the lofty ranges in their rear,‡ and by reports on the fossils of the Spiti Valley by Dr. Gerard§ and Captain Hutton.¶ Captain Henry Strachey also explored Western Tibet, including the remarkable alluvial plain of Gugé, which the

* See the account of the rocks and animal remains collected by Mr. Crawfurd in 1826-27, on the banks of the Irrawaddy, by Dr. Buckland, in "Crawfurd's Embassy," ii., App. p. 143, and in the "Transactions of the Geological Society." The collection consisted of bones of mastodons, rhinoceroses, hippotamuses, tapirs, oxen, deer, and land tortoises.

† Baron Hugel had a large collection of fossils from Perim. Captain Fulljames reported on them in the "Bengal Asiatic Society's Journal," i. p. 233. See also "Notes on the Island of Perim, in the Gulf of Cambay, by Lieut. Ethersey," "Bombay Geographical Society's Journal," vol. ii. Dr. Falconer described the Perim fossils in the "Quarterly Journal of the Geological Society," i. p. 356.

‡ "Quarterly Journal of the Geological Society," vii. p. 292.

§ "Asiatic Researches," xviii. pt. ii. p. 238.

¶ "Journal of the Asiatic Society of Bengal," (1841,) p. 198.

Sutlej has excavated to the depth of a full vertical mile;* and Dr. Thomson, in his journey through Ladak to the Karakorum pass in 1848, made very careful geological notes.†

The peninsula of India has been examined and reported upon by several ardent geologists. Colonel Sykes has written upon the trap formation of the Deccan,‡ and Dr. Malcolmson's paper on fossils of the eastern portion of the great basaltic region had for its object an endeavour to arrive at a conclusion respecting the age of the basalt which is spread over 200,000 square miles on the plateau of the Indian peninsula. The fossils were collected in 1832, on the Sichel hills, which extend from the junction of the Wurdah and Godavery towards Aurungabad.§

But perhaps the most eminent of the Indian geological observers of those days was Captain Newbold, the Assistant Resident at Kurnool, an officer who had entered the army in 1827. He made several careful sections across the peninsula, and reported upon the whole region south of a line drawn from Ganjam to Bombay. No formation has attracted more attention than the laterite, a rock peculiar to India, which was first noticed and named by Dr. Buchanan, in his work on Malabar. Captain Newbold described it very fully as a reddish brown tubular and cellular clay, more or less indurated, and often impregnated with iron. The air-exposed surface of laterite is hard and glazed, but a few inches below the surface it becomes softer, and is cut out in blocks with a spade, hardening after exposure to the atmosphere. It is used largely for building and for repairing roads, and, among other edifices, the arcaded Inquisition at Goa is built of laterite. The laterite formation covers the western coast almost continuously from Bombay to Cape Comorin, and generally from the sea to the foot of the ghauts. It is also found in detached beds in many other parts of India. It is of late origin.

* "Physical Geography of Western Tibet," in the "R. G. S. Journal," vol. xxiii. p. 1. Henry Strachey is a Gold Medallist of the Royal Geographical Society.

† "Western Himalaya and Tibet. A journey during the years 1847–48," by Thomas Thomson, M.D. (1852.)

‡ "Colonel Sykes on the Geology of a portion of the Dukhun." (4to, London, 1836.) Re-printed from the "Transactions of the Geological Society," vol. iv. (Second Series.)

§ "Transactions of the Geological Society," v. p. 537. Dr. Malcolmson, who was Secretary to the Bombay Branch of the Asiatic Society, died at Dhoolia in the Taptee valley, while engaged in the pursuit of his favourite science, in February 1844. See a notice of him in the "Bombay Times" of April 30th, 1844.

Some writers derive it from the weathering of trap rocks, but the laterite beds are sometimes conglomeritic, cover indiscriminately all kinds of formations, and rest undisturbed alike on the traps and on the cretaceous limestones of Pondicherry, while they are never invaded by trap dykes.*

General Cullen, an officer of high scientific attainments, who was for many years resident in Travancore, found beds of lignite in the laterite near Quilon.

The régur or black cotton soil was also carefully studied by Captain Newbold;† and he formed a theory respecting the origin of those nodules of lime so well known in India by the name of kunkur, which are met with as irregular overlying beds, or filling up chinks and fissures of rocks of every age. He referred their origin to the action of springs charged with carbonic acid, bringing up lime in solution, and either depositing it as the temperature lowered, or parting with the carbonic acid.‡

In 1840 Captain Newbold visited the fossiliferous limestones of South Arcot and Trichinopoly, which were afterwards carefully examined by Mr. C. Turton Kaye and Mr. Brooke Cunliffe of the Madras Civil Service. These gentlemen collected 178 fossils from the cretaceous formation near Pondicherry, described by Sir Philip Egerton and Professor Edward Forbes.§

Captain John Warren, the assistant of Colonel Lambton, had examined the petrified drift wood at Treevikera near Pondicherry in 1808,‖ which, Captain Newbold tells us, closely resembles the petrified wood in the desert near Cairo.

In the Western Presidency, Captain Grant examined the important

* See also a paper on laterite by Dr. Cole, in the "Madras Journal of Literature and Science," iii. p. 100; and another by Dr. Clark, viii. p. 334.

† Paper read before the Royal Society, March 22nd, 1838.

‡ Captain Newbold's papers will be found in the "Transactions of the Geological Society," in the "Journal of the Royal Asiatic Society," vol. vii., and in "Notes, chiefly Geological," in four parts, in the "Journal of the Asiatic Society of Bengal." The papers in the "Journal of the Asiatic Society" are on the Mineral Resources of India, in eight numbers. They contain accounts of the gold tracts, and of the mines of lead, manganese, rubies, garnets, diamonds, &c. See also the "Calcutta Review," ix. p. 314. He also wrote papers on the geology of Egypt, and on the petrified forest near Cairo. ("Quarterly Journal of the Geological Society," iv. pp. 324–49.)

Captain Newbold was an accomplished antiquary and Persian scholar, as well as a geologist. He died at Mahabuleshwur on June 2nd, 1850.

§ "Madras Journal of Literature and Science," No. 28, xii. p. 37. "Transactions of the Geological Society," vii. p. 97. Mr. Kaye died in October 1845.

‖ "Asiatic Researches," xi. p. i.

plant bearing formation in Cutch.* Dr. Christie gave an account of the geology in the Southern Mahratta country in 1836,† and Lieutenant Aytoun reported upon the geology of parts of Belgaum.‡ Colonel Meadows Taylor has described the geology of the district of Shorapore in the Deccan, where the several formations of that region unite with those of the Carnatic, accompanied by evidence of much local disturbance. His observations connect the work of Captain Newbold at Kurnool with that of Dr. Christie and Lieut. Aytoun in the Southern Mahratta country.§ Dr. Fleming described the nummulitic limestone in the Suliman range, above the Derajat.‖ In Sinde, Sir Bartle Frere has written upon the geology,¶ and also contributed a most admirable paper on the Desert and the Runn of Cutch. The same region was described by Alexander Burnes and Mac Murdo; and Sir Charles Lyell has given an interesting account of the Allah Bund, and of the effects of the earthquake of 1819, in his "Principles of Geology." Dr. Robert Thompson,** Dr. Buist,†† and Dr. H. J. Carter,‡‡ have written upon the geology of the Island of Bombay.

The nummulitic limestone formation in western India has attracted much attention, and has been carefully studied. In 1844 Dr. Malcolmson, just before his death, discovered a nummulitic bed in the Rajpeepla hills, crossing the Nerbudda valley; and Major Fulljames, in 1852, reported upon the same formation. More recently, in 1861, Mr. Alexander Rogers, the Collector of Surat, who is an accomplished and enthusiastic geologist, discovered nummulitic limestone at Turkeysur, between Surat and Broach. Thus the existence of the nummulitic formation in the Rajpeepla hills, which form the westernmost termination of the Satpoora range, was fully established.§§

* "Transactions of the Geological Society (2nd Series)," v. p. 289.

† "Madras Journal of Literature and Science," iv. p. 452.

‡ "Journal of the Bombay Geographical Society," xi. p. 20.

§ See the "Transactions of the Royal Geological Society of Ireland."

‖ "Quarterly Journal of the Geological Society," ix. p. 346.

¶ Ibid., ix. p. 349.

** In 1836. "Madras Journal of Literature and Science," v. p. 129.

†† "Journal of the Bombay Geographical Society," x. p. 167.

‡‡ "Bombay Branch of the Asiatic Society," iv. p. 161. Dr. Carter made a final geological examination of Carinja, Elephanta, Trombay, Salsette, and the other islands round Bombay. See "Journal of the Bombay Branch," Nov. 1860.

§§ A work on the nummulitic fossils of India was published in France in 1853. "Description des animaux fossiles de groupe nummulitique de l'Inde, précédée d'un "résumé géologique et d'une monographie des nummulites, par le Vicomte de Archiac "et Jules Haime." 4to. 32 plates. Paris, 1853.

Dr. Carter, then in the Indian Navy, was the most distinguished of the pioneers of Indian geology. While serving with Captain Sanders in the *Palinurus*, he examined the rocks of the Arabian coast,* and he afterwards reported upon the geology of the Islands of Bombay and Salsette. But his most valuable work consisted in the collection and classification of all the geological labours of his predecessors, to which is added a reprint of his Summary of the Geology of India between the Ganges, Indus, and Cape Comorin. This work was undertaken at the instance of Lord Elphinstone.† The plan is first to introduce the reader to the geology of the great trappean region of Western India, and then to carry him round its outskirts, in order that he may become acquainted with the geological formations of India generally. His attention is then directed to the geology of Cutch, afterwards to that of Sinde, and lastly to that of the Arabian coast. For this purpose almost all the geological papers on India that had then been written were re-printed *in extenso*.

In 1853 Mr. Greenough carefully compiled his geological map of India, showing the state of our knowledge at that date;‡ copies of which were transmitted to the Local Governments, and elicited several reports from officers interested in the subject.§

Such were the principal labours in the field of Indian geologists previous to the establishment of the official survey. They were results obtained by independent inquirers; and, such as were recorded when geology was in its infancy, are now to some extent out of date. There was of course a great want of concentration in

---

* See note at page 22.

† "Geological Papers on Western India, including Cutch, Sind, and the South-east "Coast of Arabia, to which is appended a Summary of the Geology of India generally; "edited for the Government by Henry J. Carter, Assistant Surgeon." (Bombay 1857.) See a Review of this valuable work in the "Bombay Quarterly Review," vol. vii. p. 316.

‡ "General Sketch of the Physical and Geological Features of British India; by "G. B. Greenough, Esq., engraved by A. Petermann." The map is 7 feet long by 5¾. It is described by Sir Roderick Murchison in one of his anniversary addresses as President of the Geographical Society. "R. G. S. Journal," xxiii. p. cviii.

§ "Correspondence on the subject of the Geological Map of India, compiled by Professor Greenough." (Madras 1857.) This pamphlet contains remarks by General Cullen on the laterite of Travancore; by Major Dallas and Dr. Cole on the geological features of the Ceded Districts; and memoranda by Dr. Ranking, Dr. Balfour, Dr. Hunter, and Rev. C. F. Muzzy. Mr. Muzzy wrote a paper on the geological features of Madras, Trichinopoly, and Tanjore, in the "Madras Journal of Literature and Science," i. N.S., p. 90.

these labours, and the value of many observations was lost owing to the absence of an intelligible nomenclature. Much has required revision, but at the same time the labours of those Indian geologists who were first in the field are valuable and important.

Dr. McClelland, who held the office of Geological Surveyor for two years after the death of Mr. Williams,* wrote a Report on the Geological Survey of India for the Session 1848–49, and described the coal strata of the Rajmchal hills.† He also mapped the Kurhabaree field.

The work of Dr. Oldham, the present Superintendent of the Geological Survey of India, extends over a period of upwards of 20 years. Before commencing his service in India he had been on the Irish Survey, and Professor of Geology at Trinity College, Dublin. He arrived in India in March 1851, and found that the establishment of the Geological Survey then consisted of one peon and one writer, with no European assistant, and no preparation of any field work. The few existing records were kept in a box in a small room in the Surveyor-General's office. Dr. Oldham obtained sanction for the employment of Mr. J. G. Medlicott, who had served with him for several years on the Survey of Ireland, as assistant; and in 1852 Mr. St. George was added. The only idea the Government then had of the duties of a geological surveyor was that he should go about from place to place, and report upon real or fancied discoveries of minerals. The difficulty of the position was increased by the small confidence that could be placed in much that had previously been done. The beds represented by the former Coal Committee to be the very lowest of the carboniferous period are in reality eocene or miocene resting upon nummulitic limestone; and the coal measures of the Rajmehal hills, which had been stated to be newer than or to rest upon the trap flows of that district, are in reality exactly the opposite. Dr. Oldham worked steadily on, in the face of many difficulties at the outset, to obtain a definite geological horizon from which to work up or down, and so obtain a true basis for future operations. This was, however, impracticable while he was expected

---

* See page 147.

† Dr. McClelland was secretary to a committee for the investigation of the coal resources of India. See the Report printed at Calcutta in 1841. There is also a work on the Geology of the Province of Kumaon, by John McClelland. (8vo. Calcutta, 1835.)

to go first to the eastern boundary of Bengal, then to the southern extreme of Tenasserim, and next towards Bombay.

Lord Canning really took an enlightened interest in geology, and on his arrival Dr. Oldham was able for the first time to commence a regular survey of the country. Lord Canning ordered that, unless under very special circumstances, the geological surveyors were to confine their labours to those parts of the country which had already been mapped, and steadily to proceed, as far as the maps existed, over the country from east to west. Before Lord Canning's arrival Dr. Oldham had, in 1851, proceeded to Cherra-Poonjee, with a view to examining the iron ores in the Khasia hills. He made a collection of fossils, chiefly from the nummulutic limestone of the Khasia hills, establishing the occurrence of rocks of the upper cretaceous age in Eastern Bengal.* In 1852–53 he examined the geological features of the Rajmahal hills;† and Mr. Theobald, one of his assistants, made a detailed report upon the Punjab Salt Range in 1853.‡ In 1855 Dr. Oldham accompanied Sir Arthur Phayre's mission to Ava, and wrote a memoir on the geological features of the banks of the Irrawaddy, and of the country north of Amarapoora.§

In 1856 Lord Canning placed the Geological Survey upon a proper footing. Dr. Oldham's staff was increased, the labours of the Survey were systematized, and the reports were ordered to be published in a uniform series. The operations have been directed to those districts where the Revenue and Topographical Surveyors have completed their maps, and where the most valuable practical or scientific results were to be obtained. But the geologists have been constantly hindered in their work by the want of maps, and indeed this has been one of their chief difficulties. The superintendent and his staff have also been frequently detached from their regular work to report

* "On the Geological Structure of part of the Khasi hills, with observations on the "meteorology and ethnology of that district, by Thomas Oldham, A.M.," &c. (4to, Calcutta, 1854, with geological maps). See also the "Quarterly Journal of the Geological Society," xix. p. 524. "Geological Memoirs," i. p. 94. Colonel Hannay and Captain Dalton reported upon the economic geology of Upper Assam at about the same time. "Journal of the Asiatic Society of Bengal," vii. p. 625, xxii. p. 511, xxv. p. 230. See also their report on auriferous deposits in Assam.—"Memoirs," i. p. 90. Dr. Hooker described the structure of the Khasia hills, much as Dr. Oldham did afterwards. This district is the Cossyah hills of other authors.

† "Journal of the Asiatic Society of Bengal," xxiii. p. 268., and xxv. p. 249.

‡ Ibid. Nos. 3, 4, 5, of 1853. In 1848 Dr. A. Fleming, of the 7th N. I., had also written a paper on the Salt Range. Ibid., xvii. pt. 2, p. 500.

§ "Yule's Mission to Ava," App. A., p. 309.

upon some special point for the Government, which (though useful service is sometimes performed in the interval) has delayed the progress of the Survey.

The best way to convey a tolerably clear idea of the geological work that has been done will perhaps be to take the history of the progress of the survey in each district, instead of reviewing the whole of the operations year by year; and, with this object, it will be as well to begin with the coal yielding region.

In 1856–7 Cuttack was examined by three of the staff, Messrs. W. T. and H. F. Blanford and Mr. J. G. Medlicott, from the Chilka lake to Midnapoor, and Mr. Blanford reported upon the laterite of Orissa.* The Blanfords discovered and named the important Talcheer group of rocks underlying the coal beds. The separation of the Talcheer from the coal bearing rocks is applicable in all districts. During the two following years, Mr. W. T. Blanford was zealously investigating the Raneegunge coal field,† while Mr. Medlicott was engaged in the survey of the Kurruckpoor hills and on the examination of the Kurhabaree coal district. The existence of a large supply of coal west of the river Barakur was established, and Dr. Oldham had himself explored the Cossyah hills in former years.‡ Mr. Blanford completed field maps of the Raneegunge, works which are as useful to the practical worker as the geologist, and he also brought together returns of the coal raised from the several open works and pits. In 1859–60 there were 370,206 tons of coals raised. At the close of 1861 Mr. Blanford was transferred to Burmah.

The examination of the coal country was continued in 1863 by Mr. Hughes and Mr. Willson, at Jherria§ and Kurhabaree. In the following year Mr. Medlicott was on detached duty in Assam,‖ and came to satisfactory conclusions respecting the value of coal in that district. In 1865 Mr. Hughes continued his work in the coal region,

---

* See "Memoirs," vol. i., "On the Coal and Iron of Talcheer in Cuttack." "Structure and Relations of the Talchir Coal Fields." "Geology of Midnapore and Orissa." "Laterite of Orissa." These labours are reviewed in the "Quarterly Journal of the Geological Society," xiii., p. cviii. The coal and iron of Talcheer had previously been written upon by Captain Kittoe. "Journal of the Asiatic Society of Bengal," viii. p. 137.

† "Memoirs," vol. iii., "On the Raniganj coal field."

‡ "Memoirs," vol. i., "Geology of the Khasi hills."

§ "Memoirs," vol. v., "On the Jherria coal field," by T. Hughes.

‖ "Memoirs," vol. iv., "On the coal of Assam," by H. B. Medlicott.

exploring the Hazareebagh and Bokaro * fields; and in 1866 Mr. Blanford made his first examination of the Chanda coal field, and indicated the localities where borings should be made. The Palamow coal fields could not be proceeded with for want of maps. In 1868 Mr. Medlicott traversed a wide tract of country to investigate the extent and relations of the several series of sandstones associated with coal in Bengal, as compared with those in Central India; and proceeded, in the following year, to the Nerbudda valley, to work out the coal bearing rocks in that area, which had been first visited 12 years before, when there were no maps.† In 1869 two geologists were sent to revise the maps of Bhagulpoor and Beerbhoom, the earliest coal region examined by the Survey.

These Indian coal fields are situated in the drainage basins of the rivers Dammoodah, Sone, Mahanuddy, Godavery, and Nerbudda. The oldest and best known, namely, the Raneegunge, Jherria, Bokaro, Ramghur, and Karampoora fields are in the Dammoodah drainage basin.‡ The Itkuree and Kurhabaree fields are in Chóta Nagpoor province, on the Barakur, the chief effluent of the Dammoodah, from which river it is separated, in the upper part of its course, by the lofty Parasnath hill and the wide plateau of Hazareebagh. The whole of these may be considered to have been deposited in one great estuary. In the Sone valley are the Palamow, Singrowlee, and South Rewah coal fields, the Talcheer and Belaspoor fields are in that of the Mahanuddy, and the Chanda in the Godavery.

The conclusions derived from the Survey are, that the rocks associated with coal are separated into several distinct groups. The lowest is the Talcheer group, first established by the brothers Blanford, and not containing coal. The Dammoodah series contains most of the coal beds of Bengal and Central India. It was separated from the overlying rocks by Dr. Oldham. There are also the Rajmahal group, and the tertiary series of the Cossyah hills. The data for this classification of the coal bearing rocks consist of the remains of plants.

---

* "Memoirs," vol. vi., pt. 2, "On the Bokaro coal field." G. T. W. Hughes.

† "On the Mohpani coal field in the Nerbudda valley," by H. B. Medlicott. "Records," iii. pt. 3, (1870.)

‡ An affluent of the Hoogly, rising in the province of Chóta Nagpoor, and flowing through the Bancoorah, Burdwan, and Hoogly districts of the Lower Provinces of Bengal.

In the eastern coal fields there are five well marked sub-divisions:—

1. The Talcheer beds, the lowest, in which no coal is known; so called by the Blanfords, from the district in Cuttack where they were first examined.
2. The Barakur beds, formerly called Lower Dammoodah.
3. Ironstone shales.
4. Raneegunge beds.
5. Panchet beds, or upper series. First separated as a distinct sub-division, and so named by Mr. Blanford. They are of the triassic epoch, and contain bones of labyrinthodont and dicynodont amphibia. Panchet is the name of a remarkable hill, and the title of a Rajah.

To the westward these become three:—

1. Talcheer.
2. Barakur.
3. Panchet.

Dr. Oldham's general conclusions, respecting these coal series, are that the drainage basins of India were marked out and existed at the enormously distant period when the deposition of the great plant bearing formations commenced. All the successive beds represent an enormous lapse of time, and seem to be fresh water or estuarine deposits. He also concludes that the present limits of the coal measures coincide with the original limits of deposition, and are not the results of faulting or even mainly of denudation.* The Dammoodah system is believed to represent the Permian period of European geology, together with a portion of the upper carboniferous epoch.

Dr. Oldham has, from time to time, prepared returns of the amount of coal raised. In June 1859 he furnished one of the Raneegunge fields; in 1861 returns were given in Mr. Blanford's Report;† and in June 1861 the first general statement of the out-tour of Indian coal was given by Dr. Oldham. In March 1867 he prepared a Report on the coal resources of India, for the Secretary of State, with results from 1861 to 1866; and in June 1869 he sent in a

---

* See Dr. Oldham's papers "On the geological relations and probable geological age of the several systems of rocks in Central India and Bengal," (Memoirs, vol. ii., p. 299), and "Additional Remarks" in (Memoirs, vol. iii., p. 198).

† Memoirs, iii. p. 179.

1868, coal used on railways connected with Calcutta, 66,20,837 maunds.

Return for 1868, with statistics of the methods of working the coal, and statements tabulated for each year from 1858 to 1868.

The next investigation is that respecting the alluvial deposits of the Ganges valley, which was commenced in the first year of the Survey. In 1859 the portion from the Bhagruttee northwards to the foot of the hills was examined and mapped. In 1860, Mr. Theobald was fixing the boundaries and extent of recent alluvial deposits from Burdwan to Monghyr. In 1861 the investigation was continued over the plains south of the Ganges to Patna and Shahabad; and in 1862 the examination was completed.

The geological survey of the important formations in Central India was also a great object.* In 1855, Mr. J. G. Medlicott passed from Jubbulpore westward down the Nerbudda valley; while his brother crossed the Rewah country and the river Sone to the Singrowlee coal field. Both considered that the sandstone rocks of Rewah and Bundelcund should be entirely separated from the sandstones associated with coals in Bengal and in the Nerbudda valley. Dr. Oldham visited the same country in 1856, and gave the name of VINDHYAN to the entire group, because it is best seen in the scarped mountains of that name on the northern side of the Nerbudda valley.† It includes the diamond yielding rocks of Central India, and is one of the most remarkable and interesting series in the country. Hitherto (1870), no fossils have been found in it. Its age cannot therefore be determined; but the Vindhyan rocks are older than the carboniferous series of India. In 1863, Mr. Mallet was engaged in tracing out the divisions and boundaries of this formation in Rewah, while Mr. Hackett worked out the limits of the trappean rocks in Saugor, and Mr. H. B. Medlicott was closing up the gaps in the geological mapping between Central India and the Sone valley. In 1864, Mr. Mallet revised the boundaries of the Vindhyan rocks north of the Nerbudda valley, covering 2,200 square

---

* Mr. J. G. Medlicott compiled the "Cotton Hand Book" for Bengal in 1862, for the Government.

† "Memoirs," vol. ii., p. 1, "On the Vindhyan rocks and their associates in Bundelkhund." "Geological structure of the central portion of the Nerbudda district," p. 95. "Tertiary and alluvial deposits of the Nerbudda valley," p. 279. "The Vindhyan series," vol. vii., pt. 1. Dr. Oldham proposed the name VINDHYAN in a paper in the Journal of the Asiatic Society of Bengal," xxv. p. 249. See also his paper on the Geological relations of the rock systems of Central India and Bengal."—"Memoirs," ii. p. 299. There is a useful list of all papers relating to the Nerbudda valley, published previously to the date of vol. ii. of the "Geological Memoirs," at page 387.

"Records," vol. ii., pt. 2, "Sketch of the metamorphic rocks of Bengal."

miles of ground, while Mr. Hackett examined the Gwalior country. During this year Dr. Oldham himself examined the rocks on the south bank of the Ganges, from Gya to near Bhaugulpoor. In 1867 Mr. Medlicott undertook the investigation of a wild and difficult country from Raneegunge and Hazareebagh in the Dammoodah basin to the basin of the Mahanuddy. He came again upon the old Vindhyan rocks, chiefly limestone, which cover 12,000 square miles, abutting against crystalline rocks to the north, and passing under the Deccan traps to the south and west. In 1869, Mr. Willson was at work in Jhansi, to connect with Mr. Hackett in Gwalior,* and Mr. Mallet was in the Sone valley.

A complete and connected history of the Vindhyan formations has been drawn up by Mr. Mallet: and still more recently Mr. Blanford has re-examined part of the Vindhyan series, but he could find no fossils to determine their age, which therefore still remains unsettled.

Mr. H. F. Medlicott, then Professor of Geology in the Roorkee College, commenced the examination of the Sewaliks, and upper and outer Himalaya, in 1859, during the intervals of time that his collegiate duties permitted of his taking the field. His studies were more directed to the orographical relations of these hills than to their fossils. In the following years he continued his examination to near Kangra; and the results of his labours are embodied in a valuable memoir. These are the hills in which Dr. Falconer discovered numerous mammalian remains. They are of miocene and post miocene age. Nummulitic rocks occur north of the Sewaliks, and appear to form a large proportion of the ranges in the Punjab. Representatives of these tertiary rocks extend to the east, are found at the base of the hills in Sikkim, and stretch far up the Assam valley. Dr. Hooker also found the nummulites in Tibet, north of Sikkim, at 16,000 feet above the sea. One important consequence of Mr. Medlicott's survey of this region was the discovery of a good water supply at Umballa. He reported that water bearing beds must exist there, and the trial confirmed his expectations.† Mr. Medlicott also reported upon the *reh* efflorescence which has given rise to so much anxiety, and on the waters of the rivers and canals in the N. W. Provinces.‡

* "Records," vol. iii., pt. 2, "Geology of Gwalior and vicinity."

† "Memoirs," vol. iii., "On the southern portions of the Himalayan ranges."

‡ "Journal of the Asiatic Society," xx., p. 326.

In 1862, Messrs. Theobald and Mallet were sent in the footsteps of Colonel Richard Strachey, to collect fossils, and trace out the succession of sedimentary beds on the northern slopes of the western Himalaya and in the Chini and Spiti valleys, up to an elevation of 18,000 feet. They were found to be identical with known species from Europe occurring in the same association. Triassic and oolitic beds are especially abundant about Spiti. In 1864 Mr. Mallet, in company with Dr. Ferdinand Stoliczka, who was formerly in the Austrian Geological Survey, and a colleague of Dr. Hochstetter, were despatched to the Himalaya to work out their structure, and revise the fossil fauna. Undoubted representatives were proved to occur of the European Silurian, carboniferous, triassic, lias, jurassic, and cretaceous periods, and, out of 200 varieties collected, only 32 are new.* In 1865, Dr. Stoliczka extended his investigations in the Himalaya as far as Leh, but in 1867, he went home with Mr. Oldham.

The great mass of the Himalayan ranges consists of metamorphic rocks, in places highly granitoid, in others slatey or schistose.

The operations of the Survey were extended to the Madras Presidency in 1857. The party was in charge of Mr. H. F. Blanford, and consisted of Mr. C. Oldham, Mr. King, and Mr. Geoghegan. The latter gentleman died suddenly of sun stroke early in 1858, and was succeeded by Mr. R. Bruce Foote. They were instructed first to examine the important group of cretaceous rocks in South Arcot and Trichinopoly, the fossils of which had been collected in former years by Kaye and Cunliffe, and thence to work northward. In the first year Mr. Blanford reported upon the geology of the Neilgherry hills.† The survey of the highly interesting cretaceous formations was completed in 1861‡, and in the same year King

* "Memoirs," vol. v., "Sections across N.W. Himalaya from Sutlej to Indus." "On the gypsum of Spiti." "Summary of Geological Observations in S. Ladak, Western Tibet, &c.," by F. Stoliczka.

† "Memoirs," vol. i., p. 211, "The Nilghiri Hills." Dr. Benza wrote papers on the geology of the Neilgherries and Koondahs, on that of the country between the Neilgherries and Madras, and on the geology of the Northern Circars, in the "Madras Journal of Literature and Science," in 1835–36, vols. iii. and v.

‡ "Memoirs," vol. iv., "On the Cretaceous Rocks of the South Arcot and Trichinopoly districts, by H. F. Blanford. "On the Structure of the Districts of Trichinopoly and Salem." "On the Occurrence of Crystalline Limestone in the vicinity of Trichinopoly," by W. King.—*Madras Journal*, iv. N.S., p. 271.

and Foote examined the iron deposits of Salem. Mr. H. F. Blanford then retired from the Survey.*

The other members of the party, in 1862, commenced an examination of the hill range which separates Cuddapah and Kurnool from Nellore, a very difficult and almost roadless country. In 1863 Mr. King traced the boundaries of these Cuddapah rocks, chiefly quartzites and slates, into Bellary and Kurnool. Mr. Foote was engaged during the same year in examining rocks near Madras.† He met with beds of marine fossils intercalated with others holding abundance of vegetable remains of the same species as have been found in the Rajmahal hills and in Cutch. This discovery of the wide extension of the Rajmahal series is a fact of high interest.

The Cuddapah formations appear to represent an older portion of the great Vindhyan series. The diamond beds of Southern India occur in these formations, and they show very favorable traces of lead, copper, and iron. The main object of the geologists was to work out the true succession and extent of these remarkable and interesting series of quartzite, slate, schist, and limestone beds in Cuddapah, Nellore, and Kurnool. In 1866 Mr. Foote was working along their eastern and Mr. C. Oldham up their western boundaries, while Mr. King was in the centre. They completed the area in Cuddapah and Kurnool during 1868, when the superintendent took an opportunity of testing the accuracy of their mapping, and in 1869 Mr. Foote began to work across the Raichoor Dooab towards the Bombay Presidency. Mr. King has drawn up a general report on the entire series.‡ During the hot weather in each year, the gentlemen of the Madras Survey were usefully employed in arranging and cataloguing the fossils and minerals of the Madras Central Museum, for Captain Mitchell, the curator; and Mr. C. Oldham, followed by Messrs. King and Foote, have delivered a series of lectures on geology at the Madras Engineering College. Mr. Oldham went home on leave in 1868, and died from the effects of disease contracted in India in April 1869. An able and talented

* He wrote papers on the occurrence of crystalline limestone in Coimbatore, and on the geological age of the sandstones at Trivicary, near Pondicherry, in the "Madras Journal of Literature and Science," iii. N.S., p. 60, and iv. N.S., p. 47.

† "Records," vol. iii., pt. 1, "Notes of the Geology of the Neighbourhood of Madras."

‡ "Records," vol. ii., pt. 1, "On the Kuddapah and Kurnool formations."

geologist, and a painstaking conscientious public servant, was thus lost to his country.

The Geological Survey of British Burmah was commenced in 1860, under Mr. W. T. Blanford, with the Henzada district in Pegu, where there are petroleum wells and salt springs. This district was selected because it was the only one of which there were reliable maps, and the future direction of geological researches had to depend on the publication of the results of the Topographical Survey. Mr. Blanford was transferred to Bombay in the following year, and Mr. Theobald took charge in Burmah; indeed he was single handed. He was at work in the Yoma range and on the west coast, but was much hampered in his operation by the want of trustworthy maps. The great Yoma range is composed of slightly altered sandstones and shales of unknown age, but expected to be in part at least cretaceous. Upon them, in Pegu, rest nummulitic rocks. Some peculiar serpentines are associated with the Yoma rocks. In 1864 Mr. Theobald took advantage of the publication of a sheet of the survey by Captain Fitzroy to complete the geological examination of the country contained in it, including Rangoon; and in the two following years he and Mr. Fedden were at work in the ground covered by the second sheet, east of the Irrawaddy and north of Prome. In 1864–65 Mr. Fedden accompanied an expedition through the Shan provinces of the kingdom of Burmah to the Salween river, and constructed a map of the route. In 1867 Mr. Theobald went home, after a continuous service of 18 years. But in 1868 he was again at work in the Prome district of Pegu, the east part of which he completed; taking up the western banks of the Irrawaddy, where there is a formation of nummulitic rocks, in 1869.*

Mr. Blanford took charge of the party in the Bombay Presidency, with Mr. Wilkinson and Mr. Wynne as his assistants, in 1863. He commenced at Surat, and on the shores of the gulf of Cambay, with the view of connecting his work with that of Mr. Medlicott in the Nerbudda valley, and thus completing a band of geological

---

* "Records," vol. ii, pt. 4, "On the Beds containing Silicified Wood in Eastern Prome."
" vol. iii, pt. 1, "On the Alluvial Deposits of the Irrawaddi."
" vol. iii, pt. 3, "Note on Petroleum in Burmah."

L 2

survey across India from sea to sea, on that parallel. In the following season the line from sea to sea, containing some of the most important formations in India, was completed. The hill ranges north of Guzerat are partly metamorphic and partly trap, and not far from the coast nummulitic rocks are found resting on the trap. Mr. Wilkinson also examined the Western Ghauts in the rocks of Mahabuleshwur, Rutnagherry, and Sawunt Warree; and Mr. Wynne investigated the geology of the island of Bombay, and showed how erroneous the previous conclusions respecting its structure had been in some respects.*

In 1863 Mr. Blanford was detached to report upon a supposed discovery of coal near Kotree, in Sinde, for the Bombay government.† He found it to be lignite and of no commercial value, but on his return he took the opportunity of visiting the interesting formations in Cutch.‡ In 1865 the northern declivities of the Nerbudda valley were reached, and a tract of 5,000 square miles was examined, chiefly trap with bottom rocks of granite or gneiss. In 1866 Mr. Blanford was at work in the upper Taptee and the Poorna and Wurda valleys,§ and reported upon the Chanda coal fields. He was usefully employed in Abyssinia, and in completing the publication of his results, during the greater part of the two following years; and in 1870 he returned to his old work in the Central Provinces, with Mr. Hughes and Mr. Fedden as assistants. He has since reported on the coal and lead ores in Chutteesgurh.‖ Mr. Blanford is an accomplished naturalist, as well as an able and experienced geologist, and during the period that he was employed on detached duty in Abyssinia, he did work of the highest scientific value.

After Mr. Blanford's visit to Cutch in 1863, Mr. Wynne was sent to make a fuller and more exhaustive examination of the rocks in

* "Memoirs," vol. v., "On the Geology of Bombay."

† Ibid., vol. vi., pt. 1, "On the Geology of the neighbourhood of Lynyan and Runneecote in Sind."

‡ Ibid., vol. vii., pt. 2, "On the Geology of a Portion of Cutch."

§ Ibid., vol. vi., pt. 2, "The Traps of Western and Central India," by W. T. Blanford.

" pt. iii, "The Taptee and Lower Nerbudda valleys."

"Records," vol. ii., pt. 1, "The valley of the Poorna river."

" vol. ii., pt. 4, "Lead in Raipur District."

" vol. iii., pt. 2, Ibid.

that district. There was an important question as to the relation of certain beds of fresh-water origin containing imperfect layers of coal and plant remains, with others which yielded marine fossils of undoubted jurassic age in Kuch. Mr. Blanford decided that the two groups were intercalated and not superimposed, and thus fixed the age of the plant beds. He also ascertained the extension of the Deccan trap rocks into Cutch. Mr. Wynne reported that the jurassic rocks occupied a large portion of the northern half of the province, and also formed the hilly parts of the islands in the Runn. His complete report and map have not yet appeared.*

This year Mr. Wynne has proceeded to the Punjab, to take up the geology of that important province, and has reported upon the gealogy of Mount Tilla.†

During the examination of Indian rocks, geologists have not failed to discover traces of a race of men belonging to that stone age the history of which has been so carefully examined in Europe by Sir John Lubbock and other writers. In 1864 Messrs. King and Foote discovered chiselled stone implements spread widely over the country west and north of the town of Madras, all of the ruder type, and made of semi-vitreous quartzites from the Cuddapah rocks. In 1864 Mr. Ball found a chipped implement in the Jherria coal field, and Mr. Theobald found others in Burmah. A chipped stone weapon of hard close grained quartzite was found near Neemuch by Mr. Medlicott, and in 1868 the Madras implements were traced up to the banks of the Kistnah. More recent observations have shown that these implements occur over a much larger extent of country to the north of the Kistnah river, and close to the southern edge of the region examined by Mr. Blanford on the Godavery.

The superintendence and control of all these operations have devolved upon Dr. Oldham, the Superintendent of the Survey, besides the direction of the museum and the publications. He has, in addition to his ordinary duties, been constantly called upon to make special reports to the Government on such points as the propriety

---

* "Memoirs," vol. ii., pt. 3, "Preliminary Notes on the Geology of Cutch." See also a "Report on the geological action on the south coast of Kattiwar and in the Runn of Cutch," by William Sowerby, C.E.—*Bombay G. S. Journal*, xviii., p. 96.

† "Note on the Petroleum Locality near Rewal-Pindee, by A. B. Wynne."—"Records," vol. iii., pt. 3, p. 73. "Geology of Mount Tilla," by A. B. Wynne. Ibid., pt. 4, p. 83.

of sinking Artesian wells in particular localities, on the structure of rock to be cut through for engineering purposes, on the selection of lines of railroad with reference to the position of coal fields, and on proper sites for barracks. He must have travelled over many thousand of miles, sometimes to confirm the importance of useful discoveries, at others to expose mares' nests. A brief sketch of the extent and objects of these journeys will convey some idea of Dr. Oldham's labours.

In 1860, Mr. Oldham went to Kumaon to report upon the iron works, which he considered to be essentially a practical and not a geological question. In 1862 he went to England to seek for assistants, and brought five out with him. In 1863 he was engaged on the investigation of the modes of deposit of lignite in the Salt Range, in the northern part of the Punjab. The Salt Range contains an extensive series of carboniferous, triassic, oolitic, and tertiary rocks. In 1867 he was again in England for a few months. In 1868 he went to examine some alleged coal bearing rocks near the Kistnah, but found that nothing of the kind existed in that region. Later in the year he went to Attock, to examine the rocks on the Indus through which the tunnel drift is carried. He saw nothing to prevent its being enlarged into a regular road way, so far as the nature of the rock is concerned. Afterwards he examined the Goorgaon and Dhurmsala districts in the North-West Provinces, with regard to the possibility of utilizing the kaolin clay; and in 1869 he visited the scenes of the earthquake in Cachar and Sylhet. He has since prepared a list of earthquakes that have occurred in India.* In this year he was also engaged in important work at the Chanda coal field.

The credit of discovering the Chanda coal belongs to Major Lucie Smith, the Deputy Commissioner of the Central Provinces, in 1866. Mr. Blanford was there early in 1867, and recommended borings, pointing out where they should be put down. He felt some doubt, at first, as to the ultimate value of the discovery, because the beds belong to the series known as Barakur,† which have a tendency to

* Colonel Baird Smith had previously compiled a memoir on Indian Earthquakes, in three parts.—"*Journal of the Asiatic Society of Bengal*," vols. xii., p. 257 and 1227, and xiii., p. 964.

† See page 157.

exhibit very great variation both in thickness and quality within short distances. Mr. Mark Fryar, a mining engineer, had joined the Survey at about the same time, and was sent to Raneegunge to learn the methods of coal mining in India, and get some practical acquaintance with the nature of the formations. In 1868 he was removed to Chanda, to explore the beds regularly, by boring; and two skilled borers, with the necessary tools, were despatched from England. After some unsuccessful trials, a point was selected by Dr. Oldham near Telwasa, about 10 miles north of the river Wurdah. Here 41 feet 7 inches of coal were found in a total depth of 138 feet. The investigation is still progressing, with very promising results.*

A small museum of economic geology was established at Calcutta in 1840, under the direction of Captain Piddington,† who was curator for some years before his death, and made many useful analyses. His careful experiments to ascertain the quantity of silt in the Hooghly at different seasons were especially valuable. In 1856 the museum was placed in connexion with the Geological Survey, and under the superintendence of Dr. Oldham. As early as 1859 it contained 1,100 specimens of fossils, minerals, rocks, and ores. The various members of the Survey of course contributed; so that there are good series of cretaceous fossils from Madras, of fossil plants from the Rajmahal hills, of tertiary fossils from the Spiti valley, of minerals obtained by Mr. Blanford on the Bhore Ghaut, of fossils from the Salt Range and the jurassic beds of Cutch, and from other places. But the great boast of the museum is its collection of meteoric stones. It contains specimens from 247 falls, and in this branch its collection ranks among the first in the world. A very complete geological library has also been gradually formed.

The museum is of great practical use, as its officers are constantly applied to for information, and to supply assays and analyses for companies and private individuals, as well as for the Government In 1862, Mr. Tween, the curator, made 23 analyses of coals, seven of soils, 18 of iron ores, nine of limestones, and seven of water.

---

* "Records," vol. ii., pt. 4, "Coal Field near Chanda."
,, vol. iii., pt. 2, "The Wardha River Coal Fields."

† Piddington's Memorandum on the establishment of the Geological Museum is printed in Thuillier's Manual of Surveying. Appendix, p. xxxiii.

The publications of the Geological Survey, under the direction of Dr. Oldham, consist of "Memoirs," "Records," and the "Palæontologia Indica."

The "Memoirs," which have now reached to the seventh volume, are the detailed and matured results of the survey of each district, written by the geologist who has conducted it. The volumes are fully illustrated with maps, sections, and sketches.

The "Palæontologia Indica" is a superb series, containing figures and descriptions of the organic remains procured during the progress of the Survey. The volumes already issued contain the cephalopoda and gasteropoda of the cretaceous rocks of Southern India, the fossil flora of the Rajmahal series, and the vertebrate fossils of the Panchet rocks. The Panchet fossils are described by Professor Huxley. They are bones of fossil reptiles, hitherto only known in South Africa.

The "Records" were commenced in 1868, and are published quarterly in rather small type and on thin paper, for ready transmission by post. They contain the Superintendent's annual reports, brief abstracts of the labours of members of the Survey in the field during the quarter, and other papers of general interest.*

There is a vast field still spread before the Geological Survey of India; a great work yet to be achieved, though much certainly has already been done. They must be animated by a noble devotion to the cause of science—these Indian geologists, for theirs is neither a safe nor an easy task. Out of the two dozen or so that have entered the Survey since it commenced, 34 per cent. have been struck down by death or incapacitating disease. The rest work on zealously and bravely, reflecting honour on English administration by the results of their labours, extending the sum of human knowledge, and doing much practically useful work.†

In spite all difficulties of climate, inaccessibility of districts, and slowness of means of travel, they have examined an area about four times as large as Great Britain.

---

* We have ten of Dr. Oldham's Annual Reports, 1858 to 1868 in separate covers, and the two last, for 1868 and 1869, bound up in the "Records," vol. ii., pt. 2, and vol. iii., pt. 1.

† There is a short notice of the operations of the Geological Survey of India, by H. Woodward, Esq., in the "Quarterly Journal of Science," for Oct. 1870, No. xxviii., p. 458.

A year or two more will enable Dr. Oldham to issue a general map of the geology of India, which will hold the position which Greenough's map of England, or Griffiths' map of Ireland, do with reference to general knowledge; and the map will, of course, be added to and improved as the country is opened out and examined.

XIII.—THE ARCHÆOLOGICAL SURVEY OF INDIA.

A survey of the archæological remains throughout India, which are as important as regards art, as they are indispensable to the study of history, has only of late years been considered to be a work which comes within the province of the Government to undertake. This is the more to be regretted because the loss of time is irreparable. All investigations connected with physical science are almost independent of delay, and can be made as well in one year as in another, but archæological remains are liable to deterioration, and delay causes absolute loss. Paintings fade from walls, sculptured edifices are destroyed by the vigorous growth of trees, and by ruthless modern builders in want of material, coins and inscriptions are mislaid or effaced, and all the works of man suffer more or less under the hand of time. In connection with geography, the study of archæology forms a most important branch; for, through the identification of ancient sites, the physical changes that have taken place in a country are determined.

Yet it was not possible that a survey of this nature could have been entered upon with any useful result before the English occupation, or even until long after our power was established. Mere descriptions of ruins and other remains are of little use unless the observer has mastered their history and true significance, and this was impossible until the study of the languages and literature of India was well advanced. Thus the earliest accounts of Indian archæological remains were only useful in exciting an interest in the subject, and in stimulating later enquirers to labour at those studies which alone could qualify them, and others of later generations who benefited by their works, for the task of investigating the mysteries of Indian chronology and art.

Glowing descriptions of the architectural monuments of India are not wanting among the writings of early travellers.

The Hindoo capital of Bijayanuggur is described in the works of Varthema,* Nicolo di Conti, Abder Razzak, Nikitin,† Barbosa,‡ and

* Hakluyt Society's Translation, p. 125.

† The narratives of Conti, Abder Razzak, and Nikitin will be found in the Hakluyt Society's volume, entitled "India in the 15th century."

‡ Hakluy Society's volume, entitled "The Coasts of East Africa and Malabar," p. 85.

Cæsar Frederick;* the beauties of Beejapore were noticed by Tavernier;† and Finch, Thevenot, Bernier, and others, who visited the court of the Mogul, did not fail to recount the wonders of Agra and Delhi. The cave temples of Western India also received attention from early travellers. Thevenot‡ and Anquetil du Perron explored the caves of Ellora; Linschoten, Boon,§ Anquetil, and Salt described Salsette; Salt was at Karli with Lord Valentia, and the famous cave of Elephanta was visited and described by Niebuhr, Fryer, Hamilton, Anquetil, Lord Valentia, and others.‖

The perusal of some of these authors had filled the mind of Sir William Jones with a keen interest in the literature and antiquities of the East, and his arrival at Calcutta is the epoch from which any attempt at the systematic investigation of Indian antiquities dates. The Asiatic Society at Calcutta was instituted on the 22nd of January 1784, and a centre was thus formed to which individual inquirers might forward the results of their labours, and from which they might derive assistance and advice. In the absence of an exhaustive survey under the direction of the Government, such an institution as the Asiatic Society was invaluable. Warren Hastings was obliged to decline the post of President, which he was so admirably fitted to occupy, from want of leisure to perform the duties, and Sir William Jones presided over the proceedings of the society from its first institution until his death. A branch of the Asiatic Society was formed at Bombay by Sir James Mackintosh in 1804. The Madras Literary Society, under the auspices of Sir John Newbold, the Chief Justice, was established in 1818.

The results of the early labours of English antiquaries in India are recorded in the twenty volumes of the Asiatic Researches from 1788 to 1836, in the three volumes of the Transactions of the Literary Society of Bombay, 1819-21; and in the opening numbers of the Journal of the Madras Literary Society, which was commenced in 1827.

---

* Viaggio di M. Cesare Fedrici nell' India Orientale (Venetia, 1587), p. 32.

† In Pinkerton.

‡ Travels, Part III., Chap. 45 (Eng. Trans.)

§ Governor of Bombay.

‖ See the Archæologia, vii., p. 323. Linschoten mentioned the cave of Elephanta in 1579. Dr. Fryer describes the Salsette caves in his travels published in 1698; J. Ovington, 1689; Hamilton in his Voyage, I., chap. xx., p. 338; Anquetil, Zend Avesta, I., pp. 234, 249, 419, 394.

The earliest labourers in the fruitful and important field of Indian archæology were Sir William Jones, Charles Wilkins,* Henry Colebrooke,† Francis Gladwin,‡ William Chambers, and Colin Mackenzie,§ followed by Buchanan Hamilton‖ and Horace Wilson.¶ These learned and accomplished scholars were zealously assisted and furnished with material for their researches by numerous younger explorers who forwarded to them the results of their investigations in all parts of India.

The description and delineation of architectural remains were of great importance, but the deciphering of inscriptions on pillars, metal plates, or coins was most essential to the student of Indian history, for by that means alone could dates be obtained, without which history would have no coherence. The learning and sagacity and

---

* Charles Wilkins went to Bengal, in the Civil Service, in 1770. After studying Sanscrit for several years, he translated the Bhagavat Gita, to which Warren Hastings prefixed a learned dissertation. The Court of Directors published this work in 1785. Wilkins prepared the first types for Bengalee and Persian that were ever used in India. He returned home in 1786, and in 1795 he published his translation of Sacontala. He became Librarian of the East India House in 1800, in 1808 he published his Sanscrit Grammar, and he took an active part in the promotion of the Oriental Translation Fund. He was knighted by William IV., and died in Baker Street on May 13th, 1836, aged 86.

† Henry T. Colebrooke, son of Sir George Colebrooke, Bart., the Chairman of the East India Company, was born in London in 1765. He went out to India as a writer in 1782, and in 1794 undertook the translation of a digest of Hindu Law, compiled under the direction of Sir William Jones. In 1803 he was at work on a Sanscrit grammar, and published the first volume in 1805, but abandoned the rest, owing to the publication of the grammar by Wilkins. Colebrooke became a member of Council at Calcutta in 1805, returned home in 1815, and died in 1837. His works are the "Digest of Hindoo Law" (4 vols., folio, 1798), the first volume of a Sanscrit grammar (1805), lexicon (1808), Sanscrit algebra (1817), and numerous essays in the "Asiatic Researches," "Transactions of the Royal Asiatic Society," &c.

‡ Translator of the Ayeen Akberi.

§ See page 58.

‖ Dr. Buchanan is well known for his explorations in Nepaul, Mysore and Malabar, and Burmah, and for his survey of Bengal.

¶ Horace H. Wilson went out to India as assistant surgeon in 1808, and was attached to the Calcutta mint. In 1813 he published Calidasa's "Cloud Messenger;" and in 1819 the first edition of his Sanscrit dictionary appeared. In 1826 his "Hindu Theatre" was published. In 1812 he became Secretary to the Asiatic Society at Calcutta; and, after his return to England, he was elected Professor of Sanscrit at Oxford in 1833, and Librarian to the East India Company on the death of Sir Charles Wilkins in 1836. The last years of his life were devoted to the translation of the Rig Veda. He died on May 23rd 1860, and his numerous works on Sanscrit literature and kindred subjects have been re-published since his death.

the indefatigable industry that have been brought to bear upon the deciphering of inscriptions in India have never been surpassed, and have perhaps produced the most valuable results of archæological research in that country. The importance of this branch of the investigation was felt from the very first. Colonel Polier described the famous Boodhist pillar with its inscriptions, known as the Feroze Lat,* and a paper was contributed to the Asiatic Researches on the same subject by Colebrooke.† Blunt ‡ and Ewer § described the Kuttub Minar pillar at Delhi, and Harington and Buchanan contributed papers describing the remains at Boodh Gya.‖ Charles Wilkins wrote six papers on the meaning of various inscriptions that had been forwarded to him,¶ and Colebrooke wrote an essay on inscriptions generally, especially on those found on ancient monuments.** Several were also translated by Captain Fell from Hissar and Benares, containing genealogies of Indian dynasties ††; and Lieutenant Price translated a Sanscrit inscription on a stone found in Bundelcund.‡‡ Wilson contributed translations of three copper plates found in Chuttishgur§§ and of many Sanscrit inscriptions at Abu, which throw much light on the history of the Jain temples from 1189 to 1752.‖‖ In the last volume of the Researches there are translations of various inscriptions found in the ruins of Bijayanuggur by Mr. Ravenshaw, with observations by Wilson. They consist of genealogies of the kings and grants of land.¶¶

In the total absence of authentic materials for fixing dates in Indian written histories, very great importance attaches to all genuine monuments and inscriptions on stone or metal. The principal

---

* Asiatic Researches, i., p. 379.

† " vii., p. 175.

‡ " iv., p. 313.

§ " xiv., p. 480.

‖ " i., p. 276. "Description of the Ruins at Buddha Gaya," by Dr. Buchanan Hamilton.—*Transactions of the Royal Asiatic Society*, ii., p. 40.

¶ On a copper plate found at Monghir, i., p. 123; on a stone pillar near Buddal, i., p. 131; on Boodh Gya, i., p. 284; on an inscription near Gya, ii., p. 167; on Islamabad, ii., p. 383; and another on Boodh Gya, i., p. 276.

** ix., p. 398.

†† xv., p. 387.

‡‡ xv., p. 437.

§§ xv., p. 499.

‖‖ xvi., p. 284.

¶¶ xx., p. 1.

discovery resulting from researches of this nature was made by Sir William Jones, and announced in his anniversary address delivered on the 28th of February 1793.* It had been a question where the city of Palibothra was situated, which was visited by the Greek ambassador Megasthenes. Sir William discovered in a Sanscrit book that Hirayabahu or "the golden armed," which the Greeks changed into Erannaboas,† was only another name for the river Sone. This discovery led to another of great moment, for King Chandragupta actually fixed the seat of his empire at Pataliputra at the mouth of the Sone (the Palibothra of Strabo), and was no other than the very Sandracottus who concluded a treaty with Seleucus Nicator. Thus Sir William Jones fixed the first great landmark in the ancient history of India. He reserved his proofs for a future essay, but his interesting labours were cut short by a premature death.

Detailed descriptions of ruins and other architectural remains were also contributed to the Asiatic Researches. William Chambers visited the famous ruins on the Coromandel coast known as the Seven Pagodas or Mavalipuram in 1772, and again in 1776, and described them;‡ and another more detailed account of the Mavalipuram sculptures was furnished by Mr. Goldingham, the astronomer at Madras,§ who also wrote an account of the cave of Elephanta. Sir C. Malet contributed a paper on the Ellora caves in 1794, with drawings by Lieutenant Manby;‖ and Colin Mackenzie described the pagoda of Perwuttum in a wild tract near the south bank of the Krishna,¶ and wrote an account of the Jains.** A full description of the grand Mohammedan ruins at Beejapore was written by Captain Sydenham in 1811, who also made a careful survey.†† They had been previously described by Major Moor in 1794,‡‡ and when Sir James Mackintosh visited them in 1808 he called Beejapore the "Palmyra of the Deccan."

---

* Asiatic Researches, iv., p. 11.
† Strabo, XV., c. i. and ii., 1, 9.
‡ Asiatic Researches, i., p. 123.
§ " iv., p. 69.
‖ " vi., p. 389.
¶ " iv., p. 303.
** " vii., p. 175.
†† " xiii., p. 433.
‡‡ Major Moor's "Narrative of the Operations of Captain Little's Detachment," p. 310.

The antiquaries on the Bombay side of India emulated the example of their brethren at Calcutta. Mr. Salt, Lord Valentia's secretary, wrote an account of the caves in Salsette in 1806, illustrated by drawings and copies of sculptures.* Mr. Erskine drew up his exhaustive essay on the cave of Elephanta,† the whole conception and plan of which he truly describes as extremely grand and magnificent. His account, which is correct and minute without being tedious, and is by far the best description of the cave that has been published, is illustrated by plans and copies of sculpture.‡ It was written in November 1813.§ In 1819 and 1820 Colonel Sykes wrote accounts of the ruined city of Beejapore and of the Ellora caves.‖

In Madras the leading antiquary of the earlier period was Colin Mackenzie, whose labours have already been noticed.¶ His vast collections of *sassanums* or inscriptions on stone and copper, of manuscripts and coins, have alone enabled the early history of Southern India and its dynasties to be understood and written.** To Mackenzie's researches we owe Wilson's history of the great Pandyan dynasty of Madura,†† and Dowson's paper on the Chera dynasty.‡‡

---

* Transactions of the Literary Society of Bombay, i., p. 41. The Rev. J. Stevenson afterwards wrote a paper on the rock inscriptions of the island of Salsette.—*Journal of Bombay Branch of Asiatic Society*, iv., p. 132.

† Transactions of the Literary Society of Bombay, i., p. 198.

‡ See also "An Account of the Cave of Elephanta," by Mr. Goldingham.—*Asiatic Researches*, iv., p. 407.

"On the Three-faced Siva at Elephanta," by Colonel Sykes.—*Journal of the Royal Asiatic Society*, v., p. 81.

"The Theory of the Great Elephanta Cave," by Dr. Stevenson.—*Journal of Bombay Branch of Asiatic Society*, iv., p. 261.

§ William Erskine came out to India with Sir James Mackintosh in 1804, and was for many years a magistrate at Bombay. He returned to England in 1823. When the Literary Society of Bombay was instituted in 1804 he became its Secretary. Besides his paper on the Cave of Elephanta, he wrote an essay on the sacred books of the Parsees in 1819; and his valuable translation of the Memoirs of Baber was published in 1823.

‖ Transactions of the Literary Society of Bombay, iii., pp. 55, 265.

¶ See p. 58.

** "Mackenzie Collection of Oriental Manuscripts," by H. H. Wilson. 2 vols. (Calcutta, 1828).

"1st Report on the Mackenzie MSS., by Rev. Wm. Taylor. (Madras Journal of Literature and Science, vol. vii., p. 1.) 2d, 3d, 4th, and 5th Reports in vols. viii. and ix.

†† Journal of the Royal Asiatic Society, iii., p. 199.

‡‡ " " viii., p. 1.

A correct estimate of the beauty and magnificence of Indian architectural art and of the interest which attaches to it, was furnished to our fathers by Thomas Daniell, an artist who passed the greater part of the last decade of the last century in traversing all parts of India, and executing water-colour drawings of the highest merit, of all the principal monuments and edifices. His labours were given to the world in six large folio volumes, containing 120 coloured views engraved by himself and his nephew between 1797 and 1809. Here will be found most accurate drawings of the temples and palaces at Madura and Tanjore and of the ruins at Mavalipuram, to represent the architecture of Southern India; the Taj Mahal, Akbar's tomb, and mosques at Juanpore and Delhi, as specimens of Mohammedan art; and the rock-hewn temples at Salsette and Elephanta. This work also contains an elaborate series of views of the caves at Ellora, drawn by Mr. Wales, but engraved by the Daniells; as well as numerous general views. They are drawn with such care and accuracy that they bear the test of comparison with recent photographs.

Such were the advances that were made in the investigation of Indian antiquities during what may be considered as the first period of the study of the subject. The second period is that in which James Prinsep took the lead, a man whose equal has rarely been found in acute reasoning and unflagging industry, backed by an enthusiastic love of research. He added to rare gifts of intellect an amiable and generous disposition, giving all credit to his fellow labourers and reserving none for himself, so that men worked as much to please James Prinsep as for the sake of Indian archæology. The son of an East India agent and nephew of Mr. Auriol, Warren Hastings's secretary, James Prinsep was one out of seven brothers who obtained employment in India. He was born in 1799, and was appointed assistant assay master at the Calcutta mint in 1819, serving under Horace Wilson. In 1820 he became assay master at Benares, where he executed a series of accurate drawings of streets and buildings which were published by the Asiatic Society; and in 1825 his "Views and Illustrations of Benares" appeared. In 1830 Prinsep returned to Calcutta, where he joined heartily with Major Herbert in his project of publishing a periodical called "Gleanings in Science," of which he became editor and proprietor in 1831, when Herbert accepted the post of astronomer at Lucknow.

He succeeded Wilson as assay master of the Calcutta mint in 1832, and became secretary to the Asiatic Society, altering the title of his "Gleanings" to that of "The Journal of the Asiatic Society of Bengal," the first number of which appeared on March 7th, 1832. It has been published monthly ever since. For the remaining 10 years of his life James Prinsep devoted his energies to the solution of a most difficult problem, and his marvellous success has thrown new light on ancient Indian history, while it has immortalized his name among oriental scholars.

The Buddhist remains were known to be the most important and the most ancient in India, but the numerous inscriptions connected with them were still unreadable puzzles. The inscriptions on the pillars at Delhi and Allahabad had been copied and published, but they had baffled the scholarship of Jones and Colebrooke to decipher. In the years 1835 and 1836, notices of James Prinsep's success in deciphering the inscriptions were published. In 1834 Lieutenant Burt had written a description, with drawings, of the Boodhist stone pillar at Allahabad,* which was said by the Hindoos to be the club with which the hero Bhima ground his bhang. There are four inscriptions engraven upon it in different characters. Of these the first is the same as that on the Delhi pillar, and the second is the same as the Gya inscription, the key to which was supplied by Wilkins's translation.† The name of Chandragupta, the king whose identity with Sandracottus had been established by Sir William Jones, occurs on the second inscription. But the clue was first obtained when, in June 1837, Prinsep received copies made by Captain E. Smith of sentences cut on the pillars round the famous Sanchi tope or mound, near Bhilsa, in Central India.‡ Each sentence ended with the same two letters, and it occurred to Prinsep, by a sort of inspiration, that these two letters represented the verb "to give," or "a gift." It was thus that he finally obtained a clue to the alphabet, and the language turned out to resemble the Pali of Ceylon. He applied this alphabet to the inscriptions on the *lats* or pillars at Delhi and Allahabad, and the great discovery was completed. They all proved to be the same series of edicts by the famous

* Asiatic Researches, iii., p. 106.
† " i., p. 279.
‡ "J. A. S. B.", iii., p. 488; vi., pt. i., p. 451.

Buddhist King Asoka.* The name on the pillars was Pryadasi, which Mr. Turnour,† the Pali scholar, identified with that of Asoka.

Among the most indefatigable of Prinsep's coadjutors was Lieutenant Kittoe, who investigated the ruins in Orissa, and discovered an important series of inscriptions on a rock at Dhauli, in Cuttack. He was also employed by Government to make excavations at Sarnath, near Benares.‡ At about the time that Kitto found the Dhauli inscription, a copy of the rock inscription at Girnar, in Guzerat, was made by Captain Lang, and sent to Prinsep in 1837 by Mr. Wathen; and a third series was discovered at Kapur di Giri, near Peshawar, in the far north of India. Prinsep studied the first two of these rock inscriptions with the utmost care.§ Those discovered by Kittoe at Dhauli, in Cuttack, proved to be identical with those received from Girnar, in Guzerat, being a series of inscriptions by King Asoka. The names of Antiochus the Great,‖ of Antigonus, and of one of the Ptolemies¶ occur and fix their date,

* "J. A. S. B." iii., p. 257. Restoration of No. 2 inscription on the Allahabad Lat, by Dr. Mill.
" vi., p. 1. Restoration and translation of the inscription on the Bhitari Lat in Ghazeepore, by Dr. Mill.
" vi., p. 451. Note on fac-similes of inscriptions from Sanchi, taken by Capt. E. Smith.
" iii., p. 488. Copy of the inscription on the iron pillar at Delhi.
" vi., pt. 2., p. 566. Interpretation of the inscriptions on the Feroze Shah and Allahabad Lats.
" vii., p. 219. Edicts on Girnar and Dhauli rocks.
" vii., pt. 1., p. 434. Edicts on the Dhauli rock.
" " p. 4562. More *denams*, sent from the Sanchi Tope by Capt. Burt, and translated by Prinsep.

† *See* an account of these investigations in the introduction to Turnour's Mahawanso.

‡ Lieut. Markham Kittoe wrote many papers in the Journal of the Asiatic Society of Bengal:—"Journal of his tour in Orissa" (vii., pt. 2, p. 679); "A journey through the forests of Orissa" (viii., pts. 1 and 2); "On the viharas and chaityas round Gyah" (xvi., pt. 1, p. 272); "On sculptured images on the temple of Grameswara in Cuttack" (xvi., pt. 2, p. 660); "On pillars found in the Ganges" (viii., p. 681); "Notes on the places visited by F. A. Hian" (xvi., p. 953); "Inscriptions at Juanpore" (xix., p. 454); "On antiquarian researches" (xvii., p. 536); "The temple of Durga at Badieswar" (vii., p. 828). These contributions range from 1838 to 1850. He was Curator and Librarian to the Asiatic Society at Calcutta until 1838, when he was appointed to survey the road to Bombay. He died soon after returning to England in 1853.

§ "J. A. S. B.," viii., pt. 1, p. 156.
‖ " vii., pt. 1, p. 156.
¶ " " p. 334.

while the prohibition of the sacrifice of animals either for food or ceremonies, the order that medical aid shall be supplied for animals as well as men, that for the planting of trees and digging of wells by the roadsides, and the publication of precepts, prove that the royal lawgiver was a follower of the creed of Buddha.

Important researches were successfully conducted in the north of India during the time of James Prinsep's editorship, which engaged his attention. Generals Ventura and Court, officers in the service of Runjeet Sing, opened a tope at Manikyala, in 1830, and others between Jhelum and the Indus in 1833 and 1834. They found a gold box containing coins and relics; while Masson, Honigberger, and Gerard examined some equally interesting topes near Jellalabad.* Captain William Brown, of the Revenue Survey, also gave an account of the ancient temple and famous ship model at Hissar, in Prinsep's Journal.†

The copy of the Girnar inscription was not quite satisfactory, and through Prinsep's influence, Lieutenant Postans was employed by the Bombay Government to take exact fac-similes. But James Prinsep had worn himself out by intense and continuous study. He was obliged to return home in a hopeless condition, and died on April 22nd, 1840.‡ Meanwhile, Lieutenant Postans took infinite pains to secure exactitude in his fac-similes of the Girnar inscription, which were sent to Calcutta. They arrived too late. The guiding spirit of these investigations—the heart and soul of Indian archæological research—had already passed away. Prinsep sailed for England just before the results of the labours of Lieutenant Postans arrived. The manuscripts and cloth copies were thrown carelessly aside, and rotted in a godown at Calcutta.§

---

* "Asiatic Researches," vol. xvii. "J. A. S. B.," iii., p. 313. "Remarks on the Relic in the Manikyala tope by Prinsep," iii., p. 436 and p. 556. Masson on Cabul Coins, v., p. 537.

† "J. A. S. B.," vol. vii., pt. 1, p. 429.

‡ The seven first volumes of the Journal of the Asiatic Society of Bengal were edited by Prinsep, 1832–38. See a notice of him, written by his brother, at the beginning of "Essays on Indian Antiquities, by the late James Prinsep, edited by E. Thomas" (2 vols. Murray, 1858). In this work Prinsep's essays were reprinted, owing to an increased demand for the early copies of the Journal of the Asiatic Society of Bengal, in which they first appeared.

§ "Journal of the Bombay Branch of the Asiatic Society," i., p. 257. The Girnar inscription was again copied by Le Grand Jacob and the Danish Zend scholar Westergaard; and a second copy was sent to Professor Lassen.

Prinsep's genius discovered the first positive dates in early Indian history, and opened to European scholars a mine of knowledge which has been ably followed up by his disciples. His conclusions were closely criticised, and were more fully established by the ordeal. Horace Wilson* expressed doubts of the correctness of Prinsep's identification of the Pryadarsi of the inscriptions with the great King Asoka; but he has been completely answered by General Cunningham,† and the soundness of Prinsep's interpretations are no longer impugned. The history of these discoveries, and a very complete and interesting notice of Asoka, his religion and government, was published by Sir Erskine Perry.‡

The third and last period of Indian archæological research, extending from the death of Prinsep in 1840 to the present year, has been one of great activity, the zeal and scholarship of Prinsep having been inherited by numerous successors. Cunningham and Maisey in the north, Meadows Taylor and Wilson in Bombay, Walter Elliot in Madras, have taken the lead, and they have had many followers; while photography has lately increased the means of illustrating and elucidating their researches. But it is to Fergusson that European inquirers are most indebted for having brought a knowledge of Indian architecture within their reach, and for having systematized and rendered clear the chronology and history of eastern art, while he has explained and illustrated its rare beauty and excellence. A brief notice of his labours will be a fitting prelude to the enumeration of the various archæological researches of the last thirty years.

Mr. James Fergusson, having, as far as he was able, qualified himself for the task of thoroughly investigating the architecture and antiquities of India, left England in 1829, with the intention of availing himself of any opportunities of pursuing his inquiries that might be offered him, and which his professional engagements would admit of. During his residence in Jessore, from 1829 to 1833, he repeatedly visited Dacca, Rajghur, and the few other places in the Ganges Delta which contain any remains of architectural art. In

* "Rock Inscriptions of Kapur di Giri, Dhauli, and Girnar," by H. H. Wilson.—*Journal of the Royal Asiatic Society*, xii., p. 236.

† "Bhilsa Topes," p. 100.

‡ Journal of the Bombay Branch of the Asiatic Society, iii., p. 149. Sir Erskine's notice is chiefly based on Lassen's "Indische Alterthumskunde."

1834 he went to Benares, and thence visited Agra and Delhi, returning by way of Deeg and Jeypore, Canouge, Lucknow, and Juanpore, and visiting all the cities on the Ganges as far as Gour and Moorshedabad. In 1836 he was present at the festival of Juggernath at Pooree, and visited all the places of interest in Cuttack. In 1839 he again visited most of the cities in the Gangetic valley, including Agra and Delhi, and went on as far as the Sutlej. He also passed four months in wandering through Central India, visiting most of the principal cities of Rajpootana, as far west as Abu, and thence making his way to Bombay, by Ajunta, Ellora, and Karli. He examined these caves, as well as those of Salsette and Elephanta, before leaving Bombay on his return to England in 1839. Mr. Fergusson had occasion to revisit India in 1842, and he took the opportunity of making a coast voyage from Bombay to Goa, Cannanore, and Calicut, thence crossing the peninsula by way of Tanjore, Trichinopoly, Chellumbarum, Conjeveram, and the rock-cut temples at Sadras. He thus made himself acquainted with the architecture of Southern India. During all these journeys Mr. Fergusson kept a careful record of what he saw, and made drawings of everything of interest. His next object was to give the results of his investigations to the world, and in 1843 he read a paper before the Royal Asiatic Society on the "Rock-cut Temples of India,"* which may be considered as having placed the theory of the age and uses of those monuments on a basis of certainty, which has never since been called in question. This paper was followed, in 1847, by a folio volume of plates entitled "Picturesque Illustrations of Ancient Architecture in India," with an introductory historical essay and full descriptions of the plates. He intended to have continued the work by publishing similar volumes on Buddhist, Jaina, and Mohammedan architecture, but the expense was so great and the encouragement so small that the idea was abandoned. Since that time various papers by Mr. Fergusson on the architecture of India have appeared in the transactions of learned Societies, and chapters on all its branches are given in his handbook, and with greater fulness and detail in his History of Architecture. But the great project to which all these steps were merely preliminary still remains in abeyance. Besides his own personal researches, it is understood that during the last

* Printed in vol. viii. of the Journal of the Royal Asiatic Society, and afterwards published separately in 1845, with a folio volume of plates.

30 years Mr. Fergusson has been collecting drawings and photographs, with the idea of writing an illustrated history of Indian architectural art. The expense, however, would be very great, and the encouragement is so problematical that it is to be feared that the publication of this valuable and important work may be indefinitely postponed.

Meanwhile the luminous classification of Indian architecture by Mr. Fergusson furnishes the means of reviewing the researches of the last 30 years in a more systematic way than was possible in the case of earlier labours, in days when the distinctions of time and race were only very imperfectly understood. The subject is now divided under the following heads :—

1. Prehistoric archæology of India.
2. Buddhist monuments. (The Aryans who composed the Vedas built no permanent edifices.)
3. Dravidian architecture of Southern India.
4. Bengalee architecture.
6. Rajpoot or Chalukya architecture.
7. Jaina architecture.
8. Saracenic architecture, which Mr. Fergusson divides into eight styles, as developed at different times and in various parts of India.
9. The collection and deciphering of coins, and inscriptions on metal or stone plates is a distinct and very important branch of research, through which the ancient history of India has been elucidated.

1. *Prehistoric Remains.*

The prehistoric remains in India consist of cairns, cromlechs, and other cognate remains of unknown age, and constructed by an unknown people. They are probably scattered widely, but have hitherto only been examined in a few localities. In 1820 Mr. Babington described the Kodey Kulls or Pandoo Koolies of Malabar,* which consist of several stones set upon end with their points meeting, on which a large mushroom-shaped stone is fixed. Underneath are found urns containing fragments of human bones mixed with charcoal and fine sand. The next notice of prehistoric

---

* "Transactions of the Literary Society of Bombay," vol. iii.

remains was by Captain Harkness, who published an account of some cairns he found in the Neilgherries in 1832. He was followed by Captain Congreve, who wrote a detailed account of the cromlechs and cairns of the Neilgherries;* and 12 years afterwards the Rev. J. T. Kearns, an S. P. G. missionary, published an interesting paper on the cairns, containing urns, which occur in the Tenecassy talook of Tinnevelly.† Captain Newbold discovered some ancient sepulchres, consisting of slabs of granite forming four sides and a top, surrounded by circles of stones, in a secluded valley of North Arcot, three miles from Chettoor.‡ Captain Congreve described a remarkable cromlech near Pullicondah, in the Carnatic.§ Colonel Meadows Taylor has devoted much attention to the prehistoric archæology of India, and has himself made important discoveries in the Shorapore province of the Deccan, just above the junction of the Bhima and Krishna rivers. The Shorapore remains consist of cairns, cromlechs, and kistvaens of sandstone slabs placed upright on their sides, and covered with a slab monolith which projects over them. They are scattered over the province in groups.‖ Large groups of cairns also occur near Hyderabad in the Deccan,¶ in the Raichoor Doab, in Bellary, and in the Central Provinces, where excavations have recently been made by the Archæological Society at Nagpore. Sir Bartle Frere also described some cairns and cromlechs in Beloochistan.** On the Khasia Hills, Colonel Yule, found megalithic monuments scattered on every wayside. They consist of rows of pillars some 27 feet high, cromlechs or large flat stones resting on four rough pillars, and tombs formed of four large slabs on their edges, roofed over by a fifth placed horizontally.†† The whole subject was recently discussed by Colonel Meadows Taylor

---

* "Antiquities of the Neilgherry Hills," by Captain H. Congreve (1847).—*Journal of Literature and Science of Madras*, xiv., p. 77. "Remarks on Druidic Antiquities of Southern India," by Major H. Congreve,—N.S., vol. vi., p. 205.

† Ibid., N.S., v., p. 27.

‡ "Journal of the Royal Asiatic Society," x., p. 90.

§ *Madras Journal*, xiii., pt. ii., p. 47.

‖ "Ancient remains at the village of Jiwarji, near Farozabad, on the Bhima," by Colonel Meadows Taylor.—*Journal of the Bombay Branch of the Asiatic Society*, iii., p. 179. "Cromlechs and Cairns in Sorapore," by Colonel Meadows Taylor,—*Ibid.* iv., p. 380. See also the "Transactions of the Royal Irish Academy" (1865), vol. xxiv.

¶ "Transactions of the Royal Irish Academy" (1867).

** "Journal of the Bombay Branch of the Asiatic Society," v., p. 349.

†† "J. A. S. B.," vol. xiii., pt. ii., p. 612. See also Hooker's Journal.

in a paper read before the Ethnological Society,* and he has also drawn attention to its importance in an official memorandum.† Quite recently, Mr. Boswell has reported upon the kist-vaens and rude stone circles in the Kistna district.‡

2. *Buddhist Remains.*

A wide interval lies between the cromlechs and cairns and the Buddhist remains that come next in order, for the Aryans who composed the Vedic literature and poured out soma juice to their gods in their own houses, built nothing that has endured to our time. We, therefore, come at once from the period of unknown antiquity when the cromlechs were built, to the centuries immediately preceding and following the Christian era, when Buddhism flourished in India. From B.C. 250 for five centuries all monuments in India are Buddhist. Fergusson calls this earliest style "a wooden art, painfully struggling into lithic forms." Gateways and railings of masonry were imitated from the earlier forms carved out of timber. The Buddhist remains consist of rock inscriptions,§ *lats* or pillars ‖ with inscriptions, *topes* or *stupas*, rock-hewn temples, and viharas or monasteries. The inscriptions on the rocks and pillars had already received full attention from James Prinsep and his predecessors. The topes have been examined by General Cunningham, Colonel Maisey, Sir Walter Elliot, and others.

The most important group of *topes*,¶ or vast mounds for the reception of relics, is near Bhilsa in the Bhopal State of Central India. There are about 30, but that known as the Sanchi Tope is the largest, and indeed the finest in central India, the dome being 42 feet high and faced with masonry. It is surrounded by a stone fence

* "On Prehistoric Archæology of India," by Colonel Meadows Taylor.—*Journal of the Ethnological Society*, i., No. 2, p. 157.

† "Report on the Illustration of the Archaic Architecture of India," Appendix E.

‡ Boswell's Report on the archæology of the Kistna district.

§ The rock inscriptions are at Girnar in Guzerat, at Dhauli near Cuttack, at Kapardi Giri near Peshawur, and a fourth copied by General Cunningham at Dehra Dhoon.

‖ The *lats* are, 1,—that of Feroze Shah at Delhi; 2, another of iron near Delhi; 3, that in the fort at Allahabad; 4, 5, 6, near the Gunduck in Tirhoot; and 7, was used as a roller on the Benares road by an engineer officer.

¶ An Afghan word, meaning a solid mound of masonry. It is the same as the Pali *thupo*, and Sanscrit *stupa*, a mound or tumulus.

consisting of uprights with three horizontal cross pieces, and is approached by four masonry gateways covered with sculpture. The Sanchi Tope was first injudiciously dug into by Sir H. Maddock in 1819. Captain E. Smith sent copies of the sentences carved on the pillars to James Prinsep in 1837, and Captain W. Murray made a series of drawings.* In January 1851 the Bhilsa Topes were minutely examined and opened by Major Alexander Cunningham, an enthusiastic scholar and antiquary, and a friend of James Prinsep, with whom was associated Lieutenant F. Maisey, who had previously been employed in describing the antiquities at Kalinjar.† Colonel Maisey executed a beautiful series of drawings in 1854, and a series of photographs of the Sanchi Tope was taken by Lieutenant Waterhouse. General Cunningham published a full description of the Bhilsa Topes, with an interesting sketch of the rise and progress of Buddhism, in the same year;‡ and Mr. Fergusson's superb work on "Tree and Serpent Worship," illustrated by Lieutenant Waterhouse's photographs and by lithographs of Colonel Maisey's drawings of the Sanchi Tope, appeared in 1868.§ A brief account of the Bhilsa Topes will also be found in the "History of Architecture."‖

The Amravati Tope is another magnificent Buddhist monument. It is in the Guntoor district, near the mouth of the Kistna, and elaborate drawings were made of it, and of its minutely carved stones in the last century, by Colin Mackenzie. He first visited the spot in 1797, and in 1816 he caused careful plans and maps, and 80 drawings of sculptures to be made by his assistants, which are unsurpassed for accuracy and beauty of finish.¶ Sir Walter

---

* "J. A. S. B.," vi., pt. i., p. 451.

† Ibid., pt. i., vol. xvii., p. 171; and report to the government of the N. W. Provinces, 1847. Kalinjar is mentioned in the Vedas.

‡ "The Bhilsa Topes or Buddhist monuments of Central India; comprising a brief sketch of the rise, progress, and decline of Buddhism," by Brevet Major Alexander Cunningham (Bengal Engineers). Illustrated with 33 plates. London, 1854.

§ "Tree and Serpent Worship; or illustrations of mythology and art in India in the first and fourth centuries after Christ, from the sculptures of the Buddhist Topes at Sanchi and Amravati, prepared under the authority of the Secretary of State for India in Council, with introductory essays and descriptions of the plates," by James Fergusson, Esq., F.R.S. (London, India Museum, 1868.)

‖ Fergusson's "History of Architecture," ii., p. 463.

¶ "Asiatic Researches," ix., p. 272. Three copies of Colin Mackenzie's drawings were made, one for the library of the Court of Directors, one for the Asiatic Society of Bengal, and a third for Madras. Specimens of sculpture were also sent to the India House. See "Description of the Amravati Tope in Guntoor," by James Fergusson.—*Journal of the Royal Asiatic Society*, N.S., iii., p. 132.

Elliot, who was Commissioner in Guntoor in 1840, excavated a portion of the monument, and sent 160 fragments of sculpture to Madras,* which were forwarded to the India House in 1856. Some of these sculptures were exhibited in the museum at Fyfe House, and the others, on account of want of space, were placed in store, where they remained until they were brought to the notice of Mr. Fergusson, at whose desire photographs were taken of the entire series. The whole of these remarkable sculptures have recently been arranged in the inner court of the India Office; and 52 photographs of them, with descriptions by Mr. Fergusson and a map, are published in "Tree and Serpent Worship."†

The examination of the Jellalabad Topes by Masson, and of those in the Punjab by Ventura and Court, took place in Prinsep's time, and has already been alluded to. There is another group of Buddhist ruins near Benares, called Sarnath, the principal of which is a tower 100 feet high. It was opened in 1835 by General Cunningham, who made the excavations, as well as a set of drawings of the elaborate ornament of the great tower, entirely at his own expense. Subsequently, some further excavations were made at Sarnath, at Government expense, under the superintendence of Captain Kittoe, in 1852. After his departure they were continued by Mr. Edward Thomas‡ and Professor Hall.

The cave temples have been visited and noticed by numerous travellers from the time of Thevenot, and described in detail by Mr. Fergusson§ in his "Illustrations of the Rock-cut Temples of India." Dr. Wilson, of Bombay, has also written two memoirs on the rock-cut temples. At the suggestion of Mr. Fergusson in 1850, the Asiatic Society had represented to the Court of Directors the propriety of taking steps for the preservation of the cave temples

* "Selections from the Records of the Madras Government," 2d series, No. xxxix., p. 195.

† See also "History of Architecture," ii., p. 471.

‡ "Notes on the excavations at Sarnath."—*J. A. S. B.* (1854), p. 469.

§ *Ubi sup.* See also the "History of Architecture," ii., p. 479. In 1863 Mr. Fergusson edited a small volume of 78 photographs of the caves of Ajunta and Ellora, by Major Gill, which, though containing little that is new, are interesting as confirming the accuracy of the lithographs published by Mr. Fergusson 18 years before.

and other ancient monuments,* and Dr. Wilson then prepared a descriptive list of all the rock temples in Western India.† There are 900, of which nine tenths are in the Bombay Presidency. Dr. James Bird published descriptive accounts of the sculptures in the caves,‡ Westergaard gave a brief account of some minor caves near Karli,§ Sir Bartle Frere described those at Karadh and at Waee,‖ and Colonel Sykes wrote a paper on inscriptions from Buddh caves near Joonur.¶ The Court of Directors, through the efforts of Colonel Sykes, employed Major Gill to copy the paintings in the caves, and he was engaged upon this work for twenty years. Eventually a series of oil paintings was transmitted to the India House. The paintings were exhibited in the Crystal Palace at Sydenham, where they were all burnt in December 1867, except four, which had been forgotten to be sent, and which are now at the India Office. Unfortunately some application that had been made to the originals in the caves, to bring them out more clearly for copying, has injured them irremediably, and they are now rapidly fading away.**

The *raths* or rock-hewn edifices at Mavalipuram, near Sadras, on the Coromandel coast, which were described in the last century by

---

* Karli cave was described by Lord Valentia, and fac-similes of inscriptions were taken by Dr. Stevenson and Dr. Wilson.

Ajunta caves were first mentioned in Mr. Erskine's paper; a short account of them was read before the Royal Asiatic Society, by Lieut. J. E. Alexander, in 1829 (*Trans. R. A. S.*, iii., p. 62). Mr. Ralph also described them in the *J. A. S. B.*, v., p. 557. Fac-similes, transcripts, and translations of the inscriptions were made by Dr. Bhau Dajee in 1863. See "Journal of the Bombay Branch of the Asiatic Society," vii., p. 53.

Ellora caves were first described by Sir C. Mallet in the "Asiatic Researches." Drawings were taken by Mr. Wales; and Colonel Sykes wrote a paper on them in vol. iii. of the "Transactions of the Bombay Literary Society."

Aurungabad caves were first described by Dr. Bird. Junegad and Girnar caves were visited by Dr. Wilson.

† "Memoirs on the cave temples, and monasteries of Western India," by Dr. Wilson.—*Journal of the Bombay Branch of the Asiatic Society*, iii., p. 36, iv., p. 340.

‡ Historical researches on the origin and principles of the Bouddha and Jain religions, illustrated by descriptive accounts of sculptures in the caves of Western India," by James Bird.—*Ibid.*, ii., p. 71.

§ Ibid., i., p. 438.

‖ Ibid., iii., p. 36, and p. 108.

¶ "Journal of the Royal Asiatic Society," iv., p. 287.

** At Mr. Fergusson's suggestion, the plans, photographs, and drawings of Ajunta and other temples were purchased from Major Gill by the Government in 1868; 61 negatives, 36 pencil drawings, and books containing ground plans and sketches.

Chambers and Goldingham, and are commonly known as the seven *pagodas*, are classed by Mr. Fergusson as forms of Buddhist architecture adopted by the Hindu.* He considers them to be close copies of a Buddhist storied *vehara* or monastery. The most complete descriptions of these monuments were written by Dr. Babington, who gives drawings and copies of inscriptions,† and by Sir Walter Elliot;‡ and they are also described by Bishop Heber in his journal.§ The Madras Government have recently printed all these papers together, in a small octavo volume, edited by Captain Carr, with a map drawn under instructions from Colonel Priestley.‖

3. *Dravidian Architecture.*

The Dravidian style of architecture extends over all India south of the river Kistna, except Mysore, and had its origin in the three ancient kingdoms of Pandya, Chola, and Chera. The Dravidian temples are of vast extent and magnificent design. They consist of the *vimana* or shrine, the *mantapas* or porches leading to it, the *gopuras* or lofty gate pyramids in the quadrangular surrounding walls, and the pillared halls or chooltries. In 1830 a learned native of Tanjore, named Ram Raj, wrote an essay on the architecture of Southern India. His project was to collect treatises on architecture in the native languages, collate them, and produce an exposition such as should enable a European reader to form an opinion on the system. The holy Rishi Aghastya, who brought the first Brahman colony into Southern India, is said to have written a treatise on architecture, and others were also composed in ancient times, which collectively were called Silpa Sastra, but few traces of them remain. One, called Mánasára, on the building of sacred edifices, and eight others, are extant. From these sources Ram Raz described the

---

* "History of Architecture," ii., p. 502.

† "Transactions of the Royal Asiatic Society," ii., p. 258.

‡ "Madras Journal of Literature and Science," xiii., pt. i., p. 46., and pt. ii., p. 36. "A guide to the sculptures and excavations at Mamallaipur, generally known as the "seven pagodas, by Lieut. John Braddock; archæological notes by Rev. W. M. Taylor, "and a supplementary account of the remains at Salvan Cuppam, by Walter Elliot.

§ iii., p. 216.

‖ "Descriptive and historical papers relating to the seven pagodas, on the Coro-"mandel Coast, by G. W. Chambers, J. Goldingham, B. G. Babington, Rev. G. W. "Mahon, Lieut. J. Braddock, Rev. W. Taylor, Sir Walter Elliot, and C. Gubbins, "Esq. Edited by Captain M. W. Carr."—*Madras*, 1869, 8vo.

mouldings of pedestals, the bases, pillars, shape of the padma or lotus, and other architectural details. But his descriptions and illustrations are more applicable to the modern system of temple building, and are of no great archæological value.*

The only complete account of the Dravidian temples will be found in Mr. Fergusson's History of Architecture,† and they are best illustrated in Daniell's great volumes of engravings. Descriptions will be found of some of the Southern Indian temples in the manuscript memoirs of the early Topographical Surveys, and there are scattered notices elsewhere.‡ Mr. Fergusson considers the style to be well deserving of more attention than has hitherto been bestowed upon it, and that the buildings to which it gave rise, often combine grandeur of form with great beauty of detail.

Of late years the Madras Government have, from time to time, shown an interest in the preservation and illustration of architectural monuments. In Lord Harris's time, and at the instance of Sir Walter Elliot, Captain Tripe, of the 51st Regiment, was appointed to execute a series of photographs; but he only held the office for three or four years, and it was abolished by Sir Charles Trevelyan. During that time he took photographs of most of the edifices in the southern half of Mysore, and the whole of the inscriptions on the great temple of Tanjore. But unluckily the photographs were not well fixed, and have since faded sadly. In 1857 the Madras Government ordered district engineer officers to report upon the ancient architectural remains in their several districts. This order was issued, irrespective of the tastes and knowledge of the subject of those who were expected to attend to it, and it naturally bore little fruit. Mr. Fraser, the engineer at Coimbatore, took great pains with his report, and sent in a description of temples, tumuli, cromlechs, and other monuments. Captain Harington reported upon an inscription on a rock in Ganjam, Captain Mullins upon an ancient inscription on a tank in Nellore, Captain Emery sent in annual reports on the

---

* Ram Raz was a native judge at Bangalore. He was born in about 1790, and died in 1833. His work was published by the Oriental Translation Fund. "Essay on the Architecture of the Hindus," by Ram Raz. (48 plates. London. 1834.)

† ii., pp. 558–584.

‡ See an account of the temple of Ramisweram, with a plan, by Lieut. Christopher, I. N., in the "Journal of the Bombay Geographical Society," vol. vii.

A description of the temple and other edifices at Madura will be found in "Travels in Peru and India," by Clements R. Markham, p. 415.

architectural remains in Cuddapah, Captain Prendergast described the old fort at Arcot, and Lieutenant Drewer reported upon the ruins at Gurseppah.* Dr. Hunter, the Superintendent of the Government Industrial Schools at Madras, has trained pupils in photography, and sends them out to take photographs of the most interesting remains in various parts of the Presidency. The Government have also recently employed Captain Lyon to execute a series of photographs designed to illustrate the ancient architecture of Southern India,† but there is a great want of accurate plans and descriptions.

4. *Bengalee Architecture.*

Dravidian temples are at once recognized by their pyramidal form, distinction of storeys, and separation into compartments by pilasters. The Bengalee or northern temples, on the contrary, have no trace of division into storeys, no pilasters, and a curvilinear outline, with a polygonal base. The best examples are found at Bolaneswar, in Orissa, and round the temple of Juggernath, and thence across India as far as Dharwar. The style first appears in the 6th or 7th century, but Mr. Fergusson looks upon its origin as mysterious and unaccountable, and as one of the art-problems that await solution. He is inclined to date back its invention to a period anterior to Buddhism.

5. *Chalukya Architecture.*

This style is that of Guzerat, Mysore, and Rajpootana, and originated with the Rajpoots, the Scythian hordes which entered India during the first two or three centuries after Christ. The most magnificent remains are at Hullabeed and Belloor, in Mysore, and there are others in various parts of Mysore and Dharwar. The Hullabeed temple, which was built at the same time as Lincoln and Salisbury cathedrals, is perhaps the finest example of minute and elaborate carving made subservient to unity and grandeur of general effect that is to be found in India. Mr. Fergusson considers it to be

---

* "Madras Journal of Literature and Science," N.S., vol. vi. (1861).

† "Notes to accompany a series of photographs designed to illustrate the ancient architecture of Southern India, taken for the Government and described by Captain Lyon. Edited by James Fergusson, F.R.S." (London, Marion & Co., 22 & 23, Soho Square, 1870.)

among the most marvellous exhibitions of patient human labour the world ever produced.*

6. *Jaina Architecture.*

The temples of the Jains are nearly as numerous and quite as elaborate as those of any other sect in India. The most extensive group is that on the sacred hill of Satrungya, near Palitana, where the temples exist literally in hundreds, some of great beauty and magnificence. They have been well described by Mr. Burgess, and photographed by Messrs. Sykes and Dyer of Bombay,† and also by Captain Lyon. Mr. Burgess has also illustrated the Jain temples at Girnar, which form the group next in importance in Guzerat.‡ In the same neighbourhood are the wonderful white marble temples on Mount Abu, and further on that of Sadree,§ one of the most elaborate and extensive temples of the class in India, built by a Rana of Odeypore, in about the middle of the fifteenth century. Jain temples are also found all along the western coast as far as Belgaum, and there is an important establishment of this sect at Beligola,‖ in the Mysore country. Jain temples are also found on Mount Parisnath and other places in Bengal, and throughout the Central Provinces. No temple, in its present form, is earlier than A.D. 1000, while many hundred were built within the present century. In elaborateness of detail, and in elegance of form, they, in some respects, surpass even the thirteenth century buildings of the Chalukyas.¶

---

* "Architecture in Dharwar and Mysore, photographed by the late Dr. Pigou, A. C. B. Neill, Esq., and Colonel Briggs, R.A., with a memoir by Colonel Meadows Taylor, and architectural notes by James Fergusson." (Murray, 1866, folio.)

This superb work contains 52 plates illustrative of Chalukya architecture, including the Hullabeed and Belloor temples, and the ruined city of Bijayanuggur.

See also the "History of Architecture," ii. p. 609.

† "Satrungya, photographed by Sykes and Dyar, with explanatory text by J. M. Burgess."—(*Folio. Bombay*, 1869.)

‡ "Somnath, Girnar, and Junaghad, photographed by Sykes and Dyer, with descriptive letter-press by J. M. Burgess."—(*Folio. Bombay*, 1869.)

See also the "Account of the remains of the temple at Somnath," by Alexander Burnes (1834).—*Journ. R. A. S.*, v., p. 104.

§ See "Tod's Rajasthan."

‖ "Architecture of Dharwar, Mysore, &c."

¶ For accounts of Jaina Temple, see Colonel Tod's travels in Western India. Also his "Annals and Antiquities of Rajast'han, or the Central and Western Rajpoot States."

7. *Saracenic Architecture.*

The beautiful mosques and tombs of the Mohammedans, which are scattered over nearly all parts of India except the extreme south, were the first monuments to attract the attention of travellers, and are those which have been most thoroughly examined. The various styles bear the impress of the localities in which they were originated; combining the general features of Islamism with many special details peculiar to native art. According to Mr. Fergusson's division the earliest Mohammedan style is that of the Pathans at Delhi, which possesses a certain stern severity. It includes the Kootub Minar, a careful plan of which has been made by Mr. Fergusson, and the tombs of Altumsh and Togluck. The dates of the Pathan monuments range from 1196 to 1235, and much of their detail is copied from the old Jaina edifices. The tomb of Altumsh is mentioned as a remarkable example of Hindu art applied to Mohemmedan purposes.* At Gour, where the Pathans established their Bengal capital, the buildings are peculiar for their segmental form of roof and cornice, representing the bamboo roofs of huts in lower Bengal. The large mosques and tombs at Jaunpore (A.D. 1397–1478), fine illustrations of which may be seen in the volumes of Daniell, are noticeable instances of the use of Hindu forms. At Ahmedabad the mosques and tombs are in the Jaina style in every detail. The Jumma Musjid at Ahmedabab is one of the most beautiful mosques in the east. Its 15 domes are supported by 260 pillars, and perforated stone screens of exquisite beauty exclude the glare of the sun. A series of photographs of the Ahmedabad edifices by Colonel Briggs has recently been published in a magnificent volume, to which Premchund Ramchund, a Jaina

---

(2 vols. London, 1829, 4to.) It contains a plate of a Jaina temple at Ajmeer, and others. There is also an account of the Jains in "The Cities of Gujarashtra, their topography and history," by Henry George Briggs. (Bombay, 4to. 1847.) Colin Mackenzie's account of the Jains is in the "Asiatic Researches," vii., p. 176; Dr. Bird's, on the origin and principles of their religion, in the "Journal of the Bombay Branch, A. S." ii., p. 71. "Account of the remains of the temple of Pattan Somnath," by A. Burnes (1834).—*Journal of the Royal Asiatic Society*, v., p. 104. Lieut. Postans wrote accounts of the Jaina temples at Badrasir and Badranagiri in Cutch.—*J. A. S. B.*, vii., p. 431. See also the "History of Architecture," ii., p. 620; and the "Asiatic Researches," vol. xvi. p. 284.

* "Asiatic Researches," iv., p. 313.

of Guzerat, contributed 1,000*l*.* The style of architecture at Beejapore forms an exception to the usual influence of Hindu art on Mohammedan buildings. In that wonderful city everything is pervaded by Moslem ideas. From the time of Tavernier, many observers have recorded the wonders of Beejapore. After the visits of Moore and Sydenham, Colonel Sykes contributed notes respecting the principal remains of the ruined city,† and Dr. Bird wrote a paper on the ruins of Beejapore and its Persian inscriptions.‡ In 1866 a work on Beejapore containing 46 photographs and 4 woodcuts, with memoirs by Colonel Meadows Taylor and Mr. Fergusson, was published by Murray, chiefly at the expense of a wealthy native of India named Kursondas Madhowdas.§ The Mogul architecture, represented in the tomb of Akbar, and above all in the Taj Mehal, that great triumph of art, has been thoroughly examined and illustrated, and the monuments of that period will now, there is reason to hope, be well and carefully preserved.

8. *Coins and Inscriptions.*

The collection and deciphering of coins and plates is an important branch of Indian archæological research, because, by the study of such relics alone can the chronology and sequence of the ancient dynasties be ascertained. It has been seen that much was done in this line in the time of the Asiatic Researches; and the scattered numismatic memoirs of James Prinsep‖ have been collected and reprinted. Mr. Wathen discovered and reported upon ten inscriptions on stone and copper in the Deccan,¶ and, besides the great collection of *sasanums* made by Colin Mackenzie, which

* "Architecture of Ahmedabad, photographed by Colonel Briggs. Historical sketch, by Theodore C. Hope, Bombay Civil Service. Architectural notes, by James Fergusson." (4to., Murray, 1866.) 120 photographic plates. See also "Forbes's Oriental Memoirs," iii., ch. xxx.

† "Transactions of the Literary Society of Bombay," iii. p. 55.

‡ "Journal of the Bombay Branch of the Asiatic Society, i., p. 367.

§ "Architecture at Beejapore, from drawings by Captain Hart and A. Cumming, C. E.; and photographs by Colonel Briggs and Major Loch. Memoir by Colonel Meadows Taylor, and architectural notes by James Fergusson." (Folio. Murray. 1866.)

‖ "Essays on Indian Antiquities," by the late James Prinsep. (2 vols., 1858.)

¶ "Ten inscriptions on stone and copper found on the west coast of India, and translated by W. H. Wathen, with remarks by H. H. Wilson."—*Journal of the Royal Asiatic Society*, ii., p. 378.

have already been mentioned, Sir Walter Elliot has done great service to Indian historical knowledge by his labours in this branch of inquiry. He obtained copies of 595 inscriptions, collected in Dharwar, Soonda, and North Mysore. Most of them are engraved on blocks of basalt, others are carved on pillars of temples, and a few consist of deeds on sheets of copper. The monumental stones are invariably in Canarese; the others are in Sanscrit, with Canarese words intermixed. They all record grants of land or money, or transfers of rights to temples, and relate to four dynasties reigning over the Deccan, the oldest being the Chalukya dynasty of Rajpoots.* Sir Walter Elliot also contributed two important papers on the coins of Southern India, with descriptions and plates. A large collection was formed by Colin Mackenzie, and deposited in the India Museum; and there are scattered notices of other cabinets which have enabled Sir Walter to furnish a lucid review of the subject.† He points out that the only trustworthy data, from which a knowledge of the earlier southern dynasties and kingdoms can be obtained, are the contemporary records offered by deeds inscribed on stone and copper, and by coins. In the north of India, numismatics have found zealous students in James Prinsep, Wilson, Cunningham, and Edward Thomas. In his paper on the coins of the Ghuznee Kings, collected in Affghanistan by Mr. Masson, and now in the India Office Museum, Mr. Thomas throws doubt on the assertion that Mahmud was the first Sovereign who used the title of Sultan, and shows that one of his successors, Modud (A.D. 1041), adopted the Siva bull or *nandi* as a device. Mr. Thomas, by means of coins, has also illustrated the history of the Sassanians, the epoch of the Sah Kings of Guzerat, the chronology of the Bactrian Kings, of the Gupta dynasty, of the Patan Sultans of Hindustan,

---

* First published in the "Journal of the Royal Asiatic Society," iv., p. 1, (1836), but the paper was incorrectly printed, and was re-published more accurately in the "Madras Journal," vii., p. 190.

† "Numismatic Gleanings, being descriptions of the coins of Southern India," by Sir Walter Elliot.—*Madras Journal*, iii., p. 220.

Wilson wrote a paper on the collection of Colin Mackenzie in the "Asiatic Researches," vol. xvii. Moore figured 23 specimens of coins of Southern India, which were bought by Major Price at the prize sale of Tippoo's treasury, in his "Hindu Pantheon," and a series of Mysore coins in his "Narrative of Little's detachment," p. 455. See also Prinsep's notice of Southern Indian coins in the "Journal of the Asiatic Society of Bengal," vol. vi., plate xx.

and of the Parthian Arsacidæ.* General Cunningham has contributed papers on Bactrian and Indo-Scythian coins, and on the coins of the Indian Buddhist Satraps.† The few pre-Mohammedan written histories are so confused as regards dates and the succession of Kings that nothing reliable could be established without the aid of coins and deeds; and even as regards the records of Ferishta and other Mohammedan authors, coins are of essential use as corroborative evidence. Thus there can be no doubt of the great importance of this branch of the investigation.

The extensive ruins at Brahminabad, in Sind, do not come under the head of any of the above styles, but they are too interesting to be omitted in this enumeration. The great city, entirely built of baked bricks, and nearly four miles in circumference, was the capital of a Hindu dynasty from about the seventh to the eleventh century. It was entirely destroyed by an earthquake, and nothing but one tower is intact. We are indebted to Mr. Bellasis for a detailed account of these ruins, and he discovered beautiful engravings on cornelian and agate, and other relics among the debris.‡

The above enumeration of the various branches into which Indian archæological research is now systematically divided will give an idea of the extent and scope of the subject; and, while showing how much has already been done, will also prove how much remains to be achieved. The great need has always been a proper organization, which could only be partially attempted by the Societies at the Presidencies, whose admirable efforts and encouraging assistance to individual enquiries, though most important, could not possibly bring the needful power and means to bear. An efficient archæological survey can only be carried on, with any prospect of satisfactory completeness, through the agency of the Government.

General Cunningham, the old friend of James Prinsep, whose zeal and sagacity as an antiquary he emulates, published his views

---

* In the Journals of the Asiatic Society for 1848, 1849, 1852, 1859, 1862, and 1866 there are 16 papers by Mr. Thomas on eastern coins, bound up as "Tracts on Oriental Literature," by Edward Thomas, Bengal C. S. Mr. Thomas has also written on Cufic and Sassanian coins in the Journal of the B. A. S., vol. xx. pp. 337 and 525.

† "Journal of the Asiatic Society of Bengal," ix., pp. 531, 867, xiv., p. 430, xi., p. 130, xxiii., p. 679.

‡ "An account of the ancient and ruined city of Brahminabad, in Sind, by A. F. Bellasis."—*Bombay Branch, R.A.S.*, v., p. 413 (1856.)

on archæological investigation in 1848.* But it was not until 1860 that the Government of India instituted an archæological survey, with the object of preserving ancient monuments, rendering them easy of access, obtaining correct copies of inscriptions and pieces of sculpture, and thus facilitating the studies of future antiquaries and historians. General Cunningham was the officer selected by Lord Canning to conduct the operations of this survey, and certainly no better choice could have been made. As a scholar, an antiquary, and a numismatist, Cunningham was in the foremost rank; and he had already done important service in the examination of the Sarnath and Bhilsa topes, and in other kindred work.

The year 1861–62 was the first of General Cunningham's operations as archæological surveyor. They extended over the country between Gaya and Goruckpore, on both sides of the Ganges, embracing the principal ruins in the ancient kingdom of Magadha, the centre of Indian Buddhism during the period of its ascendancy. Two Chinese pilgrims named Fa Hian (A.D. 399–414) and Hwan Thsang (A.D. 629–42), whose travels have been translated by Mr. Beal and M. Stanislas Julien,† visited India when Buddhism was in the ascendant, and described many cities and temples. It has thus been one very important and interesting object among Indian antiquaries to identify the spots mentioned by these ancient pilgrims. General Cunningham has observed‡ that as Pliny, in his eastern geography, follows the route of Alexander, so an inquirer into Indian archæology should tread in the footsteps of the Chinese pilgrims, Hwan Thsang and Fa Hian. During his labours in 1861–62, General Cunningham succeeded in identifying a number of Buddhistic ruins of viharas and stupas with buildings that are minutely described in the writings of the ancient pilgrims. At Buddha Gaya especially, several objects enumerated by Hwan Thsang were recognized from their exact correspondence

* Proposed archæological investigation," by A. Cunningham.—*Journal of the Asiatic Society of Bengal*, xvii. pr. 1. p. 335.

† The first translation of Fa Hian's pilgrimage was published by Abel Rémusat in 1836, and entitled *Fo-koue-ki*. The English translation is by the Rev. S. Beal, late chaplain of H.M.S. "Sybille."—(*Trübner*, 1869.) In 1853, M. Stanislas Julien published his "Histoire de la Vie de Hiouen Thsang et de ses voyages dans l'Inde, traduite du Chinois;" which was followed in 1857 by his "Memoires sur les contrées occidentales par Hiouen Thsang."—(2 *vols. Paris.*)

‡ "J. A. S. B.," xvii. pt. i. p. 535.

with his descriptions. Cunningham carefully examined 24 ruins during his first season, including the caves in the Barabar hills, excavated by King Asoka. Much had been gone over, in early days, by Dr. Buchanan Hamilton, but Cunningham made a more careful and accurate examination of the different ruins, took impressions of inscriptions, and recommended that some of the more important pieces of sculpture should be photographed. His first report concludes with a full account of the great Buddhist tower at Sarnath, near Benares, which had been one of the objects of his earlier research, twenty-six years before. The operations of 1861-62 bore fruit in some valuable deductions. Thus, judging from the style of an inscription at Gaya, on which the date is given as the year 1816 of the *nirvana* of Buddha, General Cunningham assigns the year B.C. 477 as the period of that event, a calculation which has been adopted by Max Muller, though a century later than the Ceylon era. By a similar calculation, the dates of the foundation of Rajagriha, the capital of Magadha, and of Nalanda, once the most famous seat of Buddhistic learning in all India, are fixed. Interesting accounts are given, in the Report, of the ruins which he identifies as the sites of these ancient cities.

In the season of 1862-63, the surveyor's tour was extended through Futtehgur, Kanouj, Roorkee, Khallsi, and Muttra, to Delhi. He examined the ruins of Sankissa, the spot on which Buddha alighted when he descended from heaven. At Khallsi he made an impression of that famous inscription of King Asoka, containing the names of five Grecian Kings, and pronounced the fifth name, which had not before been made out, to be that of Alexander II. of Epirus. At Muttra and Delhi he copied several inscriptions, and made numerous drawings and measurements. At Delhi he examined two human statues lately found inside the area of the palace walls, and the remains of two statues of elephants in black stone. He thinks it probable that these are the statues mentioned in Baber's Memoirs as standing outside the gate of Gwalior, whence they are believed to have been removed by Aurungzebe. They are now erected in the Delhi Garden, as unique specimens of Indian portrait sculpture of life size. General Cunningham made a complete examination of the ruins in the vicinity of Delhi. After a careful investigation he came to the conclusion that not a single stone remains of Indraprastha, the capital of the Pandus, the most ancient city near the site of modern Delhi.* He described, in the Report for this season, the architectural remains attributable to Hindoo and to various epochs of Mahommedan ascendancy. He made a careful impression of the very important pillar inscription of Asoka, already published by James Prinsep, and the corrections he has supplied show the justice of Burnouf's opinion, that "a new collation of the pillar inscriptions would be of the greatest value."

In 1863–64 the Surveyor explored the ruins in the Punjab, and worked at the identification of the cities and peoples described in the expedition of Alexander the Great. Commencing from the west bank of the Indus, he worked downwards, on the track of Alexander and the Chinese pilgrims, examining every site mentioned either by the Grecian writers or by Hwen Thsang. His accounts of Taxila, Manikyala, and of the scene of Alexander's battle with Porus on the Jhelum, are especially interesting. He also explored, during this season, the famous region watered by the Saraswati, including Sirhind and Thanesar.

In the season of 1864–65, General Cunningham continued his labours, explored and described the ancient cities between the Jumna and Nerbudda, and drew up an interesting account of the Dhamnâr caves.† He had now carefully examined and described the ruins and inscriptions in nine of the ancient kingdoms of Hindostan.‡ But in 1866 Lord Lawrence abolished the appointment of Archæological Surveyor, and for a season these useful and important labours were stopped. At the same time their value was appreciated by the Secretary of State for India, who considered that they fully justified the anticipations which were entertained by Lord Canning when he first conceived the idea of the survey, and that similar operations should be set on foot in other parts of

---

* The date of the occupation of Indraprastha by Yudhisthira, the eldest of the Pandus, is fixed in the latter half of the 15th century B.C., from certain positions of the planets recorded in the Mahabharata.

† Also described by Fergusson in his "Rock-hewn Temples of India."

‡ Namely, Magadha (Behar), Mithila (Tirhout), Ayodhya (Oude), Panchâla (Rohilcund), Antarbeda (the Doab), Kurukshetra (Thanesar), Madra Desa, and Sindhu Sauriva (Punjab), and Madhya-desa (Central India).

See "Reports of the operations of the Archæological Surveyor to the Government of India during the seasons 1861–62, 1862–63, 1863–64, 1864–65." There are copies in the India Office, and in the libraries of the Society of Antiquaries and of the Royal Asiatic Society.

India. The Secretary of State also expressed an opinion that the preservation of the historical monuments of India, and their accurate description by competent observers, were objects well deserving the attention of the Government.* General Cunningham's survey has borne rich fruit since his return to England, in his learned work on the ancient geography of India, in which he discusses the routes taken by Alexander the Great and by the Buddhist pilgrim, Hwan Thsang, and identifies the places mentioned by the Grecian and Chinese writers. His chief discoveries have been Aornos, the rock fort captured by the Macedonian king; Taxila, the ancient capital of N.W. Punjab; Bairât, the capital of Matsya, south of Delhi; Sankisa, near Kanouj, the spot where Buddha descended from heaven; and Nalanda, the most famous Buddhist monastery in all India.†

In 1868, Lieutenant H. H. Cole was appointed to conduct an archæological survey in the North-West Provinces and the Punjab. He was occupied until November in examining the principal ancient temples of Kashmere, with a photographer, and afterwards surveyed the ancient buildings in the neighbourhood of Muttra, accompanied by the Rev. Mr. Simpson, who took 58 photographs. In May 1869, Lieutenant Cole left Bombay for England, to make arrangements for casting one of the great stone gateways of the Sanchi tope. Three sappers were trained in the most recent methods of making elastic moulds with gelatine, and in October 1869 Lieutenant Cole returned to India with these men and the necessary materials. It took 60 carts to convey the 28 tons of material from Jubbulpore to Sanchi, which was reached in January 1870. There were 737 square feet of carved work on the gateway, to be cast in 112 pieces. The work was completed in February, and the pieces composing the "parent" cast were carefully packed, and sent to England, to be fitted together, in order that copies of the gateway may be reproduced for the museums at Kensington, Dublin, and Edinburgh. Detailed drawings were made of the other gateways.

It was decided to publish two volumes illustrative of the archæological survey conducted by Lieutenant Cole. The first containing

---

* Despatch (Public Works) June 24th, 1864, No. 28.
" " June 16th, 1866, No. 29.

† "The ancient geography of India. I. The Buddhist period, including the "campaigns of Alexander, and the travels of Hwen Thsang. By Alexander Cun- "ningham, Major-General, R.E."—(*Trübner*, 1871. 13 *maps*.)

the photographs of the Kashmirian temples, with descriptions, has already been published. The second will contain those of the buildings round Muttra, with descriptive notes, and is nearly ready. Lieutenant Cole considers that the principal aims which he should endeavour to keep in view in collecting illustrations are to show the faith and state of civilization of the natives who occupied any particular period or locality, as represented in their sculptured architecture, to offer a means of elucidating the true position of architecture in England by widening the base of observation, to instruct native builders and artizans in different Indian styles, and to furnish the means of selecting appropriate forms out of which to design municipal and other buildings for native puproses.*

In 1869 Dr. Forbes Watson of the India Office drew up a valuable report on the various means of illustrating the archaic architecture of India, by means of photographs, drawings, plans, and sections, models, moulds, and casts. In the appendices attached to the report there is a memorandum by Mr. Fergusson on the architectural objects in India, of which it is desirable to obtain photographs, with some account of the work of this kind that has already been done; and two others on objects for casts,† and on the conservancy and representation of ancient monuments. He considers that plans and descriptions, accompanied by photographs and drawings, would convey more information than castings, and at the same time aid the selection of objects that should be cast; and he urges that an officer should be appointed in each Presidency, to devote his whole time to archæology.

In August 1867 the Government of India had forwarded a circular to the Local Governments, expressing their sense of the desirability of conserving ancient architectural structures or their remains, and other works of art in India, and of organizing a system for photographing them. Lists were called for, of all such remains and works

* "Archæological Survey of India," Lieut. H. H. Cole's Report for the year 1869–70.

† He recommends that casts should be taken of various sculptures in the Calcutta, Madras, and Lahore museums, of those in the Udyagiri caves near Cuttack, of objects at the black pagoda, of the rail once surrounding the bo tree at Boodh Gya, of fragments of the Buddhist rail at Muttra, of the carved details on the old Pathan tombs and mosques, of the Somnath gates in the Agra arsenal, of the pillars and brackets of Akbar's tomb, sculptures at Elephanta, the double elephant capitals at Karli, sculptures at Hullabeed, &c.

of art in Bengal, Oudh, the North-West Provinces, the Punjab, the Central Provinces, Hyderabad, Bombay, Madras, Burmah, and Mysore. The proposal in the circular was that photographs should be executed by amateurs, and that some assistance should be given by Government, through the purchase of a certain number, if they were really good. This circular met with some response, and a considerable number of photographs were received by the Government during the two following years.* The Government of India also proposed to expend a sum of 52,000 Rs. a year for the employment of parties in Bombay, Madras, Bengal, the North-West Provinces, and the Punjab, to make complete sets of models of one or more large buildings, with accurate plans, photographs, and descriptions; and the Principals of the schools of art at the presidency towns were to train men in the art of modelling.

The interest shown by the Government of India in the preservation and illustration of ancient monuments was very encouraging, as it thus became clear that the importance of the subject was fully appreciated. But it was necessary that the researches should be conducted in a more systematic manner, and on some definite plan; and in July 1870 it was resolved that a central establishment should be formed to collect the results of former researches, to train a school of archæologists capable of conducting local enquiries, and to direct, assist, and systematize the various efforts and enquiries made by local bodies and private persons as well as by the Government. The direction of this establishment was offered to General Cunningham. India was so fortunate as again to secure the services of that eminent scholar and archæologist, and he left England, to resume those useful and interesting labours which had already occupied so

* Photographs were forwarded, of the palace at Sambulpore, the black pagoda, the caves in Cuttack, Juggernath, and others. A set of photographs were furnished of ancient buildings in Mysore, and Captain Lyon was employed to complete a series in the Madras Presidency. Reports and photographs were also sent from Rajpootana, the Central Provinces, (where a separate chapter on archæology is given in the Administration Reports,) the Hyderabad Assigned Districts (where a Committee was formed at each station to prepare archæological reports,) Nepal, and Sikkim. In Bombay Mr. Sykes was employed to take photographs of the caves and temples round Nassick, and his negatives were purchased by Government. There was also a grant of Rs. 10,714 at Bombay, which was entrusted to Mr. Terry, the acting superintendent of Sir Jamsetjee Jejeebhoy's school of art. This sum was employed by Mr. Terry in moulding, sketching, measuring, and photographing the temple of Ambernath near Bombay, with a staff of artists, moulders, and draftsmen. He produced a set of casts from the moulds, and sent in his Report in July 1869.

many years of his life, in December 1870. It is also expected that Mr. Burgess, the head of Sir Jamsetjee Jeejeebhoy's school, and an archæologist of merit, may take charge of the archæological survey in the Bombay Presidency.

So long ago as in 1848, General Cunningham had pointed out the necessity for confiding the selection of objects for preservation to an instructed archæologist, with a knowledge of ancient Indian history, and that without such a guide the labours of the best draftsmen and photographers would be thrown away. Under such trained supervision, however, much important and valuable work will be done; and a glance at the appendices by Mr. Fergusson and General Cunningham at the end of Dr. Forbes Watson's report will give some idea of the amount of work that remains to be done before the archæological survey of India approaches completion. There are portions of the Central Provinces which are rich in ancient and most interesting remains, but which are unexplored. Much also awaits investigation in Guzerat and Cutch, from Sadree to Somnath. At a place called Adjmeerghur there is a sacred tank whence flow the sources of the rivers Sone, Nerbudda, and Mahanuddy, and the spot is surrounded by temples. This region requires examination; and Mr. Fergusson thinks it possible that here the problem of the origin of that Bengalee style of architecture, which has hitherto puzzled him, may be solved. The districts round the delta of the Kistna, including the beautiful and ancient temples of Shreechellum, are full of antiquities of great interest, utterly unknown to Europeans; and the sculptures at Amravati, in Guntoor, have not yet been photographed *in situ*.* The rock inscription in Ganjam, which is another version of the Asoka edict, requires photographing. The buildings about Kalyan and Deoghur, the central region of the Chalukya style of architecture, are also still unexamined, as well as the Saracenic monuments of the Bahmany and Golconda dynasties in the Deccan; and a good survey of Vegi, the capital of a Buddh dynasty before the foundation of the Eastern Chalukya kingdom, is another desideratum.

* Mr. Fergusson, in June 1868, suggested that the photographers engaged in observing the eclipse of the sun, as soon as they had done their work, should be instructed to photograph the sculptures at Amravati, the caves and temples at Dachapully in the Palnaud district, and the caverns in Ellore. But nothing was done.

In March 1870, Mr. Boswell, the Collector of the Kistna district, submitted a very interesting report on the archæological remains in his district to the Madras Government.* It includes descriptions of natural caves, enlarged by man and used as dwelling places, of cromlechs and stone circles, of Buddhist topes and temples, and of more recent edifices. His account of the cave near Bezwada almost certainly identifies that place with the capital city visited by Hwan Thsang, while the ruins at Amravati, with their exquisite sculptures, are those of a cluster of religious buildings. Mr. Boswell anticipates that important results would follow the prosecution of further researches, especially at Amravati; and the Madras Government have given orders that steps may be taken for the preservation and protection of all sculptures and other archæological remains. They have also expressed their readiness to aid the efforts of any archæologist of eminence, who may be disposed to institute further inquiries in the Kistna district, by every means in their power.

There remains a great and important field of research for the archæological surveyors in India, and the future operations of General Cunningham, and his fellow labourers, may be confidently expected to lead to very important results. General Cunningham has been instructed first to prepare a summary of the labours of former inquirers, and of the results obtained, and then to draw up a general scheme of systematic inquiry for the guidance of his staff of assistants. He will submit an annual Report of his proceedings.†

* "Letter from J. A. C. Boswell, Esq., Officiating Collector of the Kistnah district, "to the Acting Secretary to the Board of Revenue. Madras. Dated, Masulipatam, "31st March 1870."

† Resolution of the Government of India, 2nd February 1871.

XIV.—METEOROLOGICAL AND TIDAL OBSERVATIONS INDIA.

The practical importance of meteorological observations is so great as to have ensured their registration in India, at a very great number of stations, and over a long period of time. They affect the operations of the seaman and of the husbandman, and are a vital element in the calculations of health officers, of administrators, and of engineers.* Their usefulness, therefore, has always been fully recognized; but it was long before any attempt was made to introduce an organized system of registration; all work connected with the generalization and utilization of the ever accumulating materials was left to the zeal and industry of volunteers; and even now, though excellent measures have recently been adopted, there is much to be done before a meteorological department in India can be considered as established on a perfectly satisfactory footing.

Medical officers at stations and hospitals have been expected to keep meteorological journals from a very early period, and numerous volunteers have registered observations; but, owing to the want of a central department, and to other causes, much of the earlier material is lost, and much that is preserved is of but moderate value.

In the Bengal Presidency the earliest series I have met with is the meteorological journal of Colonel Pearse† kept at Calcutta between March 1st, 1785, and February 28th, 1788. It includes observations of the barometer, thermometer, hygrometer, direction and force of wind, and rainfall, taken generally at about 7 a.m. and 2.15 p.m.‡ A similar diary was kept at Calcutta by Mr. Henry

* "It can scarcely be necessary to insist on the practical importance of this science "to the agriculturalist, to the navigator, and indeed to every branch of human affairs, "or to dilate on the benefits which must accrue to mankind in general from any successful attempts to subject to reasonable and well-grounded prediction the irregular "and seemingly capricious course of the seasons and the winds, or on the advantages, "purely scientific, which must arise from a systematic development of laws, exemplified "on the great scale in the periodical changes of the atmosphere, depending, as they "do, on the agency of all the most influential elements, and embracing in their scope "every branch of physical science."—*Sir John Herschel.*

† See page 40.

‡ "Asiatic Researches," i. p. 442.

Traill, from February 1st, 1784, to December 31st, 1785.* The hygrometers of those days were of very primitive construction. Mr. Traill used a bit of fine sponge suspended in a scale on the end of a steel yard, with a semicircular scale at the top; and Captain Kater's ingenious device for ascertaining the amount of moisture in the atmosphere has already been described.†

James Prinsep took a careful series of meteorological observations at Benares for two years, and published his general results for 1823; including the mean daily range of the barometer for each month, the monthly means and extremes of the thermometer, the hygrometric entries, the rainfall, direction of the wind, and weather.‡ General Thomas Hardwicke kept a meteorological register at Dum Dum, from 1816 to 1823. It contains daily and monthly means of seven daily observations of the thermometer; barometrical observations taken daily at sunrise, noon, and evening, with monthly means; a register of the hygrometer; an enumeration of days of rain, and prevailing winds.§

When Sir John Herschel was at the Cape he sent a circular to India, suggesting that horary observations should be taken for 24 hours together at the time of the equinoxes and solstices.‖ Several observers complied with the great astronomer's directions, in various parts of India. Mr. Barrow, the mathematical instrument maker at Calcutta, took observations of the barometer and thermometer every hour, on the 21st and 22nd of December 1835, and on the 21st and 22nd of March 1836;¶ and Colonel Colvin, assisted by Lieutenants Baker and Durand, registered horary readings at Dadapore, on a day in September 1835, and on another in March 1836.

Numerous observations were made, from time to time, by travellers and residents, while the registers of medical officers were continually accumulating. In 1798 Dr. Hunter recorded observations

---

* "Asiatic Researches," ii., p. 420.

† See note at page 48.

‡ "Asiatic Researches," xv., App. p. vii.

§ "Journal of the Royal Asiatic Society," i., App.

‖ Sir John Herschel recommended 3 and 9 a.m. and 3 and 9 p.m. as the most important hours for observation; and that hourly observations for 24 hours should be taken on the 21st of March, June, September, and December. These are called "term observations."

¶ "J. A. S. B." v., p. 51 and p. 243.

on the rainfall and climate at Oujein.* In 1835 the Rev. R. Everest wrote an essay on the revolution of the seasons, and on the correspondence between atmospheric phenomena and the changes of the moon;† and the same observer also published a valuable paper on the rain and drought of eight seasons in India, from 1831 to 1838, giving the rainfalls at Calcutta, Madras, Bombay, and Delhi.‡ Among travellers General Cunningham, in his work on Ladak, gives a series of meteorological observations taken in the Spiti valley, Kashmir, Ladak, and other parts of the Himalayan region;§ Dr. Hooker, in his journal, furnishes a series of observations registered in Darjeeling, Khasia, and Cachar, the Behar hills, the valley of the Sone, Mirzapore, and the Kymore hills, which include minima, maxima, and means of the thermometer, the wet and dry bulb, and solar and terrestrial radiation;‖ and Colonel Richard Strachey made some hourly observations of the barometer in August 1849, at 18,400, 16,000, and 11,500 feet above the sea, in the mountains of Tibet.¶ A notice of the climate of Kumaon and Gurhwal will be found in Mr. Henry Strachey's paper.** Dr. Royle took a series of observations at Saharunpore from 1826 to 1830, and wrote an account of the meteorology of the plains and mountains of N.W. India;†† and Drs. Hooker and Thomson have given a sketch of the meteorology of India, in the Preliminary Essay to their *Flora Indica*.‡‡ It would be a hopeless task to attempt a complete enumeration of all the observations of this kind, or of those kept by medical officers and others at fixed stations; but the enquirer will find abstracts of a great number of registers in the volumes of the journal of the Asiatic Society of Bengal.§§

---

* "Asiatic Researches," vi., p. 53.

† "J. A. S. B.," iv., p. 257. ; vi., pt. i. p. 303.

‡ "J.A.S.B.," viii., pt. i. p. 313.

§ Cunningham's "Ladak." On climate pp. 171–190, and tables, p. 442.

‖ Hooker's Journal," ii., p. 357. Appendix A, on Meteorology.

¶ "R. G. S. J," xxiii., p. 64. Colonel Strachey's observations at great heights tend to show that the atmospheric pressure is subject to the same sort of fluctuations on the Tibetan table land as prevail in the lower regions elsewhere.

** "R. G. S. J," xxi., p. 72.

†† "Illustrations of Himalayan botany," i., p. xxx.

‡‡ Flora Indica, i., p. 74.

§§ At Simla, vol. v., p. 825; at Bijnore, ii., p. 206; Bombay, v. p. 821, Katmandu; v. p. 824, and xii, p. 768; at Tirhoot, v. p. 822; Socotra, v. p. 821; Bangalore, v. p. 296; Darjeeling, vi., pt. i., p. 308; Rangoon, vol. xxii.; Agra, xxii.; Bankura, i.; Chin-

From time to time endeavours have been made to classify and utilize the ever accumulating meteorological observations of medical officers in India. In 1852 Dr. Lambe drew up an abstract of the registers of 126 stations in Bengal and the N.W. Provinces for the year 1851, giving the monthly mean temperatures and rainfalls.*

The Messrs. Schlagintweit, who were in India from 1854 to 1858, published the meteorological volume of their work in 1866.† The meteorological registers received by the Medical Board at Calcutta were handed over to them in 1857, comprising a series of 38 folio volumes in manuscript. The observations, thus obtained, were taken at no less than 250 stations. They consist of entries for temperature and rainfall, and sometimes for readings of the wet and dry bulb thermometers, and in the sun's rays. The results, from this great mass of material, are a series of tables of monthly means of temperature, with maxima and minima, in some instances, for two and sometimes for three years.‡

A regular series of meteorological observations has been kept at the Surveyor General's Office at Calcutta from 1829 until the present year, and monthly and yearly abstracts of them have been published, first in the "Gleanings in Science," and since 1832 in the "Journal of the Asiatic Society of Bengal." At first the hours of observation were sunrise 10 a.m., noon, and sunset; but afterwards they were altered to sunrise, 9.50 a.m., 2.40 p.m., 4 p.m., and sunset;§ and since 1856 the observations have been taken every hour. Observations of maxima and minima temperatures

---

sura, ii.; Gazipore, ii.; Lucknow, xxiii.; Mussoorie, iv.; Cherraponji, i.; Mozufferpore, ii.; Nagpore, ii., p. 239; Singapore, ii.; Nushirabad, ii., p. 128, and v.; Dadapore, v.; Umballa, iv. Sir John Malcolm registered the barometer and thermometer five times a day, at Mundleysir in July, and at Mhow in January 1821. *Central India*, ii., p. 350. See also a meteorological register at Shillong and Cherraponji for August 1860, and a register of temperature at Kamptee and Muhtoor hills for May 1860, in the "Report on the Sanitary Establishments for European Troops in India," (No. iii., Calcutta, 1862.) Abstract of meteorological observations made at Futtehgur by John C. Pyle in 1850. See "*British Association*," xx., p. 40.

* "J. A. S. B.," vol. xxi. p. 383; and *British Association Reports*, xxi., p. 52.

† "Meteorology of India; an analysis of the physical conditions of India," vol. iv., (1866.)

‡ A list of works on the subject of Indian meteorology will be found in this volume of the Messrs. Schlagintweit's work.

§ Observations at sunrise, noon, and sunset involve computations for determining diurnal barometric oscillations.

first appear in 1818. The abstracts were also published in the "Calcutta Journal of Natural History;" but, as the registers were bulky, little used if given in detail, and useless if too much abridged, Dr. McClelland, the editor, discontinued their publication, and gave instead the general results to be deduced from these records for the year 1843-44 in a series of tables. These tables show the monthly means, maxima, and minima of the thermometer and barometer; the monthly rainfall, direction of wind and weather.* In 1848 Colonel Thuillier prepared a tabular statement of the number of rainy days, and the quantity of rain which fell in Calcutta, for every month from the year 1829 to 1847.†

Since 1868 the abstracts of the results of the hourly meteorological observations taken at the Surveyor General's Office at Calcutta have been published separately in monthly parts. They give daily means of the hourly observations of the barometer and thermometer, for means, maxima, and minima; daily and hourly means of the wet bulb, dry bulb, dew point, dry bulb above dew point, mean elastic force of vapour, mean weight of vapour required for complete saturation, mean degree of humidity, and the maximum solar radiation, rainfall, direction of wind and weather. Two tables have also been published showing the mean monthly and the mean hourly variations of temperature and humidity for fifteen years, from 1855 to 1869, as determined in the Surveyor General's Office at Calcutta. Facsimiles of the indications given by the anemometer at the time of the cyclones of May 16th and June 9th, 1869, showing the direction and pressure of the wind per square foot, have also been published.

A valuable series of meteorological observations was taken at Simla, under the direction of Major Boileau, between 1841 and 1846. They consisted of registers of temperature, of maxima and minima, of readings of the dry and wet bulb thermometers, from which were deducted the dew point, tension, and temperature, dew-points by Daniell's hygrometer, solar and terrestrial radiation, wind and quantity of rain. The observations were made hourly for six

* "Reduction of the meteorological register kept at the Surveyor General's Office at Calcutta for the year 1st Nov. 1843 to 31st Oct. 1844, by J. McClelland." Calcutta Journal of Natural History, v. p. 533.

† "J. A. S. B.," vol. xvii. pt. i., p. 312.

days in the week.* Dr. Lloyd, of Dublin, reported that the Simla observatory, under Major Boileau's superintendence, was in all respects admirably organized; and pointed out the great value of an extended and complete series of observations made at an altitude of 8,000 feet.†

A complete series of meteorological observations has been registered at the astronomical observatory at Madras, from the year 1796 to 1870, by the astronomers who have successively been in charge. The earliest I have seen are for 1819.‡ The hours of observation were then at sunrise, noon, 2 p.m., sunset, and 9 p.m.; and the entries were the readings of the thermometer, rain gauge, wind and weather. The series from 1822 to 1843, taken by Mr. Goldingham and Mr. Taylor, successive astronomers, was published in a folio volume with plates.§ From 1837 the hours of observation were 10 a.m., 4 p.m., and 10 p.m. A further series of observations by Mr. Taylor, Major Worster, and Major Jacob, from 1841 to 1850, has also been published.‖ Hourly observations were taken of

---

* All the Simla observations had been printed, and were packed at Agra, ready for transmission to England, when the mutiny broke out, and they were burnt. The manuscript monthly abstracts of the observations from September 1841 to the end of 1845 are preserved, and are now in the hands of the Royal Society, but the mass of the original observations was lost in the fire. The Simla observations were among the most extensive and carefully made records ever taken, and their loss is a great calamity as regards science, as well as a source of deep disappointment to General Boileau. That officer also published a useful volume of tables: "A collection of " tables astronomical, meteorological, and magnetical; also for determining the alti- " tudes of mountains, by Lieut.-Colonel J. T. Boileau, computed at the office of " H. E. I. Co.'s magnetic observatory at Simla." (Umballa, 1850.) See also *J. A. S. B.*, xiii., p. 135.

† *Reports of the British Association*, xiv., p. 3.

‡ There are the following manuscripts in the Geographical Department of the India Office:—

"Meteorological Journal kept at the Madras Observatory for 1819."

"Meteorological Journal kept at the Madras Observatory for 1824."

"Meteorological Journal kept at the Madras Observatory in 1830."

§ There are printed meteorological observations taken at Madras in 1841, 1842, 1843, 1844, and 1845.

See also—"Meteorological register kept at the observatory at Madras for the " years 1822–1843; by John Goldingham and Thomas Glanville Taylor." (Plates. Folio. Madras. 1844.)

‖ "Meteorological observations made at the Honorable East India Company's obser- " vatory at Madras, by the late T. G. Taylor, Esq., F. R. S., Captain Worster, M. A., " and Captain Jacob, Astronomers, 1841–50."

The meteorological abstracts from the Madras Observatory have been published

barometric pressure, thermometer, humidity of the air, direction and force of the wind, rainfall, evaporation, and state of the weather; and in 1853 Dr. Balfour published a series of barometric sections. The register has since been regularly kept by Mr. Pogson, the present astronomer, up to the current year. The observations at the Madras Observatory are now taken three times a day, and the results are published in the Fort St. George Gazette and in one local paper. The hourly observations were taken for twenty years, and the series is now nearly worked up for publication. Rain returns have been kept at 350 stations, more or less regularly, since 1852, under the control of the Revenue Board. They will furnish an interesting rain map of the Madras Presidency, showing the comparative influences of elevation above the sea-level, and proximity to the coast.*

In 1846 the Court of Directors gave orders that a series of meteorological observations should be taken at a considerable height above the level of the sea, on the Neilgherry hills; and sent out a set of instruments for the purpose. Mr. Taylor, the Madras astronomer considered that no set of observations could really be considered valuable unless they were made on the summit of the peak of Dodobetta, 8,640 feet above the sea, and within the influence of both monsoons. A bungalow was accordingly erected, and on the 12th of January 1847 the instruments were fixed, under the charge of John de Cruz, an assistant of the Madras Observatory. The instruments were an Osler's anemometer, a standard barometer, thermometers, and rain gauges; and the hours of observation were at 9.40 a.m. and 3.40 p.m., the supposed hours of maxima and minima. At this great elevation, as in Colonel Sykes's Deccan observations, to be noticed presently, there is not a single day throughout the year in which the pressure at 3.40 p.m. is higher than that at 9.40 a.m. On the 21st and 22nd of each month horary observations were taken for 24 consecutive hours.† Work was

in the "Journal of Literature and Science of Madras" since 1833. There was a long hiatus in the publication of the journal from 1840 to 1847; but in the latter year the monthly meteorological abstracts re-appeared, and have been continuously published ever since. They are signed by Mr. Norman Robert Pogson, the present Astronomer at Madras, since 1861.

* Proceeding of the Astronomical Society, vol. xxiii., p. 178.

† "Meteorological Observations made at the meteorological bungalow on Dodobetta "Peak, 8640 feet above the sea, in 1847–48, under the directions of T. G. Taylor, Esq., "F. R. S." See also Colonel Sykes's paper, *Phil. Trans.* 1850., pt. ii. (xv.)

commenced in February 1847, and was continued until about 1858, when the Dodabetta Station was abolished, by Sir Charles Trevelyan. Observations for temperature, rainfall, and directions of wind at Ootacamund and Kotergherry on the Neilgherries, will be found in Ouchterlony's report of the survey made in 1847, where there are also some remarks on the climate.*

The foundation of the observatory at Trivandrum was due to the great interest taken both by the late Rajah of Travancore and by General Fraser, the Resident at his court, in the sciences of astronomy and meteorology. Mr. John Caldecott received the appointment of astronomer, and the building was erected in 1836, on a hill 190 feet above the sea.† Mr. Caldecott died in December 1849, and, during an interregnum of two years, Mr. G. Spershneider registered the observations. The Trivandrum observations will be found in several numbers of the Madras Journal of Literature and Science, and the means of Mr. Caldecott's hourly observations, between 1837 and 1842, were published by Professor Dove.‡ General Cullen also had observations taken to ascertain the rainfall, from 1842 to 1846, at Cochin, Quilon, Allepy, Cape Comorin, and other points on the Travancore coast.§ But the best and most extensive observations in Travancore were made by Mr. John Allan Broun, who formerly had charge of Sir Thomas Brisbane's observatory at Makerstown in Scotland, and arrived at Trivandrum, as Astronomer to the Rajah of Travancore, in January 1852. He continued the series of meteorological observations at Trivandrum, and after

* "Geographical and Statistical Memoir of the Neilgherry Hills." Presented to Parliament, and also printed in the Madras Journal., xv., p. i. There is a series of meteorological observations taken on the Neilgherry Hills by J. Glen, from 1829 to 1836, in the Journal of the Physical and Medical Society of Bombay. See also "Travels in Peru and India, by Clements R. Markham," pp. 359 and 382; and tables in McIvor's Annual Reports on Chinchona cultivation.

† See a sketch and plan of the building in the "Madras Journal of Literature and Science," vol vi., p. 56 and p. 339. Mr. Caldecott also published "a notice accompanying a series of meteorological observations made at Trivandrum."—*Report, British Association*, (pt. 2., 1840,) p. 28. "Observations on the temperature of the earth in India."—*Proceedings of the Edinburgh Royal Society*, i., p. 432 (1845,) and "Observations on the ordinary temperature of the ground at Trivandrum from May 1842 to Dec. 1845."—*Transactions of the Edinburgh Royal Society*, xvi. p. 379; and *Proceedings*, ii., p. 29.

‡ "*British Association.*" *Reports*, ix., p. 28.

§ General Cullen also published a series of barometrical levellings in the Madras Presidency.—"*Reports. British Association*," xv., p. 22; xvi., p. 42; and xvii., p. 39.

two years consumed in the undertaking, he established a branch observatory on the summit of the peak of Aghastya-mulla, 6,200 feet above the sea. In reaching this lofty site, paths had to be cut through jungles infested by wild elephants, and there were delays, owing to labourers running away, from fear and cold.*

The Aghastya-mulla Observatory was at last completed in March 1855; and from its platform the whole south of the Indian peninsula is seen, from Cape Comorin to Cochin on one side, and to Adam's Bridge on the other; an almost unequalled view. Mr. Broun has given a most interesting account of the observatory, and of the difficulties overcome in its construction, in his Report of 1857. The assistants at this lofty observatory were arranged into three sets of four men each, according to their castes, the first set being Syrian Christians, the second Brahmans and Sudras, and the third Roman Catholics, relieving each other every three months. The observations were commenced on July 1st, 1855; but during Mr. Broun's absence in England in 1860 the observatory was allowed to fall to pieces. On his return in 1863, he had it rebuilt, and a second series of observations was taken, which extended over ten months. Mr. Broun also caused a series of hourly observations to be taken in different years, simultaneously with those at Trivandrum and Aghastya, at stations near the latter, and at 5,000 feet lower level, one east and one west. This series had special reference to questions connected with the atmospheric pressure, temperature, humidity, and evaporation. In 1859, a similar series of hourly observations was taken at five different stations rising about 1,200 feet one above the other, in connection with the same meteorological questions. In all these series the best instruments were used. Base lines were measured by Mr. Broun. on both sides of the Aghastya-mulla peak, in order to ascertain trigonometrically the exact height of the observatory, and the lower stations. When the Travancore Government decided on abolishing the observatories in 1865, Mr. Broun obtained leave for the continuation of a limited series to be made by the two oldest and best of his native observers; and a Syrian Christian, his principal assistant, is still in charge, and forwards monthly reports and abstract of meteorological observations to Mr. Broun, in Europe.

---

* Report on the "Observatories of his Highness the Rajah of Travancore," by John Allan Broun, F.R.S., *Director*. (*Trivandrum*, 1857.) *Reports. British Association*," xxiv., p. 25; xxvii., p. 30.

There is every reason to believe that this series, which is of great importance in reference to many questions of interest, will be continued. The great mass of results has yet to be reduced and published. This will be done by Mr. Broun, at the expense of the Travancore Government.

Sir John Herschel's suggestion, that horary observations should be taken for 24 hours together on four fixed days of each year, received due attention from the Madras observers. Such observations were registered, both at the Madras and Trivandrum observatories, on December 20th and 22nd, 1836, in January 1838 at both places, and also by Dr. Gilchrist at Hoonsoor in June and September 1838, in April 1839, and again in 1840.* Dr. Mouat, also, at Bangalore, took horary observations, in conformity with Sir John Herschel's circular, on the 21st and 22nd of March 1836. His previous meteorological observations extended over the years 1834 and 1835.†

Registers of observations have been published, which were taken in the hill regions of Wynaad and Coorg. Captain Minchin observed at Manantoddy in Wynaad during the year 1832, and gives the monthly mean temperature at daylight, noon, the mean and greatest heat, and the number of days of rain.‡ In Coorg the register was kept at Mercara by Dr. Baikie, who published his notes on the climate, with a table giving the monthly means of the barometer, thermometer, and hygrometer, observed at 6 a.m., 10 a.m., and 5 p.m.§

A diagram showing the meteorological condition of Secunderabad for the year 1864 was lithographed and published at Madras in 1866. It gives the amount of ozone, atmospheric pressure, rainfall, temperature of the air in sun and shade, the amount of humidity, and prevailing winds. The work is valuable, and does great credit to the industry and zeal of its author, Dr. W. Arnold Smith.‖

In the Bombay Presidency a regular register of the thermometer was kept for 26 years, from about 1816, by Mr. Benjamin and

* Madras Journal of Literature and Science, v. p. 214, vii. p. 144., viii. p. 397, ix., p. 454.

† J. A. S. B., vol. v., p. 296.

‡ Madras Journal, i., p. 38.

§ Ibid. iii., p. 338.

‖ There are several copies of this diagram in the Geographical Department of the India Office.

Mr. George Noton, of the Company's service; but the leading meteorologist of India, who first classified, and drew sound deductions from his work, was Colonel Sykes. This accomplished observer kept a register in the Deccan and at Bombay from 1825 to 1830, and gave his results to the world in an elaborate paper which was read before the Royal Society in 1835.*

Colonel Sykes points out that the great features in his barometrical indications are the diurnal and nocturnal tides, embracing two maxima and two minima in the 24 hours, the former between 9 and 10 a.m. and 10 and 11 p.m., and the latter between 4 and 5 p.m. and 4 and 5 a.m. In many thousand observations there was not a solitary instance in which the barometer was not higher at 9 to 10 a.m. than at sunrise, and lower at 4 to 5 p.m. than at 9 to 10 a.m. His hygrometric observations, and those for the direction of the wind, were very complete and satisfactory. The great feature as regards wind in the Deccan is its extreme rareness from the north or south. Whirlwinds are common in the hot months; columns of dust in the form of trumpets, chasing over the treeless plains, and carrying sand, straw, clothes, and baskets to a height of 200 feet in the vortex of heated air. The deductions derived from the observations by Colonel Sykes are important and numerous. In the first place, they removed the doubts, previously entertained by Humboldt, as to the suspension of the atmospheric tides during the monsoon in Western India; next, Colonel Sykes proved the existence of four atmospheric tides in the 24 hours, two diurnal and two nocturnal, and each consisting of a maximum and minimum tide; as well as the occurrence of the tides within the same limit hours as in America and Europe. He discovered that the greatest mean diurnal oscillations took place in the coldest months, and the smallest tides in the damp months of the monsoon in the Deccan; that the diurnal and nocturnal occurrence of the tides was regular, without a single case of intervention; and that the diurnal and annual oscillations were trifling, compared with those of extra-tropical climates. He found that the annual range of the thermometer was less than in Europe, but that the diurnal range was much greater. He also described the remarkable circular and white rainbows in the Deccan, the peculiarities of the winds,

* "Philosophical Transactions," No. x (1835), p. 161. "On atmospheric tides and the meteorology of the Deccan, by Lieut. Colonel W. H. Sykes, F.R.S."

the frequency of calms, the quantity of electricity in the atmosphere under certain circumstances, and the singular opacity of the atmosphere in hot weather. The tables which accompany this important paper show the oscillations of the barometer, the barometric observations at Poona, Bombay, and Mahabaleshwur, the hygrometric observations, the register of the ombrometer, and the prevailing winds.

The Bombay observatory at Colaba was first established under Mr. Curnin in 1823, but the records previous to 1840 are scanty and imperfect. In the end of the latter year a set of instruments, originally intended for Aden, were transferred to Bombay, and Mr. Arthur B. Orlebar, who was Elphinstone Professor of Astronomy and Mathematics, took charge of the observatory, at the request of Colonel Sykes. His series extends over the year 1841–42, and on the 15th of July 1842 Dr. George Buist assumed charge of the Colaba observatory.* The results of Dr. Buist's meteorological observations from 1842 to 1844 are published monthly in the Journal of the Bombay Branch of the Asiatic Society. He had three native assistants, and horary readings were registered of the barometer, thermometer, wet and dry bulb, and direction of the wind.† Dr. Buist had devoted much attention to meteorological subjects. He collected a vast amount of data, and the newspaper he edited at Bombay is full of information respecting phenomena connected with the weather. Dr. Buist published the results of a comparison of the observations of nine different barometers read every half hour for 24 successive hours;‡ a catalogue of remarkable hail storms from 1822 to 1850, in India;§ and a notice of remarkable meteors.‖ He put thermometers for recording solar and terrestrial radiation

* Dr. Buist published an account of "the Observatories of India" in the "*Times of India*," June 15th, 1850.

† "Meteorological Observations, Bombay, 1842, Dr. George Buist, L.L.D.," 1843.

"Journal of the Bombay Branch of the Asiatic Society," i., pp. 49–90, 145–200, 255–354.

"Provisional Report on the Meteorological Observations at Bombay for 1844." (Cupar, 1845.)

"Journal of the Bombay Branch," i., p. 287, and printed separately.

"Journal of the Bombay Geographical Society, ix., p. 184 and p. 1.

‡ "Journal of the Bombay Branch," i., p, 207, and printed separately.

§ "Journal of the Bombay Geographical Society," ix., p. 104, and xii., p. 1, and "*British Association Reports*," xx., p. 31, and xxiv., p. 35.

‖ Ibid. ix., p. 197.

into use at the Colaba observatory, and constructed a diagram of hourly barometric curves at Bombay, comparing them with those at Madras and Trivandrum. Dr. Buist endeavoured to make the study of meteorology interesting; and in his very pleasantly written paper on the climate of Western India, he complained that "picturesque and descriptive meteorology had almost altogether been buried under minute instrumental details."*

Dr. Buist furnished General Sabine with observations taken in 1843, consisting of the mean temperature, mean barometric pressure, mean tension of the atmosphere, and mean gaseous pressure at every second hour. These data formed the subject of a paper read before the British Association by General Sabine in 1845,† and assisted in the explanation of the diurnal variation of barometric pressure. General Sabine had already noticed, from observations taken at Toronto, that the aqueous and gaseous constituents of barometric pressure, when presented separately, exhibited, in their variations, a striking accordance with variations of temperature. The data supplied by Dr. Buist tended to confirm these deductions, which suggest an extension in height and consequent overflow of the column of air in the higher regions of the atmosphere, over the place of observation in the day time, when the surface of the earth is gaining heat by radiation, and a contraction when the temperature is diminishing.

Dr. James Murray was actively engaged in meteorological studies in the Deccan during the time that Dr. Buist was at work in Bombay. He registered a series of observations at Sattara from 1844 to 1847, consisting of means, maxima, and minima, and daily ranges for each month; and had previously completed a series at Mahabaleshwur, extending from 1829 to 1843,‡ which had been commenced by Drs. Walker and Morehead.

---

* "Sketch of the Climate of Western India, by Dr. Buist." *Reports of the British Association*, xx., p. 29.

† *British Association Reports*, xiv., p. 73. Reprinted in the "Madras Journal of Literature and Science," xiii., p. 106.

‡ See his "Observations on the climate of the Mahabaleshwur hills."—*Journal of the Medical and Physical Society of Bombay*, i. p. 79 (1838); and "Notes on the meteorology of the Sattara Territory for 1848."—*Journal of the Bombay Geographical Society*, vol. ix., p. 13 (1850.)

See also his paper entitled "Practical observations on the nature and effects of the hill climates of India;" in which he gives the mean temperature at Simla, Ootaca-

Professor Orlebar resumed the charge of the Colaba observatory in 1844, and superintended the registration of hourly readings in 1845.* He prepared a series of hygrometric tables, based on those of Major Boileau.† In 1846 the Colaba observatory was handed over to Captain Montriou,‡ of the Indian Navy, who had the observations registered every two hours. His elements were atmospheric pressure, temperature of the free air, of the stratum of air in contact with the ground, of the ground six feet below the surface, of the wet and dry bulbs, the force and direction of the wind, rainfall, evaporation, and clouds. He also gives tables of means. Captain Montriou was succeeded by Lieutenant Fergusson, of the Indian Navy, who held the appointment until 1864.§ In his time the instruments were in an open shed-like building at Colaba, fitted with screens to regulate the absence of glare and sunshine. The observations were horary, and he published summaries of results, with diagrams of diurnal changes of the meteorological elements, and of variations of temperature.‖ Lieutenant Fergusson was succeeded by Mr. Morland, and Mr. Chambers has continued the series down to the present year.

In 1850 Colonel Sykes contributed another valuable paper, embodying the results of the further progress that had been made in India up to that date. It is entitled "A discussion of the "meteorological observations taken in India at various heights, "embracing those at Dodabetta on the Neilgherry hills at 8,640 feet "above the sea."¶ The paper contains many important generalizations, and the additional information gives occasion for a further examination of the phenomena of horary oscillations, and the times

mund, Darjeeling, Kotagherry, Landoor, Mahabaleshwar, &c.—*Transactions of the Medical and Physical Society of Bombay*, vol. vii., p. 3. (1844.)

* "Meteorological Observations, Bombay, 1845." Arthur B. Orlebar." (Bombay 1846. 4to.) "On magnetic and meteorological observations at Bombay, by A. B. Orlebar." *Reports. Brit. Ass.*, xvi., p. 28.

† "Journal of the Bombay Branch," ii., p. 309.

‡ "Observations made at the Bombay observatory for 1847." C. W. Montriou, Commander, I.N." Part II., meteorological. (Bombay, 1851. 4to.)

§ "Meteorological Observations." Bombay, 1853, Lieut. E. F. T. Fergusson, I.N. Also 1857 (Bombay, folio, 2 vols. 1855,) and 1859–64.

‖ A Report on the subject of the rainfall in the Deccan, and on the climatic disturbance apparent during 1861 and 1862, was published in 1863. See "Bombay Selections," No. 78, N.S.

¶ "Philosophical Transactions" (1850), pt. ii. xv.

of ebb and flow of atmospheric tides at an increased number of observing stations, some of them, like Dodabetta, at great elevations above the sea. Among other deductions, Colonel Sykes points out that climate is not absolutely dependent on latitude, but is affected by numerous local circumstances. Thus the three hill stations of Mahabaleshwur, Mercara, and Uttray Mullay in Travancore are exactly the same height above the sea,* but widely separated as regards latitude. The mean temperatures of Mahabaleshwur and Mercara are almost identical, while Uttray Mullay, which is much nearer the equator, is 3° 35′ lower. It is within the influence of both monsoons. Colonel Sykes points out great anomalies in the hours of the occurrence of maxima and minima of temperature at Madras, and remarks upon the range of temperature at Calcutta, Sattara, Mahabaleshwur, and Dodabetta. The Dodabetta temperature, at 8,642 feet, compared with that of Mahabaleshwur, at 4,500 feet, has a decidedly diminished daily, hourly, and annual range. The probable sources of error in the degree of humidity in the air, as represented by the wet bulb observations in India, are discussed at some length, and Colonel Sykes recommends caution in generalizations from a limited number of local observations for the determination of the dew point.† He then gives a most valuable comparative summary of the amount of rainfall in various latitudes, and at different heights above the sea, showing that, on the ghauts, the elevation of greatest fall is 4,500 feet above the sea; and that there is an extraordinary difference between points on the western rim of the ghauts and others a few miles further east. At Mahabaleshwur the fall in 1849 was 338 inches, and at Paunchgunny, only 11 miles to the eastward, 58 inches. The phenomena of winds, fogs, and electricity are also discussed. Colonel Sykes's paper is accompanied by tables showing the mean oscillations of the barometer at Calcutta, Bombay, and Madras; and the mean horary oscillations at Calcutta from 1845 to 1848, and at Bombay and Madras from 1843 to 1845.

Of late years the increased attention that has been paid to sanitary measures, to the causes of periodical famines, and to the phenomena

* 4,500 feet.

† A paper by Dr. Forbes Watson, illustrative of Colonel Sykes's remarks, and showing the small value to be attached to observations of the hygrometric state of the air in India, as obtained by means of the dry and wet bulb thermometer, will be published shortly.

of cyclones, has led to a more systematic study of the laws affecting the changes of the atmosphere in India. It has been seen how zealously the study of the law of storms was pursued,* on the publication of Colonel Reid's work, by Piddington at Calcutta, Biden at Madras, and Buist and Thom in the Bombay Presidency. At about the same time the Government of India gave some attention to the more complete registration of meteorological data, with reference to the prospects of the harvests. On the 21st of January 1846 the collectors were ordered to submit reports, and in 1847 they were supplied with thermometers and rain gauges. For three years these statistics were given in the Annual Revenue Reports, but in 1852 the instruments were made over to the medical officers at the several stations, who were charged with the duty of keeping registers of the rainfall and temperature. It appears, however, that these records were not satisfactorily kept. The hours of observation were nominally at sunrise, 10 a.m., 4 p.m., sunset, and 10 p.m.

In 1863 Mr. Glaisher prepared a report upon the meteorology of India from all the data that were then accessible. His most reliable sources of information were the observatories at Madras and Bombay, but he also availed himself of a great mass of observations taken at other stations. He found those for humidity of the air to be far too few, as well as those for solar evaporation. Mr. Glaisher discussed his materials with a view of rendering the results applicable for the purposes of the Army Sanitary Commission, and especially endeavoured to indicate, at different seasons of the year, the height at which the English climate is most nearly approached. The most valuable and reliable section of his report is that on the fall of rain in India. All the materials that could then be collected were examined and utilized by Mr. Glaisher; but they were far from satisfactory, and he expressed a hope that future meteorological observations in India might be carried out under some general system, and on a uniform plan, both with respect to instruments, their position, and general instructions.†

Admiral FitzRoy's introduction of the system of warnings and forecasts in England gave a fresh impetus to similar investigations

---

* See page 34.

† Report upon the Meteorology of India in relation to the health of the troops, by James Glaisher, F.R.S. In the Report of the Royal Commission on the Sanitary State of the Army in India. I., pp. 781-943. (*London*, 1863.)

in the east. The Admiral's "weather book" was published in 1863, and in March 1865 a Meteorological Committee was appointed at Calcutta, to consider the best means of establishing a system of observations for the protection of that port. The Committee recommended the appointment of observers, generally assistants in the Electric Telegraph Department, to be stationed at a series of points round the coast of the bay of Bengal, and in some other directions, which should be in telegraphic communication with Calcutta. They were supplied with instruments for observing the barometric pressure, humidity of the air and rainfall, and were to observe at 9 30 a.m. and 4 p.m. Their observations were to be transmitted daily by telegraph, and to be received at the meteorological observatory attached to the Surveyor General's Office at Calcutta, whence, if necessary, they were to be communicated to the master attendant. The Committee also recommended that the thermometrical observations should be restricted to six first-class stations; namely, Patna, Monghyr, Hazareebagh, Berhampore, Shillong, and Goalpara.* Sheds of uniform pattern were ordered to be erected for dry and wet bulb, maxima, and minima thermometers. The second-class stations are those still under the Medical Department, where the rainfall only is registered.

These measures were followed by the appointment of meteorological reporters to the Governments of the Punjab, the North-West Provinces, and Bengal. Dr. A. Neil was appointed for the Punjab in 1866. The records from the various stations,† comprising registrations of atmospheric pressure, humidity, temperature, rainfall, and force and direction of the wind, are forwarded to him monthly, besides daily registers of rainfall at 32 stations, from the Revenue Returns; and he prepares an annual condensed report on the general barometric phenomena, with barometric and wind charts.‡

---

* Jessore, Gaya, Cachar, and Debrooghur have since been added.

† The stations are Lahore, Mooltan, Shahpoor, Dera Ismael Khan, Peshawur, Rawul Pindee, Sealkote, Sreenaggur, Bahawulpore, Leh, Dalhousie, Rungi, Loodiana, and Hoshiarpur.

‡ There have been three Punjab annual reports. "Annual Reports of the Meteorological Observations registered in the Punjab," by Dr. A. Neil. 1867, 1868, 1869.

Dr. Neil also supplied a summary of the weather in the Punjab for 1868, which is printed in the 5th Report of the Sanitary Commissioner with the Government of India (1868), p. 13.

Dr. Murray Thomson, the meteorological reporter for the North-West Provinces, assumed charge in February 1865. In the first year he received returns every month from 23 stations, of which three were in the Himalaya, above 5,000 feet, and the rest on the plains at elevations from 1,800 feet at Ajmeer to 250 at Benares. Six of these are first-class stations, where there are complete sets of instruments; namely,

Roorkee,	Ajmeer,
Nynee Tal,	Jhansi,
Agra,	Benares.

The officers in charge are generally the civil surgeons of the stations, and the barometers are read at all the extreme periods of the daily oscillations. Two volunteers also supply valuable meteorological data; namely, Dr. Bow from Chunar, and Mr. Hennessey, of the Great Trigonometrical Survey, from Mussouree, and afterwards from Dehra. The second-class stations, where observations are taken at 6 and 10 a.m. and 4 and 9 p.m., are the civil and military hospitals. Dr. Murray Thompson, in the first year, delivered lectures on meteorological instruments and their use, at the Agra Medical School. His report for 1866 contains a general retrospect of the weather, and monthly tables of the barometric readings at 10 a.m. and 4 p.m. of the dew point; elastic force of vapour; relative humidity; the thermometer exposed and in shade, and six inches below the surface of the ground; the rainfall and winds.* In 1868 the number of stations was 14; namely, Chakrata, Dehra, Roorkee, Nynee Tal, Meerut, Bareilly, Futtehgur, Agra, Lucknow, Ajmeer, Goruckpore, Allahabad, Benares, and Jhansi. Each year, from the materials submitted to him, Dr. Murray Thomson draws up an annual report, giving a retrospect of the weather, remarks on the climate, and tables of means.†

* "Report on meteorological observations in the N. W. Provinces," by Dr. Murray Thomson, 1866. It is published as Appendix C. to the third Annual Sanitary Report for Bengal. (Calcutta 1867.)

† "Report on the Meteorological Observations in the North-West Provinces for 1868," by Dr. Murray Thomson, Reporter on Meteorology. Printed in the "Selections from the Records of the Government of the N. W. Provinces." Second series, vol. iii., No. 1, (1870).

Dr. Murray Thomson supplied a summary of this report to the Sanitary Commissioner, and it is printed in the 5th Report, p. 13.

The Sanitary Commissioner in the Central Provinces has also taken steps to establish a number of meteorological stations, on the same plan as those in the North-West; but only the Nagpore observations have yet been received.

The rainfall is also carefully registered by the canal officers, and a great deal of information on that branch of the subject will be found in the various irrigation reports.

On the 1st of April 1867 the office of meteorological reporter to the Government of Bengal was established, to carry on the system of storm warnings for the protection of the port of Calcutta, and to perform duties similar to those of the meteorological reporters who had already been appointed for the Punjab and the North-West Provinces. He was also to examine existing records, and undertake their supervision, and conversion into a form in which they might prove useful. The reporter's work was thus divided into two branches; the collection of data, and its utilization.

The appointment was accepted by Mr. H. F. Blanford, who had already done good service, in the geological survey in 1857-62, on the Neilgherry hills,* among the crystalline limestones of Coimbatore and the sandstones of Trivicary, as well as with his brother in Cuttack in 1856. The office work consists of sending daily reports to the newspapers, weekly to the Calcutta Gazette, monthly abstracts and rainfall reports from 66 stations to the Board of Revenue, and of preparing storm warnings and special reports. In 1868 the first and second-class stations were equipped, and in 1869 they were in good working order, while some additional stations were established. The elements recorded at the first-class stations are the atmospheric pressure, mean and extreme temperatures of the air, solar and terrestrial radiation, humidity, rainfall, wind, and proportion of clouds; and the hours for observation are 4 a.m., 10 a.m., 4 p.m., and 10 p.m.† The stations are at Akyab on the Arracan coast, False Point Lighthouse near the mouth of the Mahanuddy, Cuttack, Saugor Island at the mouth of the Hooghly, Chittagong, Calcutta, Jessore, Dacca, Darjeeling, Silchar, Shillong on the northern slope of the Cossyah hills, Goalpara, Berhampore, Monghir, Hazareebagh, Gya, and Patna. Mr. Blanford also receives reports from Benares, Roorkee, Madras, and Port Blair; from Mr. Nursingrow's observatory at Vizagapatam, where the register is uniform with those

---

* See page 161 (*note.*)

† Most of the stations are in charge of electric telegraph assistants, and the instruments supplied to each station are two mercurial barometers, dry and wet bulb and maximum and minimum thermometers, a grass minimum radiating thermometer, a Robinson's anemometer, rain gauge, and wind vane.

of the Bengal stations; from the manager of the Tea Company's garden in Upper Assam; and of the rainfall from the Chinchona plantations in Sikkim, and on the Cossyah hills. Mr. Blanford has also set on foot a system of meteorological registration in the Indian seas, on a small scale, and registers are now kept on board six of the British India Steam Navigation Company's vessels. All the barometers, except those at Madras, Benares, and Roorkee, have been compared with the Calcutta standard. The third-class stations, of which there are 36, only record the rainfall.

In his annual reports, Mr. Blanford digests the information he receives from the numerous stations, and shows the results in a series of tables. These include the monthly means of atmospheric pressure,* the monthly mean pressure at all the stations reduced to the sea level, the maximum, minimum, and mean monthly temperatures, humidity, serenity, comparison of serenity, solar radiation and mean temperature in hot weather months, rainfall, comparison of rainfall with averages, summary of observed winds, and monthly wind resultants. There is also a sketch of the normal character of the monsoons, with notices of the storms on May 1st and 13th, June 5th and 10th, and October 7th and 8th of 1869.† Mr. Blanford supplies memoranda on the chief characteristics of the meteorology of each year to the Sanitary Commissioner.‡ "The accumulation of "trustworthy and systematic observations," Mr. Blanford reports, "which far exceed anything previously available for Bengal, has "admitted of a more scientific discussion than had previously been "practicable; and a beginning has been made to educe from the "tabulated and reduced results, some general conclusions."

The Sanitary Commissioners in the three Presidencies have greatly promoted meteorological science, in the well-founded expectation that systematic observations over wide areas would enable them to form conclusions as to the effects of climate on the diseases of the

---

* He communicated a paper on barometric irregularities to the "Journal of the Asiatic Society of Bengal," 1870, pt. ii., No. 2.

† See also the "Report on the Calcutta cyclone of October 5th, 1864," by Colonel Gastrell and Mr. H. F. Blanford, noticed at page 36.

‡ Mr. Blanford has submitted three annual reports, "Reports of the Meteorological Observer to the Government of Bengal," 1867, 1861, 1869, and an Administration Report for 1869–70.

See also the 5th Report of the Sanitary Commissioner with the Government of India (1868), p. 13.

country. In 1865 the Madras Sanitary Commissioner, Mr. Ellis, prepared and submitted a scheme for recording meteorological observations at each of the chief, civil, and military stations, which received the sanction of the Supreme Government.* The stations are to be under the superintendence of the senior medical officer, and the registers will all be forwarded to Mr. Pogson, the astronomer at Madras, for reduction, who will prepare annual reports. He drew up a memorandum on the meteorological character of the year for the Sanitary Report of 1868,† but had not had time to prepare the returns for publication which he had received from the stations in the districts. These will appear in future years.

The meteorological registers at the Bombay Observatory have always been regularly kept, and yearly abstracts by Mr. Chambers, who has been the Superintendent since 1856, are published with the Reports of the Municipal Commissioner.‡ These abstracts give the pressure of the air, temperature, dew point, humidity, rainfall, and force of the land and sea winds for each month. Half yearly Meteorological Reports, by Mr. Chambers, are also regularly transmitted to the Astronomer Royal. But no general system for observing at numerous stations and of sending the records to a central reporter for reduction, such as exists under the other Local Governments, appears to have been established at Bombay.

The machinery is, however, available for making important scientific deductions from observations taken at points scattered over the greater part of India, all of which are in regular communication with central stations. Mr. Blanford has pointed out that the distribution of relative pressures is an important object of inquiry, because the local character of the south-west and probably of the north-west monsoon is greatly affected by its variations in different years. There are other points which require a very wide field of

---

* The stations are Kamptee, Secunderabad, Vizagapatam, Bellary, Bangalore, Negapatam, Salem, Masulipatam, Cannanore, Trichinopoly, Rangoon, Jakatalla, Tinnevelly, Madura, Coimbatore, Kurnool, and Cochin.

† See the Reports of the Sanitary Commissioner for Madras, 1866 and 1868, p. 114.

‡ Annual Reports of the Municipal Commissioner of Bombay, 1866. App. L, p. 45. Do. for 1867, p. 52. Do. for 1868, at the end of Dr. Lumsdaine's Report, the Health Office, p. 6. Do. for 1869, by Dr. Hewlett. See also "Reports of the Superintendent of the Government Observatory, Colaba." 1866, 1868, 1869, 1870. "Normal Winds of Bombay," by Charles Chambers, Esq., F.R.S.—(*Bombay Builder*. *June* 1869.)

Statistics of the rainfall will be found in the "Bombay Times" Directories.

observations for their elucidation; and thus Bengal, or any one local province, cannot usefully be treated independently of the other parts of India. It is to be hoped that, before long, it will be possible to include the data of a wide area, and, indeed, of the whole Indian Empire, in one general Meteorological Report. "The business of a meteorological department," says Mr. Blanford, "is to "discuss as well as to record facts, to compare and correllate them "under the guidance of accepted physical laws, and to endeavour "to trace out the causes which operate in producing the normal "features of our seasons, as well as those of their irregularities, the "important influence of which on the welfare of the country has, "of late years, been too painfully obvious. In order to do this, "however, with any degree of completeness, a uniform system of "registration must be extended much beyond the limits of Bengal."

Tidal Observations.

The earliest recorded tidal observations in India, which I have met with, were taken at the Kidderpore dock-head, on the Hooghly, by Mr. James Kyd,* for 22 years, from 1806 to 1827.† Mr. Kyd did not publish his results in tables, but showed them on a series of diagrams, which he accompanied by some suggestive remarks. He observed that in the Hooghly there were two long unequal tides, eight months of flood and four of ebb. He assumed that the south-west wind in March caused the currents to set up the Bay of Bengal, and raise the sea several feet at its head, and in the Hooghly, long before the freshes from the rivers are felt. This cause continues till October. Then the river freshes of August and September, and the change of wind, give the currents a set in the contrary direction. The rise of the Ganges affects the Hooghly early in July, and its level is bodily raised, the low water (neaps) at the time of the freshes being even higher than the high water (also neaps) of the dry season. Mr. Kyd suggests that the Damooda, Roopnarain, and Hidgelee rivers occasion the height of low water in the season of freshes, by acting as a dam, and preventing the

* Mr. Kyd was an East Indian, who set an example of independent enterprise to his countrymen, in forming a large docking establishment at Kidderpore, which afterwards became the property of the Government.—*Calcutta Review*, iii. p. 249.

† "Asiatic Researches, xviii. p. 259.

ebbing of the waters quickly into the sea. Another local phenomenon of the Hooghly tides which he could not satisfactorily explain is, that in the north-east monsoon the night tides are highest, and in the south-west the day tides. The bores in the Hooghly only occur on the highest spring tides.

Mr. Kyd's observations were continued in 1828 and 1829 at Mud Point, on Saugor Island, and a further series of tidal registrations was published by James Prinsep.*

While these early tidal observations were being taken in the Hooghly, the subject was being carefully studied in England by Sir John Lubbock† and Dr. Whewell. Their papers on co-tidal lines in the Philosophical Transactions excited general interest; but on the chart which accompanied Dr. Whewell's essay,‡ though a numerous series of cotidal lines in other parts of the world was given, the coasts of India presented nearly a blank. In the same year in which the essay was published, Dr. Whewell's "suggestions to "persons who have opportunities to make or collect observations of "the tides" appeared in the Journal of the Asiatic Society of Bengal;§ and the Governor-General, at the same time, requested that the Society would undertake to promote inquiries on the Indian coasts to complete the cotidal lines for the Bay of Bengal.‖ It was considered that the most important branch of the investigation was that for the determination of the diurnal inequality or difference between day and night tides, which depends on the declination of the moon north or south of the equator; and the Society sent a circular on the subject to members residing at coast stations.¶ Dr. Whewell also expressed a hope that tidal obser-

* "Gleanings in Science," Nov. 1829 and Jan. 1830.

† "Philosophical Transactions," 1831.

‡ "Phil. Trans., 1833." "Essay towards an approximation to a map of cotidal lines." Dr. Whewell wrote 14 memoirs on tides in the Philosophical Transactions from 1833 to 1850. "Researches on the tides, and their diurnal inequalities," were published separately. (London, 1848.) See also Professor Airy's article on "Tides and Waves," in the *Encyclopædia Metropolitana.*

§ "J. A. S. B., ii., p. 151.

‖ "J. A. S. B., iv., p. 401.

¶ "J. A. S. B.," vi., p. 401. James Prinsep expressed his confident belief that "all who had seen Professor Whewell's laborious map of the tidal wave, traced in its "course over the whole surface of the globe, would willingly contribute to the per- "fection of so interesting and useful a problem."

vations would be made from an extensive range of places in India.*

The first result of these measures was the contribution of a table of the times of high water at the principal places between Calcutta and Point Palmyras, which was prepared by Mr. P. G. Sinclair. Then the results of observations made on the tides at Madras in 1821, by means of a tide gauge fixed near the north-east angle of Fort St. George, was published.† In 1837, observations of tides were made by Lieutenant H. Siddons at Chittagong, in conformity with the circular of the Asiatic Society,‡ and a succinct review of observations of tides made in the Indian Archipelago in 1839 was also published,§ as well as the registers of the rise and fall of the tide at Prince Edward's Island in 1840–41, and at Singapore in 1834–35.‖ Professor Whewell also received the Singapore observations which were taken by Mr. Scott, the Master Attendant, and he notices the enormous diurnal inequality.¶

A special series of tidal observations was ordered to be taken in the Hooghly in 1869, with reference to the effect of a cyclone wave if the river was embanked. Tidal observations are also taken at Kidderpore dockyard; and the Master Attendant at Calcutta predicts tide tables, giving the anticipated time of high and low water for every day, which are published annually. But the tables, when compared by Mr. Parkes with the register furnished from the Master Attendant's Office, were found to be so erroneous that they can be of no practical use. For the complete investigation of the Hooghly tides observations should be made near the mouth of the river.

The earliest register of tides on the west coast of India will, I think, be found in a table shewing the rise of the spring tides in Bombay harbour, during night and day, for 1832, which was communicated by Benjamin Noton Esq.** When the Colaba observa-

* "J. A. S. B.," iv., p. 517. "Though we have some detached observations on the "coast of India, we have nothing which gives us a correct view of the progress of the "tide." Dr. Whewell, in a paper read before the British Association, "On our "ignorance of the tides." (1851) xx., p. 27.

† "Madras Herald, June 3rd, 1835.

‡ "J. A. S. B., vi., p. 949.

§ "J. A. S. B.," x., p. 302.

‖ "J. A. S. B." xi., pp. 149 and 263, and xix.

¶ "7th series of researches on the tides. On diurnal inequalitiest a Singapore." *Phil. Trans.* 1837, p. 75.

** "J. A. S. B." ii., p. 247. And in "Rushton's Gazetteer" for 1842.

tory was first established, Captain Daniel Ross suggested a contrivance for registering tides by means of a large float and pulley in a well 22 feet deep, with a register house over it, just above high-water mark; but it was found impracticable to connect the well with the sea by a cutting. Nothing was, therefore, done until Dr. Buist took charge of the observatory, in July 1842, when the self-registering tide gauge was put into working order, and the well was connected with the sea by a siphon pipe.* The tides have since been observed at the Colaba observatory, though with much irregularity. The registers, while Captain Montriou was in charge, have been published for 1846, 1847, and 1848. Serjeant Dunn, of the Sappers and Miners, a very active and intelligent man, was the actual observer, and the series for 1846 is partially reliable; but those for subsequent years are very doubtful. Captain Montriou remarked that the law of tides had been found to differ materially from that which had been determined relative to the tides in Europe.† Captain Ross, as Master Attendant at Bombay, constructed a set of tables from observations made at the dock head, from May 1835 to December 1840.‡

In the paper which accompanies Captain Ross's tables, Dr. Buist observed that the amount of information respecting the tides of the west coast of India was then singularly meagre in amount and incomplete in kind. Great tidal irregularities prevail at Mahim, Tannah, Panwell, and Nagotna; and there are remarkable local currents dependent upon tides, but none of these phenomena have been carefully observed. Further irregularities are said to have been subsequently caused in the tides by the construction of the Bandora and Mahim causeway.

Tide registers were kept by the Surveyors of the Indian Navy, and were always sent in with the field books and journals of the respective ships. These have never been published; but the tide tables, annually issued at the Admiralty, give the time of high water at the full and change of the moon, and the ranges of tides at springs and neaps, for 98 places on the coast of India. The geographical arrangement of the table follows nearly the same order as the progress of the

* "Journal, Bombay G. S., vi., p. 235.

† "Observations made at the Bombay Observatory," by Capt. Montriou and Lieut. Fergusson. (Bombay 4to.) See those for 1847 and 1862 especially.

‡ "Journal, Bombay G. S., vi., p. 243.

great tidal wave from S.W. to N.E.* The tidal wave strikes Western Hindostan, from the west, at right angles to the mean direction of the shore line, thus causing very little difference in the times of high water along the whole length of coast, except when the wave has to run up indentations of the land, such as the gulfs of Cambay and Cutch. From Mangalore to Jyghur (100 miles south of Bombay) no tidal stream is observed along the coast, except just off the mouths of rivers;† but along the Northern Concan the flood stream sets to the north, and increases until, in the gulf of Cambay, it finishes with the well-known bore which was described by Lieutenant Ethersey. This tidal bore sets in like a straight wall of water with a head 5 or 6 feet high, each succeeding wave decreasing more and more, until the whole gulf is reduced to the same level with the sea outside.‡

South of Mangalore the flood stream is from the N.W. Kurrachee and Porbunder receive the tidal wave earlier than any other parts of India; and thence the flood tide sets eastward along the coast of Sind and Cutch, north above Porbunder, and south-east along the Kattiwar coast to Diu head. Off Diu head there are frequent eddies caused by the ebb stream of the gulf of Cambay running westward, while the flood stream from Porbunder is running to the east.

Captain Taylor has suggested other causes for tidal irregularities. Where evaporation is so great as it is in the Indian seas, there are doubtless local movements of the ocean dependent on that cause. At Cochin the stream, flowing into the backwater, is sometimes constant for twenty hours, although the regular but inconsiderable rise and fall has been marked on the tide guage.§

It was also observed by Captain Taylor that, in the S.W. monsoon, in the harbours on the west coast of India, more especially in Jyghur, Viziadroog, and Carwar, the water in the daytime was on a higher level by 2 or 3 feet than in the dry season. The three above-

---

* See "Findlay's Directory for the Navigation of the Indian Seas" (2d ed. 1870) p. 77. Imray's "Seaman's Guide to the Navigation of the Indian Ocean;" and "Horsburgh's Indian Directory."

† "The West Coast of Hindostan Pilot," compiled by Commander A. D. Taylor, I.N. (1866) p. 8.

‡ "R. G. S. Journal," viii. p. 96 and p., 202. For a notice of Lieut. Ethersey's Survey, see p. 18.

§ "Taylor's West Coast Pilot," p. 8. A tidal register was kept at Cochin so long ago as when Dr. Buist wrote his remarks in 1836.—*Bombay G.S. Journal*, vi. p. 250.

mentioned ports are formed by points of land running out to seaward on their southern sides. Captain Taylor suggests that the great body of water brought down by the rivers, at that season, is stopped by the force of the monsoon blowing upon the shore, and that the observed phenomenon of the water in these harbours being at a higher level in the rain is thus partially accounted for.

Mr. William Parkes, the Consulting Engineer of the Kurrachee Harbour Works, has computed very accurate tide tables, both for that port and for Bombay. His data for Kurrachee were sets of observations taken at Manora Point from December 1857 to March 1858, and at Keamari from March 1st to August 31st, 1865.

His calculations were made with a view to determining the laws which govern the tides of the Indian seas, where the diurnal inequality gives to alternate tides an elevation or depression in height, and an acceleration or retardation in time. The theory of these diurnal inequalities has been elaborately investigated by the Astronomer Royal and others. The desideratum is to bring the art of tidal prediction for Indian ports, where there is a large diurnal inequality, to the same degree of precision as has been arrived at in the case of English tides, where the irregularity is unimportant. At Kurrachee the diurnal inequality sometimes affects high water to the extent of two hours and low water 40 minutes, and as regards height, as much as 12 inches at high and 36 at low water. These effects are far too great to be neglected in the prediction of tides.

Mr. Parkes based his investigation on the fact that the diurnal inequality was caused by a diurnal tide which alternately raises and depresses, accelerates and retards, the semi-diurnal tides; and the problem was to find the relation between the movements of the sun and moon, and the varying times and heights of this diurnal tide. The result of the calculations has been very satisfactory; and the rules for the prediction of tides for the port of Kurrachee have been drawn up, and the tables computed, by combining the semi-diurnal and diurnal tides.* The tidal observations at Kurrachee, taken at Manora Point by a self-acting register in charge of Mr. Humby, since 1865, are now becoming of great value, at a very small cost;

* "Report on the tides of the Port of Kurrachee," by W. Parkes, Esq., C.E. 1866. See also a paper read before the Royal Society, "On the Tides of Bombay and Kurrachee," by William Parkes, M. Inst., C.E.—*Phil. Trans.* 1868, xxix., p. 685. Mr. Parkes has computed the Tide Tables for Kurrachee and Bombay for the years 1866, 1867, 1868, 1869, 1870, and 1871.

and have served to suggest further corrections in the formulæ by which the tables are calculated.

The data used by Mr. Parkes for his Bombay tide tables were the registers taken at the Colaba observatory by the self-acting tide gauge in 1846. From these materials the Bombay Time Tables are computed, and Mr. Parkes, in his report, gives the modifications necessary for making the rules given for the prediction of tides at Kurrachee applicable to Bombay, as well as a diagram of curves of semi-monthly inequalities of time and height. The Bombay Tables have been compared with tidal observations taken from January 28th to June 4th, 1867, by Mr. Ormiston, the Government engineer of reclamations, by direct reading from a graduated staff at every ten minutes.

Sir William Thomson, using materials furnished by Mr. Parkes as part of the basis of his argument, has suggested a new mode of investigating tidal observations, which is being worked out under the auspices of a Committee of the British Association.*

It is very important that the investigation of the laws of the tides of the Indian seas should be extended to other ports than Bombay and Kurrachee, both from a purely scientific and from a practical point of view. But so incredibly long does it take for such measures to pass from the stage of discussion to that of action that the suggestions of Dr. Whewell, made in 1832, and the importance of which were fully recognized by the Government of India at the time, have borne little fruit. Mr. Parkes, the value of whose accurate tide tables are fully appreciated at Kurrachee and Bombay, has recently renewed the attempt of Dr. Whewell. He urges that a series of observations, extending over twelve months, should be taken at several judiciously chosen points round the coast; and that a competent person should be appointed to the special duty of systematically collating these observations, deducing from them formulæ for the computation of tide tables, and annually issuing the tables. Such an investigation would be as valuable to practical seamen as to men of science.

---

* "Reports, British Association," 1868, 1870.

XV.—ASTRONOMICAL OBSERVATIONS IN INDIA.

"A laudable curiosity prompts to inquire the sources of knowledge, "and a review of its progress furnishes suggestions tending to pro- "mote the same or some kindred study. We would know the "names at least of the individuals to whom we owe successive steps "in the advancement of knowledge." The above remark is equally applicable to all the sections of this memoir, but it was made by Mr. Colebrooke, when he introduced the ancient Indian astronomers, and opened his dissertation upon their systems. Of all the sciences which have been cultivated in India under the auspices of the Government, astronomy alone has a history which goes back ages before the English occupation, and which requires, in this enumeration of those to whom, in India, we owe successive steps in the advancement of knowledge, a wider range than is included within the last century. Rennell and Voysey, the fathers of Indian geography and geology, flourished within the memory of living men; but we must go back to the 5th century for the era of Aryabhata, the sage who stands at the fountain head of the history of Indian astronomy.

Aryabhata must have flourished before the sixth century. He affirmed the diurnal revolution of the earth on its axis, accounting for it by a current of aerial fluid, extending to a height of 114 miles above the earth's surface; and he calculated the earth's circumference to be 25,080 miles. He believed the moon and primary planets to be dark, and only illumined by the sun; and he possessed the true theory of lunar and solar eclipses. He is also the earliest author that is known to have treated of algebra.* In his *Surya Siddhanta* he deduced from observations the values of the mean motions of the sun, moon, and planets, and of their apsides and nodes, and calculated eclipses. Mr. William Spottiswoode at one time had an intention of translating the *Surya Siddhanta*, and he has actually enabled an

* Colebrooke on Indian algebra.

enquirer to understand the ancient astronomer's system, by giving his rules in modern mathematical language and formulæ.*

Vahara-mihira, another astronomer, flourished in the generation after Aryabhata.

Brahmegupta, who wrote in 628. A.D., set himself the task of correcting the earlier system, which had ceased to agree with the phenomena, and of reconciling computation with observation. His *Brahma Siddhanta*, in 21 chapters, contains calculations of the mean motions and true places of the planets, of lunar and solar eclipses, of the rising and setting of planets, of the position of the moon's cusps, and of observations of altitudes by the gnomon. The principles of his astronomical system are given in a compendious treatise on spherics. He frequently quotes from Aryabhata.

Bhascara, a later astronomer, completed his work on algebra, arithmetic, and mensuration in about 1150 A.D.†

The systems of the earlier of the ancient Hindu sages were communicated to the astronomers of the court of the Abbasside Caliph Almamun at Baghdad; and the knowledge derived from this source, combined with the learning of Ptolemy, after being cultivated by the more enlightened sovereigns of Central Asia, came back again to India, with the descendants of Timour.

The Arabs began to study astronomy under the Caliph Almamun, and in 827 the Almagest was translated into Arabic. Al Batany, the most celebrated of their astronomers, noticed errors in the positions of stars in Ptolemy's catalogue, in consequence of that astronomer's error with regard to the precession of the equinoxes; and in 882 he determined the amount of this precession with greater accuracy. Dr. Halley calls Al Batany "Vir admirandi accuminis

---

* "On the Surya Siddhanta, and the Hindu method of calculating eclipses, by "William Spottiswoode." (1863.) *Journ. R. A. S.*, xx., p. 345. Dr. Bhau Daji wrote "Brief notes on the age and authenticity of the works of Aryabhata." *Journ. R. A. S.* i., (N.S.) xiv., p. 322. See also Dr. Kern—"On some fragments of Aryabhata." *Journ. R. A. S.*, xx., p. 375. Lassen's "Indische Alterthumskunde," ii., p. 1136. Burgess's translation of Aryabhata, and Fitz Edward Hall on the Arya Siddhanta, in the *Journal of the American Oriental Society*, vi., pp. 145–559. Bentley's "Historical View of Hindu Astronomy" (London 1825.) Mrs. Manning's "Ancient and mediæval India," i., 362.

† "Algebra, with arithmetic and mensuration, from the Sanscrit of Brahmegupta "and Bhascara. Translated by H. T. Colebrooke," (Murray, 4to 1817.)

"ac in administrandis observationibus exercitatissimus." Ebn Younis observed three eclipses at Cairo between 977 and 979, and Aboul Wefa, who died in 986, composed a catalogue of the fixed stars.* The learning thus fostered on the banks of the Tigris spread to the east and west,† and the Mongol Holagou Khan established an observatory at Maraga in Azerbijan, where Nasr Eddin composed his Eelkhanee tables in the thirteenth century.

Ulugh Beg, the grandson of Timour, was for many years governor of Mawer-ul-nahr during the reign of his virtuous father Shah Rokh, and reigned himself from 1447 until he was assassinated by his own son in 1449. Ulugh Beg attracted to his court all the most celebrated astronomers, from various parts of the world. He erected a college and observatory at Samarcand at which a hundred people were constantly occupied in the pursuits of science; and among other instruments he had a quadrant, the radius of which equalled in length the height of the dome of St. Sophia.‡ Having found that certain stars in Ptolemy's catalogue, reduced to his own epoch, did not coincide with observations made at Samarcand, Ulugh Beg and his learned assistants undertook to re-observe the whole of the stars in Ptolemy's catalogue, and to construct a new set of astronomical tables. This was ultimately accomplished. The tables, called *Zig Ulugh Beg*, are divided into four parts, referring to treatises on epochs and eras, on the knowledge of time, on the courses of planets, and on the positions of fixed stars. Ulugh Beg re-observed all Ptolemy's

---

* "Asiatic Miscellany, i., p. 34.

† Abu Obeydah Moslema, a native of Madrid, who had studied in the east, was the most renowned astronomer of Mohammedan Spain. He was well acquainted with the movements of the heavenly bodies. He reformed the *kiblah*, giving the true bearing of Mecca from Spain, and his work on the manner of constructing and using astrolabes is preserved in the library of the Escurial. He is also said to have translated the Almagest of Ptolemy, and to have constructed some excellent astronomical tables. See an account of his life in *Casiri*, i., p. 378, c. 2., and ii., p. 147, c. 2. and *Gayangos's Al Makkari*, i., pp. 149, 427, 465. Moslema died at Cordova in 1007 A.D.; so that he was the contemporary of the eastern astronomers Ebn Younis and Aboul Wefa.

‡ At least so the Turks, who had it from Persians of credit, told Professor Greaves. But Mr. Baily thinks it was more probably a gnomon. The Spanish Ambassador, Ruy Gonzalez de Clavijo was at Samarcand thirty years or more before Ulugh Beg built his observatory. This is to be regretted, as Clavijo described all he saw at Samarcand very minutely. See "Narrative of the Embassy of Clavijo to the court of Timour," translated and edited, with a life of Timour, by Clements R. Markham, (printed for the Hakluyt Society, 1859.,) p. 169.

stars but 27, which were too far south to be visible at Samarcand.* One of these was *Soheil* or *Canopus*, a star which was first seen by the great Timouride astronomer's cousin Baber, when he crossed the Hindoo Koosh, on his way to bring the learning of Aryabhata, increased by that of Ptolemy and Ulugh Beg, back to its native source on the plains of Hindoostan.

Thus the Timouride emperors at Delhi boasted of a famous astronomer among their collateral ancestors;† but none of the family had since turned their attention to the subject, and it was from among the Rajpoot princes, whose valour was a main support of the Delhi throne, that the greatest Indian astronomer since the days of Aryabhata was to arise. The rajahs of Dhoondar, of the race of Cuchwaha Rajpoots, and descended from Rama the king of Ayodya, were the first among the native rulers who became vassals of Mohammedan emperors. Bhagwandas, the Prince of Dhoondar, was the friend of the great Akbar, and his daughter married Akbar's son, the Emperor Jehanghir. Maun Sing, another Dhoondar Prince was the most brilliant courtier and the most successful general at the Delhi court. Jey Sing, the great astronomer, succeeded as Rajah of Dhoondar in 1699, and was famous as a general and a statesman, but above all as a man of science. Amber was the ancient capital of his state, but in 1728 he founded another capital, the only one in India which is built on a regular plan, with streets bisecting at right angles; and he called it after himself—Jeypore. It is six miles from Amber, which is included in the lines of its fortifications. Under Mohammed Shah of Delhi, the Rajah Jey

* The tables of Ulugh Beg were first brought to the knowledge of Europeans by the great orientalist and mathematician, John Greaves, Savilian Professor at Oxford, 1642–48. See "Life of Greaves, and miscellaneous works," 2 vols. 8vo, 1737 (London.) Dr. Thomas Hyde also translated and published the whole catalogue in 1665, with an account of the life of Ulugh Beg. "Tabulæ long. ac lat. Stellarum fixarum ex observatione Ulugh Beighi, Tamerlanis magni nepotis," &c., 1 vol. 4to, Oxon. 1665. The work was reprinted, with corrections, by Sharpe, in 1767. M. Sedillot translated the tables of Ulugh Beg, with the preliminary discourse. In 1843 was printed in vol. xiii. of the *Memoirs of the Astronomical Society*:—"The Catalogues of Ptolemy, Ulugh "Beigh, Tycho Brahe, Halley and Hevetius," with a preface to each catalogue by Francis Baily. The Ulugh Beg tables here given are reprinted from Sharpe's edition of Hyde; which is from a collation of three Persian MSS. at Oxford. See also, "Asiatic Miscellanies," i., p. 51. Kinneir often quotes the tables of Ulugh Beg, in determining the latitudes of places in Persia.

† Ulugh Beg was a first cousin of Baber's great grandfather.

Sing served as Subadar of Agra and Malwa, and he was also chosen to construct a new set of tables to supersede those of Ulugh Beg. They were called Zig Mohammedshahy, in honour of the emperor, and were completed in 1728.

The instruments formerly in use appear to have been in brass, but they did not come up to Jey Sing's ideas of accuracy, owing to the smallness of their size, to their imperfect graduation, to the shaking and shifting of their planes, and to the wearing of the axes. He therefore, invented enormous instruments of his own, of masonry work; and to confirm and check the truth of the observations, he formed five observatories, each with a complete set of instruments, at Delhi, Jeypore, Muttra, Benares, and Oojein. Those at Delhi have been minutely described by Dr. Hunter,* and Sir Robert Barker† has given an account of the instruments at Benares, with illustrations.

The Delhi observatory was outside the walls of the town. The large equatorial dial is of stone, with edges of white marble for graduation. The gnomon in the centre is 56 feet 9 inches high. A masonry wall has a graduated semicircle for taking altitudes of bodies east and west, from the eye. Another is in the plane of the meridian, having a double quadrant described in it, with the two upper corners of the wall as centres, for observing altitudes of bodies passing the meridian north or south of the zenith. One degree on these quadrants is 2⅞ inches long, and the degrees are divided into minutes. There are also two buildings of peculiar construction, for taking simultaneous observations of the altitudes and azimuths of heavenly bodies.

At Oojein observatory there was a double mural quadrant on a wall 27 feet high, and 26 feet long. On the west side of the wall there was a stair to the summit, and the east side was smooth and graduated. At the top, near the corners, were two iron spikes, 25 feet 1 inch from each other; and with these spikes as centres, and a radius equal to their distance, two arcs of 90°, intersecting each other, are graduated on the wall. The divisions are into 6°, 1°, 6′, and 1′. By this instrument Jey Sing, who, as Subadar of Malwa, had a palace at Oojein, made the latitude 23° 10′ N. Dr. Hunter,

* "Asiatic Researches," v., p. 177.

† "Philosophical Transactions," vol. 69, pt. 2, p. 5. The Benares Observatory is also described, with wood cuts of the instruments, in Dr. Hooker's Journal.

by several careful observations, made it 23° 10′ 24″ N. Oojein appears to have been the prime meridian of early Hindu geographers.*

At Muttra the instruments were on the roof of a room in the fort, and were small and imperfect; but at Benares they were large, and equal to those at Delhi and Oojein. A drawing of the beautiful balcony of Jey Sing's observatory at Benares is given by James Prinsep, and the masonry equatorial dial at Delhi is among the drawings engraved by Daniell.†

Jey Sing, with his instruments at Delhi, determined the obliquity of the ecliptic to be 23° 28′ in 1729, within a year of Godin's determination, which only differed by 28″. The great Rajpoot astronomer also constructed a table of the daily places of stars, and, hearing that other tables had been previously published in Europe, he sent skilful persons to Portugal, with a certain Father Manuel, to procure them. Xavier da Silva was despatched to India with the tables of De la Hire, the first edition of which had been published in 1680 and the second in 1702. Jey Sing also had Euclid and Napier's logarithms translated into Sanscrit. His own tables, which were completed in 1728, give the mean longitude and motions of the sun and of his apogee for 30 years, equation of time, and the motions of the moon and planets. Down to Colonel Tod's time, all computations were made and almanacks constructed by the tables of Jey Sing.

This great and wise prince intended to have completed his career, by getting up the *aswameda yuga*, or horse sacrifice. After a reign of 43 years he died in 1748, and three of his wives ascended the funereal pyre, on which Hindu science expired with him.‡

Dr. Hunter was acquainted with a grandson of Vidhyadhur, a Jain, and one of the chief coadjutors of Jey Sing, who inherited his ancestor's learning and traditions. Dr. Hunter himself, as well as Colonel Pearse and others, towards the end of the last century, took many astronomical observations, but they were made more for the purposes of a survey than in the interests of pure astronomy, and

---

* See Lieut. Conolly's paper on Oojein.—*J. A. S. B.* (1837) p. 813.

† Plates xix. and xx. See also "Life in ancient India," by Mr. Spiers, pp. 422 and 460.

Dr. Hunter gives a complete translation of the preface to Jey Sing's tables, with the original text.—*Asiatic Researches*, v., p. 177.

‡ For a very interesting account of Jey Sing, his family, and his principality, see *Tod's Rajasthan*, ii., p. 345.

have already been noticed. Colonel Hodgson, the Surveyor General of India from 1821 to 1827, was an astronomer, and a series of transit observations were made under his superintendence at Calcutta.* He also determined the longitudes of Calcutta, Madras, and Futtehgurh, by lunar transits, and eclipses of Jupiter's first satellite; the difference between his Madras result, and that of the astronomer Goldingham, being less than a second of time.†

The King of Oude established an observatory at Lucknow on a considerable scale, and Major Herbert was induced to hand over his editorial labours at Calcutta to James Prinsep, and take charge of it in 1832, but he died at Lucknow on September 24th, 1833. This observatory was supplied with a mural circle of six feet, an eight feet transit, and an equatoreal by Troughton and Simms. In about 1841 Major Wilcox assumed charge of it, and made a valuable series of observations with the help of native assistants; but he died in October 1848, and in 1849 the King of Oude abolished the observatory. The records were gradually eaten away by insects, and when the mutinies broke out, the instruments were destroyed.‡ Thus all the work of this once first class observatory has been lost to the world, and its records have perished without rendering any result to science.

The Madras Observatory has been the centre of astronomical work during the British occupation of India. It was founded in the days of Sir Thomas Munro, and has ever since been directed by a succession of able astronomers. Besides the value of the work that has been performed at Madras to astronomical science, the observatory is specially important because the longitudes of the Great Trigonometrical Survey depend on the meridian passing through it. The various determinations of the Madras Longitude, with reference to the Survey, have already been discussed in a previous section of this Memoir; and it is here only proposed to give a brief sketch of the other labours of the astronomers.

---

* "Transactions of the Astronomical Society, iii., pt. ii., p. 358.

† Hodgson's was 5h. 21m. 8·64s. Goldingham's 5h. 21m. 9·4s. John Anthony Hodgson was born at Bishop Auckland on July 2nd, 1777, and was educated at Durham. He went to India, as a cadet, in 1799, and in 1817 was selected, with Herbert, to survey the sources of the Ganges and Jumna. He was Surveyor General from 1821 to 1827. In 1845 he went out to India again as Major General of the Rohilcund Division, and died at Umballa on the 28th of March 1848.

‡ Report by Major Tennant.—*Proceedings of the Astronomical Society*, xvii., p. 63.

The Madras series of observations commenced in 1787, and the observatory building was erected in 1792, and furnished with a 20-inch transit, and a 12-inch altitude and azimuth instrument by Troughton. Mr. John Goldingham was the first astronomer; and his labours have already been noticed, in the discussion on the longitude of Madras.* He was an antiquary and an architect, as well as an astronomer; and wrote papers on the seven pagodas, and on the cave of Elephanta. He also built the banqueting room at Madras. He retired in 1830, and died at Worcester, at an advanced age, in 1849.†

Thomas Glanville Taylor, who succeeded Mr. Goldingham, was born at Ashburton, in Devonshire, on November 22nd, 1804; a year before his father Thomas Taylor was appointed Assistant to Dr. Maskelyne at Greenwich. Young Taylor was brought up as an astronomer, and in 1822 he was placed on the establishment of the Royal Observatory, taking charge of the night transit observations. He also gave Sabine much assistance in his pendulum operations. In the spring of 1830, at the recommendation of Mr. Pond, then Astronomer Royal, he was appointed to the charge of the Madras observatory. At the same time a new five-foot transit instrument was supplied, and Mr. Taylor began his series of observations of moon culminating stars with it, in 1831–33, whence a new determination of the longitude of Madras was obtained.‡

---

* See page 49.

† His labours at the observatory are printed in 5 folio volumes:—

"Astronomical Observations," by John Goldingham, 4 vols. (fol.), Madras 1825–27.

"Madras Observatory Papers," by John Goldingham, Astronomer. (Madras 1827.)

See also "A paper on the longitude of Madras, as deduced from observations of eclipses of the first and second satellites of Jupiter, 1817–26, by J. Goldingham."—(*Pro. As. Soc.*, i. p. 13.) A notice of the life of Mr. Goldingham will be found in the *Pro. As. Soc.* x. p. 80.

		h.	m.	s.
‡ Goldingham's result was		5	21	9·35.
Hodgson's	„	5	21	8·64.
Taylor's	„	5	20	57·28.

On June 13th, 1845, a paper was read before the Astronomical Society, giving Taylor's recomputed results, from 442 observations of the moon's first limb, and 86 of the second limb. Mr. Riddle, of the Greenwich School, in a paper read on April 10th, 1840, entered at length on the method of computing longitudes by moon culminating observations. He makes the—

						h.	m.	s.
Longitude of Madras,	from	54	observations at	Greenwich and	Madras	5	20	55
„	„	56	„	Cambridge	„	5	20	55
„	„	65	„	Edinburgh	„	5	20	58

See Proceedings of the Royal Astronomical Society, vi., p. 247., v. p. 49., xv. p. 110.

Mr. Taylor also made a catalogue of fixed stars,* on which Mr. Baily based his great catalogue. The observations, during Mr. Taylor's time, were regularly published in four volumes. He visited England in 1840. After his return, he met with a severe accident at Trivandrum, a fall occasioned by extreme short sight, from which he never quite recovered. Owing to his daughter's illness, he again went home, but too late to see her, and died on May 4th, 1848, leaving a widow and three sons.

Captain Jacob succeeded Mr. Taylor as Astronomer at Madras. William Stephen Jacob, son of the Rev. S. Jacob, was born at Woolavington in Somersetshire on November 19th, 1813. He was at Addiscombe in 1828, and sailed for India in 1831, where he was appointed to assist Colonel Shortrede in the surveys in the Bombay Presidency. Between 1837 and 1841, assisted by Sir Andrew Waugh, he completed the Bombay Longitudinal Series, which was an excellent piece of work. He went to England in 1843, but returned in 1845, and during the three following years he took astronomical observations at Poona with a five-foot equatoreal by Dollond, and made a catalogue of double stars.† In 1848 he was appointed to the charge of the Madras observatory. Captain Jacob was an accomplished astronomer, a careful and accurate observer, and an able computer; but the climate of Madras did not agree with him, and he suffered much from ill health. In 1850 he was occupied in revising and perfecting Taylor's catalogue of stars, and on the orbits of *α Centauri*, (which investigation he had made peculiarly his own,) and other double stars. In 1853 he sent home a catalogue of 144 double stars, as a continuation of his Poona catalogue.‡ Neptune was also observed since 1849, and careful measures were taken of Saturn and his ring.§

---

* Upwards of 8,800 stars. In the second volume of observations by Taylor, there is a catalogue of 11,015 stars collected from the five volumes of Madras observations, including all those in the Astronomical Society's and Piazzi's Catalogues visible at Madras, reduced to Jan. 1st, 1835, being about the middle period of the observations.

"Results of Astronomical Observations made at the H. E. I. C. Observatory at Madras," by J. G. Taylor, 4 vols. (Madras 1831–37.) (*J. A. S. B.*, ii. p. 380. *Pro. A. S.*, v. p. 27., vi. p. 187., ix. p. 62.)

† Memoirs of the Astronomical Society, xvii. p. 79.

‡ Trans. A. S., vol. xvii., Pro. A. S., x. 87., xi. 103., xv. 133.

§ In 1854 another volume of Madras observations was published, containing those for 1848–52, with an Appendix bringing some of them up to 1854.

Captain Jacob has also written, "Catalogue of 317 stars selected from the B. A. Cata-

In 1854 Captain Jacob was obliged to go home on sick leave, and Major Worster, of the Madras Artillery, assumed temporary charge of the observatory. He was engaged in examining 400 stars affected by proper motion to the extent of 0·5″ annually.

In 1856 a new meridional circle by Simms, was ordered for the Madras observatory, which arrived in 1857; Captain Jacob having resumed charge in December 1855. He commenced a series of equatorial observations of the satellites of Jupiter and Saturn; but he was again obliged to go home, owing to ill health, in April 1858, and Major Worster once more took temporary charge of the observatory. A useful catalogue of stars was prepared under his management. After recruiting his health, Captain Jacob purchased a nine-inch aperture telescope, and set out, under the auspices of the Astronomical Society, to establish an observatory in the Bombay Presidency. He landed at Bombay on August 8th, 1862, but died at Poona on the 16th, and the hopes that had been raised as to the results to be derived from the labours of so accomplished an observer came to an end.

Major Tennant of the Great Trigonometrical Survey, who had assisted at the measurement of the Kurrachee base, assumed charge of the Madras observatory on October 13th, 1859; but he only held the post for a short time, and in 1860 Mr. Pogson was appointed Astronomer. Norman Robert Pogson was already well known as an observer of variable stars, and as the discoverer of several small planets, and he had been in charge of Dr. Lee's observatory at Hartwell since 1858. In 1862 he undertook equatorial observations of Mars and neighbouring stars, for determination of Sun's parallax, with the old equatorial at Madras.* A new Transit Circle was completed and set up in June 1862, which Mr. Pogson has employed for the determination of the positions of comparison stars used for equatorial observations, of all observable variable stars, and of such small planets as come to opposition south of the equator.† In 1863 the for-

---

logue, being such as are supposed to have large proper motions," by Captain Jacob, *Mem. A. S.*, xix. p. 61.

"On the ring of Saturn and on Jupiter's Satellites," by Captain Jacob.—*Mem. A. S.* xxx. p. 236.

"Micrometrical measures of 12 double or multiple stars," by Captain Jacob.—*Mem. A. S.*, xix., p. 68.

"On Jupiter's mass," by Captain Jacob.—*Mem. A. S.*, xxviii.

* "Month. Not., A. S.," 1862.

† "Pro. A. S.," xix., p. 141; xxiii., 178.

mation of a catalogue of new small southern stars was commenced, as zero points for the Southern Celestial Survey which Mr. Pogson had taken in hand. In 1865 the construction of a room with a revolving dome, for the new equatorial, was completed. This new instrument is by Troughton and Simms. The former one, by Lerebours and Secretan, is also in working order. During 1865-66 the observations with the Transit Circle were made throughout the year by the two head native assistants; and between 1862 and 1866 they took 9,618 complete observations of right ascension and polar distance, averaging 2,443 a year; a large per-centage referring to stars in the southern hemisphere, the positions of which had not been previously determined at any other observatory. The old equatorial was chiefly used in the construction and revision of an atlas of variable stars.* On May 17th, 1866, a new minor planet was discovered from the Madras observatory, and named (87) "Sylvia,"† and another named "Camilla" was discovered in November 1868. The Madras mean time of the flash of the evening gun is noted, to facilitate the rating of chronometers in the roads. Mr. Pogson's chief difficulty has hitherto been the preparation of work for publication,—the great desideratum; owing to the want of an efficient establishment. One of the most valuable of his undertakings will be the share of the Madras observatory in the great survey of the southern heavens. The arrangement is that the southern heavens shall be divided into zones for mapping and publication, and that shares of the work of examining them shall be taken by the three southern observatories at the Cape, Melbourne, and Madras. The following division has been arranged:—

Zones, 1.—Equator to 20° S.
2.— 20° to 40° S.
3.— 40° to 60° S.
4.— 60° to 80° S
5.— 80° to the Pole.

Mr. Pogson commences with Zone 2, and then follows with 1. Mr. Ellery, at Melbourne, takes 4 and 3; and Sir Thomas Maclear, at the Cape, undertook 5. Mr. Pogson has also commenced upon the application of precession to Taylor's Madras catalogues, to reduce them to the epoch 1875.‡

* "Pro. A. S.," xxvii., p. 122.
† "Mon. Not., A. S.," xxvi., p. 311.
‡ "Mon. Not., A. S.," xxv., p. 118.

In 1836 Mr. John Caldecott, the commercial agent to the Travancore Government at Alipee, pointed out to General Fraser, the Resident, the advantages to science to be derived from the establishment of an observatory at Trivandrum. The latitude is 8° 30′ 35″ N., and observations taken in such a position were considered likely to yield valuable results, owing to its proximity to the equator. Trivandrum is, also, only about 70 miles south of the magnetic equator. Rama Kermah, the late Rajah of Travancore, who was a learned and cultivated prince, entered warmly into the project, and appointed Mr. Caldecott his astronomer, with authority to build an observatory at Trivandrum. The building was planned and erected by Captain Horsley of the Madras Engineers in 1837, on a laterite hill two miles from the sea, and 195 feet above it, whence there is a magnificent view. On one side is the sea bordered by groves of cocoa-nut trees, on the other the rich undulating country, bounded by the many peaked ghauts. Mr Caldecott went to England for instruments in December 1838, and returned in April 1841 with a transit instrument by Dollond, two mural circles, an equatorial, altitude and azimuth, and magnetic and meteorological instruments. Mr. Caldecott forwarded complete copies of his observations to the Court of Directors and the Royal Society, and in 1846, leaving the Rev. Dr. Spershneider in charge of the observatory, he came home to try and obtain the aid of some of the scientific Societies in publishing them, but without success. He returned to Trivandrum in 1847, and died there on December 17th, 1849.

The observatory was in charge of Mr. Spershneider for two years, but in 1851 the Rajah of Travancore appointed Mr. John Allan Broun, who had been in charge of Sir Thomas Brisbane's observatory at Makerstown from 1842 to 1850, to be the astronomer at Trivandrum. Mr. Broun arrived on January 11th, 1852; but he found the astronomical instruments in so unsatisfactory a condition that he thought it best to devote his chief attention to magnetism and meteorology. An account of his meteorological work, and of the establishment of an observatory on the summit of Aghastya-mulla has been given in the previous Section. He also built a house adjoining the observatory at Trivandrum, with a row of Doric columns supporting an entablature imitated from that by Inigo Jones on the church in Covent Garden, and a terrace. In July 1852 he commenced a series of lectures on the instruments, their objects, and the results derived from them; and in course of time he succeeded in training a very efficient set of assistants. In 1853 he built rooms for a new set of magnetical instruments which were obtained from England, and his magnetic investigations are of great value and importance. He obtained a complete set of hourly magnetic observations at Trivandrum from March 1852 to March 1865, and at Aghastya from June 1855 to July 1858, and during ten months in 1863. Mr. Broun also made a short series of hourly magnetic observations simultaneously at three different stations, relative especially to the diurnal variation of magnetic declination. One was as nearly as possible on the magnetic equator, about 30 miles north of Trivandrum, the other at the observatory, and the third at Cape Comorin. In 1859–60 he made a magnetic survey of the west coast of India, for the purpose of ascertaining the position of the magnetic equator which passes through Travancore, and the variations of intensity about the line of no inclination. Stations were chosen at intervals along the coast, which were eventually extended up to the Bombay. The horizontal intensity was found to be nearly the same from Bombay to Cape Comorin.

The present Rajah of Travancore resolved to discontinue the observatory establishment, and Mr. Broun left Trivandrum in March 1865. But it was arranged that a limited series of observations should be continued by the two most experienced native assistants, who still forward monthly reports and abstracts of observations to Mr. Broun, which are of great importance with reference to several questions of interest. Mr. Broun is now engaged in preparing his work for the press, and the whole will be printed at the expense of the Travancore Government.*

* A history of the observatory, and a most interesting account of the establishment of the branch observatory on the Aghastya-mulla peak will be found in the "Report on the observatories of His Highness the Rajah of Travancore, at Trivandrum and at the peak of Agustier on the Western Ghats," by John Allan Broun, F.R.S., Director of the Observatories. (*Trivandrum*, 1857.) This is the only report that has been printed. Mr. Broun has contributed papers to the Transactions of the Royal Society of Edinburgh (vol. xxii. and xxiv., p. 669), on horizontal force of the earth's magnetism, and on the bifilar magnetometer, on diurnal variation of the magnetic declination at Trivandrum, deduced from 12 years' observations, and on an examination of diurnal observations at nine other stations; for which he received the Keith biennial prize. In the Comtes Rendues of the Academy of Sciences for July 4th, 1870, Mr. Broun's paper on the secular variation of the magnetic declination, as deduced from observations made at Trivandrum, 1853–70, is published. In the Philosophical Magazine for July 1858 is Mr. Broun's letter to Sir David Brewster on the results and views derived from his

The Bombay observatory is confined to magnetic, tidal, and meteorological observations, and to observations for time to rate the chronometers in the harbour. Major Jacob's desire that an astronomical observatory should be established in the Western Presidency has never been fulfilled.

The Madras observatory is now the sole point for astronomical work in India, and the only successor of the famous establishments founded by Jey Sing. It has been presided over by a succession of six able and accomplished astronomers, it has produced results which entitle it to take rank with the observatories of Europe, and its present Director is engaged in the prosecution of labours which are of great importance to astronomical science.

---

observations in Scotland and India. See also British Association Reports, ix., p. 38; xv., p. 22; xxiv., p. 28; xxvii., p. 30; xxix., p. 20, 24, 27, 74; and "Proceedings of the Royal Society," xvi., p. 59.

XV.—PHYSICAL GEOGRAPHY OF INDIA.

The operations which have been enumerated in the previous sections are intended to furnish minute and exact information respecting the topography of every part of India; the heights, positions, and ramifications of its mountain masses; the courses of its rivers and streams; the nature of its coast line; the geological character and climate of its various regions; while a part of the object of an archæological survey is to investigate the physical changes that have taken place within historic times, by a comparison of the information supplied by ancient writers with the actual state of the country. Such is the material by the aid of which it is the task of the physical geographer to form a systematic view of the various regions, with reference both to the action of natural causes on their physical conditions, and to the changes produced by human means. It will be the object of the present section to supply information respecting the various attempts that have been made to utilize the material that has been collected, and to deduce generalizations from numerous classes of observations, as well as to point out where material is to be found for generalization, in regions or on subjects where nothing of the kind has hitherto been attempted. With this object the travellers who have explored portions of the Himalayan range will be enumerated, and an endeavour will be made to give an idea of the views some of them have enunciated respecting the physical structure of that great mountain mass. Some account will then be attempted to be given of the writers who have formed general views on the great river basins, and of those who have written on the physical geography of other parts of India. A sketch of the botanical geography, with an enumeration of the principal works on Indian botany, will then be given, and some information respecting the writers on the importance of forests and on forest conservancy will follow, with reference to the effect of human agency on physical geography. Finally there will be an allusion to the physical geography of the Indian seas, and to the value of maps showing the various features which compose a physical and statistical atlas.

The structure of the great Himalayan mass which bounds India to the north is the branch of the subject to which attention is naturally drawn in the first place, and it is that to which both travellers and systematic geographers have devoted the largest share of their labours.

The reports of a long series of travellers necessarily preceded the first attempt at generalization. Those who first penetrated into the apparently inextricable labyrinth of snowy peaks, such as the Missionaries Desideri, Freyre, and Antonio di Andrada,* were simply appalled at the horrid aspect of the mountains, and at the eternal winter. The English officers who afterwards contemplated the mighty barrier from the plains became desirous of ascertaining the real height of the peaks, and of exploring the hidden sources of the great rivers. It was with these objects that Colonel Hodgson, Herbert, and Webb were ordered to survey the mountains between the Sutlej and the Kali, that Hardwicke penetrated to Sreenuggur, and that Baillie Fraser first crossed the range, on the southern slope of which the Jumna rises. A few years later, Moorcroft and Trebeck explored the upper courses of the Indus and the Sutlej, and reached the Mansarowa lake, while Dr. Gerard ascended the Spiti valley.† Mr. Bogle and Captain Turner were sent by Warren Hastings on an embassy to the Lama of Tibet, and crossed the eastern Himalaya from Bhootan to the valley of the Sanpu; a feat which has never since been achieved by any modern traveller, though Dr. Hooker penetrated some distance beyond the water parting.‡ Opportunities offered by embassies to Nepal enabled Kirkpatrick, Crawford, and

---

* "Letires Edifiantes," xv., 183.—*Royle's Illustrations.*

† See page 149. Webb's Survey is in the *Asiatic Researches*, xi., p. 447. See also a paper by Mr. Colebrooke on the Sources of the Ganges.—*Asiatic Researches*, xi., p. 429. "Journal of a Tour through part of the Snowy Range of the Himalaya mountains," by James Baillie Fraser (London, 1820). "Travels in the Himalayan provinces," &c., by William Moorcroft and George Trebeck, in 1819–25 (2 vols., 1841). See also R. G. S. Journal, i., p. 232. "Observations on the Spiti Valley," by Surgeon J. G. Gerard.—*Asiatic Researches*, xviii., p. 239. The original MS. Journal of Herbert's Survey in 1818 is preserved in the Geographical Department of the India Office.

‡ "An account of an Embassy to the Court of the Teshoo Lama in Tibet," by Captain Samuel Turner (London, 4to, 1800). The Journal of Mr. Bogle has never been printed.

Buchanan Hamilton to collect some information respecting the central portion of the great chain.*

Captain Herbert, whose writings deserve to be better known, was the first geographer who attempted to give a general view of the physical character of the Himalaya. Writing in 1818, his information was necessarily limited, but he had before him the results obtained by most of the travellers whose works I have enumerated, and he had some personal knowledge of the Western Himalaya from the Kalee to the Sutlej. The physical features of Central Asia were unknown to him, and he laments the deep obscurity which then covered the geography of that interesting region. His conception of it was a vast central space from the circumference of which rivers flowed in all directions, and he perceived that a line connecting their sources must be of great elevation, compared with other parts of Asia external to such a line. He knew also that this interior space was surrounded by mountains, and supposed it to be a very lofty plateau. But with part of the southern boundary, the stupendous mountains traversed by Webb, Turner, and himself, he was familiar. He was the first to point out that the line of water parting was by no means synonymous with that of greatest elevation. In exploring the Western Himalaya he could distinguish no continuous chain of elevations on a cursory glance. There seemed to be nothing to lend a clue to the development of the mountain masses, and there appeared an assemblage of elevated peaks confusedly heaped together. But he soon perceived that, by tracing the courses of the rivers and their tributary streams, a clue would be found to lead an observer out of this labyrinth. As regards the part of the Himalaya from the Sutlej to the Kalee,† instead of a succession of parallel ranges rising one behind another in regular array, he made out a continuous chain forming an irregular curved line, with the Sutlej bounding it to the north, and bending round its convex side, while the sources of the Ganges rise within its concavity. He calls this the Indo-Gangetic chain, and his description of it is precise and accurate. His next

* "An account of the kingdom of Nepal," by Colonel Kirkpatrick, in 1793 (London, 1811), with a map by Colonel Gerard.

"An account of the kingdom of Nepal, by Francis Buchanan Hamilton, M.D., 1802–3 (Edinburgh, 1819). At the end a table of the heights of 8 peaks, measured by Colonel Crawford is given. The plants collected by Buchanan Hamilton were described by Don, in the "Prodromus Floræ Nepalensis."

† A chief branch of the Gogra.

chain is that separating the sources of the Jumna and Ganges, which was crossed by Baillie Fraser. He adds, that the ramifications of ridges would almost bid defiance to any analysis, but for the assistance derived from observing the courses of the rivers. Herbert also observed that the ridge separating the Ganges and Indus basins was by no means the highest ground, and that the most elevated peaks were on a series of transverse ridges which ramify from the Indo-Gangetic chain, over which they tower several thousand feet. He traced a connected line of peaks, not under 21,000 feet in height, and intersecting the watercourses; and both Webb and Herbert gave 27,000 feet as the height of Dhawala-giri.* In his valuable memoir, Herbert also speculates upon the relation between the height of the sources of rivers and the length of their courses, and gives a most interesting account of the Doons, the parallel chain of the Sewaliks, the forest belt at their bases, and the Terai region beyond.†

After the time when Herbert was engaged on his survey, a number of able geographers and naturalists explored the Himalaya mountains. Vigne‡ and Falconer penetrated into Balti and Ladak, Jacquemont§ and Hugel‖ explored Cashmere, Cunningham¶ thoroughly examined the Ladak region, Dr. Thomson** reached the summit of the Karakorum pass, Captain Gerard gave an account of Spiti and Koonawur,†† and the Stracheys‡‡ surveyed Kumaon and

---

* Actually 26,826 English feet.

† "Report of the Mineralogical Survey of the Himalaya Mountains, by Captain J. D. Herbert," *J. A. S. B.*, xi. pt. i. p. x.

‡ "Travels in Kashmir, Ladak," &c., by G. T. Vigne. (2 vols., 1835.)

§ "Voyage dans l'Inde," par Victor Jacquemont, 1828–32. (Paris, 1841.)

‖ "Kaschmir und das Reich der Siek." Carl von Hügel (4 vols. Vienna, 1840). Translated into English by Major Jervis (London, 1845). See also *R. G. S. Journal*, vi., p. 343.

¶ "Ladak; physical, statistical, and historical," by A. Cunningham, Major, Bengal Engineers (1854).

** "Western Himalaya and Tibet, a narrative of a journey during the years 1847–8," by Thomas Thomson, M.D. (1852).

†† "Account of Koonawur, in the Himalaya," by Captain A. Gerard. Edited by Lloyd. (Map. 8vo. 1841.)

‡‡ "On the physical geography of the provinces of Kumaon and Gurhwal in the Himalaya mountains, and of the adjoining parts of Tibet," by R. Strachey, Esq., of the Bengal Engineers.—*R. G. S. Journal*, xxi., p. 57.

"Physical Geography of Western Tibet," by Captain H. Strachey of the Bengal Army.—*R. G. S. Journal*, xxiii., p. 2. Published separately in 1854; and his "Journey to Lake Manasarowa." Published at Calcutta. 8vo. 1848.

Western Tibet. The valley of Katmandu had an able generalizer in Mr. Hodgson,* who was for many years the British Envoy in Nepaul; and in 1848 Dr. Hooker† threw a flood of light on the geography of the Sikkim portion of the eastern chain.

Dr. Forbes Royle discusses Himalayan geography in his great work illustrating the botany of the mountains.‡

Cunningham, in his work on Ladak, gives a general view of the physical features of the Western Himalayas. Their most striking characteristic is the parallelism of the mountain ridges, which stretch through the country from S.E. to N.W., their general direction determining the course of the rivers, and the valleys lying along the head waters of the Indus, Sutlej, and Chenab. He divides the mountain region into six distinct ranges:—§

1. The Karakoram range, from the sources of the Gilgit and Yasan, to that of the Shayok.

2. The Kailas or Gangri range, traversing Western Tibet, along the right bank of the Indus from its source to its junction with the Shayok, and onwards to the junction of the Hunza and Nager.

3. The Trans-Himalayan range branches off from Gangri to the south of Garo, and extends to Zanskar in an unbroken line. Here the river rushes dark and turbulent through a vast chasm which human foot has never trod. Thence the range continues to the Dras, where it is cut through by a narrow gorge called the wolf's leap; and thence to the great southern bend of the Indus, at the junction of the Gilgit.

4. The Great Himalaya, which is the natural boundary between India and Tibet, is a mighty chain 650 miles long, pierced in three places by the Sutlej, its affluent the Para, and the Indus.

5. The Mid-Hamalaya, or Pir Panjal, consists of four distinct masses, the Bisakar, Lahul, Pir Panjal, and Swát.

---

* "On the physical geography of the Himalaya," by B. H. Hodgson, Esq.—*J. A. S. B.*, xviii., pt. 2., p. 761.

† "Himalayan Journal," by J. D. Hooker. (2 vols. 8vo. 1854).

"Notes, chiefly botanical, made during an excursion from Darjiling to Tonglô."—*J. A. S. B.*, xviii., pt. 1., p. 49.

‡ "Illustrations of the botany and other branches of the natural history of the Himalayan mountains," by J. Forbes Royle. (London, 1839. 2 vols. 4to.)

§ Csoma de Körös says, that from the first range on the Indian side to the plains of Tartary the Tibetans count six chains of mountains.—*J. A. S. B.*, i., p. 121.

6. The Outer Himalaya. This classification only applies to the portion of the system from the bend of the Beas to the Indus.

Henry Strachey, in his general sketch of Western Himalayan geography, adopts the native Tibetan nomenclature. He considers the general plan of the mountain system to be a series of parallel ranges running in an oblique line to the general extension of the whole; the great peaks being generally on terminal butt ends of the primary ranges. The chief watersheds are often found to follow the lowest of the ridges, and the channels of drainage to cross the highest, deep fissures intersecting the mountains, often directly transverse to the main lines of elevation. No traveller, except the Pundit sent by Major Montgomerie in 1866, has ever visited any part of the great transverse watershed separating the Indus and Sutlej from the Sanpu; though the western shores of Lake Mansarowar were reached by Moorcroft and Hearsey in 1812, and by the Stracheys in 1846 and 1848. Henry Strachey describes the alluvial beds in the Himalaya, and the wonderful gorge where the Sutlej flows over bare rocks with walls of alluvium on either side upwards of a mile high. Richard Strachey gives a very clear and interesting description of the Sewaliks, rising abruptly from the plains along the whole southern edge of the Himalaya, with a steep outward face, and a gentle declivity sloping inwards, and forming the Doons or shallow valleys, by meeting the foot of the next range of mountains. He also explains the nature of the country at the base of the Sewaliks, the waterless belt covered with forest, and the line of swampy Terai beyond, where the drainage of the higher country breaks out in copious streams in the country east of the Ganges. The fact of this Terai region terminating at the Ganges is accounted for by the slope being less to the eastward of that river. The limit of the snow line on the different ranges is discussed by Cunningham, Richard Strachey, and Captain Thomas Hutton.*

Dr. Thomson, who was the first traveller, after the Chinese pilgrim Fa Hian, to reach the summit of the Karakorum pass,† has discussed the physical structure of the Western Himalaya with great ability. He considers that the only feasible mode of division is afforded by the courses of the different rivers. If these be taken as

* "J. A. S. B.," xviii., p. 954.

† He found its height to be 18,660 feet.

guides, the mountains will be found to resolve themselves into two great systems. Dr. Thomson gives Herbert the credit of having first pointed out the impropriety of regarding the mountains as a single chain parallel to the plains. He proposes to call Herbert's Indo-Gangetic the Cis-Sutlej, and the chain commencing at Kailas the Trans-Sutlej range. These would be the Mid-Hamalaya and Great Himalaya of Cunningham's system. Dr. Thomson also described the alluvial deposits in the Himalayas, and the shells that are found in them.

The generalizations of Cunningham, the Stracheys, and Thomson refer to the Western Himalayas, and are not intended to apply to the ranges eastward of the Nepal frontier. Mr. Hodgson, during a long residence at Katmandu as Resident, thought much over the configuration of the mountains towering above the valley to which his personal observation was confined. In his paper on the physical geography of the Himalaya* he describes the Nepaul division of the system as consisting of three river basins, those of the Karnali, Gunduck, and Cosi, separated by peaked ridges, parallel to each other, and at right angles with the main chain.

Sikkim has been explored by Dr. Hooker and Dr. Campbell, and the former traveller examined two passes in Eastern Nepaul. As a physical geographer, Dr. Hooker, combining his own acute observation with an intimate knowledge of the results obtained by others, has furnished his view of the composition of the great mountain mass. A prodigious chain traverses Asia from east to west, and south of it flow the Indus and Brahmaputra, in different directions, rising nearly together. The chain between these rivers and the plains of India is the Himalaya, connected with the Kuen-lun in rear, at the sources of the two rivers. The axis of the main Hima-

* "J. A. S. B.," xvii. pt. II., p. 761.—It is to be regretted that Mr. Hodgson has never published a work on Nepaul in a complete form. His scattered papers on the topography, ethnography, philology, and above all on the zoology of Nepaul are very numerous. Besides 4 books on the Buddhist religion, on the aborigines of India, and on Indian education, Mr. Hodgson has contributed no less than 170 papers to various periodicals, chiefly the Journal of the Asiatic Society of Bengal, the Transactions and Journal of the Agri-Horticultural Society of India, the Proceedings of the Zoological Society of London, and McClelland's Journal of Natural History. In the examination of the anatomy of the birds and quadrupeds of Nepaul, Mr. Hodgson received much assistance from Dr. Campbell, who also resided 8 years at Katmandu, before he commenced his career of more active usefulness at Darjeeling.

layan chain lies far back, and nearer to the two great rivers than to the plains; while from the central axis successions of secondary ranges descend on either side. These secondary ranges vary in direction, some being almost perpendicular to the main range, and others forming a very acute angle with it. All ramify very much, giving off chains of a third order, which separate the tributaries of the great rivers. Dr. Hooker thus considers the system as consisting of a main range, with numerous secondary chains branching from it, but all connected with the central axis, and not forming distinct mountain ranges. Most of the loftiest peaks are on the secondary chains. He compares the Sikkim Himalaya to Norway. The narrow valleys of Sikkim are analogous to the Norwegian fiords, the lofty snowy peaks to the islands on the coast, the broad rearward axis is the same in both cases, and the Sanpu valley occupies the relative position of the Baltic. Dr. Hooker points out that Herbert's proposition of the line of great peaks intersecting the river basins, and not forming the true axis, was the first enunciation of a very important fact in physical geography.

Humboldt made his Russian expedition in 1829, and published his "Fragmens Asiatique" in 1831,* while his "Asie Centrale" appeared in 1843,† some years before the above explorers had completed their labors. But in 1833 Klaproth had produced his map of Central Asia, based on a great mass of Chinese material, and on the work of missionaries employed by the Chinese Government,‡ and Humboldt also obtained much information from Stanislas Julien, and Carl Ritter. From these data Humboldt formed his theory of the mountain system of Central Asia, as consisting of four great chains, the Altai and Tian-Chan on the north, and the Kuen-lun and Himalayas on the south, issuing from the central knot of Bolor or Pamir. But he furnishes little information respecting the

---

* "Fragmens de Geologie et de Climatologie Asiatique." (2 vols. 8vo., Paris, 1831.)

† "Asie Centrale, Recherches sur les Chaines de Montagnes et la Climatologie comparée. (3 vols. 8vo., Paris, 1843.)

‡ Klaproth. "Carte de l'Asie Centrale, dressée d'apres les cartes levees par ordre de "l'Empereur Khian-loung par les Missionaires de Peking, et d'apres un grand "nombres de notions extraites et traduites de livres Chinois." (1833.) The Mis- "sionaries were Fathers Felix d'Arocha, Espinha, and Hallerstein, who appear to "have observed the latitude of Khotan.

Himalaya, and refers his readers to the collections made by Carl Ritter.*

The complete topographical survey of the Western Himalaya, conducted under the superintendence of Major Montgomerie, the detailed accounts of its glaciers by Major Godwin Austen, and the examination of the structure of its southern portion by Mr. H. B. Medlicott, have rendered our knowledge of that section of the region both accurate and complete. But, to the eastward of the Nepaulese frontier, nothing has been done since the days of Hodgson, Campbell, and Hooker.

The most recent systematic attempt to give a general idea of the physical structure of the Himalayan region will be found in the sketch map and memoir prepared by Mr. Trelawney Saunders, after a study of all the foregoing authorities.

The Himalayan region is included between the plains of India and the upper courses of the Sanpu, Sutlej, and Indus, and extends from the gorge of the Indus to the gorge of the Sanpu or Bramaputra, a distance of 1,400 miles. Its general structure, according to the view of Mr. Saunders, is briefly as follows:—The Himalaya culminates in two parallel ranges running through its entire length, and these he would call the Northern and Southern Himalaya respectively. Nearly all the great snowy peaks to the eastward of the Sutlej, which have been fixed and measured by distant triangulation, are in the southern range; while the same part of the northern range has so far received scarcely any attention. It is, however, the northern range which forms the water-parting between the Ganges basin and the Sanpu. A series of valleys separates the two ranges, and through them flow the upper courses of the Jhelum, Chenab, Spiti, Baspa, Ganges, and numerous affluents of the Ganges and Bramaputra, in the direction of the Himalayan axis, until they break through the southern range to join the main streams in the plains of India. The Indus, Sutlej, and Sanpu form a continuous trough in the same axial direction, and divide the Himalaya from

* "Une immense masse de materiaux dus aux dominateurs actuels de l'Inde, comme "aux courageux efforts de Jaquemont et de Hugel, a été reunie et discutée recemment dans l'excellent ouvrage de M. Ritter."—*Asie Centrale*, ii., p. 439. He alludes, of course, to Ritter's "Die Erdkunde von Asien." (9 vols.); the Himalayan part of which was published previous to the explorations of Cunningham, Hooker, Thomson, and the Stracheys.

the Karakoram and Gangs-ri mountains. The Karakoram divides the Indus from the basin of Lake Lob. The Gangs-ri divides the Indus, Sutlej, and Sanpu from the extremely elevated plateau of Tibet, which is drained by inland lakes. The northern limit of this very high plateau is formed by the Kuenlun mountains, which descend to the comparatively low plain of Gobi. The Gangs-ri and Kuenlun meet the Karakoram mountains at the head of the Karakash valley. The Himalaya unites with the Karakoram, Hindoo-Koosh, and Bolor or Pamir mountains, in the central knot of Tagh Dumbash or Poosht-i-Khar.

The general character of the highlands beyond the eastern extremity of the Himalaya and Assam, towards China and Burmah, has also been defined by Mr. Saunders, from a combination of the scraps of intelligence which contain our present knowledge of this remarkable part of the Indian frontier.

Although the scale is very small, the map by Mr. Saunders shows these features with much clearness and precision, and the position of each peak and spur of importance is accurately defined.

There is still a great field for exploration in the Himalayan region. The whole of the Nepaul portion of the ranges for a distance of 500 miles, and the greater part of Bhotan, a long reach of the Indus, the valley of the Sanpu eastward of Lassa, and the mountain region still further to the east, where the Irawaddy, Salween, Cambodia, and Yangtse rise, are entirely unknown.

The rivers flowing from the Himalaya, and forming the two great systems of the Indus and Ganges, have been studied with minute attention. Upon the water supply brought down by these streams from the Himalayan snows the very existence of the millions inhabiting the plains of India depends. The physical laws regulating the direction and volume of the rivers are of such practical importance that they have formed the subject of close investigation for many years, and this great section of Indian physical geography has thus been minutely and elaborately examined.

The best general account of the Indus and its five tributaries, before they enter the plains, will be found in Cunningham's Ladak. He traces them from their sources, and describes the peculiar knee-bends in each, at the points where, after flowing down the long lateral valleys in the Himalaya, they burst through the chain, and alter their courses to reach the plain. He also gives an account of the tremendous cataclysms which periodically take place, especially in the valleys of the Indus and Sutlej. These floods appear to be caused by the fall of huge masses of rock, or of parts of a glacier, which block up the rivers until at length the pent-up waters burst forth with irresistible fury. Dr. Falconer considered the Indus cataclysm of July 1841 to be one of the most remarkable natural catastrophes hitherto recorded as having occurred on the continent of India.* A great flood is also recorded of the Sutlej, which took place in 1819. The shoulder of a mountain gave way at Seoni, about 20 miles north-west of Simla, where the river flows between precipitous cliffs. The fallen mass choked the bed for a height of 400 feet, the river ceased to flow for 40 days, when it burst the obstruction, and rushed down in an irresistible wave a hundred feet high.

It is in tracing the alterations that have taken place in the courses of rivers, and in studying the physical causes which have given rise to these changes, that archæology has rendered most useful service to physical geography. By a careful study of the historians of Alexander's campaign, of the Chinese pilgrims, and of the Ayeen Akberi, General Cunningham has collected most interesting evidence respecting the former history of the Punjab rivers and of the Lower Indus. The Punjab rivers have frequently shifted their channels. Thus, in the time of Akbar, the Chenab and Indus united at Uch; now the junction takes place 60 miles lower down, at Mittankote. Mooltan was once on two islands in the Ravee; it is now 30 miles from that river. The confluence of the Beas with the Sutlej only dates from about 1790, and the whole bed is now part of a complicated network of dry channels.† A very complete knowledge of the present aspect of the Punjab and its rivers may be obtained from a study of the reports of irrigation officers.‡

The course of the Indus from Mittankote to the sea has been the subject of equally close study with reference to the improvement of

---

* J. S. A. B., x., pt. 2, p. 615, and xviii., p. 231; Vigne, ii., p. 362.

† General Cunningham's Ancient Geography of India.

‡ Selections from the Records of the Government of India.—*Punjab Reports*, 1849–56.

"Agricultural resources of the Punjab," by Lieut. R. Baird Smith (1849).

Memorandum on the Baree Doab Canal, by Colonel Crofton. April 3rd, 1868.

Colonel Napier's Report on the inundation canals. Sept. 11th, 1852.

"On the rivers of the Punjab," by W. Purdon, C.E. 1860.

irrigation in Scinde. At the time of Alexander's invasion, and down to the visit of the Chinese pilgrim, Hwen Thsang, the Indus flowed to the eastward of its present course, down the bed now known as the Eastern Narra. But it is believed by many geographers that a gradual westing of all rivers flowing north and south is the natural result of the earth's revolution from west to east, which gives their waters a permanent bias towards their western banks.* At last the Indus turned the northern end of the Alor range, and cut a passage for itself through the gap in the limestone rocks between Roree and Bukkur, in about 680 A.D. Sinde is described by Sir William Baker and Colonel Fife as an alluvial plain, almost every portion of which has, at some time or other, been swept by the Indus or its branches. The land is always highest at the river banks. The silt with which the waters are charged is deposited during the season of overflow most abundantly near the edge of the stream, thus forming a natural glacis, the crest of which is on the river bank, while the slope falls away gradually towards the boundary of the valley. A continuance of this process raises the level of the river-bed until, during some extraordinary flood, at intervals of many centuries, it bursts its embankment, and takes to one of the lower tracts. Thus the bed and banks are continually rising.†

The changes in the valley of the Indus have also been effected, to a great extent, by earthquakes, which entirely destroyed the great city of Brahminabad some centuries ago,‡ and threw up the Allahbund in more recent times.§ But a discussion of Indian earth-

---

* This fact, in physical geography, was first enunciated by the Russian naturalist, K. E. von Baer.

† Lieut. Postans.—*J. A. S. B.* (1838), p. 103.
Capt. McMurdo.—*J. A. S. B.*, i., p. 33.
Capt. McMurdo.—*Journ. R. A. S.*, i., p. 223.
Capt. Del Hoste.—*J. A. S. B.* (1840), p. 913.
"On the canals and forests in Scinde." Report by Colonel Walter Scott.
Baker's Report on the Eastern Narra. Oct. 14th, 1844.
Merewether on the Bigaree Canal. Oct. 1856.
Colonel Fife on irrigation in Scind. October 1855.

‡ Bellasis on the ruins of Brahminabad.—*Journal of the Bombay Branch of the Asiatic Society.*

§ "Remarks on the Alla Bund and drainage of the eastern part of the Scinde basin," by Capt. W. E. Baker.—*Bombay G. S. Journal*, vii., p. 186.
See also Lyell's Principles of Geology.
"Memoir on the eastern branch of the Indus, giving an account of the alterations

quakes, as a branch of physical geography would, of itself, occupy a volume.

The physical features of the Thurr, or desert, to the eastward of the Indus valley, of the Runn of Cutch, of the valley of the Looni, and of the Aravally hills, protecting the Ganges basin from the encroachments of the sand-drifts, were first fully described by Colonel Tod,* who was followed by Alexander Burnes,† and a most interesting paper on the Runn of Cutch and neighbouring region by Sir Bartle Frere will appear in the Journal of the Royal Geographical Society for 1870.‡

The vast plain of India, including the lower parts of the basins of the Indus and Ganges, extends uninterruptedly along the base of the Himalaya, and nowhere attains a greater height than 900 feet, from the Arabian Sea to the Bay of Bengal. But, at its highest point, where the water-parting separates the Jumna from the Sutlej, there is an interval where the floods of the classic Saraswati once watered the land of Kuru, on their way to the Indus, but where now the streams have ceased to be perennial, while the desert fast encroaches on the once rich kingdom of Sthaneswara. The causes of the physical changes in this interesting tract of country have been discussed by several able writers.§ In 1840 Sir William Baker ran a line of levels across it from Kurnool to Loodiana, finding the greatest elevation above the Jumna and Sutlej to be 68 feet, and he afterwards carefully surveyed the courses of its river beds. Captain Brown, of the Revenue Survey, also examined and described the water-parting region between the basins of the Indus and Ganges.‖

---

caused by the earthquake;" also, "A theory of the formation of the Runn, 1827-28," by A. Burnes.—*Trans. R. A. S.*, iii., p. 550.

* "Annals and antiquities of Rajasthan," by Lieut.-Colonel James Tod. (2 vols. London, 1829.)

† "Countries on the N.W. frontier of India," by Alexander Burnes.—*R. G. S. Journ.*, iv., p. 88.

"Description of the saltworks at Panchpadder, in Marwar," by Alexander Burnes. —*J. A. S. B.*, ii., p. 365.

‡ "Notes on the Runn of Cutch and neighbouring region," by Sir H. Bartle Frere. —*R. G. S. Journ.*, xl., p. 181.

§ Colvin, Fergusson, Baker, Cunningham.

‖ General Cunningham's ancient geography of India.

Captain W. Brown (Revenue Surveyor) on the Bhuttee States.

Report on the Cuggur and Soorsooty, by Captain W. Brown.

Baker's Report on the Cuggur, Sept. 17th, 1841.

"Report on a line of levels between the Jumna and Sutlej rivers," by Lieut. W. E. Baker.—*J. A. S. B.*, ix., p. 688.

Report on the Bangur lands of Bawulpore, by Mr. Barns. 1870.

The basin of the Ganges, with its tributary rivers and their peculiarities, has been minutely examined and described by the officers who have constructed those irrigation works which will be the proudest and most enduring monuments of British rule in India; and the lower part of the valley of the Bramapootra has been almost as fully treated of, in the published reports of officers on Assam and the north-eastern frontier, from the time of Bedford and Wilcox. But the physical laws which regulate the great Indian river systems have been most ably discussed by Mr. Fergusson in his paper on recent changes in the delta of the Ganges.* He points out the law by which all rivers oscillate in curves, the tendency of rivers in alluvial soils to raise their banks, and so confine themselves in their beds, and the mode in which deltas are gradually raised. On the first point Mr. Fergusson shows that all rivers oscillate in curves whose extent is directly proportionate to the quantity of water flowing through them, any obstruction or inequality causing oscillation, which goes on increasing until it reaches the mean between the force of gravity tending to draw it in a straight line and the force due to the obstruction tending to give it a direction at right angles with the former, the extent of the curves being proportioned to the slope of the bed. With reference to the tendency of rivers in alluvial soils to raise their banks, he calls attention to the important fact that water resists water far better than earth does. A river can attack its banks in detail, and carry the bits away, but still water, by producing a state of rest, forces a river to deposit its silt exactly where it is most useful in forming a barrier against further incursions, and so finally repels its advance. In India these expanses of still water, called jheels, are at about the same level as the river. In the rains they rise with it, so that, when it overtops its banks, it meets this body of still water, and deposits its silt along the limits between the moving and the stationary mass. The mode by which it now appears that deltas are raised is by a river flowing through some low part of the country, gradually embanking itself, then raising its bed until the body of its water is higher than the country round. Into this it eventually falls, and commences a similar process of embanking itself, till, in the course of time, it is forced to seek a lower bed. Thus the whole delta is gradually raised by continual shifting of

* "Quarterly Geological Journal," xix., p. 321.

the plains of the rivers. Mr. Fergusson forms the conclusion, from a long and careful study of these Gangetic phenomena, that from 4,000 to 5,000 years ago the sea, or at least the tide, extended as far as Rajmehal, and that Bengal proper was a vast bay or lagoon. The gradual raising of the delta, which caused the lower part of the Ganges basin to become inhabitable, is indicated by the positions of the capital cities, which were first on the water parting between the Ganges and Indus basins, and were established lower down the Ganges valley by successive dynasties as the progress of the physical changes rendered the former lagoons and swamps fit places for the abodes of men. The first cities really in the plains were Hastanapura on the Ganges and Ayodya on the Gogra, which flourished from 2,000 to 1,000 B.C. Then Canouj was built; at a later date Palibothra or Patna; the early Mohammedans made Gour, opposite Rajmehal, their capital; and finally Dacca was built in 1604 near the mouth of the river. Thus in 3,000 B.C. the only practically habitable part of the alluvial plain of India was the water-parting between the Sutlej and Jumna. The rest has only become fit for man's occupation within the historical period, and hundreds of square miles of the delta have become habitable since the days of Clive. Great changes have taken place since Rennell's survey. In 1785 that great geographer found the Bramapootra flowing through Sylhet with a width of a mile and a half in the dry season. Now the same bed is a mere creek, or rather chain of ponds, while the volume of water has passed into the Jennai (then an insignificant stream), some 70 miles further westward than the bed it occupied in the beginning of the century. Then the Teesta joined the Ganges at Jaffiergunge; now it flows into the Bramapootra. Earthquakes have aided the more gradual action of water in effecting changes in the delta. In 1762, in the great earthquake at Chittagong, a large tract was submerged, and now forms the Sylhet jheels, through which Dr. Hooker sailed, while other parts were elevated.* Mr. Fergusson points out another important hydrographic law, namely, that the mouths of tributaries shift upwards along the main stream in consequence of the decrease of slope caused by the rise of the delta, which obliges the tributaries to increase the angle at which they fall into the Ganges. Careful

* "Phil. Trans.," lviii., p. 251; "Hooker's Journal," ii., p. 256.

observation of the rate at which this takes place would show the progress of the rise in the delta. "Hitherto," says Mr. Fergusson, "dipping tumblers from the sides of budgerows" (to ascertain the quantity of silt in suspension) "has been supposed to be sufficient "to gauge the growth of continents; but the safest test of the "elevation of the delta is the progress of the retrocession of the "tributaries."

It has been seen that both in the Indus and Ganges basins earthquakes have formed an important element in the changes that have taken place. This branch of the subject has received much attention, and descriptive lists of earthquakes in India have been drawn up by Colonel Baird Smith, and more recently by Dr. Oldham.*

South of the Ganges valley, long flat topped spurs descend towards the Jumna, and almost reach the river to the eastward of Gwalior. But further east they recede, and form an amphitheatre of precipices, shaping the plain of Bundelcund into a bay surrounded by sandstone cliffs, which again advance to the Jumna near Mirzapore. This is the northern face of the plateau of Malwa, and highland of Bundelcund and Rewah, which is bounded to the south by the valleys of the Nerbudda and Sone. These two valleys form a continuous and almost straight line of depression across India, from the gulf of Cambay to Patna on the Ganges. Thus the plateaux of Malwa and Bundelcund, or, as it may more properly be called with reference to physical geography, the Vindhyan table land, forms a great triangle, with the line of the Nerbudda and Sone as one side, the Ganges valley as another, and the Aravalli mountains separating it from the Looni basin and the desert, as a third. To the south the great rock escarpment of the Vindhyan hills terminates the table land, and overhangs the valley of the Nerbudda, presenting the appearance of a weather-beaten coast line. From its summit there is no abrupt descent to the north, corresponding to their southern declivity; yet the northern slope, though slight, commences at the very edge of the escarpment above the Nerbudda, where the Betwa, Dessaun, and Sonar rivers rise, and flow northwards to the Ganges. The escarpment of Vindhyan rocks, here called the

* See also the paper on earthquakes, and especially on that in the N.W. part of the Bombay Presidency, on April 29th 1864, by D. J. Kennelly, Esq.—*Bombay, G. S. J.*, xviii., p. 288.

Kymore hills, continues along the north flank of the Sone valley. It is said that on the remarkable hill of Amarkuntak, the three rivers Sone, Nerbudda, and Mahanuddy rise from one tank. This is not true, but their sources are really only a few miles from each other. This region has been best described by Dangerfield,* Franklin,† Jacquemont,‡ Oldham,§ and Medlicott;‖ while Dr. Hooker crossed and described the Kymore hills.

The Nerbudda itself forms one of the most important and interesting features of the physical geography of Western India. To the north of its valley are the flat topped cliffs of the Vindhyan hills, from 300 to 800 feet high; and to the south is the Mahadeo or Satpoora range, sloping gently towards the Nerbudda, and with its abrupt face to the southward, forming the northern boundary of the Taptee valley. The Satpoora hills have been described by Rigby;¶ and the Taptee valley by Edwards.** Both the Vindhya and Satpoora ranges are abrupt and scarped to the south, and slope off gently on their northern sides. Dr. Impey wrote a full description of the physical character of the Nerbudda valley in 1855,†† it was reported upon by Evans, Keatinge, and Del Hoste,‡‡ and has since been carefully examined by the Geological Surveyors.

The extensive region bounded by the Ganges, the Sone, the Mahanuddy, and the Bay of Bengal, and drained by the Damooda and other streams, has received very close investigation on its northern side, where the mineral treasures of the Rajmahal hills have long attracted attention;§§ but the southern and western parts of the tract are less known. A party of the Topographcial Survey is now engaged in the exploration and mapping of part of this region.

The plateau of the Deccan has been best described by Colonel Sykes; and no account of Mysore has yet appeared to supersede the

* Malcolm's Central India.

† Geological Society, Trans. III. 2d. S.

‡ Voyage dans l'Inde.

§ J. A. S. B. xxv. p. 249.

‖ Geological Memoirs.

¶ Journ. Bombay G. S. xi. p. 69.

** „ „ G. S. xi. p. 16.

†† Bombay Selections. No. xiv. N. S.

‡‡ Journal, Bombay G. S. viii. 119 and 174, and i. 174.

§§ See "Notes upon a tour through the Rajmahal hills, by Capt. Sherwill, R. E." J. A. S. B. xx. p. 544; the Geological Memoirs; and Dr. Hooker's Journal, and his paper in the J. A. S. B., xvii. pt. II. p. 355.

admirable work of Dr. Buchanan; but the schemes for navigation and irrigation, and the works already executed, have led, more recently, to frequent and minutely detailed examinations of the basins through which flow the rivers which traverse the peninsula, and fall into the bay of Bengal.

The Mahanuddy, rising in the mountainous region which bounds the Chutteesgurh plateau, has a comparatively short course, and numerous tributaries converging from a limited circumference to a common centre. Thus a single storm will often affect the whole area of the basin. This peculiarity has caused those destructive floods in Cuttack which necessitate a system of carefully constructed embankments. Captain Harris, from his position in charge of these works, has studied the meteorological phenonoma of the Mahanuddy basin with close attention; but the best general description of the region is by Sir Richard Temple.*

The basin of the Godavery is very fully described in the reports of Colonel Haig; the Kistna and Cauvery, with the smaller streams along the coast, have also been minutely described in numerous irrigation reports;† and the eastern hills of the peninsula have been for several years the scene of the labours of Mr. King and his colleagues of the Geological Survey.

The western ghauts, extending from the Taptee to Cape Comorin, with one remarkable gap at Palghat, and the peculiarities of their western drainage system, would require a large volume for their satisfactory description.

No general work of the kind exists, and the different portions or districts can only be studied in detail.

The northern portion is included in various accounts of the Deccan; but I know of no detailed geographical description of Nuggur and Munjerabad, nor of Coorg and Wynaad, apart from the manuscript memoirs of the old surveys. The best general account of Coorg is given in Colonel Sankey's interesting report on the roads,

---

* Selections (India P. W. D.), No. xliii., Journal, R. G. S., xxxv. p. 70, (1865.)

† See, on these subjects, Major Orr's Report on the works of the Madras Irrigation Company at Kurnool, dated January 8th, 1861, Sir William Denison's Minute of March 2d, 1861, and Colonel Ludlow's Report of October 1862. For an excellent general account of the works on the deltas of the Godavery, Kistna, and Cauvery, see Colonel Baird Smith's Report (London 1856). For the Kistna, see also Major Anderson's Report of January 6th, 1863.

and I have myself reported upon the Wynaad district.* Ouchterlony's report gives details of the geographical features of the Neilgherry and Koondah hills,† and the first account of the Anamallays appeared in Dr. Cleghorn's "Forests and Gardens of Southern India." The Pulneys have been described by Captain Ward, Captain Beddome, Dr. Wight, and by myself; and I have also reported upon the mountainous region between Travancore and Madura.‡ Yet wide tracts of the western ghauts are undescribed, and others are still unexplored. Malabar was explored, early in this century, by Dr. Buchanan, and his is still the standard work on the subject; but the system of back waters along the coast, and all the phenomena connected with the western drainage of the ghauts, is a branch of physical geography which would still repay careful study.§

The distribution of plants, and their influence upon the climate, and, through the climate upon the physical character of a region, is one of the most important branches of geographical science; and it is one which, in India, has been studied from a very early period. The first Indian herbalists, however, collected and examined plants without reference to any such general views. It was to learn their healing virtues that the holy sage Aghastya explored the wonders of the vegetable kingdom,‖ that Ibn ul Bakhtar came all the way from distant Spain to collect the plants of India,¶ and even that the Portuguese physician Cristobal da Costa made his botanical observations.** The first great Indian work on plants was the "Hortus Malabaricus," undertaken under the auspices of Henry von Rheede, the Dutch governor of Malabar. The specimens were collected by Brahmans between 1674 and 1676, and sent to Cochin, where drawings were made by the missionary Mathœus, and descriptions in

* "Chinchona Blue Book," (1870) pp. 61–93; "Travels in Peru and India, p. 402; "Madras Journal, vi., p. 280, v., p. 280, and 1857; "Forests and Gardens of South India," p. 289–302.

† See also the earlier report on the Neilgherries by Messrs. Fox and Turnbull.—*Bombay G. S. J.*, iv., p. 9.

‡ "Chinchona Blue Book," (June 1866,) p. 283.

§ "On the inland navigation of Travancore."—*R. G. S. Journ.* xxxvi., p. 195. (1866.) See also Mr. Kennedy's interesting report to the Madras Government on the back-water navigation, and the works required at Cochin, dated Oct. 9th, 1862.

‖ "Aghastier Vytia Anyouroo." A medical Sastrum frequently quoted in Ainslie's Materia Medica.

¶ Escurial, MSS. Casiri.

** His observations form the basis of "Ausius. Exoticorum libri decem." (Antwerp 1563.)

Malayalim were translated into Latin by Hermann von Doulp, the secretary to Government at Cochin. The work was published at Amsterdam in 12 folio volumes, with 794 plates, between 1686 and 1703; and a commentary on it, by Dr. Buchanan Hamilton, has since been printed in the Transactions of the Linnæan Society.*

William Roxburgh was born at Underwood, in Scotland, on June 29th, 1759. He entered the Madras medical service in 1786, and John Kœnig† of Courland came out to India in the service of the Danish Government in 1768. These two eminent men, with Sir William Jones, Buchanan Hamilton, Hunter, Carey, and Rottler, formed themselves into a society for the promotion of botany; and Roxburgh was the first to reduce the plants of the east to the form of a flora. In the early part of his career he resided at Samulcottah in the Northern Circars, and wrote some valuable papers for Dalrymple's Oriental Repository, on the cultivation of rice, sugar, and pepper. In 1793 Roxburgh became the first Superintendent of the botanical gardens at Calcutta‡, where he remained until 1814, when he went home, and died at Edinburgh in April 1815. Roxburgh caused 2,000 coloured drawings of plants to be made, 300 of which were published by the East India Company in three large volumes entitled "The Plants of Coromandel," between 1795 and 1816. The published plants were selected chiefly for their useful qualities, and included the sandal wood tree, catamaran, nux vomica, teak, areka catechu, minosa Arabica, and terminalia chebula. Roxburgh's "Flora Indica" (3 vols. 8vo.) was published between 1820 and 1832.§

Wallich received Dr. Roxburgh's mantle, and succeeded him as the leading Indian botanist. Nathaniel Wallich was a Dane born at Copenhagen on the 28th of January 1786. He went out to India as surgeon of the Danish settlement of Serampore, and was taken prisoner when that place was captured by the English. His great

---

* Vols. xiii. xiv. xv.

† Kœnig's herborium and MSS. are in the British Museum.

‡ The gardens were commenced by Captain Kyd in March 1786.

§ The first volume of Roxburgh's "Flora Indica" was edited by Drs. Carey and Wallich, and published in 1820, the second in 1824. Dr. Roxburgh's sons brought out the three complete volumes in 1832. Copies of all Dr. Roxburgh's unpublished drawings were made by the late Sir William Hooker, on a reduced scale.

In the "Hortus Bengalensis" a list of all the plants described in Roxburgh's Flora is arranged according to the Linnæan system, with native names, habit, time of flowering, and references to the plates in Von Rheede's "Hortus Malabaricus."

There is an obituary notice of Dr. Roxburgh, with a portrait, in the 38th volume of the Transactions of the Society of Arts.

attainments as a botanist soon secured for him the transfer from a prison to the charge of the Government gardens at Calcutta, as Dr. Buchanan Hamilton's successor, in 1815. Dr. Buchanan Hamilton had taken Dr. Roxburgh's place for a year. During the next thirteen years Wallich added enormously to the extent of the collections. In 1820 he made a botanical excursion to Nepaul, and in 1824 he commenced the publication of his "Tentamen Floræ Nepalensis." In 1825 he was sent to inspect the timber forests of Oude and Rohilcund, and made large collections of plants; and in 1826 he enjoyed further opportunities as a member of the mission to Ava. He also employed many collectors in various parts of India. In 1828 Dr. Wallich came to England with an enormous collection of plants, which he distributed among the principal botanists of the day. He made a catalogue, consisting of 253 folio pages, of the specimens retained at the India House (7683). In 1832 Wallich's original herbarium was presented to the Linnæan Society by the East India Company. It consists of about 7,000 specimens, and has become a standard work of reference.* While he was in England Dr. Wallich also completed his "Plantæ Asiaticæ Rariores," a magnificent work in 3 folio volumes, containing 300 coloured plates, which was published by the East India Company in 1832. In 1833 Dr. Wallich returned to India, and resumed his labors at the gardens with unremitting zeal. From 1836 to 1840 he distributed no less than 189,932 plants to 2,000 different gardens. He was engaged in examining the capabilities of Assam for tea cultivation in 1843, but in 1847 was obliged to go home from ill health; and this most zealous and able public servant died in London on the 28th of April 1854, aged 69. His successors at the Calcutta gardens have been Drs. Falconer, Thomson, Anderson, and King.

William Griffith must be mentioned as one of the leading Bengal botanists. Born in 1810, he arrived at Calcutta as assistant surgeon in 1835, and was appointed to accompany Dr. Wallich to Assam. He traversed the unexplored tracts near the Mishmee mountains, between Sudeya and Ava, collecting insects and plants; and in February 1836 he made a journey from Assam to Ava, and down the Irawaddy to Rangoon. Next, as surgeon to Pemberton's embassy, he traversed 400 miles of the Bhootan country, returning

* There is also a set of the Wallichian Herbarium at Kew. Dr. Hooker has since rescued 12 or 14 waggon loads of dried plants from the cellars of the India House, and arranged and distributed them, within the last ten years.

to Calcutta in June 1839. In November of the same year he joined the army of the Indus in a scientific capacity, and went from Cabul to Khorassan, making large collections of plants. Dr. Griffith died in February 1845. The great object of his life was the preparation of a general scientific Flora of India. He devoted 12 years of unremitted exertions to this work; collecting 2,500 species from the Khasia hills, 2,000 from Tenasserim, 1,000 from Assam, 1,200 from the Mishmee country, 1,700 from Bhootan, 1,000 from the neighbourhood of Calcutta, and 1,200 from the Naga hills.*

The public garden at Saharunpore was established in 1779 by Zabita Khan, who appropriated the revenues of seven villages for its maintenance; Gholam Kadir, and the Mahratta chiefs after him, continued the grant; and in 1823 Lord Hastings ordered the establishment to be converted into a botanical garden of 400 acres, to which was afterwards added a nursery of trees for the canal banks.† Dr. Forbes Royle was the first Superintendent, and, in his "Illustrations of the botany of the Himalayan Mountains," he was the first to attempt to demonstrate the prominent features of the geographical distribution of North Indian plants, in reference to the elevations and climates they inhabit, and to the botany of the surrounding country. In his paper on the geographical distribution of the Flora of India, Dr. Royle makes some most interesting remarks on the vegetation of Indian lakes, and suggests the process by which the coal formations have been deposited. The lakes are often covered with numerous stems, leaf and flower stalks of a variety of plants closely interlaced and matted together; and cattle are even said to graze upon the grasses with which the lakes become covered; the matted growth being strong enough to bear their weight.‡

Dr. Royle was succeeded at Saharunpore by Drs. Falconer and Jameson.

---

* "Posthumous papers bequeathed to the H. E. I. C., and printed by order of the Government of Bengal; being journals of travels by the late William Griffith, Esq., arranged by John McClelland, M.D." (Calcutta, 1847. 8vo.)

They include his journals of travels in the Mishmee country, Upper Assam, to Ava, Bhootan, Candahar, and Cabul.

† J. A. S. B., i., p. 41.

‡ "General observations on the geographical distribution of the Flora of India, and remarks on the vegetation of its lakes, by Dr. Forbes Royle."—*Reports of the British Association*, xv., p. 74 (1846.)

Dr. Wight stands at the head of the botanists of the Madras Presidency. His "Prodromus Floræ Peninsulæ Indiæ Orientalis" is pronounced by Dr. Hooker to be the most able and valuable contribution to Indian botany that has ever appeared.* In 1853 Dr. Wight returned to England with an enormous collection of plants, chiefly from the hill districts. In 1830 Dr. Graham made a catalogue of the Bombay plants, and he has been followed by Law, Dalzell, Gibson, Birdwood, and others.†

The "Flora Indica" of Drs. Hooker and Thomson will combine all the information that has hitherto been collected on the subject of Indian botany. In 1851 the Court of Directors refused to promote this great national object, though strongly memorialized by the British Association; yet a first volume, with a most valuable and interesting preliminary essay, was published in 1855. It is now in contemplation that Dr. Hooker should edit a Flora of British India, by engaging and superintending the labours of various botanists as authors. The number of species to be described is computed at 12,000, and all will be included in four volumes, 8vo., of 800 pages each. All plants found between Tibet and Ceylon and Singapore, and from the Indus to the Irawaddy, are to be included. After enumerating the works of previous botanists and the labours of various collectors,‡ the Preliminary Essay by Hooker and Thomson

---

* By Robert Wight and G. A. W. Arnott (2 vols. 1834.) Dr. Wight has also published, "Illustrations of Indian Botany," commenced in 1838; "Icones Plantarum Indiæ Orientalis," (2,101 plates,) and "Spicilegium Neilgherrense" (coloured plates). Dr. Leschenault, the director of the botanic gardens at Pondicherry, and Mr. Gardner of Ceylon, also explored the Flora of the Neilgherries.

† "The Bombay Flora, or short descriptions of all the indigenous plants in the Bombay Presidency," by N. A. Dalzell and A. Gibson. (Bombay 1861.)

"Catalogue of the economic products of the Presidency of Bombay;" compiled by Assistant Surgeon Birdwood, M.D. (Bombay, 1862.)

‡ Richard Strachey collected 2,000 species in the Himalaya, and distributed them to several European museums. Munro made a large collection in Madras, Coorg, Agra, and Simla; Falconer in Tibet; Schmid in the Neilgherries, Coorg, and Canara (named by Miquel); Lobb in Cossyah and Malabar; Law in Bombay; Dalzell in the Concan; Sykes and Gibson in the Deccan; Stocks in Sinde; Madden in Simla and Kumaon; Vicary in the Punjab and Sinde; Edgeworth in Moultan and Bundelcund; Fleming in the Salt Range; Jameson at Mussoorie; Thomson 3,000 species in Rohilcund, Kashmir, Tibet, and the Punjab, and in the Himalaya; Hooker 1,000 in Behar and the Gangetic valley, 3,500 in Sikkim, 3,000 in the Cossyah hills, 1,000 in Cachar and the Sunderbunds; Griffith in Bhootan. Jacquemont's collection was published by Cambessides and Decaisne, 180 plates, 4to. (Paris, 1844.)

gives a lucid sketch of the physical features and vegetation of the provinces of India.

The authors, in giving a comprehensive view of Indian botany, divide the country into 18 botanical provinces, including Ceylon, with reference to physical features.* The total number of Indian species is from 12 to 15,000, but there is almost a total absence of absolutely local plants, while India contains representatives of almost every natural family on the globe. The general physiognomy of the greater part of the Flora approximates more to that of tropical Africa than to any other part of the world. The plains are very poor in species, and there are few countries in which the vegetation presents so little beauty, or such short seasons of bloom. In the Carnatic, where the Flora has been thoroughly investigated, the vegetation is neither rich nor varied; and there are no forests except on the flanks of the mountains. In Malabar, where there is abundant rainfall, the luxuriant vegetation is Malayan; while in the Concan, further north, where the country is more open, and heavy forests are rarer, there is a mixture of African types. On the Deccan the Flora is not extensive, and in Berar and Khandeish little is known of it. On the Vindhyan table land the Flora resembles that of the eastern ghauts, but the Malwa Flora is scarcely known. In Sinde, where there are about 400 species, nine tenths are indigenous to Africa; and the vegetation of the Punjab is very like that of Sinde. There is nearly complete identity of vegetation between Sinde and Egypt.

The Himalayan region, as regards its botany, is divided longitudinally into east, central, and west; latitudinally into exterior, interior, and Tibetan; and altitudinally into tropical, temperate, and alpine. In the eastern portion Dr. Hooker explored the dense forests of Sikkim, which extend up to 12,000 feet, collecting 2,770 species of flowering plants and 150 ferns. Many European types do not reach beyond the western Himalaya, while others, such as

---

* Namely,

1. Ceylon,	10. Behar,
2. Malabar,	11. Bundelcund,
3. Concan,	12. Malwa,
4. Carnatic,	13. Guzerat,
5. Mysore,	14. Sindh,
6. Deccan,	15. Rajwara,
7. Khandeish,	16. Punjab,
8. Berar,	17. Upper Gangetic plain,
9. Orissa,	18. Bengal,

besides the Himalayan region.

walnuts, ivy, junipers, and yews, extend over the whole range. As many as 222 British plants are found in India; but to the eastward of Kumaon the European types rapidly disappear. The *deodara* or cedar of Lebanon is only found to the west of Nepaul. Very few European plants extend into that central part of the region, and fewer still into Sikkim. This is probably connected with the gradually diminishing rainfall to the westward. The phenomena of vegetation are less dependent upon the mean temperature of the year than upon that of the season of growth, and it is therefore important to know the mean temperature of each month.

The effects of human action on the physical condition of the earth's surface have been very great; and the planting and destruction of forests have been among the chief agents in the changes thus caused.* It is true that too much importance has been attributed to the influence of forests, as if they were the principal causes of the moisture of a climate. Lieutenant W. H. Parish, in a very interesting paper on this subject,† has well pointed out that temperature, the pressure of the atmosphere, and its electrical state are the chief agents towards the formation of rain, and that mountain chains and forests are merely local causes. Humboldt considers that forests exercise a triple influence on climate, by protecting the soil against the rays of the sun, producing a constant evaporation, and increasing the radiation through the leaves. The entire destruction of many forests has certainly rendered India liable to those dreadful calamities which always follow a deficiency of rain; and, during the troubles attendant on the fall of the Mohammedan empire, many districts were denuded of their trees, and converted into dreary wastes. The attention of the English rulers was first turned to the subject by the rapid failure of the supply of timber for ship building in the Malabar forests, and Dr. Gibson was appointed as conservator of the forests in the Bombay Presidency. Broader views, however, soon began to be entertained, and a regularly organized system of forest conservancy is now established throughout India. Much valuable information on this subject will be found in the work of Dr. Cleghorn, to whose skill and ability as an administrator the present success of forest conservancy in India is mainly due; in the reports of Dr. Brandis, the present accom-

---

* The best and most instructive work on this subject is "Physical Geography, as modified by human action," by George P. Marsh. (London, 1864.)

† "J. A. S. B." xviii., p. 791.

plished Inspector General of Forests; and in the writings of Dr. Balfour and others.* On the western ghauts, owing to the introduction of coffee cultivation, many thousands of acres have been cleared of forest, and it is impossible to exaggerate the importance of ascertaining the nature of the changes caused by these clearings, and the best means of obviating the evils that may arise from them; for on the water supply from the ghauts depends the irrigation of a large part of the peninsula. Among other measures, I believe and trust that the Chinchona plantations, formed within the last ten years on most of the mountains of India, will be as useful as the trees they have supplanted, in preventing evaporation, regulating drainage, and receiving the moisture which is wrung out of the passing clouds.†

The nature of the soil is another cause which produces modifications in climate, owing to greater or less power of radiating heat. Sandy soils become rapidly and intensely hot, and when the rays of the sun are withdrawn they readily radiate to the atmosphere the heat they have acquired. Clayey soils, on the other hand, become slowly heated, and as slowly part with heat. Swampy ground chills the air; thus, if marshes are drained or forests cleared, the temperature is raised.

The changes that take place along the coasts, and are still in progress, have only been partially investigated. For this purpose the examination of charts of the same places, made at different periods, is very important. At Cochin, for instance, round the Vypeen point, the action of the S.W. monsoon and of the backwater

---

* "Forests and Gardens of Southern India," by Hugh Cleghorn, M.D. (London. 1861.)

"Timber Trees of India," by Dr. Balfour. (Madras. 1862.) A new edition appeared in 1871.

"Useful Plants of India," by Major Heber Drury. (Madras. 1858.)

"Handbook of Indian Botany," by Major Heber Drury. (Madras. 2 vols.)

"Index to the native and scientific names of Indian plants and products," by Dr. Forbes Watson. (India Office. 1866.)

"Trees of the Madras Presidency," by Captain Beddome. (Madras. 1863.)

"Timber Trees of India," by George Bidie, M. B. (Madras. 1862.)

"Timber Trees of Upper Assam."—*Journal Ag. and Hort. Socy. of India*, iii., pt. ii., p. 6–10.

Dr. J. L. Stewart is about to publish his "*Flora Sylvatica*" of the Punjab and N.W. Provinces.

† "On the effects of the destruction of forests in the western ghauts of India, on the water supply," by C. R. Markham, R. G. S. Journal, xxxvi. p. 180 (1866); see also Chinchona Blue Books, presented to Parliament, *passim*.

produces incessant change.* Such phenomena as the Alipee mud-bank, and others connected with the relations between the Malabar backwaters and the ocean, require further study and examination;† as do also the bores in the Gulf of Cambay, and at the mouth of the Salween, and other tidal phenomena, the changes at the mouths of rivers, and the so-called "swatches of no ground" off the mouths of the Indus and Ganges. A complete and thorough investigation of the evidence of upheaval and depression round the sea shores of India is also a desideratum. Indeed "the physical geography of the Indian Seas" is a valuable and important volume which has yet to be written.

An attempt has been made in this section to give a general idea of the points of chief interest that have been discussed by physical geographers in connection with India; with references to their writings. It is of course only possible to furnish a cursory view of so vast a subject, within such narrow limits. A great mass of accurate and well digested observation has been accumulated, to all of which it has not been possible to refer; but very rich veins of good metal will reward the explorer who searches among the selections from Government Records, the volumes of the Asiatic Society of Bengal, and those of other societies established in India. There is ample material already garnered to enable a physical geographer to follow up and form generalizations on any branch of his science, while fresh stores are constantly being collected by the Topographical and Geological Surveyors and by other observers. Surveyors are expected to send in a full account of the geographical features of the districts under survey, with notes on their aspect, climate, superficial configuration, forests, rivers, soils, productions, &c.‡

Few attempts have hitherto been made to produce really good maps to illustrate the physical geography and statistics of India. In 1833 Mr. Walker brought out a set of maps to show the European connection with India; but these are merely skeleton maps, giving the political boundaries, and those for military, revenue, and judicial purposes. A second edition, with five additional maps, was published in about 1848.

---

* See Kennedy's Report, Oct 9th, 1862.

† See, on this subject, "On the Inland Navigation of Travancore; an account of the Alipee mud bank and the Wurkallay Barrier," by C. R. Markham, R. G. S. Journal, xxxvi. p. 195, (1866.)

‡ "Manual of Surveying for India," p. 634. The last volume of selections from Survey Reports contains accounts of Buraich, Seonee, Raepore, Chandu, Kamroop, Gowalpara, and the Dooars. (No. lxxiv.)

The best series of illustrative maps is that prepared by Mr. Edward A. Prinsep, the settlement officer in the Sealkote district of the Punjab. Their design is admirable, and they display both taste and skill in their execution. They are invaluable, as far as they go, and it is much to be desired that similar maps should be prepared in other parts of India. These are confined to the Sealkote district, and the series of sixteen shows at a glance the details of every branch of information required by a revenue officer, and much that is most useful to a general enquirer.* Mr. Prinsep also made a map of the Umritsur Division of the Punjab, showing the general features of the hills and plains, rivers and canals, the roads, and limits of fiscal and civil divisions. There are also lines showing the zones of rainfall, and the depth of wells throughout the division.†

In 1870 Mr. Prinsep published a very interesting series of maps of the Punjab, showing the State canals acting on improvable waste lands, the depth of wells, the rainfall and zones of drought, and the parts of the country already irrigated.‡

A series of skeleton maps of the Central Provinces has been lithographed to accompany the Administration Reports, showing, very roughly, the lines of railways, mineral resources, and positions of forests. They are quite of a different character from Mr. Prinsep's maps, both as regards design and execution; yet they are welcome as showing the interest that is taken in these matters.

We may look forward, hereafter, to seeing general maps of India, as well as those of particular districts, with strictly accurate outlines, prepared for the purpose of illustrating botanical and other branches of physical geography, forest tracts, areas of cultivation, irrigation works, systems of communication, and other features which compose a physical atlas; as well as statistics, and revenue details.

---

* I. "Report on the revised fiscal settlement of Sealkote district in Amritsur division," effected by E. A. Prinsep. (Lahore, 1865.)

II. "Statistical account of the Sealkote district," geographically sketched by E. A. Prinsep, settlement officer, 1855–60. The maps shew the agricultural tribes arranged according to occupancy of land; political and fiscal divisions; rent-free aspect of the district; physical features and zones of fertility; productive power as influenced by rain or aided by irrigation; different kinds of soils; acres under different kinds of produce; police divisions, and haunts of criminal races; roads and lines of traffic; statistical aspect of area, agriculture, and population; and prevailing tenures and modes of assessment. The maps were lithographed at the Surveyor General's Office at Calcutta.

† Scale 4 inches to the mile. Lithographed by Walker in 1863.

‡ At the end of his "How to make State Canals without borrowing," being a few suggestions by Edward A. Prinsep, Settlement Commissioner, Punjab. (Lahore, 1870.)

XVII.—THE GEOGRAPHICAL DEPARTMENT OF THE INDIA OFFICE.

A Department for the systematic utilization of geographical work has been considered to be an important and indeed an essential element in the Home Government of a great Colonial Power, ever since Columbus first sailed from Palos. Bishop Fonseca was alive to its necessity, and as soon as the Royal Council of the Indies was formed, in 1524, for the Home Government of the vast trans-Atlantic possessions of Spain, a Geographical Department was regularly organized. In those days it was called the Office of the Cosmographer of the Indies, but, allowing for the difference of time, the duties were the same as those which should devolve upon a similar Department at the present day. The utilization of geographical knowledge was as important, and the value of science in all branches of administrstion was as great, then as now.

It was the duty of the Cosmographer's Department, in the Office of the Council of the Indies, to furnish geographical knowledge to officers and servants of the State; to supply instruments; to apprise officers in the Indies of the times for observing; to collect and enter in books all routes and journeys made in the Indies with care and accuracy; to construct maps and charts in accordance with the descriptions received, and to record all such descriptions, and other reports of a like nature. Finally, the Cosmographer was called upon to train up a class of efficient geographers; and this was one of the most important parts of his duty. He gave three-yearly courses of lectures, which were attended by young officers and pilots. The course for the first year consisted of the four rules of arithmetic, the rule of three, extraction of square and cube root, fractions, and Sacrobosco's "De sphæra mundi." The second year's course comprised the six first books of Euclid, arcs and chords, right sines tangents and secants, the tables of King Alfonso, George Purbach's theory of the planets, and the fourth book of the spherical triangles of Muller (or Juan de Monte Regio, as the Spaniards called him). The third year's course included the Almagest of Ptolemy, cosmography and the art of navigation, the use of the astrolabe and its mechanism, the use and adjustments of other instruments, and the method of observing the movements of the heavenly bodies.*

This wise care for the instruction of their officers as geographers, on the part of the Council of the Indies, was one of the most admirable parts of their system, and one which would be well worthy of imitation. For the rest, the labours of their Geographical Department were of inestimable value, and a knowledge of them will always be indispensable to students in the wide field of research which they embrace. The one great fault of the Spanish officials was their love of secrecy, but even this arose, in great part, from their sense of the value of the information that had been collected, and it ensured, at all events, due care in the preservation of the records. All branches of knowledge connected with geography were not utterly neglected, nor were precious documents destroyed by cartloads, or left to rot and perish.

When the East India Company was first formed in London, its enlightened managers had not then a great empire to administer, like the Council of the Indies at Seville; but very few days had elapsed before they saw the necessity for a Geographical Department as part of their system of management. Correct geographical information was, they well knew, as necessary for a body of merchants as for the administrators of an empire; and two months after the incorporation of the Company we find Richard Hakluyt, the illustrious founder of the East India Geographical Department, preparing memoranda of the chief places where sundry sorts of spices do grow, gathered out of the best and latest authors; of the prices of precious stones and spices; of what is good to bring from the Indies by him that is skilful and trusty; of certain commodities of good request gathered out of authors that have lived and trafficked in those parts; and of other information of a like nature.† A few years afterwards

* "Ordenanzas del Consejo Real de las Indias, por el Rey Felipe IV., 1636," ccxxxviii. to ccxliii. Also in the "Recopilacion de leyes de los reynos de las Indias, Carlos II." Lib. ii., Titulo xiii., Leyes i., to v. (Tom. i., p. 185.)

It should be remembered that the Cosmographer's Department of the Council of the Indies was quite distinct from that of the "Piloto Mayor" at the "Casa de Contratacion." The latter was analogous to the present Hydrographer's Department at the Admiralty.

† "Divers Voyages, by Richard Hakluyt," printed for the Hakluyt Society, and edited by Mr. Winter Jones (1850), p. 151.

Calendar of State Papers (Colonial, 1513–1616), para. 284.

Edward Wright was added to the Department, to compile the maps and charts; and the collection of geographical information in the form of logs and journals was commenced.*

For a century and a half the labours of the Geographical Department were chiefly confined to the preparation of charts and the record of voyages; but with the acquisition of Bengal by Lord Clive commenced the land surveys of Rennell, "the Father of Indian Geography." When Major Rennell returned from his severe labours as a surveyor in Bengal, he devoted the remainder of his life to the interests of Indian Geography at home. He was the unpaid but most efficient head of the Geographical Department of the India House. His Bengal Atlas was already published by order of the Company in 1781;† but in March 1788 his famous map of India appeared, and the memoir followed in 1792. This is the starting point in the history of Indian Government map making, and the memoir furnished a complete account of the material upon which Rennell's map is based. The map of D'Anville, published in 1751 and 1752, was still the basis upon which the new work was to be founded, but Rennell collected much additional material. He had the route surveys of General Goddard from the Jumna to Poona, of Captain Reynolds through Malwa, of Colonel Fullarton in Coimbatore, of Colonel Call in Tinnevelly, and those made in the wars with Hyder and Tippoo; besides the marches of Bussy in the Deccan. On the Bengal side he had his own admirable surveys; but D'Anville's map was still the best authority for the Punjab and the course of the Indus, as it was until very lately for the upper basin of the Brahmaputra. Rennell's interest was excited by the accounts he had obtained, from the notes of Captain Kirkpatrick, of the remains of old irrigation works north of Delhi, the canal of Shah Feroze and the new cut of Shah Jehan, and he regrets that the descriptions of them were so obscure. He also discussed in his memoir the question of the identity of the Brahmaputra with the Sanpu, advocating that view against a counter theory of D'Anville; and he identified some of the Punjab rivers with those mentioned by Arrian and Pliny. It is unnecessary to say that, though Rennell continued to labour zealously in the interests of

* Calendar of State Papers (Colonial, 1513-1616), para. 284.

† "Bengal and Behar Atlas," by James Rennell, 1781, published by order of the East India Company. The maps are dedicated to the memory of Lord Clive, to Warren Hastings, Sir Hector Munro, Mr. Verelst, &c.

Indian geography for the remainder of his life, his works were by no means confined to the scenes of his active service. He welcomed all geographical material, and warmly supported all explorers. When the engineers who accompanied the Indian armies, in their various campaigns, produced new work, it was Rennell who promptly brought it to the knowledge of their countrymen at home.* In 1798 he was assisting Mungo Park in the arrangement of his African travels. His great work, the "Geographical System of Herodotus examined and explained," was published in 1800, and in 1816 it was followed by his "Geographical Illustrations of the Retreat of the Ten Thousand." He also devoted many years to the collation of the log books of the Indiamen for 40 years back, and his valuable results, entitled "Investigations of the Currents of the Atlantic," &c., were published by his daughter, Lady Rodd, with several large charts, after his death.

Rennell lived to a great age, and never ceased to devote his time to the interests of Indian geography. After he had reached his 87th year he possessed in full vigour all his intellectual faculties, and, though suffering little short of martyrdom from frequent attacks of the gout,† he still devoted many hours of each day to his favorite pursuit. There is but one thing to regret in the great geographer's career. His early prejudice in favor of route surveys led him to withhold from Colonel Lambton that hearty support which would have been invaluable, from such a quarter, when the Trigonometrical Survey was in its infancy. But he became convinced of the superiority of Lambton's method long before his death, and welcomed with joy the 6-sheet map of India by Walker,‡ which was partly based on triangulation. He was remarkable for true, patient, and persevering research; his critical judgment was seldom at fault, and his work is always reliable.

Rennell died on the 29th of March 1830, at the great age of 88, and was buried in Westminster Abbey, where there is a mural monument to his memory.§

---

* "On the Marches of the British Army in India, during the Campaign of 1791," by James Rennell. (1793.)

† "Quarterly Review," Vol. 39, p. 179 (1829).

‡ Allen's.

§ A memoir of Major Rennell, reprinted from the "Address of the President of the Royal Society," on November 30th, 1830, is given in *Gleanings in Science*, iii., *p.* 409, (*Calcutta*,) 1830.

See also "Notice Historique sur la vie et les ouvrages de James Rennell, par M. le Baron Walckenaer" (4to, Paris, 1842).

Major Rennell never held any official appointment after his return to England. His great services to India were all rendered from motives of zeal. His contemporary and active fellow labourer, Dalrymple, was the recognized official Hydrographer in those early days.

Alexander Dalrymple, the seventh out of 16 children of Sir James Dalrymple, was born at New Hailes on the 24th of July 1737. He received little or no education, and it was not until after he had gone out to Madras as a writer in 1752 that he taught himself accounts and the French and Spanish languages. In 1759 he was sent on a voyage to the Eastern Islands, and acquired much nautical experience. In 1765 he returned to England, and published several charts and plans of coasts and anchorages. He went back to Madras as a Member of Council, under Lord Pigot, in 1776, and finally went home in 1777. Two years afterwards he received the official appointment of Hydrographer to the East India Company. Dalrymple was a most indefatigable collector of geographical materials. Rennell acknowledges the assistance he received from the Company's Hydrographer in the preparation of his great map of Hindustan; and Dr. Vincent was indebted to Dalrymple for the maps and charts to illustrate his great work, "The Voyage of Nearchus." Dalrymple was, indeed, a most industrious and untiring workman. He translated and published several voyages from the Spanish;* and Admiral Burney, in the preface to his great work on voyages in the Pacific, says that the above translations of Dalrymple were his *vade mecum*, and that he was largely indebted to their author. Dalrymple advocated the existence of a southern continent, and was anxious to sail with Captain Cook in the "Endeavour," but was prevented, because he had not been bred in the Navy. He gave innumerable tracts to the world on various subjects.† In 1790 he made a useful suggestion to the East India

* "A historical collection of the several voyages and discoveries in the South Pacific Ocean, being chiefly a literal translation from the Spanish writers, by A. Dalrymple,' London, 1770, 2 vols. With an extraordinary dedication, stating to whom it is *not* dedicated. He gives Magellan from Herrera and Barros, Juan Fernandez from the Memorial of Arias, Mandana and Quiros from Figueroa and Torquemada, Le Maire and Schouten, Tasman and Roggewein. At the end there are many curious woodcuts.

† Bound up in three volumes in the Geographical Society's library.

Company, which was approved, and 200*l*. was granted for the purpose. The scheme was, to publish tracts from time to time on the geography, commerce, and products of the East. The result was "The Oriental Repository," in two volumes, which contains several papers of considerable interest, especially those on the cultivation of various Indian products, by Dr. Roxburgh. Dalrymple's strictly official work is represented by 58 charts, 740 plans, and 57 views of coasts; in all, 855 plates, besides 50 nautical memoirs.* In 1795 the office of hydrographer to the Admiralty was created, and Dalrymple was the first to hold it, together with the same post at the India House. He filled it until 1808, when he was suddenly called upon to resign by Lord Mulgrave. He declined to do so, and was summarily dismissed on the 28th of May. On the 31st he published "The Case of A. Dalrymple," bitterly complaining of the treatment he had received. It broke the old man's heart, and he died on the 19th of the following June.†

On Dalrymple's death, Captain Hurd succeeded him at the Admiralty, but his post at the India House remained for some time vacant, until an accumulation of nautical materials led to the appointment of Captain Horsburgh, who had made himself known by the publication of several valuable charts of the China seas. Sir Charles Wilkins, the librarian, had charge of the original maps, memoirs, and other records, while Horsburgh performed the duties of hydrographer.

James Horsburgh was born of humble and respectable parents at the small village of Elie, on the south-east coast of Fife. He commenced his career as a cook and cabin boy, and eventually rose to be captain of the "Anna," East Indiaman, in which he sailed from England in 1802, returning in 1805. In a paper printed in the "Philosophical Transactions," he detailed his meteorological observations, and in 1806 he began to collect materials for sailing directions. After some years of indefatigable research, he completed his East India Directory, which has gone through eight editions, and is still the recognized guide for the navigation of the Indian

* A large number of Dalrymple's charts and plans are bound up together in a volume preserved in the Geographical Department of the India Office. The number is 454.

† There is a memoir on Dalrymple, prepared by himself, in the "European Magazine," Nov. and Dec. 1802.

seas.* Under Horsburgh's superintendence at the India House, which began in 1810, many valuable charts were compiled and published.

Dalrymple was more an industrious collector of materials than a compiler. The map of India which succeeded Rennell's was by that great cartographer, Aaron Arrowsmith. This was the last great map based on route surveys. The materials were furnished from papers and drawings belonging to the Duke of Wellington, Sir John Malcolm, Dr. Buchanan, and Colonel Colin Mackenzie. It was published in 1816, in nine sheets, on the scale of 16 miles to an inch.

But the labours of the topographical surveyors of the Madras Military Institute, based on the triangulation of Colonel Lambton, began to attract attention as soon as their results arrived in England, and the necessity for the publication of more accurate and detailed maps of India than had hitherto been produced, was soon acknowledged. Aaron Arrowsmith was of course consulted. He constructed a projection for a new atlas of India, on the scale of four miles to an inch, and the Madras survey maps were placed in his hands. The result was the publication of his atlas of South India, from Cape Comorin to the Kistnah, in 18 sheets, on the scale proposed, which appeared in July 1822.

The question of the publication of the results of the great trigonometrical and topographical surveys, which had now been in progress for upwards of 20 years, was carefully and anxiously considered by the Court of Directors, and Colonel Salmond, then Military Secretary, was, for some years, in consultation with Colonel Mackenzie, the Surveyor General at Calcutta, on the subject. Colonel Hodgson, Mackenzie's successor, returned to England, in the hope and expectation that the great work would be entrusted to him. It, however, would no doubt have been given to Aaron Arrowsmith, who had already made the projection, and, indeed,

* It was preceded by Laurie and Whittle's "Oriental Pilot." The first edition of Horsburgh's Directory appeared in 1808, the second in 1817, the fifth in 1841, the eighth and last, in 1864.

Captain Horsburgh became a Fellow of the Royal Society in 1806. In 1816 he published his "Atmospheric Register for indicating storms at sea." In 1830 he contributed a paper to the Royal Society on "Icebergs met with in the Southern Hemisphere."

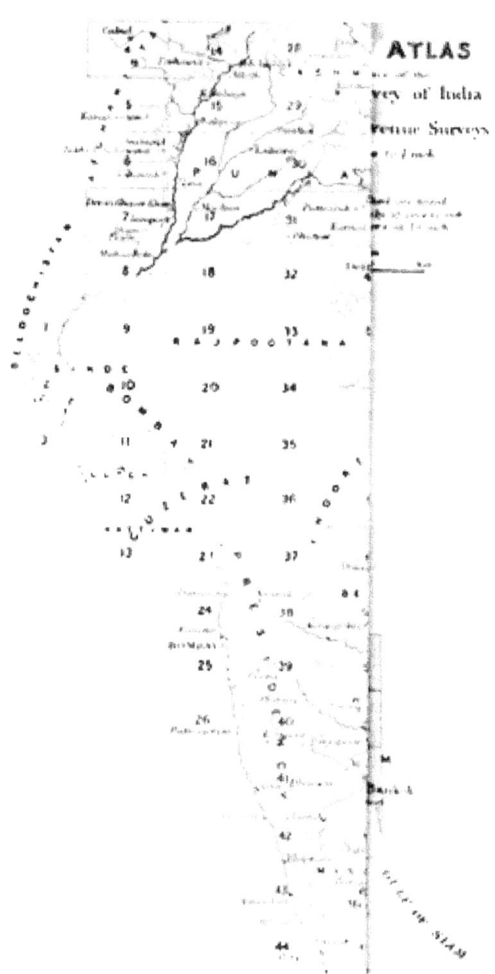
ATLAS
vey of India
Surveys
RAJPOOTANA

published several sheets in the best style of the day; but, just at that time, the veteran cartographer died. The East Indian Directors then appointed Mr. John Walker to compile and engrave the sheets of the great atlas of India.

Mr. Walker comes of a family of map engravers. His father had worked for Dalrymple, and his name appears on the maps in Vincent's Nearchus, on that in Salt's Abyssinia, on those in the Arctic voyages of Parry and Franklin, and on many others of that period. His name was also immortalized by Sir Edward Parry on a lofty cape in the far north, which is well known to many an Arctic traveller. The son was thoroughly trained, and the amount of judgment and ability he brought to the great task he undertook is shown by the often disputed but ever approved excellence of his work.

The Indian Atlas was designed to occupy 177 sheets, 40 inches by 27, and the globular projection and scale (4 miles to the inch), originally proposed by Mr. Aaron Arrowsmith, were adopted. The scheme embraces the region from Kurrachee to Singapore, and includes Ceylon. Since 1825 Mr. Walker has combined the various documents sent home by the surveyors in India, prepared the sheets for publication, engraved them on copper, and issued them to the Surveyor General in India and to the London Agent.

Sir Charles Wilkins, the librarian who had charge of all geographical records, died in Baker Street, at the great age of 85, on the 13th of May 1836. Captain Horsburgh, the hydographer to the East India Company, died at Herne Hill, at the age of 74, on the 14th of the same month of the same year. Mr. Walker was then engaged to take charge of all the records that had previously been under the care of Sir Charles Wilkins, in addition to his other duties. As Captain Horsburgh's coadjutor and successor, Mr. Walker produced nearly a hundred charts, many of which are of a large size, and the majority continue to be the chief authorities followed by navigators in the Eastern seas to this day. He also continued to engrave the sheets of the Atlas and other maps. Engraving was his special work. The care of records and conduct of geographical business required departmental agency for its efficient discharge. None was furnished. All geographical work ceased to be performed; the records were lost or left to rot, and even the correspondence book was destroyed. But Mr. Walker's duties as a cartographer were admirably performed.

The first sheets of the Atlas were of course those for which the Madras Topographical Surveys furnished the materials. The first was published in 1827. Then followed one of Bundelcund from Captain Franklin's work, and the Himalayan region from Hodgson's and Herbert's surveys. These, however, have since undergone complete revision. In 1860, and again in 1863, remonstrances were received from India, at the delay in the execution of the sheets, after the materials for them had been sent home. With a view to obviating this delay, a proposal was made by the Surveyor General in July 1864 that the sheets of the Atlas should henceforth be brought out in quarter sheets. Mr. Walker concurred that this arrangement would expedite the work, and it was accordingly adopted. There has always been the highest testimony to the accuracy and excellent style with which Mr. Walker has produced the Atlas sheets.

But Mr. Walker's work is by no means confined to the sheets of the Atlas. He has engraved seven maps of the triangulations, including Lambton's operations, Everest's great Arc Series, and Waugh's N.W. Series, the last forming a chart of five feet by six in extent. Of general maps of India, he has drawn and engraved one on six sheets for Messrs. Allen, a skeleton map on six sheets for the Government, a map in two sheets, and some others. Simm's large plan of Calcutta, drawn in 1848–49, was reduced and engraved by Mr. Walker in four sheets.* From 1846 to 1848 a number of maps of districts in the Bengal Presidency were required to be reduced from the Revenue Surveys to a ¼ inch scale, and lithographed. Those of the North West Provinces were, as has been seen, prepared and published at Allahabad, under the orders of Mr. Hugh M. Elliot, the Secretary to the Board of Revenue. But those of the Lower Provinces were sent home to be lithographed in England. Of these 31 were executed by Mr. Walker, and a few appear to have been entrusted to Mr. Wyld, in 1848.† Mr. Walker also executed a Revenue Map of the North West Provinces, and one of the Ajmeer District.

The most beautiful specimens of Mr. Walker's lithography are his production of Colonel Robinson's remarkable survey of Jhelum

* The manuscript is deposited in the Geographical Department of the India Office.

† Balasore, Bijnour, Goruckpore, Ghazeepore, Jounpore, Moradabad, Patna.

and Rawul Pindee in eight parts, on 28 sheets; and his maps howing the results of Captain Montgomerie's surveys in Jummoo and Cashmere. There are four sheets on a scale of two miles, and four on a scale of four miles to an inch.

A map of the Julinder Division of the Punjab, maps for General Cunningham's and again for Mr. Vigne's travels, the map for Wood's Oxus, one of Gwalior in four sheets, one of Nagpore and Wurdah, and a carefully compiled map of the North West Frontier of India on two large sheets, are also among Mr. Walker's works.

The manuscript maps forming the results of the Hyderabad Survey were sent home and taken in hand by Mr. Walker, and he completed 13 circars on a scale of a mile to an inch. The rest remain to be done.

Mr. Walker engraved the two sheets of Colonel Scott's excellent general map of the Madras Presidency, and another general map of the Bombay Presidency in three sheets. He constructed a map of Arabia in two sheets, one of the routes between Constantinople and Delhi, and engraved a series of elaborate maps illustrating the Assyrian Vestiges, by Captain Felix Jones, in four sheets, and the Surveys in Mesopotamia by Selby, Collingwood, and Bewsher, in two sheets. Add to this 87 out of the 200 charts published from surveys executed by officers of the Indian Navy.

Such is an enumeration of the work performed by the veteran geographer of the East India Company. It is work of which he may well be proud, and places him in the first rank of the geographers of the present century.

In 1868 the question was raised whether the time had not come when the remaining sheets of the Atlas might with advantage be taken up by the Surveyor General himself, and engraved at Calcutta. Hitherto the difficulties in the way of such a course had consisted in the want of means and the absence of an efficient staff. These difficulties had to a great extent been surmounted during the time that Colonel Thuillier had been in charge, who had year by year increased the efficiency of the lithographic and drawing branches of his office, and continually introduced new improvements. The advantages of the arrangement were obvious. It was most desirable that the sheets should be compiled and prepared within easy distance of the Surveyors who had made the original drawings, and to whom reference could at once be made for the solution of any point that might arise. Much time might also be expected to be saved. Even in an economical point of view the change would probably be advantageous, as soon as the natives of India had learnt the art of engraving and hill etching.

The change was accordingly sanctioned, and Colonel Thuillier was deputed to make the necessary arrangements in England during the year 1868. He arranged with Mr. Walker that all plates of sheets of the Atlas actually in progress, or for which materials had been sent to England, should be finished by Mr. Walker; and that the rest should be undertaken by the Surveyor General in India. Thus time would be given for Colonel Thuillier to organise his increased staff at Calcutta. Up to this time Mr. Walker had completed the engraving of 84 of the Atlas sheets.*

Colonel Thuillier returned to India with a staff of carefully selected English engravers, in January 1869; and we may look forward with confidence to the success of the new arrangement for the publication of the Atlas, which he has thus inaugurated.

The whole work from the preliminary reconnaissance for the surveys to the publication of the maps will now be done in India, under the immediate eye of one chief; while plenty of useful work will remain to be performed in the India Office.

Since 1836 all geographical and kindred subjects had been deprived of separate departmental supervision, and the maps, journals, and other records had been cast aside to rot and perish. Those which were not lost were frayed and dust-stained, and finally a quantity were sold as waste paper. Ancient journals of great navigators, abstracts of which alone exist in the Pilgrims of Purchas, have disappeared; and many of the later memoirs and surveys of the time of Colin Mackenzie, and even a volume of the Great Trignometrical Survey Series, are missing.

Yet, after all these deplorable losses, there remained a most valuable collection of maps and records; and the re-constitution of a Geographical Department at the India Office, such as had been found essential to efficient administration alil . by the Council of the Western Indies in Seville and by the founders of the East

---

* Mr. Walker has since engraved 25 more quarter sheets. Eight whole sheets and one quarter sheet remain to be taken up, and will be proceeded with in due course. This leaves about 82 sheets to be prepared and engraved in India before the whole grand undertaking of the Indian Atlas is finally completed.

Indian Empire in London, was urgently needed. The Surveyor General, while he was in England in 1868, represented the necessity for such a step, and the great inconvenience that had long been felt from having no separate Department of the India Office in direct communication with the Survey Departments of India. Such a branch of the Home Government would attend to the hitherto neglected duties of receiving, analyzing, and arranging for general reference and use, all geographical and geological documents; of quickly disseminating all maps of a general character emanating from the great national surveys of India; and of transacting all business connected with the surveys and other scientific branches of the service. It was also represented to be essential, in order to meet the increasing demands for geographical information, that there should be proper arrangements for ready reference to, for the exhibition of, and for the immediate issue, for public purposes, of all geographical materials. The serious detriment to the public service caused by no Geographical Department having existed for several years was shown in the total loss of maps and memoirs representing recent surveys, which can never be replaced; in the long delays that had occurred in noticing important proposals for scientific purposes; and in the failure to make announcements of great moment to mariners or men of science, which had been duly reported from India.

In consequence of these representations, the geographical and other kindred business of the India Office was placed in charge of the compiler of this memoir, and Mr. Trelawney Saunders was appointed Assistant Geographer. This arrangement took effect in the autumn of 1868, and has practically continued in force ever since. Thus the labors of the re-constituted Geographical Department of the India Office extend over a period of two years.

A perusal of the foot notes in the previous sections of this memoir will give a general idea of the value and importance of the maps and records that have survived, and which are now preserved in the Geographical Department. They were found in a state of indescribable confusion, and undergoing rapid deterioration; and it occupied Mr. Saunders, whose experience at the Geographical Society had thoroughly qualified him for the task, for 165 days, six hours each day, to reduce the chaotic mass to anything like order. The arrangement of this valuable and in some respects unique collection of geographical records was completed in May 1869.

The next work was the establishment of a system for bringing the maps emanating from the great national surveys of India within the reach of geographers and other enquirers in Europe. Hitherto, it had only been possible to procure the sheets of the Atlas, and the numerous useful maps produced in India could not be obtained by the public, and indeed were unknown. In December 1869 three agents were appointed in London* for the sale of all maps published in the Surveyor General's Office at Calcutta, or in the office of the Superintendent of the Great Trigonometrical Survey, and the whole of these maps are now within the reach of any purchaser. Mr. Saunders has completed "A Catalogue "of Maps of the British Possessions in India and other parts of "Asia, issued by order of the Secretary of State for India," which may also be had from the agents. It contains a synopsis of the political divisions of India, furnishing the key to the arrangement of the catalogue; an index map to the Indian Atlas, carefully and accurately constructed; the catalogue itself, giving the full titles of all the maps; and a general index. Fresh editions will be prepared as new material is received from India.

The valuable collection of manuscript maps and other documents, including many drawn by Rennell, Colebrooke, Mackenzie, Burnes, Wood, and other Indian worthies, is also open to enquirers for reference and inspection, and it is hoped that a complete catalogue of its contents will be issued before the end of the ensuing year. The study of comparative geography is a necessity for the historian and the antiquary. It is also of practical importance to men of science and engineers. The examination of a series of maps of a river or of a harbour, from the first ever drawn to the results of the latest survey, is a thing rarely to be obtained, but one of great interest, and often of practical utility. Efforts have been made towards the improvement of the manuscript collection in this respect. A complete set of copies of ancient Portuguese plans of towns and ports along the west coast of India,† the originals of which are in the British Museum, is in course of preparation for the

---

* 1. W. H. Allen & Co., 13, Waterloo Place.
2. Edward Stanford, 6, Charing Cross.
3. Henry S. King & Co., 65, Cornhill.

† The list of them will be found in the "Catalogo dos manuscriptos da Bibliotheca Eborense, Cunha Rivera," i., p. 302.

Geographical Department. There is also a very precious collection of 110 maps and charts of the Indian coasts, the dates of which range over a period of a century and a half, among the Royal Archives at the Hague. The whole of these are being copied for the Geographical Department, through the kind intervention of Commodore Jansen of the Dutch Navy.*

Arrangements have been made for a regular exchange of maps with the Russian and Netherlands Governments in duplicate, one set being sent to the office of the Surveyor General at Calcutta, and the other being retained in the Department. It is hoped that before long similar arrangements will be made with other Governments. The advantage thus gained is twofold. Geographical information is obtained, while, as the Surveyor General has observed, "the possession of such splendid specimens of engraving and lithography, for the instruction of members of his Department, is exceedingly valuable."

Exertions have been made to recover some of the lost treasures, and not wholly without success. The original manuscript of a journal kept by Captain Knight during a voyage towards the North Pole in 1606 has been discovered amongst a heap of rubbish. It is to be printed and edited by Sir Leopold McClintock. This interesting enterprize, which ended in the mysterious disappearance of Knight himself on the Labrador coast, was previously only known through a meagre abstract in Purchas. A like success has attended an attempt to recover the results of Captain Selby's survey of the sea of Nejf, and part of the course of the Euphrates, which had been lost during the time that there was no separate Geographical Department. The original maps and field books had fortunately been left at Baghdad. They were sent for; 14 maps and 5 field books were duly received, and Lieutenant Collingwood has been employed to reproduce the maps for engraving. The ground they cover is most important, including the ruins of Birs Nimroud, Cufa, Meshed Ali, and Kerbela, and showing the region into which the waters of the Euphrates are being drained. The loss of such a survey, executed at considerable expense and with uncommon zeal by the able officers in charge of it, would have been

* The list of these Dutch maps of the coast of India is given in the "Inventaris der Verzameling Kaarten berustende in het Rijks Archief," (1867,) pp. 130–64.

† See p. 30.

most serious. Lieutenant Collingwood completed his work in June 1870, and the maps will now be lithographed. Like success has not attended an effort to recover Captain Selby's surveys of part of the Shat-el-Arab, nor the original drawings of the Red Sea survey for the hydrographer of the Admiralty.

The manuscript maps in the collection, many of them most precious relics of illustrious geographers and explorers, were never backed, nor adequately cared for. During the period that no separate Geographical Department existed, they were frayed and torn, stained with dust, and left in a most disgraceful state. No blame whatever attaches to Mr. Walker, who had not the means of providing against this destruction of the records. The whole collection is now being gradually and steadily cleaned and backed.

During the two years that Mr. Saunders has occupied the post of Assistant Geographer, he has been chiefly employed in cataloguing and arranging the collection; but he has also had time to execute maps requiring much careful research, and to prepare several valuable geographical memoirs. His "Memoirs of the mountains and river basins of India," with two maps, were published in the form of a quarto pamphlet early in 1870. The distinctive feature of the maps is, that the Himalaya mountains are given in a new form, the great peaks being represented in a culminating outer range, separated by a chain of elevated valleys from an inner range, which forms the water-parting between the basins of the Ganges and Sanpu. The Tibetan highland is also clearly defined, and the various elevations above the sea are admirably shown by varying depths of shading, and by sections. The map of the river basins also shows their extent at a glance, and the memoir is accompanied by a table of the areas of the basins, and lengths of the main streams. His map of the central part of British Burmah, to illustrate the Journals of Captain McLeod, Dr. Richardson, and subsequent travellers, is also a valuable addition to geographical knowledge, as it combines the routes of eight distinct explorers. The collation of their observations, and the combination of different and sometimes conflicting authorities, is work which requires the experience and sagacity of a practised geographer for its satisfactory performance. The completion of the lithography of the sheets of the Hyderabad Survey, left unfinished by Mr. Walker, has also been taken in hand. Several other pieces of work of a similar character have been undertaken from time to time, according to the requirements of the service.

The uses of the Geographical Department at the India Office will in future be, to keep up direct communication with the survey and other scientific branches of the service in India, and to transact all business connected with them; to disseminate and utilize the results of their work; to keep on record, and ready for the use of enquirers, what remains of the once magnificent collection of geographical materials, and to add to it; and to produce all geographical and other scientific work that requires to be executed in England. There is every reason to expect that the public service and the interests of science will be furthered in no small degree by the careful performance of these duties.

Members of the Great Trigonometrical, Topographical, and Revenue Surveys of India.

SURVEY DEPARTMENT.

Names.	Appointment.	Date of Appointment.	Remarks.
Colonel H. E. L. Thuillier, C.S.I. (*Royal Artillery.*)	Surveyor-General of India and Superintendent of the Topographical Surveys.	12th March 1861	Joined the Surveys, 1836. Deputy Surveyor-General, 1847-61.
Colonel J. T. Walker - - (*Royal Engineers, Bombay.*)	Superintendent of the Great Trigonometrical Survey.	„	On furlough 18 months, from Dec. 1870.
Colonel J. E. Gastrell - - (*Staff Corps.*)	Deputy Surveyor-General and Superintendent of the Revenue Surveys.	11th March 1867	On furlough two years, from Dec. 1869.
Colonel D. C. Vanrenen - (*Royal Artillery.*)	Deputy Surveyor-General, with the superintendence of the Revenue Surveys in the Upper Provinces.	„	
Major J. Macdonald - - (*Staff Corps.*)	Officiating Deputy Surveyor-General, with the superintendence of the Revenue Surveys in the Lower Provinces, and Boundary Commissioner, Bengal and Behar.	19th Feb. 1867 -	Also Officiating Superintendent of the Mathematical Instrument Department.
Captain W. G. Murray - - (*Staff Corps.*)	Assistant Surveyor-General, attached to Surveyor-General's office.	„	
Lieutenant J. Waterhouse - (*Staff Corps.*)	Assistant Surveyor-General in charge of the Photographic Branch, attached to the Surveyor-General's office.	23rd July 1866.	

GREAT TRIGONOMETRICAL SURVEY OF INDIA.

Names.	Appointment.	Date of Appointment.	Remarks.
Colonel J. T. Walker - - (*Royal Engineers, Bombay.*)	Superintendent - -	12th March 1861	On furlough 18 months, from Dec. 1870. He joined the Survey Department, Dec. 1st, 1853.
Major T. G. Montgomerie - (*Royal Engineers.*)	Officiating Superintendent. Deputy Superintendent, 1st grade.	25th Nov. 1862 -	Dehra Doon. He joined the Survey Department, Nov. 25th, 1852.
Captain J. P. Basevi - - (*Royal Engineers.*)	Deputy Superintendent, 1st grade.	1st April 1866 -	In charge of Pendulum party. Joined the Department, Jan. 18th, 1856.
J. B. N. Hennessey, Esq. - -	„ „	- - -	Computing Officer. Joined the Department in 1844.
Lieutenant-Colonel D. J. Nasmyth. (*Royal Engineers, Bombay.*)	Deputy Superintendent, 2nd grade.	8th Dec. 1866 -	On furlough for two years.
Captain H. R. Thuillier - (*Royal Engineers.*)	„ „	1st Oct. 1867 -	In charge of the Kumaon and Gurhwal Topographical Survey.
Captain C. T. Haig - - (*Royal Engineers, Bombay.*)	„ „	„	On leave for two years, from Sept. 1869.
Captain J. Herschel - -	„ „	„	In charge of No. 1 extra party. Bangalore. (Astronomical.)
C. Lane, Esq. - - -	„ „	- - -	Spirit-levelling operations.

Names.	Appointment.	Date of Appointment.	Remarks.
Major H. R. Branfill (*Late 5th European L.C.*)	Deputy Superintendent, 3rd grade.	1st June 1865	In charge of the Madras party. Bangalore.
Captain T. T. Carter (*Royal Engineers.*)	„ „	21st April 1864	On furlough.
Captain W. M. Campbell (*Royal Engineers, Bombay.*)	„	1st Feb. 1867	On furlough for two years from Dec. 1868.
Lieutenant H. Trotter	„ „	24th Jan. 1869	In charge of the Kattywar party.
H. Keelan, Esq.	„ „	- -	In charge of Sumbulpore Meridional Series.
W. C. Rossenrode, Esq.	„ „	-	Eastern Frontier Series. Burmah.
G. Shelverton, Esq.	„ „	- -	Beder Longitudinal Series.
Captain A. Pullan (*Staff Corps.*)	Assistant Superintendent, 1st grade.	20th Jan. 1864	On furlough for two years, from Dec. 1869.
Lieutenant W. J. Heaviside (*Royal Engineers.*)	„ „	1st March 1868	On furlough for two years.
Lieutenant M. W. Rogers (*Royal Engineers.*)	„ „	15th Dec. 1868	In charge. Bombay party Bangalore.
Lieutenant J. Hill (*Royal Engineers.*)	„ „	18th Dec. 1866	Kumaon and Gurwhal.
W. H. Cole, Esq., M.A.	„ „	1st Sept. 1867	Computing Office.
Lieutenant A. W. Baird (*Royal Engineers.*)	Assistant-Superintendent, 2nd grade.	4th Dec. 1868	On leave for two years, from April 1870.
Lieutenant J. R. McCullagh (*Royal Engineers.*)	„ „	12th Feb. 1869	General Survey. Poona.
		Date of Joining the Department.	
W. H. Scott, Esq.	Surveyor, 1st grade	1st March 1827	Chief draughtsman. Dehra Doon.
H. R. Duhan	„ „	22nd April 1843	Author of the History of the Surveys, in the "*Professional Papers.*" Superintendent's Personal Assistant. Head Quarters.
W. G. Beverley	„ „	1st July 1854	Kumaon and Gurwhal Survey.
J. McGill	„ „	17th Dec. 1851	Kattywar Survey.
E. C. Ryall	Surveyor, 2nd grade	24th April 1855	Kumaon and Gurwhal.
J. Peyton	„ „	3rd Feb. 1850	„ „
H. Beverley	„ „	14th June 1855	Eastern Frontier Series. Burmah.
A. W. Donnelly	Surveyor, 3rd grade	19th June 1855	Levelling operations.
L. H. Clarke	„ „	26th Nov. 1855	Sumbulpore Meridional Series.
C. J. Neuville	„ „	1st Dec. 1855	Brahmapootra Series. 1868-9.
W. Todd	„ „	11th Jan. 1856	Kattywar Survey.
A. De Souza	„ „	19th Feb. 1856	Kattywar Survey.
J. Low	Surveyor, 4th grade	1st Oct. 1857	Kumaon and Gurwhal. 1868-69.
H. B. T. Keelan	„ „	17th Aug. 1858	Longitudinal series W. of Calcutta.
F. Bell	„ „	17th Aug. 1858	Beder Longitudinal Series.
R. Scott	Assistant Surveyor, 1st grade	25th Oct. 1844	Superintendent's Office.
F. W. Ryall	„ „	1st April 1859	Kumaon and Gurwhal.

Names.	Appointment.	Date of Joining the Department.	Remarks.
G. W. E. Atkinson	Assistant Surveyor, 1st grade	1st April 1859	Kumaon and Gurwhal.
G. A. Andige	„ „	Oct. 1859	Cape Comorin Base Line, 1868-69.
J. Wood	„ „	12th Nov., 1860	Latitude observations.
C. W. Braithwaite	Assistant Surveyor, 2nd grade	14th May 1860	Kumaon and Gurwhal.
G. A. Harris	„ „	23rd July 1861	Brahmapootra Series.
J. W. Mitchell	„ „	1st Sept. 1861	Madras party.
H. W. Prychers	„ „	22nd Sept. 1862	Longitudinal Series, W. of Calcutta.
G. Belcham	„ „	1st Nov. 1862	Cape Comorin Base Line, 1868-69.
L. J. Pocock	„ „	10th July 1863	Kumaon and Gurwhal.
A. L. Christie	„ „	7th Aug. 1863	Cape Comorin Base Line, 1868-69.
W. J. O'Sullivan	„ „	1st Oct. 1863.	
N. Gwinne	„ „	19th Oct. 1863	Kattywar Survey.
W. C. Price	Assistant Surveyor, 3rd grade	1st Nov. 1863	Madras party.
C. H. McAfee	„ „	6th Nov. 1864	Kattywar Survey.
T. H. Rendell	„ „	11th Oct. 1864	„
E. J. Connor	„ „	1st March 1865	Eastern Frontier Series.
J. W. McDougall	„ „	1st March 1865	Cape Comorin Base Line. 1868-69.
H. P. W. Todd	„ „	15th July 1865	Kumaon and Gurwhal. 1868-69.
E. N. Wyatt	„ „	1st Sept. 1865	Kattywar Survey.
C. Bryson	„ „	29th Oct. 1865	Kumaon and Gurwhal.
O. V. Norris	„ „	24th April 1866	Cape Comorin Base Line 1868-69.
J. Bond	„ „	18th Oct. 1866	„ „
C. D. Potter	„ „	29th Oct. 1866	„ „
E. P. Wrixon	„ „	25th Oct. 1865	Beder Longitudinal Series.
A. Moore	Probationary Assistant Surveyor, 4th grade.	1st March 1866	General party.
J. Hickie	„ „	29th April 1868	„
W. Feilding	„ „	3rd May 1868	„
G. B. Cusson	„ „	6th May 1868	„
C. Goslin	„ „	13th Nov. 1868	„
T. Kinney	„ „	17th June 1868	Kumaon and Gurwhal.
E. F. Litchfield	„ „	28th Nov. 1868.	
E. W. Lawson	„ „	1st May 1869	Bombay party.
A. Bryson	„ „	20th Sept. 1869	No. 4 extra party.

TOPOGRAPHICAL SURVEY OF INDIA.

Names.	Appointment.	Date of Appointment.	Remarks.
Colonel H. E. L. Thuillier, C.S.I. (*Royal Artillery.*)	Superintendent - -	12th March 1861	Calcutta.
Colonel G. H. Saxton - - (*Madras Staff Corps.*)	Deputy Superintendent, 1st grade.	1st April 1865 -	Central Provinces and Vizagapatam Agency Survey. Ootacamund.
Major G. C. Depree - - (*Staff Corps.*)	„ „	25th Oct. 1866 -	On leave for two years, from Dec. 1868.
Major H. H. Godwin Austen - (*Staff Corps.*)	Deputy Superintendent 2nd grade.	1st Jan. 1868 -	On leave for two years, from April 1870.
Captain A. B. Melville - - (*Staff Corps.*)	„ „	1st April 1869 -	
Captain W. G. Murray - - (*Staff Corps.*)	„ „	„	Surveyor-General's Office.
Lieutenant G. Strahan - - (*Royal Engineers.*)	Deputy Superintendent, 3rd grade.	1st July 1866 -	Rajpootana Survey. Mussoorie.
J. O. N. James, Esq. - -	„ „	1st April 1866 -	Assistant to Surveyor-General on duty at Head Quarters. Previous service from July 29th 1845 in subordinate branch.
J. B. Girdlestone, Esq. - -	Assistant Superintendent, 1st grade.	1st Jan. 1867 -	Joined the Survey in 1863. Formerly a midshipman in the Indian Navy.
Lieutenant R. V. Riddell - (*Royal Engineers.*)	Deputy Superintendent, 3rd grade.	1st Oct. 1867 -	Bundelcund Survey.
Lieutenant C. Strahan - - (*Royal Engineers.*)	„ „	1st Dec. 1867 -	Gwalior and Central India Survey.
Lieutenant A. E. Downing - (*Late Staf N.I.*)	Assistant Superintendent, 1st grade.	7th Nov. 1867 -	On leave, from 12th Dec. 1868.
Captian W. F. Badgley - - (*Staff Corps.*)	„ „	6th May 1868 -	On leave, from 23rd Jan. 1869.
Lieutenant H. T. Sale - - (*Royal Engineers.*)	„ „	18th Dec. 1868 -	Chota Nagpore Survey.
Lieutenant T. H. Holdich - (*Royal Engineers.*)	„ „	„	Gwalior and Central India Survey.
H. Hearst, Esq. - - -	„ „	1st Oct. 1869 -	Rajpootana Survey. Previous service since 1854 in subordinate branch.
Lieutenant J. R. Wilmer - (*Royal Artillery.*)	Probationary Assistant Superintendent, 3rd grade.	24th Aug. 1869 -	Bundelcund Topographical Party.
		Date of Joining the Department.	
N. A. Belletty, Esq. - -	Surveyor, 1st grade - -	13th July 1847 -	Coosyah and Garrow Hills Survey.
C. H. T. Neale - - -	„ „ - -	21st April 1855 -	On leave for two years, from Aug. 1870.
J. P. Bonrne - - -	„ „ - - -	5th Sept. 1856 -	Geographical Examiner. Head Quarters.
A. C. Chamarett - - -	„ 2nd grade - -	2nd June 1852 -	Head Quarters.
H. J. Boist - - - -	„ „ - -	26th July 1852 -	Gwalior and Central India Survey.
G. A. McGill - - -	„ 3rd grade - -	8th April 1855 -	Chota Nagpore Survey.
D. Atkinson - - -	„ „ - -	4th Aug. 1856 -	Draughtsman. Head Quarters.
J. Vanderputt - - -	„ 4th grade - -	1st Sept. 1856 -	Chota Nagpore Survey.
R. W. Chew - - -	„ „ - -	13th Sept. 1856 -	Central Provinces and Vizagapatam.

Names.	Appointment.	Date of Joining the Department.	Remarks.
J. Harper	Surveyor, 4th grade	8th Aug. 1857	Central Provinces and Vizagapatam.
A. J. Wilson	Assistant Surveyor, 1st grade	1st Dec. 1860	Bundelcund Survey.
J. A. May	" "	1st Oct. 1860	Central Provinces.
R. D. Farrell	" "	"	Gwalior and Central India.
F. Adams	" "	"	Central Provinces.
E. S. P. Atkinson	" "	15th Aug. 1861	Rajpootana.
A. G. Wyatt	Assistant Surveyor, 2nd grade	1st Nov. 1861	Chota Nagpore.
M. J. Ogle	" "	1st July 1863	Cossyah and Garrow Hills.
C. F. Hamer	" "	3rd Aug. 1863	Bundelcund.
C. A. R. Scanlan	" "	8th Sept. 1863	Gwalior and Central India.
R. Todd	" "	1st Nov. 1863	Rajpootana.
A. Chennell	" "	1st May 1864	Bundelcund.
T. E. M. Claudius	" "	10th Aug. 1863	Central Provinces.
C. Tapsell	" "	2nd Aug. 1864	Rajpootana.
A. James	" "	15th June 1864	Chota Nagpore.
G. K. Allnutt	Assistant Surveyor, 3rd Grade	1st Sept. 1864	Gwalior and Central India Survey.
C. Kirk	" "	1st Oct. 1864	Bundelcund.
W. Stotesbury	" "	"	Rajpootana.
F. Kitchen	" "	4th Oct. 1864	"
J. A. Barker	" "	19th Sept. 1865	Chota Nagpore.
E. F. Wainwright	" "	1st May 1865	Bundelcund.
T. D. Ryan	" "	18th Sept. 1865	Gwalior and Central India.
W. J. Cornelius	" "	15th Aug. 1866	" "
W. F. Pettigrew	" "	12th Sept. 1866	Central Provinces.
P. J. W. Doran	" "	1st Feb. 1867	Cossyah and Garrow Hil
W. W. McNair	" "	1st Sept. 1867	Rajpootana.
H. T. Kitchen	Assistant Surveyor, 4th Grade	1st Nov. 1867	Bundelcund.
A. Cooper	" "	1st Dec. 1867	Central Provinces.
J. H. Wilson	" "	1st April 1868	Chota Nagpore.
W. H. Lilley	" "	1st May 1868	Bundelcund.
W. Robert	" "	1st Aug. 1869	Cossyah and Garrow Hills.
F. E. Warde	" "	1st Sept. 1870	Rajpootana.
C. T. Templeton	" "	"	Gwalior and Central India.

REVENUE SURVEYS UNDER THE GOVERNMENT OF INDIA.

		Date of Appointment.	
Colonel J. E. Gastrell (*Staff Corps.*)	Superintendent	11th March 1867	On leave for two years, from Dec. 1869.
Colonel D. C. Vanrenen (*Royal Artillery.*)	Superintendent (Upper Circle)	"	Calcutta.
Major J. Macdonald (*Staff Corps.*)	Deputy Superintendent, 1st Grade, Officiating Superintendent (Lower Circle.)	1st April 1866	Calcutta.
Lieutenant-Colonel H. C. Johnstone, C.B. (*Staff Corps.*)	Deputy Superintendent, 1st Grade.	"	N.W. Frontier (Murra).

Names.	Appointment.		Date of Appointment.	Remarks.
J. H. O'Donel, Esq. - -	Deputy Superintendent 1st Grade.		- - -	Cooch Behar.
Major F. C. Anderson (*Staff Corps.*) -	„	„	1st April 1868 -	Oude (Nynee Tal).
Major A. D. Vanrenen - - (*Staff Corps.*)	„	„	8th July 1860 -	N.W. Provinces (Landour).
Major R. E. Oakes - - (*Staff Corps.*)	„	2nd Grade	7th April 1867 -	On leave for two years from July 1870.
Captain J. Scone - (*Staff Corps.*)	„	„	6th Nov. 1868 -	Lower Provinces (Hazareebaugh).
R. B. Smart, Esq. - -	„	„	- - -	Raepore (Nagpore).
Captain W. J. Stewart - - (*Staff Corps.*)	„	3rd Grade	1st April 1866 -	Lower Provinces. Hooghly Surveys (Barrackpore).
W. Lane, Esq. - -	„	„	- - -	Ramree and Kyouk Phyoo.
Captain D. Macdonald - (*Staff Corps.*)	„	„	1st April 1868 -	Sinde.
Captain F. Coddington - (*Staff Corps.*)	„	„	28th July 1867 -	Central Provinces (Poona).
Captain A. D. Butler - - (*Staff Corps.*)	„	„	„	Nowgong.
Captain J. H. W. Osborne - (*Late 64th N. I.*)	„	„	1st April 1870 -	Lower Provinces. Assam.
Lieutenant W. Barron - (*Staff Corps.*)	„	„	„	On leave for one year from Jan. 1870.
Captain H. C. B. Tanner - (*Bombay Staff Corps.*)	„	„	„	Central Provinces (Kurrachee).
Lieutenant D. C. Andrews - (*Staff Corps.*)	Assistant Superintendent, 1st Grade.		30th Dec. 1866 -	Assam.
Captain W. H. Wilkins - (*Staff Corps.*)	„	„	27th April 1867	Central Provinces (Jubbulpore).
Lieutenant E. W. Samuells - (*Staff Corps.*)	„	„	25th Jan. 1868 -	On leave for two years from Feb. 1869.
Lieutenant J. E. Sandeman - (*Staff Corps.*)	„	„	6th Oct. 1868 -	On leave for two years from Dec. 1869.
Lieutenant H. L. Smith - (*Staff Corps.*)	„	2nd Grade	18th June 1867	Central Provinces (Poona).
Lieutenant S. H. Cowan - (*Staff Corps.*)	„	„	17th March 1868	On leave for two years from March 1870.
Lieutenant H. S. Hutchinson (*Staff Corps.*)	„	„	13th Aug. 1868 -	On leave for 20 months from April 1870.
Lieutenant E. H. Steel - (*Staff Corps.*)	„	„	20th May 1869 -	Lower Provinces (Assam).
Lieutenant R. Beavan - - (*Staff Corps.*)	„	„	9th Nov. 1869 -	Lower Provinces (Hazareebaugh).
R. C. Barrett, Esq. - -	„	„	- - -	Reypore (Nagpore).
E. J. Jackson, Esq. - -	„	„	- - -	Cooch Behar.
J. Campbell, Esq. - -	„	1st Grade	- - -	Bareilly (Nynee Tal).
E. T. S. Johnson, Esq. -	„	„	- - -	Bhawulpore.
H. R. Gastrell, Esq. -	„	3rd Grade	- - -	Sinde.
H. B. Talbot, Esq. - -	„	„	- - -	Seebsaugur.
G. Housden, Esq. - -	Revenue Surveyor, 1st Grade		- - -	Peshawur and Derajat.
G. S. Swiney, Esq. - -	„	„	- - -	Ramree.
W. H. Patterson, Esq. -	„	2nd Grade	- - -	Bijnour.
J. Pickard, Esq. - -	„	„	- - -	Ramree.
J. W. Kelley, Esq. - -	„	„	- - -	Head Draftsman.

Names.	Appointment.	Date of Appointment.	Remarks.
C. Brownfield, Esq.	Revenue Surveyor, 3rd Grade		Lower Provinces (Nowgong).
G. H. Blyth, Esq.	„ „		Assam. Luckimpore.
W. Sinclair, Esq.	„ „		Chunda (Poona).
C. W. Campbell	„ „		Gonda (Nynee Tal).
E. Loftie, Esq.	„ „		Sinde.
F. Grant, Esq.	„ „		Chundwara (Jubbulpore).
R. Barclay, Esq.	„ 4th Grade		Cooch Behar.
J. Todd, Esq.	„ „		Hazareebagh.
W. R. Vyall, Esq.	„ „		„
W. A. Wilson, Esq.	Assistant Surveyor, 1st Grade		Assam. Luckimpore.
P. Cowley, Esq.	„ „		Bhawulpore.
B. H. Hillon, Esq.	„ „		Hooghly (Barrackpore).
R. H. Littlewood, Esq.	„ „		„ „
G. R. Buttress, Esq.	„ „		Hazareebagh.
S. M. Smylie, Esq.	„ „		Ramree and Kyouk Phyoo.
G. Rae, Esq.	„ „		Chindwara (Jubbulpore).
W. S. Buttress, Esq.	„ „		Raepore (Nagpore).
J. S. Pemberton, Esq.	„ „		„ „
T. W. Reilly, Esq.	„ „		Chindwara (Jubbulpore).
C. David, Esq.	„ „		Draftsman.
P. H. W. Brady	„ „		Nemaur.
L. G. Hill, Esq.	„ 2nd Grade		Lower Provinces (Nowgong).
A. M. Lawson, Esq.	„ „		Nemaur.
J. H. Barter, Esq.	„ „		„
J. T. T. Cosen, Esq.	„ „		Chunda (Poona).
M. Wray	„ „		Bijnour.
J. H. O'Donel (Junr.), Esq.	„ „		Bareilly (Nynee Tal).
J. A. Swyny, Esq.	„ „		Gonda (Nynee Tal).
W. H. Reynolds, Esq.	„ „		Peshawar and Derajat.
H. T. Hanby, Esq.	„ „		Gonda (Nynee Tal).
A. J. Gibson, Esq.	„ „		Peshawar and Derajat.
H. Dowman, Esq.	„ „		Sinde.
J. N. Storlke, Esq.	„ „		Hooghly (Barrackpore).
T. D. Moran, Esq.	„ „		Cooch Behar.
G. H. Cooke, Esq.	„ „		Hazareebagh.
J. D. Lynch, Esq.	„ „		Seebsaugur.
E. Little, Esq.	„ „		Chindwara (Jubbulpore).
R. B. Smart, Esq.	„ 3rd Grade		Lower Provinces (Nowgong).
E. Lincoln, Esq.	„ „		Assam (Luckimpore).
C. W. F. Sayers, Esq.	„ „		Nemaur.
J. Newland, Esq.	„ „		Chund (Poona).
W. Bourne, Esq.	„ „		Bijnour.
T. Patterson, Esq.	„ „		„

Names.	Appointment.	Date of Appointment.	Remarks.
Hurrising - - -	Assistant Surveyor, 3rd Grade	- - -	Peshawar and Derajat.
G. B. Scott, Esq. - -	„ „	- - -	Peshawar and Derajat.
F. Foord, Esq. - -	„ „	- - -	Sinde.
J. Comar, Esq. - -	„ „	- - -	„
T. Dunne, Esq. - -	„ „	- - -	„
W. J. Lane, Esq. - -	„ „	- - -	Cooch Behar.
R. C. Ewing, Esq. - -	„ „	- - -	Hazareebagh.
D. A. King, Esq. - -	„ „	- - -	Ramree and Kyouk Phyoo.
L. J. S. Evans, Esq. - -	„ „	- - -	Raepore (Nagpore).
J. E. P. Linke - -	„ „	- - -	Draftsman.
J. O'Tool, Esq. - -	„ 4th Grade	- - -	Lower Provinces (Nowgong).
S. Scallan, Esq. - -	„ „	- - -	„ „
R. L. Thompson, Esq. - -	„ „	- - -	Nemaur.
A. Hall, Esq. - - -	„ „	- - -	Chanda (Poona).
W. H. Penrose, Esq. - -	„ „	- - -	„
S. O. Madras, Esq. - -	„ „	- - -	Bignour.
J. Lincoln, Esq. - -	„ „	- - -	„
J. Swiney, Esq. - -	„ „	- - -	Bareilly (Nynee Tal).
B. Anderson, Esq. - -	„ „	- - -	„ „
G. L. B. Scott, Esq. - -	„ „	- - -	„ „
G. W. Jarbo, Esq. - -	„ „	- - -	Gonda „
J. B. Scott, Esq. - - -	„ „	- - -	„ „
A. C. W. Lemarchand, Esq. -	„ „	- - -	„ „
W. J. Smith, Esq. - -	„ „	- - -	Peshawar and Derajat.
T. Shaw, Esq. - - -	„ „	- - -	Luckimpore.
A. C. Low, Esq. - - -	„ „	- - -	Hooghly (Barrackpore).
A. Lane, Esq. - - -	„ „	- - -	Cooch Behar.
H. Hexter, Esq. - -	„ „	- - -	Hazareebagh.
C. W. Wilson, Esq. - -	„ „	- - -	„
G. B. Younge, Esq. - -	„ „	- - -	Chindwara (Jubbulpore).
A. Hutchinson, Esq. - -	„ „	- - -	Reepore (Nagpore).
J. MacHutton, Esq. - -	„ „	- - -	„
T. Freeman, Esq. - - -	„ „	- - -	Assam (Luckimpore).

SURVEYOR GENERAL'S OFFICE.

(46, *Park Street, Calcutta.*)

Names.	Appointment.	Date of Appointment.	Remarks.
A. E. Byrne, Esq. - -	Registrar and Accountant.		
J. O. Byrne, Esq. - -	Chief Clerk.		
E. H. C. Powell, Esq. - -	Second Clerk.		
H. S. Pemberton, Esq. -	Record Keeper.		
M. Francis, Esq. - -	Store Keeper.		
H. R. Vallis, Esq. - -	Assistant Store Keeper.		
C. W. Coard Esq. - -	Hill Engraver and Foreman -	September 1868.	

Names.	Appointment.	Date of Appointment.	Remarks.
F. J. T. Walsh, Esq.	Hill Engraver	September 1868.	
J. M. Dalziel, Esq.	Outline and Writing Engraver	„	
M. H. West, Esq.	„ „	„	
H. James, Esq.	„ „	„	
Alfred Houghton, Esq.	Copper Plate Printer.	October 1869.	

OFFICE OF THE SUPERINTENDENT OF REVENUE SURVEYS.

(15, *Middleton Street, Calcutta.*)

Names.	Appointment.	Date of Appointment.	Remarks.
J. P. Adel	Registrar.		
A. C. Cunningham	1st Assistant.		
J. McKie	2nd „		
F. W. Kelly	Head Draftsman.		
C. David	Draftsman.		
J. C. F. Lieke	„		

MADRAS REVENUE SURVEY.

Names.	Appointment.	Date of Appointment.	Remarks.
Colonel F. J. H. Priestley (*Staff Corps.*)	Superintendent	22nd Feb. 1855	Present Appointment 18th August 1857.
Major W. H. Hessey (*Staff Corps.*)	Deputy Superintendent	3rd Nov. 1854	Coimbatore and Salem (No. 1 Party).
Lieutenant Colonel W. Crewe (*Staff Corps.*)	„ „	13th Aug. 1858	Cuddapah and Kistnah. On sick leave (No. 3 Party).
F. O. Puckle, Esq., M.A.	„ „	10th Mar. 1858	Tinnevelly (No. 4 Party).
Major W. Barber	„ „	21st June 1861	Madras (No. 5 Party).
W. Beaumont, Esq.	„ „	21st May 1858	„ „
H. O. C. Cardoso, Esq.	1st Assistant Superintendent	24th Feb. 1859	Kurnool (No. 2 Party). On sick leave.
J. H. Wright, Esq.	„ „	21st May 1858	Madras (No. 5 Party).
Captain J. G. Clarke	„ „	22nd June 1863	Kurnool (No. 2 Party).
Captain O. D. Barnes	„ „	19th June 1861	Madras District. On sick leave.
H. Gompertz, Esq.	„ „	12th Aug. 1854	Cuddapah (No. 3 Party). On sick leave.
Captain A. O'H. Clay	„ „	1st Nov. 1861	Cuddapah.
Lieutenant W. Prouth	„ „	1st Oct. 1864	No. 1 Party.
Captain H. O. Graham	„ „	23rd Aug. 1863	Tinnevelly (No. 4 Party). On furlough.
J. J. Tomlinson, Esq.	„ „	3rd May 1865	Ganjam (No. 6 Party).
H. O. Dunsford, Esq.	2nd Assistant Superintendent	10th Jan. 1860	No. 2, Demarcation Party, Ganjam.
J. A. Tomlinson, Esq.	„ „	12th Aug. 1859	Cuddapah (No. 3 Party).
Lieutenant R. M. Clerk	„ „	11th May 1865	Coorg.
Lieutenant W. H. M. Franklyne.	„ „	6th Nov. 1866	Tinnevelly (No. 4 Party).
Captain C. C. Sargeaunt	„ „	20th Feb. 1867	On sick leave.
J. H. Cook, Esq.	„ „	21st Jan. 1868	Coimbatore (No. 1 Party).
E. L. M. Barber, Esq.	„ „	„	No. 4 Party.

Names.	Appointment.	Date of Appointment.	Remarks.
Captain C. A. Liardet	2nd Assistant Superintendent	6th Oct. 1868	Madras (No. 5 Party).
J. H. Merriman, Esq.	„ „	4th June 1868	Kurnool (No. 2 Party).
F. T. Bagshawe, Esq.	Probationary Assistant Superintendent.	19th May 1869	Cuddapah (No. 3 Party).
Captain F. H. Thompson	„ „	„	„ (No. 1 Party).

BOMBAY REVENUE SURVEY.

Names.	Appointment.	Date of Appointment.	Remarks.
Lieutenant Colonel W. C. Anderson.	Survey and Settlement Commissioner.	- - -	Berar and S. Division.
Lieutenant Colonel J. T. Francis.	„ „	- - -	Northern Division.
Lieutenant Colonel G. A. Laughton.	Superintendent	- -	Conducting the Survey of Bombay Island for the Municipality.
Major C. J. Prescott	„	- - -	On furlough. Guzerat.
Major W. Waddington	„	- - -	„ Tannah and Ratnagherry.
N. B. Beyts, Esq.	„	- - -	(Acting.) Guzerat.
H. M. Grant, Esq.	„	- - -	(Acting.) N. Division.
Major F. A. Elphinstone	„	- - -	Settlement Officer. Berar.
Major M. R. Haig	Settlement Officer	- - -	Sinde. Right bank of Indus.
Major E. L. Taverner	„	- - -	„ Left bank of Indus.
Major R. Wallace	Deputy Superintendent	- - -	S. Mahratta country.
J. R. Gibson, Esq.	„ „	- - -	Bombay. Acting for Colonel Laughton.
R. R. Benyon, Esq.	„ „	- - -	Berar.
Captain A. G. Dols	„ Settlement Officer	- - -	Sinde. Right bank of Indus.
Captain C. E. Fisher	„ „	- - -	„ Left bank of Indus. On leave.
W. Wilkins, Esq.	„ „	- - -	Acting. Sinde.
W. Lane, Esq.	Revenue Surveyor	- - -	Sinde. (In Europe.)
Captain D. Macdonald	„	- - -	„ (Acting.)
R. H. Light, Esq.	Assistant Superintendent	- - -	On special duty. Poona.
W. S. Prince, Esq.	„ „	- - -	S. Mahratta Country.
R. C. Benyon, Esq.	„ „	- - -	„
Lieutenant G. Coussmaker	„ „	- - -	„
Lieutenant G. L. Fagan	„ „	- - -	„
Lieutenant G. W. Godfrey	„ „	- - -	„
Lieutenant G. C. Sartorius	„ „	- - -	„
A. P. Young, Esq.	„ „	- - -	„
R. S. Pelly, Esq.	„ „	- - -	„
A. S. Bulkley, Esq.	„ „	- - -	Guzerat.
J. C. Hall, Esq.	„ „	- - -	„
Lieutenant D. C. Pedder	„ „	- - -	„
Lieutenant R. Westmacott	„ „	- - -	„
Lieutenant H. D. Cathcart	„ „	- - -	„
Lieutenant G. E. Hancock	„ „	- - -	„

Names.	Appointment.	Date of Appointment.	Remarks.
H. H. Summers, Esq. - -	Assistant Superintendent -	- - -	Guzerat.
W. B. Prescott, Esq. - -	" "	- - -	"
A. B. Forde, Esq. - -	" "	- - -	"
Lieutenant C. Hexton -	" "	- - -	North Division.
W. Harrison, Esq. - -	" "	- - -	"
J. R. Gibson, Esq. - -	" "	- - -	"
H. K. Disney, Esq. - -	" "	- - -	"
J. W. Young, Esq. - -	" "	- - -	"
Lieutenant C. Echalaz -	" "	- - -	"
M. A. Cummings, Esq. -	" "	- - -	"
W. Fletcher, Esq. - -	" "	- - -	"
J. W. Scott, Esq. - -	" "	- - -	"
E. Mears, Esq. - -	" "	- - -	"
Lieutenant J. G. McRae -	" "	- - -	On sick leave.
E. A. Francis, Esq. - -	" "	- - -	"
Lieutenant W. C. Black -	" "	- - -	"
R. B. Pitt, Esq. - -	" Settlement Officer -	- - -	Berar.
E. A. Hobson, Esq. - -	" "	- - -	"
A. Guerin, Esq. - - -	" Superintendent -	- - -	"
Captain G. Mackenzie -	" "	- - -	"
Captain C. C. Pemberton -	" "	- - -	"
P. T. Willaume, Esq. - -	" "	- -	"
Lieutenant F. Plummer -	" "	- - -	"
W. Ashburner, Esq. - -	" "	- - -	"
W. Turnbull, Esq. - -	" "	- - -	"
H. S. Spring, Esq. - -	" "	- - -	"
Lieutenant R. Price - -	" "	- - -	"
C. L. Morant, Esq. - -	" "	- - -	"
J. B. Morgan, Esq. - -	Supernumerary Assistant Superintendent.	- - -	Guzerat.
R. T. Wingate, Esq. - -	" "	- - -	S. Mahratta Country.
J. H. D. Dunsterville, Esq. -	" "	- - -	"
Lieutenant J. H. Rawlo -	" "	- - -	"
E. R. Critchell, Esq. - -	Sub-Assistant Superintendent	- - -	Guzerat.
F. D. Souza, Esq. - -	" "	- - -	"
W. E. Waite, Esq. - -	" "	- - -	"
J. C. Whitcomb, Esq. - -	" "	- - -	N. Division.
G. Botham, Esq. - -	Supernumerary "	- - -	Berar.
Lieutenant Ward - -	" "	- - -	"
G. Berrie, Esq. - - -	1st Class Assistant - -	- - -	Sinde. Right bank of Indus
J. F. Nash, Esq. - -	" - - -	- - -	" "
J. Dowman, Esq. - - -	" - - -	- - -	" Left "
C. H. Marsh, Esq. - -	2nd " - - -	- - -	" Right "
T. R. Fernandez, Esq. - -	" - - -	- - -	" Left "

Names.	Appointment.	Date of Appointment.	Remarks.
G. F. Mathieson, Esq. - -	3rd Class Assistant - -	- - -	Sinde. Left bank of Indus.
E. Steele, Esq. - - -	" - - -	- - -	" "
H. V. Fitzgerald, Esq. -	Supernumerary " - -	- - -	" Right "
R. Giles, Esq., B.A. - -	" - - -	- - -	" " "
W. A Boulton, Esq. - -	" - - -	- - -	" Left "
Khodur Mull - - -	Sub-Assistant - -	- - -	" " "
Moen Mahomed - - -	" - - -	- - -	" Right "

INSPECTION OF INSTRUMENTS FOR THE INDIAN SURVEYS.

(Observatory, Belvidere Road, Lambeth.)

Lieutenant Colonel A. Strange, F.R.S.	Inspector of Scientific Instruments. Lambeth Observatory.	1862.	

MATHEMATICAL INSTRUMENT DEPARTMENT.

(No. 9, Park Street, Calcutta.)

Major J. Macdonald - -	Officiating Superintendent.		
E. Wehlisch - - - -	Mathematical Instrument Maker.		
T. Bolton - - - -	Assistant.		
R. O'Brien - - - -	Head Clerk.		
J. V. Halden - - - -	Storekeeper.		

GEOGRAPHICAL DEPARTMENT

IN THE OFFICE OF THE SECRETARY OF STATE FOR INDIA IN COUNCIL.

Clements R. Markham -	Assistant Secretary - -	Oct. 8th, 1868 -	Secretary to the Royal Geographical Society. Honorary Secretary to the Hakluyt Society.
John Walker - - -	Geographer - - -	June 18th, 1836	Compiler and engraver of the Indian Atlas and charts since 1827.
Trelawney Saunders - -	Assistant Geographer - -	Aug. 17th, 1868 -	He was acting until 1869, when he was appointed by an Order in Council, dated November 11th.
Henry Jones - - -	Map Mounter - - -	26th Jan. 1870.	

MEMBERS of the GEOLOGICAL

(Those who have died in the Service are in Small

Name.	Official Position in 1870.	Date of Joining the Survey.	Date of Retirement or Death.	Periods of Leave in England.	Salary 1870-1.
					In Rupees per month.
A. H. WILLIAMS	-	Feb. 1846	Died 1848	-	-
R. G. HADDON	-	1847	Died 1851	-	-
—— JONES	-	1847	Died 1848	-	-
J. McClelland	-	1846	Left 18	-	-
JOHN JOHNSON	-	Dec. 1848	Died 1850	-	-
Wm. Theobald	Assistant 1st Class	1848	-	2 years	800 0 0
—— *Gomess*	-	1849	Left 1852	-	-
Thomas Oldham	Superintendent	March 1851	-	None	1700 0 0
J. G. Medlicott	-	Dec. 1851	Left in July 1862	None	-
R. J. St. George	-	July 1853	Left in December 1853	None	-
H. B. Medlicott	Deputy Superintendent.	March 1854	-	6 months	1100 0 0 (includes 100 as Dep. Sup.)
J. S. KENNEDY	-	1855	Died in February 1856	None	-
W. T. Blanford	Deputy Superintendent.	Oct. 1855	-	6 months	1000 0 0 (includes 100 as Dep. Sup.)
H. F. Blanford	-	" 1855	Left in December 1861	None	-
C. E. OLDHAM	-	April 1856	Died in March 1869	One year (only lived 6 months out of the 12).	-
W. K. LOFTUS	-	Feb. 1857	Died in July 1859	None	-
W. L. Willson	3rd Class Assistant	March 1857	-	12 months, with 3 extension, 1861-2.	500 0 0
Wm. King	Deputy Superintendent.	" 1857	-	1 year	800 0 0 (includes 100 as Dep. Sup.)
J. GEOGHEGAN	-	April 1857	Died in May 1858	None	-
H. CHILD	-	June 1857	Died in June 1858	None	-
R. B. Foote	2nd Class Assistant	Sept. 1858	-	15 months, with 4 months extension.	700 0 0
F. R. Mallet	3rd Class Assistant	Feb. 1859	-	1 year	800 0 0
A. Tween	Curator	May 1859	-	6 months private affairs, 15 months sick leave with 3 months extension.	500 0 0
F. Fedden	3rd Class Assistant	Oct. 1860	-	6 months	500 0 0
R. TRENCH	-	" 1860	Died in May 1861	None	-
C. A. Hacket	3rd Class Assistant	Nov. 1861	-	None	500 0 0
A. B. Wynne	2nd Class Assistant	" 1862	-	20 months	600 0 0
C. Wilkinson	-	" 1862	Left in February 1865	None	-
T. W. H. Hughes	3rd Class Assistant	" 1862	-	None	500 0 0
Hugh Kane	-	" 1862	Left in March 1864	None	-
F. Stoliczka	Palæontologist	Dec. 1862	-	None	650 0 0
V. Ball	3rd Class Assistant	Oct. 1864	-	None	500 0 0
M. H. ORMSBY	-	March 1866	Died in June 1870	Sick leave 18 months	-
Mark Fryar	Mining Geologist	May 1868	-	None	600 0 0
T. H. Turner	Assistant Curator	April 1869	-	None	250 0 0

Survey of India.

(Capitals, those retired from the Service in Italics.)

Travelling and Horse Allowances.	Districts in which he has served, with Dates.	Remarks, previous Service, &c.
Rupees.		
- - -	Raneegunge coalfield, 1846-7. Ramghur, 1848	Previously on Geological Survey of Great Britain. Died of jungle fever.
- - -	Do. do. do.	Died of general debility and liver, the result of exposure.
- - -	Do. do. do.	Died of jungle fever after a few days illness.
- - -	Kuhurbali and Rajmahal Hills	Of Bengal Medical Service. Temporarily in charge of Survey after death of Mr. Williams.
- - -		Died of fever.
250 0 0	Ramghur, 1848. Rajmahal Hills, 1849-50. (Punjab, 1850 to 52.) Rajmahal Hills, 1852 to 54. Burma, 1854-5. Orissa, 1855-6. Nerbudda Valley, 1856-7. Kattywar, 1857-58. Ganges Valley, 1858 to 60. Pegu and Arracan, 1862 to 1870.	
- - -	Calcutta and Cossyah Hills 1850-1	Still alive. Now Comr. of Sunderbunds.
300 0 0	India generally and Burmah	LL.D., F.R.S., F.G.S. Formerly Director Geological Survey of Ireland.
- - -	Rajmahal Hills, 1851 to 53. Nerbudda Valley, 1854 to 57. Midnapoor, 1857-58. Sonthal pergunnahs and Behar, 1858 to 60. Sone Valley Rewah, 1860 to 62.	B.A. Joined Educational Department as Inspector of Schools.
- - -	Rajmahal Hills, 1853	B.A., C.E. Joined East India Railway as Engineer.
130 0 0	Nerbudda Valley, 1854-5. Sub-Himalaya, 1855-6. Bundelcund, 1856-7. Shut up (Mutiny), 1857-8. Sub-Himalaya, 1859 to 62. Sone Valley, 1862-3. Behar, 1863-4. Assam, 1864-5. Rajpootana, 1865-6. N.W. Frontier Districts, 1866-7. Garrow Hills, 1867-8. Sone Valley, 1868-9. Ouchmari Hills, 1869-70.	M.A., F.G.S., C.E.
- - -	Nerbudda Valley	B.A. Died of fever, liver, and dysentery.
130 0 0	Orissa, 1855 to 58. Rajmahal Hills, 1856-57. Raneegunge, 1858 to 60. Pegu and Arracan, 1860 to 67 and 1869-70. Bombay Presidency, Malwa, and Central Provinces, 1862 to 70. Abyssinia, 1867-9.	A.R.S.M., F.G.S.
- - -	Orissa, 1855-6. Trichinopoly, 1857 to 61	A.R.S.M., F.G.S. Now Professor of Physical Science in Presidency College, Calcutta.
- - -	Rajmahal Hills, 1856-7. Madras Presidency, 1857 to 68	B.A. Died of blood-poisoning from guinea-worm, contracted on service.
- - -	Rajmahal Hills, 1856-7	Died of liver abscess.
130 0 0	Bengal, 1857 to 65. Central India, 1866 to 70.	
130 0 0	Madras Presidency, 1857 to 69	B.A.
- - -	Madras Presidency, 1857-8	B.A., C.E. Died from sunstroke.
- - -	Orissa, 1857-8	A.R.S.M. Died of cholera.
130 0 0	Madras Presidency, 1858-70	Royal School of Mines.
130 0 0	Raneegunge, 1859.	
150 0 0	Raneegunge, 1859-60	A.R.S.M.
130 0 0	Pegu, 1860 to 63. Bengal, 1864-5. Berar, 1866-7. Cutch, 1867-69. Nagpore and Berar, 1869-70.	Royal School of Mines.
- - -	Upper Sone Valley, 1860-1	Previously on Geological Survey of Great Britain. Died of phthisis aggravated by exposure.
130 0 0	Bengal, 1862. Gwalior and Rajpootana, 1865-8. Jubbulpoor, 1869-70	Royal School of Mines.
130 0 0	Bombay Presidency, Malwa, and Nerbudda Valley, 1862-5. Cutch, 1867-9. Punjab, 1869-70.	F.G.S. Previously on Geological Survey of Ireland.
- - -	Bombay Presidency, 1862-5	A.R.S.M. Health broke down, resigned in consequence.
130 0 0	Bengal, 1862-8. Central Provinces, 1869-70	A.R.S.M.
- - -	Sone Valley, 1863-4	B.A., M.D. Health broke down, resigned in consequence.
130 0 0	Himalaya, Bengal	Ph.D., F.G.S., Previously on Geological Survey of Austria.
130 0 0	Bengal, 1864-8. Chota Nagpur, 1868-70	B.A.
- - -	Bengal	LL.D., C.E. Died of debility, induced by sunstroke, and liver.
200 0 0	Central Provinces	
- - -	Calcutta.	

www.ingramcontent.com/pod-product-compliance
Lightning Source LLC
Chambersburg PA
CBHW021122270326
41929CB00009B/1004

* 9 7 8 3 7 4 2 8 7 4 8 6 3 *